The Infanticidal Logic
of Evolution and Culture

The Infanticidal Logic of Evolution and Culture

A. Samuel Kimball

Julian,
On the one hand, "a gift is not signed, and especially not thankfully; a gift cannot come from any I, any sender who would say I.
On the other hand, to think is and must be to thank, and especially against Descartes' inescapable illusion.
From one I to another in thoughtless, transgressive regard, then, thank you, Julian, for your great, wonderful, inspiriting support and measureless generosity.

Sam

DELAWARE

Newark: University of Delaware Press

Associated University Presses
2010 Eastpark Boulevard
Cranbury, NJ 08512

The paper used in this publication meets the requirements of the American National Standard for Permanence of Paper for Printed Library Materials
Z39.48-1984.

Library of Congress Cataloging-in-Publication Data

Kimball, A. Samuel, 1959–
    The infanticidal logic of evolution and culture / A. Samuel Kimball.
       p.   cm.
    Includes bibliographical references and index.
    ISBN-13: 978-0-87413-952-5 (alk. paper)
    ISBN-10: 0-87413-952-X (alk. paper)
    1. Infanticide—History.   2. Infanticide—Social aspects.   3. Infanticide—
Religious aspects.   4. Infanticide in literature.   5. Bible. O.T. Genesis—Criticism,
interpretation, etc.   6. Greek literature—History and criticism.   I. Title.
    GN482.5.K56 207
    304.6′68—dc22   2006030917

Contents

Parents cannot regard their Child, as, in a manner, a Thing *of their own making*, for a Being endowed with Freedom cannot be so regarded. Nor, consequently, have they a Right to destroy it as if it were their own property, or even to leave it to chance; because they have brought a Being into the world who becomes in fact a Citizen of the world. . . .

—Kant, *The Philosophy of Law* (114–15)

. . . he remembered his child, coming in out of the glare: the sullen unhappy knowledgeable face. He said, "Oh God, help her. Damn me, I deserve it, but let her live forever." This was the love he should have felt for every soul in the world: all the fear and the wish to save concentrated unjustly on the one child. He began to weep; it was as if he had to watch her from the shore drown slowly because he had forgotten how to swim. He thought: This is what I should feel all the time for everyone, and he tried to turn his brain away towards the half-caste, the lieutenant, even a dentist he had once sat with for a few minutes, the child at the banana station, calling up a long succession of faces, pushing at his attention as if it were a heavy door which wouldn't budge. For those were all in danger too. He prayed, "God help them," but in the moment of prayer he switched back to his child beside the rubbish-dump, and he knew it was for her only that he prayed. Another failure.

—Graham Greene, *The Power and the Glory* (249–50)

"Some must be sacrificed for all others to be saved. At first I took that as revelation for the future. Now I see that it is as much about how we got here as about where we are going. I think that one sentence is the greatest burden I have ever known."

"You're right. Nothing would have been changed, except that my people would now be a dead race."

—*Babylon 5*, "Ship of Tears" (UPN 47, May 4, 1996)

By sacrifice will you procreate!

—*Bhagavad-Gita* (3.9)

Acknowledgments

I PRESENTED AN EARLIER VERSION OF CHAPTER EIGHT, ENTITLED "Oedipus' Five Riddles and Psychoanalytic Pedagogy," at the International Federation for Psychoanalytic Education conference, Toronto, 14 October 1995; *Soundings* (University of Tennessee) published a revised version of this talk, "'Troubles at Our Feet': The Five Riddles of Oedipus" (83.1 [Spring 2000], 201–39).

A longer version of chapter eleven, "Conceptions and Contraceptions of the Future," which includes some material now in chapters two and six, originally appeared in *Camera Obscura* 50 (2002), 69–107. I am thankful to Duke University Press for permission to use the material in this article.

A research stipend from the University of North Florida Office of Academic Affairs (summer 2000) helped underwrite this project.

I am indebted to many colleagues and friends for their questions, suggestions, translations, sometimes their hesitations and resistance, and their encouragement: Barnaby B. Barratt, Jeannette Berger, Mike Bullock, Jamal Chaouki, David Courtwright, Joe Flowers, Dennis V. Higgins, Jess Kimball, Alex Menocal, Dana Mondiano, John Maraldo, Mary Jo Maraldo, Guy Patton, Johnny Randall, Rick Roth, Sheila Roth, Eric Robinson, Shira Schwam-Baird, David Schwam-Baird, Mikush Schwam-Baird, Pam Selton, Rebeca Siegel, Brad Simkulet, Michael Singer, Herb Smith, Jillian Smith, Barrie Ruth Straus, Bryan Swanson, Libby Thomas, Ellen Wagner, and Michael Woodward.

I owe special thanks to Hank Beardsley and Al Siebert for their shadow-lifting friendship; to my father, Arthur G. Kimball, for his unstinting editorial help and encouragement; to Patrick Plumlee for our decade-long discussion of evolutionary biology, which led directly to this project; to Shep Shepard for his unflagging interest and support and his exceptional editorial care and acuity; to Mike Wiley for his lucid feedback and editorial recommendations; to Gregory Goekjian for guiding me through my first encounter with the work of Jacques Derrida and thereby for propelling me into an altogether unexpected future; to John Leavey for the educational opportunity of a lifetime as a student in his courses; to Tim Donovan for his scintillating expositions of Derrida and the example of his own brilliant work; to Henry Staten for explaining how to rewrite the initial draft of this book and for his priceless encouragement; and to Julian Wolfreys for his inspiriting support.

I am grateful to my students for their intellectual engagements with me on the subject matter of this project. I extend my gratitude to those outside of academia who understand the collective social gain that comes from the commitment of the nation's colleges and universities to produce new knowledge and to demonstrate its significance for the moral development of students, bearers of the democratic future and common good to come.

My sense of an uncommon good has deep roots in the rapport I have with, and the love I have received from, my sisters and my brothers and our parents.

Finally, I would like dedicate this book to my wife, Pamela Inez, to whom I am indebted beyond all possibility of reckoning—for her love, her humor, the example of her resilience, her generosity of spirit. . . .

Preface

An initial stimulus for this study came from the work of David Bakan, in particular his analysis of sacrifice in the book of Job. In *Disease, Pain, and Sacrifice: Toward a Psychology of Suffering* (1968), Bakan inspects "the latent content in the Book of Job that led the biblical mind to defend against its manifestation" and suggests that this content centers on the encrypted theme of the father's sacrificial-cum-infanticidal violence. The result is that the text challenges the Freudian understanding of "the identifications and conflicts in the father-son relationship." Job, Bakan proposes, apprehends what Freud resisted, namely "that the Oedipus complex might itself be a reaction of the child to the infanticidal impulse of the father—Laius leaving Oedipus to die as a child—and a defensive response of the child against aggression."[1]

In *The Duality of Human Existence: Isolation and Communion in Western Man* (1966), Bakan counters Freud's contention that the murder of the father inaugurates the history of human religion. "If there was some original holocaust of the kind that Freud envisaged, it appears less likely that it was the killing of the father by the son than the killing of the children by the father."[2] When he looks at the multiple allusions to child killing throughout the Bible, Bakan finds evidence of a recurrent effort to psychologically bind the father's infanticidal impulse by means of such practices as circumcision or such celebrations as Passover. To this end Christ's fate signals an important development in the representation of paternal aggression, since Jesus dies as a son: "*It was as the Son of Man, the son of man with the tendency to infanticide, that he suffered and died.*"[3] His undeserved death as a holy innocent "was *full* payment, a 'real' infanticide."[4]

In *Slaughter of the Innocents: A Study of the Battered Child Phenomenon* (1971), Bakan identifies the bio-economic payoffs of getting rid of one's child by killing it outright or by degrees. In his influential *Folkways* of 1906, W. G. Sumner notes that "Abortion and infanticide are primary and violent acts of self-defense by the parents against famine, disease, and other calamities of overpopulation, which increase with the number which each man or woman has to provide for."[5] According to this hypothesis, more carefully formulated versions of which are well-supported by current anthropological data, infanticide represents a rational—that is, self-interested or utility-maximizing—response to the perceived economic

11

burden of birthing and rearing the child. It is an economic—more precisely, an economizing—choice in relation to the costs and benefits parents or prospective parents confront in determining to what extent they shall invest in their children.

Bakan's three works situate the meaning of infanticide in relation to the cultural continuity this cross-generational violence jeopardizes. "A group which does not spare resources for the raising of children and teaches those children to care for their children in turn guarantees its future for itself." A group that begrudges its children the care they need jeopardizes its future. "If we understand the meanings of child abuse," therefore, "we come to understand the general problem of the relationship among the generations."[6] Infanticide focuses that problem, especially if, as Bakan argues, "in some way, and at some level of consciousness, the aim of those who abuse a child is to kill the child."[7] Such a motivation renders human groupings vulnerable to destruction from within: "If we can come to understand how parents can abuse their own children, we may learn how a group may survive in an integral fashion beyond the limited existence of its individual members."[8]

Bakan's conditional hope requires that "we" come to understand intrafamilial violence not only in its most overt manifestations but also in its covert expressions. In addition to the multiple kinds, degrees, and methods of physical and emotional abuse, "infanticide has other forms. Besides the actual beating and murder of children, we can recognize the infanticidal impulse in child neglect and undereducation, the poverty associated with the too rapid multiplication of people, and total war, which does not separate children from adults." Bakan concludes with the terrible irony that, "in our times, the absence of contraception is conducive to these other forms of infanticide."[9] This study formalizes and generalizes the analytic procedures that enable Bakan to read an infanticidal signification into phenomena that might appear to have nothing infanticidal about them. The result, however, is that this study finds the logical form of infanticide not only in the empirical phenomena Bakan explores but in the structure of the very realities Bakan privileges as antidotal to infanticide: love and care, existence and survival, the future, and cooperation and community.

A second intellectual stimulus for this study has come from René Girard's well-known hypothesis that violence is immanent in the very nature of human mimesis, which is the sacrificial source of all beliefs, attitudes, and behaviors—that is, of all cultural phenomena, indeed of humanness itself. However, Girard, like Bakan, I believe, remains tied to certain metaphysical presuppositions concerning the empirical world, assumptions the contradictoriness of which Jacques Derrida has delineated in the course of his many deconstructions. Behind this study, then, is an encounter with the works of Derrida, which clarified for me the limits of any anthropo-psychological approach to the infanticidal as empirical act only.

One other influence—the evolutionary perspective of Richard Dawkins and Sarah Blaffer Hrdy—helped give final shape to this work. In the course of their respective researches—Hrdy's reconceptualization of the reproductive benefits of infanticide among animals and Dawkins' redescription of natural selection in terms of the so-called selfish gene and extended phenotype —these two empiricists have nevertheless advanced convergent lines of reasoning that, far from being antithetical to deconstruction, in fact offer a hitherto unrecognized basis for developing a Derridean critique of evolution theory from within that very theory. Despite the antipathy of evolutionary biologists to deconstruction, certain Derridean notions help clarify and extend key implications of neo-Darwinian thought. In sum, the present study reexamines the concept and rubric of infanticide vis-à-vis the analytic possibilities opened up by Derrida's deconstructions. It endeavors to demonstrate that the logical form of the structure of infanticide is the logical form of the structure of evolution, hence of life, including the human life-world; in other words, that empirical infanticides are but one manifestation of the world's infanticidism—world here including the sacred. This demonstration, in turn, provides a point of departure for exploring how Western culture, going back to its Jewish, Greek, and Christian roots, has apprehended and misunderstood, embraced and repudiated, recalled and repressed, named and encrypted not only the specter of an empirical death—the body of the killed child—but an entirely other order of infanticidal haunting. For the Western world has always known that life is and cannot avoid being infanticidal. Such an insight—in conjunction with its denial, better its encryption—ought to be investigated as the Western world's constitutive legacy, the heart and soul of its tradition. Because the knowledge of the infanticidal has not been able to be explicitly avowed without the risk of violent reaction, the West has had to conceal its realization, secreting its apprehension between the lines of its most revered texts in the hopes of thereby keeping it alive long enough for it to be transmitted to posterity—in the words of Leo Strauss, "to a time when no one would suffer any harm from hearing any truth."[10] Or, since the truth in question is that no truth can be completely harm-free, to a time when it is possible to publicly and collectively acknowledge this consequence of the world's infanticidal horizons and to do so in ways that would help demystify the costs of existence.

Introduction

INFANTICIDE IN WESTERN LITERATURE

INFANTICIDE—FATAL VIOLENCE AGAINST INFANTS AND CHILDREN, more generally against a person of a successor generation—is a recurrent, though seldom remarked, theme in much Western literature. Infanticide, of course, has received spectacular representation in Euripides' *Medea* and in the biblical narrative of Abraham's call to sacrifice his son Isaac. In both works, the real or threatened destruction of the child is central to the deepest meanings and ramifications of the narratives. More typically, however, texts mention or allude to infanticide but do not otherwise describe or depict it. The result is that infanticide has been relegated to the margins of the work, sometimes remarked but mostly ignored.

The most conspicuous example has to be Sophocles' Oedipus, one of Western literature's paradigmatic figures of suffering. Readers know that Laius and Jocasta wanted their newborn son to die, that to avoid having blood on their hands they ordered their servant to abandon him on the mountains, and that to warn others from rescuing the infant they bound his feet together, perhaps piercing his ankles. Readers know that Oedipus receives his name—"Swell Foot"—from this savage act of maiming. In short, readers know that Oedipus is born not just to infanticidal parents but to infanticidal rulers. Might this knowledge not be pertinent to the meaning of Oedipus' career and thus to the aesthetic shape of the tragedy? As a child, would Oedipus not have wondered about how he came to be crippled, how he came to have a compromised infancy? When he learns of the widespread rumor that he is a bastard, would he not have asked his parents—especially his mother, Merope, whose name means "articulate speech"—point blank whether or not he was adopted? Is it an accident that, raised by a verbally adept surrogate mother, he would be able to solve the riddle of the Sphinx and that he would defeat the monster whose name ("the Binder") recalls the mutilating aggression directed against his infant body? When he comes to Thebes as a stranger from Corinth, could Oedipus not have chosen any name he wished, as immigrants, in fact, often do? In announcing that he is an "oedipus," a

"swell-foot," does he really not know that his name signifies the consequences of the aggression by which his parents, figures of the Theban
law itself, endeavored not just to kill him but to eliminate all trace of his
existence? Perhaps. Or perhaps there is something about the motif of infanticide that has been difficult for the West to integrate into its vision of
the world.

In fact allusions to infanticide pervade Greek culture and literature
and constitute a largely unexplored influence on European thought. Infanticidal figuration is conspicuous, for example, throughout the Greek
mythic tradition, from Kronos' cannibalistic incorporation of his children to the cross-generational aggression among the descendants of
King Pelops, whose son Atreus serves up to his brother Thyestes the
flesh of his own children, and whose grandson Agamemnon sacrifices his
daughter Iphegenia at the outset of the Trojan War. In depicting the origin of the world, Greek myth dramatizes the irruption of an infanticidal
violence in the genealogies of the very figures — gods on the one hand,
kings and queens on the other — who bear the greatest responsibility
for ensuring cosmic, social, and familial order. That the mythic struggle
for power among the Greek pantheon should involve infanticidal aggression, that this form of violence should then be repeated by the human descendants of the gods, and that the classical tragedians reenacted the infanticidal terms of the mythic tradition — all this signals the centrality of
infanticide to the Greek conception of life. The question is, why? Why
should the motif of infanticide be in evidence at the heart of the Greek
imagination?

That infanticide is crucial to the New Testament vision as well raises
a similar question. Why is it important that, after Joseph eludes the efforts of King Herod to locate the infant Jesus, the king is so enraged that
he orders the massive slaughter of "all the children in and around Bethlehem who were two years old or under"?[1] Is the infanticidal context —
indeed, the infanticidal consequence — of Jesus' advent incidental to his
destiny? When Jesus lifts up a little child and declares, "whoever welcomes one such child in my name welcomes me" (Mark 9:37), might he
be signaling that whoever rejects him rejects the child? Since he is the
"Son of God," isn't his impending crucifixion infanticidal? Does he not
hint at this meaning when he announces that those who are "children
of God" and "of the resurrection" are those who "cannot die anymore"
(Luke 20:36)? Why does he evoke the "days of vengeance" and then warn,
"Woe to those who are pregnant and to those who are nursing infants in
those days!" (Luke 21:23)? If Jesus alludes — repeatedly — to the specter
of infanticidal jeopardy, surely he does so for reasons that are central to
his message. If so, what are these reasons? The answers, I believe, help
explain why infanticide keeps reappearing throughout Western literature.

Although it is not the intent of this book to provide a history of this recurrence, even a cursory listing of major European authors who have employed the motif of infanticide suggests how persistent it has been. With respect to the European epic tradition, for example, such a list begins with Homer, Ovid, and Virgil, passes through Dante, and extends to Milton and Goethe, among the many others who represent the infanticidal demise of children at some point or other in their works. This list encompasses as well an extraordinary range of the major modern European authors, especially dramatists and fiction writers. It includes any number of playwrights, among then Corneille, Ibsen, Strindberg, Anouilh, Beckett, and Pirandello. It includes such poets as Schiller, Blake, Wordsworth, Arnold, Rilke, Trakl, Yeats, and Eliot. It also includes such continental fiction writers as Dostoevsky, Kafka, Brecht, Mann, Hermann Hesse, Günter Grass, Elias Canetti, Ilse Aichinger, Alain Robbe-Grillet, Raymond Queneau, Christa Wolf, Primo Levi, and Alexander Solzhenitsyn, to name but some of the more notable figures. It includes Sartre, whose narrator in *Nausea* repeatedly alludes to infanticide as he comes closer and closer to his existential revelation when he beholds the roots of a chestnut tree in a public garden—that is, in a scene that reinterprets the mythic advent of self-consciousness in relation to the Tree of Knowledge in Genesis. It includes as well Camus, whose central character in *The Plague* organizes his narration in part around the protracted suffering and death of a child. More recently, it includes George Konrad's *The Case Worker,* the narrative brilliance of which turns on its astonishing catalogs of abused and damaged children.

It includes any number of British authors from Malory and Shakespeare (and not only in the tragedies) to Mary Shelley, Sir Walter Scott, George Eliot, Charles Dickens, and James Joyce. The register of authors who have incorporated references to infanticide could be extended indefinitely. Among Spanish writers of the new world it includes, for example, such tradition-reshaping authors as Carlos Fuentes, Jorge Luis Borges, and Gabriel Garcia Marquez. It also necessarily includes, more recently, the literature of the Holocaust, in which the apocalyptic implication of infanticide and genocide, the one in the other, discloses certain non-transcendable conceptual limits to mimetic representation. It includes as well numerous works of film, one of the most exemplary of which is *M,* German director Fritz Lang's chilling account of a compulsive child murderer.

In the literary tradition of the United States, allusions to infanticide are at the heart of the first novel, *Wieland* (1798), by the first professional American author, Charles Brockden Brown, which reinterprets the story of Abraham and Isaac. They punctuate the action of and provide a key structuring principle in James Fenimore Cooper's *The Last of the Mohicans*

(1826). They are implicit throughout *Moby-Dick* (1851) and are explicit almost from the first page of Hawthorne's "The Custom-House" introduction to *The Scarlet Letter* (1850). They are evident in no less than six twentieth-century Pulitzer prize-winning plays by O'Neill, Albee, and Shepard. They are pivotal throughout Faulkner's corpus. They are at the dramatic center of Morrison's *Beloved*, Styron's *Sophie's Choice*, and Heller's *Something Happened*. Representations of infanticide occur in Nevil Shute's meditation on nuclear apocalypse, *On the Beach*; in Bellow's *Herzog*, whose title character witnesses a trial in which a young woman is accused of brutally murdering her child; in Updike's *Rabbit, Run*, when Rabbit's inebriated wife accidentally drowns their first child; in Malamud's *The Fixer*, which opens with the ominous discovery of the dead body of a child; in Auster's *City of Glass*, which situates cross-generational violence against a child at the heart of its mystery; in James Ellroy's *White Jazz*, when Dudley strangles Joan Herrick's three-day-old infant, as well as in *L.A. Confidential*, in which the Atherton case, involving the savage dismemberment of children, provides the horizon of the novel's vision of evil; in all of the novels by Andrew Vacchss, whose outlaw protagonist is driven by the memory of having been savagely mistreated to exact revenge years later on any child abuser who crosses his path; in such short stories as Raymond Carver's "A Small Good Thing" or Lorrie Moore's "Terrific Mother"; in the fiction and poetry of Sylvia Plath; in the large and growing body of "abortion literature"; in numerous avant-garde works, including Kathy Acker's *Empire of the Senseless* and Art Spiegelman's *Maus* I and II; in any number of horror films; in countless works of detective fiction (Scott Turow's *Reversible Errors* contains numerous, seemingly marginal or passing references to infanticide which are nevertheless central to the story's existential vision); in apocalyptic science fiction cinema (three of which are the subject of this project's concluding chapter); and in countless works of popular culture. Much of Stephen King's work, for example, and not just his horror fiction, focuses on the vulnerability of children to aggressive parents. Most recently, his novel *The Green Mile* and the film adaptation of it turn on the brutal murder of two young girls. His recent adaptation, *Kingdom Hospital*, of the Danish television series, *The Kingdom*, involves the murder of children. The initial storyline of David Lynch's and Mark Frost's *Twin Peaks* revolves around a father's murder of the daughter he has raped for years. Shortly after *Finding Nemo* begins, the bright colors of the Disney film disappear as the father wakens to discover that all but one of his near-hatchlings have been devoured. The final episode of one of the most widely watched television series, *M.A.S.H.*, revolves around Hawkeye's at first euphemistic but eventually explicit, shocking admission of his traumatizing responsibility for forcing a Korean mother to smother her infant when its crying threatens to draw the attention of enemy troops nearby.

So prevalent has been the occurrence of infanticide in literature that it appears in the works of no less than fifteen Nobel Prize winners. However, only in the novels of one (Toni Morrison) have critics directly addressed the motif of infanticide, and even then not in relation to the place of this theme in the cultural trajectory of the Western world. The subject of infanticide, therefore, raises two questions: why have allusions to this particular form of violence occurred so often, and why have they gone largely unnoticed, let alone explained?

Why should Western texts return again and again to the figure of the endangered or destroyed child? The answer is that through the image of infanticide they have intuited something fundamental about the nature of existence, which the critical tradition has been loathe to face.

INFANTICIDE VERSUS THE INFANTICIDAL

To understand why infanticide has recurred so frequently in literature but has scarcely ever been commented on requires distinguishing between *infanticide* and *the infanticidal.* Infanticide refers, literally, to the killing of infant offspring but includes the destruction of the young in general, one's own or those of others, among animals and humans. As will be seen in chapter 2, evolutionary biologists have broadened the category of infanticide still further, so that it encompasses the direct or indirect death of offspring at any stage in the life cycle. Whether it is defined more narrowly or more broadly, the concept of infanticide as it is used in the sciences refers to the empirical act or its outcome.

However, the adjective form of infanticide—infanticidal—is ambiguous. One can use the word *infanticidal* to designate an act, an attitude, an intention, or a practice without a literal infanticide taking place. Anyone who puts his or her children at risk (for example, by not strapping them into a safety seat when driving) is behaving in an infanticidal manner even if no infanticide occurs. A society that pursues certain policies or economic practices (such as directing health and educational resources in a manner that discriminates against some of its members) jeopardizes the well-being of children. In either case, the effects of repeated risk and jeopardy do not have to eventuate in infanticide in order to be infanticidal. The infanticidal effects, intended or not, of behaviors and of the beliefs and attitudes that motivate them can accumulate so slowly and covertly and by such small degrees that they may not end in the demise of the child, who may escape such a fate before the consequences of inadequate care, neglect, or abuse become perceptible, let alone lethal.

In the absence of infanticide, infanticidal effects can nevertheless be accruing stealthily, little by little, over time. Moreover, they might be the indirect consequence, once again intended or unintended, not of individual actions but of institutional practices and broad social processes — economic, political, military — the nature and results of which a culture takes for granted or otherwise does not conceptualize in infanticidal terms. Under these and other circumstances it is possible for the infanticidal to be transpiring here and now, before everyone's eyes, and not register as such. That is in effect what has happened throughout the history of Western literature.

Because it is always possible that infanticidal attitudes, intentions, actions, or processes will not eventuate in infanticide, the infanticidal — what I propose to designate by the terms *infanticidality, infanticidism,* and *infanticidity* — cannot be reduced to a simply empirical object of study. Reduced to infanticide (the literal death of an infant or child), "the infanticidal" (as that which does not necessarily result in infanticide) nearly disappears. Hence the necessity for a mode of investigation that takes as its subject not the killing of infants and children but the logic, structure, and economy of that which is infanticidal whether or not there is actual death at hand. These features of the infanticidal, I argue, are intrinsic to the processes of evolution; they appear, as well, to be inherent in the most foundational of cultural institutions and practices.

THE INFANTICIDAL AS BIOLOGICAL LIMIT

The infanticidal horizon of evolution derives from the most fundamental biological necessity: in a world of finite energy and material resources and limited reproductive opportunities, all living things must economize to survive — that is, transfer more of the costs of their existence onto the environment or onto their competitors than their competitors are able for their part to transfer. As a corollary necessity, living things must produce relatively more offspring able to survive and reproduce in turn than do their competitors. Reproductive success, then, is not absolute but relative; reproduction is not successful unless it is more successful (alternatively, less unsuccessful) than that of one's competitors. This means that relative reproductive success for oneself entails relative reproductive failure for others. To win reproductively is thus logically equivalent to imposing an infanticidal fate on those that lose reproductively; the very characteristics that enable an organism to outreproduce its competitors render reproductivity infanticidal. Every conception and birth expresses the deathliness at the heart of Darwinian existence. Insofar as reproduction is a Darwinian contest, it is an engine not of life alone but of life and death, indeed of life as death, of life as a process of driving other life to — infanticidal — extinction.

The first chapter elucidates this (infanticidal) deathliness that is part and parcel of reproduction. The second chapter shows in detail how, in constituting the condition of evolutionary possibility, the features of the infanticidal explain why evolution necessarily will lead to the demise of the life to which it has given rise. Together, the two chapters of part 1 conclude that the infanticidal cannot be escaped. The subsequent chapters (parts 2–4) argue that certain key Judaic, Greek, and Christian texts have endeavored to acknowledge and address the significance of this inescapability against enormous and pervasive cultural pressures to mystify it. In showing how texts foundational to the West have broached the thought not just of infanticide but of the infanticidal, this study aspires to elaborate the terms of an interdisciplinary discourse from which contemporary research on infanticide has been isolated.

THE INFANTICIDAL AS CULTURAL LIMIT

Having arisen as a result of the natural selection by which life competes with life, humankind remains tied to the necessity of economization. It is unlikely that any human society has not recognized the sacrificial-cum-infanticidal implications of its economizing, no matter how indirect, halting, incomplete, or conflicted is its articulation of this awareness. Indeed, one of the most basic human perceptions is doubtless that existence costs. So fundamental is this insight that it is implied in the etymological kinship of the two terms — "existence" and "cost" are Latin cognates from a common Indo-European stem — that make up this redundant predication. The knowledge that "existence costs" compresses into a single proposition the consequences of the bio-economic burden that any group of people — any family, any line of descent, any society, any culture — must negotiate: once again, how to deflect the costs of individual and collective existence elsewhere than onto itself, elsewhere than onto its own members, or, where this is not possible, onto its most expendable members.

Throughout its history the West — that is, the regions, peoples, and traditions that have come under the general sway of the Greek and then the Christianized Logos — has sought to control the costs of existence by economizing on them according to the imperatives of its basic philosophical concepts, institutions, and practices. The cultural formations that organize this economization — three of the most far-reaching of which have been stratified social institutions that funnel resources up a narrowing hierarchy of privilege and power; military conquest for territory, tribute, and slave labor; and the deification of the paternal — are manifestly sacrificial.

Western thought has rationalized this sacrificial economization in any number of ways, most dramatically, for example, by positing the infinite, world-begetting generativity of the Word. Whether or not the *Logos* provides access to a spiritual realm where the necessity of economization might be imagined not to occur, the belief that it does cannot eliminate the sacrificiality of mortal existence. For this reason economization sooner or later eventuates in a crisis over the allocation of resources — that is, in a crisis concerning the material basis of existence — of sufficient magnitude that its infanticidal consequences begin to be glimpsed.

In representing such crises, the culturally foundational texts this study examines have confronted the seeming paradox that the desire for an escape from the infanticidal — including the forms of political economy this desire underwrites — increases the risk of infanticide. These texts — few in number — not only analyze the cultural circumstances in which infanticide occurs in conjunction with dreams of transcendence, but push through to the thought of the infanticidal as such, to the non-transcendable infanticidism of the world. However, most of the Western literature that has discerned the sacrificiality of economization, especially in its patriarchal forms, has resisted its infanticidal implications and has wound up affirming the purity and perfection of the paternal function in its ideal — that is, its transcendental, hence its seemingly holiest — form. In doing so, however, these texts have unwittingly abetted the rationalization of the violence that the position of the father as worldly origin requires.

A number of scholars have shown how. In *Dreams of the Burning Child*, for example, David Lee Miller has adapted the comparative religion studies of Nancy Jay to demonstrate that the spectacle of the sacrificed son — one of "the most striking feature[s] shared by the canonical texts of English literature, along with their classical and biblical antecedents" — is ironically organized by the contradictory logic of patrilineal descent and patriarchal authority, which for their part demand such spectacles.[2] The contradictoriness results from treating the category of the father as if it did not depend on the category of the child. A person is a father only if he has a child. If he kills his child, he ceases to be a father. The category of father thus depends on the category of child. The logic of paternal transcendence, however, requires that the father be categorically independent of all other categories.

On the one hand, then, in order to establish his ontological and epistemological claims to being the (transcendental) source of life, the father must always be able to destroy his children, in particular his sons. If he did not have such power over life and death, even of his own offspring, then his authority would not be absolute but limited and contingent. For this reason infanticide is the (non-transcendable) condition of the possibility of paternal transcendence. On the other hand, in threatening to kill the child, and all the more so in carrying out the threat, the father undermines and even abolishes the very paternity that patriarchal institutions would represent as having transcendental value and thus as being transcendentally immune to disruption or abrogation. Patriarchal authority cannot gain control over the infanticidal by unleashing specific manifestations of the infanticidal—infanticide or other empirical forms of violence—and yet that is just what the patriarchal function has aspired to accomplish.

For example, at the end of the *Odyssey*, Homer's hero returns to Ithaka to reclaim his position as the paternal leader of his people and symbolically his children. Threatened by the sons of his countrymen, however, Odysseus slaughters them all. In other words, in order to assert the (heroic) paternal values—the strength and resourcefulness to survive deadly challenges, a resolute homeward orientation, and an inexhaustible phallic generativity—which he represents as king, Odysseus becomes a force of infanticide: he kills those in whom the future of Ithaka is vested and threatens to plunge his kingdom into an apocalypse of self-destruction. When Zeus—"Father of us all, and king of kings," Athena calls him[3]—intervenes, the Olympian god does not undo the (infanticidal) price of Odysseus' restoration; he remarks its inescapability. At the end, then, a father and the "true son"[4] at his side "would have cut the enemy down to the last man, leaving not one survivor."[5] If Telemakhos is a "true son," as he is characterized earlier in the epic, it is because he fights in alliance with, not against, the "true" father. Here, as elsewhere, the *Odyssey* intuits that the supposed truth of the paternal progenitor and his offspring is inseparable from (infanticidal) violence, which the *Odyssey* mystifies by giving it Zeus's sacred, paternal imprimatur.

This mystification occurs in the grounding metaphor of Western philosophy, which conceives of thought itself as a species of (masculine) conception. To apprehend one of the quintessentially human activities as an ideal form of the body's reproductivity is to posit thought as fundamentally generative. But this presumes that thought both provides access to a force of ontological generation and is indeed a manifestation of this force. If, however, cognitive capacities have arisen as a result of evolutionary selection, then thinking is necessarily circumscribed by the general evolutionary economy of the infanticidal. To represent thinking as conceiving is therefore to mystify its nature. If to think is to conceive, it is thus not *not* to conceive. To think is, perforce, to be unable to conceive what is inconceivable within the limits of the metaphorical system of thought as conception. It is to be cut off from the infanticidity that prevents thought from being a purely conceptive force of being, or that makes even the most conceptive thought infanticidal.

What makes the logic of the infanticidal border on the inconceivable is not primarily its complexity but its counterintuitive role in the very self-reflexivity by which humans have conscious access to their own minds. If consciousness at its most generative is possible by virtue of that which within life leads to the death of the individual, to the extinction of the genetic lineage, and eventually to the disappearance of the biological altogether, then this condition of thought's possibility is at the furthest distance from the way consciousness seems to produce itself from out of itself. Thus, consciousness would seem to be radically alien to the conceptuality by which Western thought has represented this self-production of itself; once again, it would be the inconceivable within the conceivable.

Evolutionary theory broaches this inconceivability through the phenomenon of infanticide, which unexpectedly opens the possibility of an infanticidal limit to the order of the biological. Long before the modern era, however, certain Judeo-Christian and Greek texts approached the inconceivable through an intuition about the infanticidal limits to culture. These texts can be read as participating in the "symbolic economy of [sacrificial] witnessing," in Miller's phrase,[6] by which the patriarchal tradition blocks the recognition of its own contradictions, which it nevertheless preserves and transmits from generation to generation.

However, these texts can also be read as attempting to think of the paternal against the way it has traditionally been conceived, as struggling to "counter-conceive" the paternal function in other than the idealizing, transcendentalizing terms that have derived from what Henry Staten calls "the massive historical phenomena of Platonism and Platonizing Christianity."[7] If the West defines itself principally in terms of an epochal investment in the possibility of such transcendence, nevertheless some of its most cherished texts have resisted the ontological vision that underwrites this investment. To this end they have refused the (infanticide-provoking) dream of an escape from finitude, a dream seemingly fulfilled in the infinitude of a Logos that guarantees the conceptivity of the concept.

In evoking the theme of infanticide, especially of the child assaulted by a father and thus imperiled by the very paternal authority that depends on the child for its future, the texts at hand have thereby initiated a collective work of mourning through which this cultural dream might be given up. They have offered in its place two converging recognitions. The first is of the infanticidal implications of the costliness—the lost opportunities that are the price—of all choice. This is the recognition that, as the endpoint of a line of reflection, decision is part of the thinking process that is itself infanticidal. This is also the recognition that, as the action by which one cuts off all the other possibilities that might have been selected, all the other futures, for which the infant or child has long been the most familiar symbol, decision is always infanticision, that is, choice marked by the inescapability not of infanticide but of infanticidal consequence. The second recognition is that openness to the world's infanticidity is not the occasion for despairing at the loss of an idealized paternal function but for affirming what this loss may enable yet to come. Providing this double recognition, the texts in question give back to the Western cultural tradition, in the spectral image of the dead child in particular and of infanticidal figuration more generally, the denied meaning of the (Western) quest for transcendence. They thereby anticipate and provide an opening to a radically other, hitherto inconceivable, cultural future and to a reflection on the responsibility for such futurity.

THE JUDAIC, GREEK, AND CHRISTIAN INTIMATIONS OF THE INFANTICIDAL

The apprehension that the costs of economization are another name for a violence that is unavoidably sacrificial of, in fact infanticidal toward, other human life is, this study claims, one of the most intimate insights of the Judaic, Greek, and Christian traditions. So troubling has this prospect been, however, that it has evoked the most powerful of resistances from within the very traditions that have been led to acknowledge it. The result has been uncanny: the keeping hidden from view of a perturbing and dangerous awareness, which, century after century, millennium after millennium, has nevertheless been continuously passed on across the generations.

This strange and covert sending from one generation to the next organizes some of the most important narratives in the Judaic as well as Homeric and classical Greek traditions. The texts to be examined here are in each case overtly preoccupied with the reproductive politics of cross-generational transfer and the vulnerability of genealogical continuity to infanticidal disruption.

The three chapters of part 2 examine how Genesis negotiates this disruption by trying to develop the difference — and the consequences of the difference for understanding the sacred — between infanticide and the infanticidal. A meditation on beginnings — on the creation of the cosmos, of life in general, of human life in particular, of history, of the promise, which is to say of a time to come — Genesis is preoccupied with securing the future through the begetting of children. Begotten of God, the world becomes the backdrop for the history of human begettings and the sacredness of the "blessing" that will be imagined through them.

And yet from the outset Genesis repeatedly alludes to infanticidal violence. Indeed, whenever it alludes to *toledot* (literally "begettings"), the term that bears "the characteristic contribution of Genesis to the Torah," according to J. P. Fokkelman,[8] the specter of infanticidal violence hovers in the background. As chapter 3 demonstrates, it is present in the account of the first sin and punishment and Cain's subsequent murder of Abel, in the story of the Flood, in the episode of Noah's nakedness, and in the brief history of the Babel disaster. It is also present in the account of Abraham's accession to the role of the first patriarch, especially with respect to his attempted intervention in the punishment of Sodom and Gomorrah, to the covenant of circumcision, and to the exiling of Ishmael. Why? The story of the *akedah*—the "binding" of Isaac—suggests an answer. In the shocking drama of Abraham's obedience to the divine call to immolate his son, the Genesis narrative anticipates one of the most basic temptations of the patriarchive—the desire to represent God simply as the source of a pure generation that would be free of the infanticidism that the *akedah* insists is inextricable from the sacred.

The *akedah* has typically been interpreted as a test of Abraham's faith in a God who repudiates the practice of sacrifice. God directs Abraham to sacrifice his son, and, when Abraham obeys, directs him not to sacrifice. Nearly all readings of the *akedah* embrace with relief this seemingly reassuring resolution. They can do so, however, only by treating the first command as a means by which God would manifest the self-evident moral authority of his second command. Such a teleological hermeneutic maneuver supposedly enables the text to dramatize a coherent, nonsacrificial meaning, thereby removing the specter of divine infanticidity attaching to God's initial call.

Chapter 4 argues, to the contrary, that all teleological readings of Abraham and Isaac betray an anxiety they cannot name concerning the structural inevitability of the violence which these readings mistakenly insist that ethics can transcend. These readings thus miss the significance of Kierkegaard's insight and Jacques Derrida's elaboration of it, the subject of chapter 5, that the *akedah* redefines faith as a response to the limits of the ethical. For those who cling to the possibility of transcendence, the thought of such limits cannot be tolerated because it threatens to abolish the ethical as a transcendental ground. Kierkegaard, Derrida, and the *akedah* narrative itself know otherwise—namely, that the ethical is itself possible only this side of the untranscendable horizon of the infanticidal.

Turning from the first patriarch in the Judaic tradition to representations of the paternal in the Greek philosophical tradition, chapter 6 investigates what Robert Con Davis has termed "the paternal romance," the cultural practices by which the Western world has attributed to the social role of the father a metaphorical power of conception, a power it then literalizes and transcendentalizes. In the process the paternal romance represses the infanticidism of the symbolic order. The study's central examples come from the *Odyssey*, Sophocles' *Oedipus the King*, and the Gospel of John, the subjects of the next three chapters.

The *Odyssey*, the subject of chapter 7, illustrates the perverse logic by which the denial of the symbolic order's constitutive infanticidality eventuates in a crisis of infanticide (Odysseus' aforementioned return home and decimation of the suitors, sons of his peers, the kingdom's fathers). The epic reveals its ambivalence toward the symbolic order by contextualizing Odysseus' identity as an injured son who mimetically redirects against his opponents the infanticidal aggression aimed at him throughout his life, especially by Poseidon. In thus living up to the meaning of his name as one who "odysseuses"—that is, suffers and causes others to suffer—Odysseus acts out the infanticidal meaning of Greek culture's most basic religious practice, the paternal institution of the burnt offering. This meaning is readable through its inscription on Odysseus' body of the scar he acquired in adolescence and through this scar's symbolic encoding of his name.

Chapter 8 argues that Sophocles' Oedipus apprehends in his scars and name the infanticidal aggression that Odysseus acts out and that Oedipus' own kingdom harbors. Oedipus, I believe, would bring this aggression into the open. To that general end he scripts the ironies to which he appears, but only appears, to fall victim. He does so for two reasons: first, in order to name the father's violence and the cultural practices by which that violence would be covered up; and, second, in order to communicate the still more confounding difficulty attendant upon apprehending the infanticidal cost of existence in general.

Proleptically anticipating the tradition that will arrogate to itself a paternally guaranteed interpretive mastery greater than that of the riddle-solving Oedipus, Sophocles' king understands not only the father's empirical violence but the infanticidal violence of the symbolic order, of that which establishes the supposed oedipal destiny of the human subject. Risking persecution in the form of an indictment for alleged crimes against his biological parents, Oedipus would bring to light the attempted infanticide those parents sought against him and thus the infanticidal source of the plague that bedevils Thebes. Were he to succeed, he would be showing how the Theban crisis of infanticide arises as a symptomatic reaction against the general infanticidity attaching to all conception, whether the child-to-be is wanted or not, and to the symbolic order through which conception is able to take place.

In the figure of Oedipus, Sophocles anticipates but falls short of the world-transforming Eucharistic discourse through which Jesus delivers himself and those for whom he dies not from but to the infanticidal—not from but to the non-transcendable infanticidity of the Divine Logos itself. Whereas pagan sacrifices—such as the burnt offerings and meat meals of Greek religion—hide the infanticidism of the gods and those who would worship them, the Eucharist brings the infanticidal violence of the body's hunger as well as of the Spirit's Word to the very tip of the tongue. In the Eucharist, then, Jesus transforms pagan sacrifice—which is always in the name of an economization at an enemy's expense—into an absolute self-sacrifice, a sacrifice of the Logos by the Logos, by which the incarnate figure of this Word would announce that there is no step beyond the infanticidal, no transcendence of it, because the infanticidal delimits the entirety of the existence made by the Word.

If the world is bounded by an infanticidal horizon, what becomes of the human future? In response to this question, the final chapter turns to three science fiction films for their depictions of humans threatened by their technological or hybrid progeny. In representing humankind's victory over its Darwinian enemies, the first two films, *The Matrix* and *Terminator 2*, distance (alienate) themselves from the infanticidal implications of their plots and themes; in contrast the third, *Alien Resurrection*, confronts these implications head-on. Whereas *The Matrix* and *Terminator 2* figure the enemy as a nonbiological, self-replicating alien, *Alien Resurrection* ultimately imagines it in the uncanny likeness of a human fetus. *Alien Resurrection* thus faces—literally so—what the other two films cannot concerning the infanticidal meaning of the violence by which humans would ensure their (temporary) survival into the future. More provocatively, *Alien Resurrection* suggests that human survival is compromised by the very "persons"—they are human simulacra, one a cyborg, the other a genetically enhanced human clone—who destroy the alien invaders. In these manufactured beings given human bodies, the film represents the end of humankind as having already occurred—invisibly—before the audience's eyes, the same unseeing eyes that Oedipus beseeches to see the infanticidism of the world.

Projecting one among possible futures, a future that barely escapes annihilation by another possible future, *Alien Resurrection* in effect remarks the monstrousness of the demand for a response to the numberless possible futures lost in the advent of any actual future. The future, Derrida has written, "can only be proclaimed, presented, as a sort of monstrosity,"[9] or as what Thomas Keenan calls a certain "enigma within humanity."[10] Personifying this monstrous enigma in the agonizing death-screams of a grotesque, half-human, half-alien hybrid neonate, *Alien Resurrection* beholds in terror the infanticidal prospect that has haunted the Western imagination from its outset.

The Risks of Cross-Disciplinarity

Anyone who would venture out of his or her discipline to speak or write of matters on which others are expert by virtue of their in-discipline education and training must earn the right to enter the intellectual territory staked out by the disciplines in question. At the same time, disciplines are themselves historically contingent institutions, the claims of which are and must be subject to critical inspection. No discipline has a simple and unproblematic authority over its subject matter. This study is therefore offered in the name of a cross-disciplinarity that aspires to respect — by working through and elaborating the consequences of, and on certain issues presuming to challenge — the intellectual achievements of the specific disciplinary researches with which it engages.

In bringing together a group of disparate texts from widely different disciplines, this study recognizes that the infanticidal is not confined to specific historical moments but is nevertheless manifest in its empirical embodiments only in history. Thus, this study affirms that the forms and patterns of the empirical phenomenon of human infanticide must be historicized, that the imbricated particularities of infanticide among specific communities, regions, countries, or cultures at certain periods in their respective histories must be carefully delineated in relation to the economic, political, and social contexts within which violence against infants and children occurs. Moreover, it affirms all the more the necessity of historicizing to the extent that the effort at contextualizing is a means of countering the idealizing maneuvers by which a culture would reify itself as universal and would claim for itself a transcendental meaning and value.

Part of this historicizing work must be to inspect the conceptual and methodological limits, outlined above, to any empirical study of infanticide. Empirical approaches — no matter how rigorous they are in their definitional, descriptive, methodological, fact-finding, analytical, and interpretive protocols — cannot identify, operationalize, or otherwise specify the infanticidal as such, for the infanticidal is not reducible to an empirical category. If infanticide is determinable as an event that transpires in the worlds of animals and humans, the infanticidal is not, for at a certain level of analysis it is one of the very conditions of these worlds. If so, then it requires a mode of inspection that traverses disciplinary boundaries and the periodizations and other demarcations that the practitioners of the disciplines in question have determined to be operative for their respective fields. In crossing some of these borders, the interdisciplinary movement of the present project does not seek to evade the materiality of history; to the contrary, it aims at understanding how Western

culture itself has repeatedly sought this impossible goal of worldly transcendence by conceiving of itself in idealizing, self-purifying, universal-
izing terms, terms that conceal precisely the infanticidal consequences of
existence reproductively embodied in history.

In risking a cross-disciplinary analysis, this study seeks to promote dialogue among researchers devoted to empirical methodologies, those
committed to hermeneutic and other broadly interpretive procedures,
and those endeavoring to engage the practices of critique, especially
where those practices are associated with the name of Jacques Derrida
and his deconstructions. Some readers may be hesitant about this over-
ture. And yet, in its understanding of the costs of survival and reproductive success, costs that in a Darwinian universe an organism must
deflect from itself, evolutionary theory itself performs a critique of one
of the most elementary conceptual oppositions in Western culture—the
hierarchized opposition of life and death and the subsidiary oppositions
of reproduction and reproductive curtailment, parental investment and
infanticide, conception and contraception. In pursuing the ramifications
of evolutionary biology's incipient deconstruction, this study aspires, on
the one hand, to further the value of this field's fundamental insights for
cross-cultural analysis; on the other hand, it aims as well to demonstrate
the pertinence of deconstruction for understanding how, in its empiricism, biological discourse remains invested in, even while beginning to
fashion a counter-discourse to, Western culture's epochal, metaphysical
commitment in the transcendental value of life.

To deconstruct the just-mentioned oppositions is to affirm what others
have shown about how violence must not be considered as alien but as
integral to and even constitutive of the self. As Hent de Vries and Samuel
Weber explain: "Thinkers from Nietzsche through Adorno to Levinas
and Derrida have long suspected . . . that violence is not necessarily the
exclusive characteristic of the other but rather, and perhaps even above
all, a means through which the self, whether individual or collective, is
constituted and maintained."[11] Suspicious of classical conceptions of
subjectivity, of the dream of a selfhood purified of violence, these thinkers
have launched a counter-conception of the self as made possible by an irreducible violence immanent in the very process of subject formation.

To deconstruct the investment in an idealized subjectivity is not merely
to dissolve the essentialist, categorical oppositions on which it relies—
self versus other, life versus death, conception versus contraception, care
versus infanticide, and so on. As Dominick LaCapra has written, "the deconstruction of binary oppositions need not result in a generalized conceptual blur or in the continual suspension of all judgment and practice."[12]
To the contrary, to deconstruct the epochal conceptual-cum-conceptive
investment in transcendence is to open the nature of political economy

to reinspection in terms of the ineluctable costs of existence, individual and collective, which must be negotiated anew as the possibility of a transcendental relief of all such debt disappears. As Thomas Keenan avers, "we are not interested simply in undermining . . . foundational or essentialist ethico-political discourses, but in demonstrating that what we call ethics and politics only comes into being or has any force and meaning thanks to this groundlessness. We have politics because we have no grounds, no reliable standpoints." For this reason, "responsibility and rights, the answers and the claims we make as foundations disintegrate, are constitutive of politics." Deconstruction, Keenan continues, "is not an antiauthoritarian discourse, an attack on grounds, but . . . an attempt to think about this removal as the condition of any political action."[13] To think in this spirit is, this project claims, to counter-conceive; it is, as certain fundamental Western texts evince, to approach the infanticidal as the non-transcendable backdrop of all decision, hence of all responsibility.

The Infanticidal Logic
of Evolution and Culture

I

The Biological Scope of Infanticide and the Infanticidal

1

Existence Costs

More individuals are born than can possibly survive.
—Darwin, *The Origin of Species* (359)

... a belief in the "sanctity of life" finds no support in Nature.... As far as Nature is concerned, the individual life is cheap.
—Hardin, *The Limits of Altruism* (116)

THE ARGUMENT

EVOLUTION IS A THEORY NOT PRINCIPALLY OF LIFE BUT OF ECONOmization. Economization among living things involves deflecting more of the costs of existence onto others or the environment than competitors for their part are able to deflect. Such economization is fundamentally sacrificial. More importantly, it is necessarily infanticidal. The infanticidal cost of life is a consequence of the thermodynamic limit to the evolutionary economy, and this limit imposes the fate of eventual extinction on each and every lineage singly and all lineages collectively. Since infanticide destroys not only a particular offspring but the potential future that would have been opened by this offspring's survival, infanticide stands as a figure of evolution in general. It does so because the evolutionary future entails not only the end of (some) living things for the sake of (other) living things but the inevitable end of life itself.

THE EVOLUTIONARY ECONOMY

In his foreword to Gary Larson's whimsical ecological tale, *There's a Hair in My Dirt: A Worm's Story*, evolutionary biologist E. O. Wilson announces the non-whimsical economic premise of biology, which is that nature is irreducibly exploitive: "while it is true that all organisms are dependent on others, the ecological web they create is built entirely from mutual exploitation." As the antithesis "mutual exploitation" suggests, cooperation and reciprocity derive from, are effects of, and conform to biology's reality principle, which takes shape as a kind of bottom line: "[t]here is no free lunch, and what one creature consumes another must provide." This economic necessity constitutes an "iron rule of Nature."[1]

What another creature provides is often its own life. Killed and eaten, the one living thing pays the survival costs of the other without having acquired a corresponding gain for itself. Even when an organism manages to survive and "cooperate," however, it does so only strategically, only in relation to the competitive pressures of its surroundings; to the extent that it acts in concert with rather than in opposition to certain other organisms, it does so only out of self-interest: "I know of no instance in which a species of plant or animal gives willing support to another without extracting some advantage in turn," Wilson says. If there were no advantage, the strategy of supporting another would quickly be selected against; it would soon disappear from the repertoire of behaviors available to succeeding generations of the organism in question. What lives is always "bought with a price, paid mostly by the naive and unsuspecting."[2] The survival of living things is invariably at the expense of other living or quasi-living things—animals, plants, microorganisms, viruses.

The evolutionary challenge for any life form, by itself or in (self-serving) collaboration with other life forms, is to outcompete those organisms vying with it for a share of available resources. To the extent that a living entity can transfer more of the energy costs of its survival onto its surroundings, including others, than its competitors are able to deflect onto their environments, it will be selected for over time by virtue of its greater reproductive success. In this sense, to survive—more accurately, to outreproduce one's competitors—is always to be engaged in the direct or indirect sacrifice of other life. Conversely, to live is to be the target of such economizing in turn. Always en route to outliving or being outlived by its rivals, no creature escapes the necessity of diverting the expense of its existence away from itself while simultaneously trying to avoid paying the deflected costs of other organisms' equally opportunistic lives. The evolutionary program knows no other economy, and the economy it does know is sacrificial.

Thus, existence costs, and evolution is the measure of the fatality that is inherent to that cost. As Darwin declares, not "to keep steadily in mind that each organic being . . . has to struggle for life and to suffer great destruction," not to realize that living creatures are "constantly destroying life" and being destroyed in turn, is to "quite misunderstand" nothing less than "the *whole economy* of nature."[3] The economy of evolution is sacrificial. Concerning the violence of this economy "nothing is easier than to admit in words the truth of the universal struggle for life, or more difficult," Darwin says, "than constantly to bear this conclusion in mind."[4] Compelled by the "exquisite adaptations" and "beautiful co-adaptations" of "organic beings in a state of nature," he notes, "we forget that each species, even where it most abounds, is constantly suffering enormous destruction . . . from enemies or from competitors."[5]

The fact that the destruction of species is so enormous constitutes, according to Will and Ariel Durant, "the first biological lesson of history."[6] It is with this essential fact about the material basis of culture that William H. McNeil begins his classic study of human civilization. *Plagues and People* opens by stipulating that human existence, like animal existence, must be understood in terms of an economy of predation, parasitism, and disease, which is to say in terms of an economy of death, the material condition of all creaturely existence:

> All animals depend on other living things for food, and human beings are no exception. Problems of finding food and the changing ways human communities have done so are familiar enough in economic histories. The problems of avoiding becoming food for some other organism are less familiar, largely because from very early times human beings ceased to have much to fear from large-bodied animal predators like lions or wolves. Nevertheless, one can properly think of most human lives as caught in a precarious equilibrium between the microparasitism of disease organisms and the macroparasitism of large-bodied predators, chief among which have been other human beings.[7]

In other words, a general economic history of the human life-world would have to begin with the "precarious equilibrium" of our individual and collective survival in relation to two fundamental modalities of "disease" — ultimately of death — namely, microparasitism and macroparasitism. One of the most basic expressions of life's costliness, the two parasitisms together "constitute a sort of 'background noise' against which human life has always been lived" — and always will be lived.[8] "Like all other forms of life, humankind remains inextricably entangled in flows of matter and energy that result from eating and being eaten."[9]

Our ability to create "new niches in that system" of predatory exchange most decidedly does not signify our transcendence of its underlying economic entailment — namely that life costs and that survival, however it is defined, requires transferring the expense as much as possible onto creatures other than oneself and niches other than one's own. In this regard the history of humankind's accelerating command of the biosphere does not represent an escape from such parasitism. To the contrary, "the enveloping microparasitic-macroparasitc balances limiting human access to food and energy have not been abolished, and never will be," McNeil declares.[10]

The disease history of human populations provides voluminous evidence of the emergence of new patterns of micro- and macroparasitism. For example, that history evinces the way the transition from hunter-gatherer social organization to sedentism—the achievement that inaugurates "civilization"—was itself achieved at the cost of increased vulnerability to parasites. The advent of larger and larger population centers—cities—appears to have increased the total parasite burden for humans. "Larger groups of people, sedentism, food storage, domestic animals, and trade and transport all exact a *price* in addition to conferring benefits," Ralph Nathan Cohen writes. "The evolution of civilization has probably broadened the range of infections to which human beings are exposed and has probably increased both the percentage of individuals infected and the size of the common dose of infection by tending to increase the reproductive success of the various parasites." The success of one parasite tends to promote the success of others by compromising the body's immunity. Thus, for example, "the influenza virus often opens the way for bacterial infection of the lungs"; thus, too, "the presence of either malaria or hookworm increases the probability that an individual will die from measles."[11] Paradoxically, the collective reproductive success of humans has increased the parasitic "background noise" of life. That noise provides an index of the evolutionary economization that makes life, including human life, possible only as the sacrifice of life.

THE INFANTICIDAL CHARACTER OF THE EVOLUTIONARY ECONOMY

This economization has manifestly infanticidal consequences. In the following formulation of the rampant infanticidism throughout the biological world, Darwin evokes an image of the cheerful face of an all-providing nature in order to unmask the innumerable predatory mouths ordinarily concealed when nature is so personified: "We behold the face of nature bright with gladness, we often see superabundance of food; we do not see or we forget, that the birds which are idly singing round us mostly live on insects or seeds, and are thus constantly destroying life; or we forget how largely these songsters, or their eggs, or their nestlings, are destroyed by birds and beasts of prey."[12] Perhaps because these creatures of the air are able both to soar above the earth and to convert the medium of their flight into the very breath of song, they have come to represent in countless mythopoetic traditions the human soul freed from bondage to an appetitive body. Yet it is these very animals, Darwin notices, whose ravening beaks "we do not see or we forget," drawn as we are to the "face of nature bright with gladness." That face, however, feeds not just on other life but on the offspring of other life.

The entirety of nature's economy, in fact, issues from the prodigality of reproduction and the equally prodigious infanticidal destruction that,

Darwin emphasizes, follows inevitably from the struggle for existence.[13] In Bertrand Russell's succinct summation: "All living things reproduce themselves so fast that the greater part of each generation must die without having reached the age to leave descendants."[14] As Russell acknowledges, the outcome of this process is an infanticidal reproductive war in which the young and newly begotten are vulnerable not only to predation by other species but to competition for scarce resources by their own kind. As a result of such intraspecific competition, "there will be a constant tendency in the improved descendants of any one species to supplant and exterminate in each stage of descent their predecessors and their original progenitor" along with their non-improved descendants. For this reason it is not alone "the original parent-species itself" that is doomed to extinction, however, but "many whole collateral lines of descent" as well,[15] since the death of the parent generation always implies the destruction, in part or in whole, of its actual or potential lines of descent. Such is the Darwinian legacy that the parent-generation and its successor generations are linked by the infanticidal processes of natural selection, which lead to the annihilation (in the losing organisms) of the very generational connection these processes have been evolved to sustain (in the winning organisms).

That procreativity is in its essence simultaneously a force of generativity *and* demise enables Alfred W. Crosby to conclude that "Every ecosystem is in danger of being smothered by the reproductive excesses of its members, but is usually saved from this fate by the appetites of its members—that is, the participating organisms obligingly eat up each other's excessive offspring."[16] Crosby considers this observation a matter of "kindergarten ecology."[17] An expression of his condescension, the phrase incorporates a vision of nature's infanticidism: if every ecosystem is a kindergarten, literally a children's garden, it is thus an infanticidal killing field in which "excessive offspring" are destroyed.

Evoking what he calls a "danger" manifest in "every ecosystem," Crosby all but calls procreativity infanticidal. Another name for the appetites that sustain an organism as it tries to maximize its reproductive success, infanticide is the paradoxical means by which "every ecosystem is usually saved" from that very reproductivity. Unimpeded, this reproductivity, by virtue of its inherent excessiveness, would destroy the biosphere. Without infanticidal checks, reproductivity would be utterly extinctive. The predatory control of reproductivity, then, is necessary for reproductivity to be a force of life rather than of catastrophic population-wide death. And yet the curbing mechanism is nothing other than the "appetites" of competing organisms, appetites that are expressions of metabolic needs and of the reproductivity such metabolism supports. Appetitiveness and the reproduction it sustains are infanticidal. The check on one organism's appetitiveness and reproduction is another organism's appetitiveness and reproduction; the ostensible control on what threatens the ecosystem is itself a form of that very threat. Ecosystems, then, are infanticidal matrices that support life by inducing massive death. They are constituted by a dynamic checking and balancing that is thoroughly infanticidal.

The infanticidal implications of reproductive success, easy enough to demonstrate, are burdensome to accept, for they signal the mistakenness of the common belief that evolution is principally the set of processes by which life proliferates. To the contrary, evolutionary change gives rise to life only as that life economizes on—lives off of by destroying—itself within a thermodynamic horizon that condemns all living things to extinction.

THE THERMODYNAMIC LIMIT TO THE EVOLUTIONARY ECONOMY

Writing in the third century BCE, the Stoic philosopher Epicurus declares that "nothing is created out of that which does not exist: for if it were, everything would be created out of everything with no need of seeds."[18] Two centuries later the Roman poet Lucretius reiterates this seminal insight: "nothing can be produced from nothing."[19] If nothing is got *from* nothing, it is also the case that nothing is got *for* nothing. The "need for seeds" is no exception, for the life these seeds produce is inscribed in an economy that is ultimately entropic, the cost of biological existence being bound by the laws of thermodynamics. A living entity achieves its complex orderliness by "increasing the entropy of its surroundings," Depew and Weber explain.[20] All "living systems . . . *pay what they owe* to the second law by building internal kinetic pathways that send things in their environment, *instead of themselves*, to thermodynamic equilibrium."[21] These pathways are part of the ("autocatalytic") means by which living things dissipate the accumulation of entropy—that is, divert it away from themselves. The self-organizing complexity of living things able to extract energy from their environments and convert it to their uses is always purchased at the cost of an increase in entropy somewhere else. That is why the "macroscopic order" of the life that makes up the biosphere "arises not as a violation of the second law of thermodynamics but as a consequence of it."[22]

What obtains at the organismic level occurs at the ecological: every ecosystem must pay a continuous thermodynamic cost, an entropy price in the form of dissipated heat, for capturing and channeling the biologically useful energy of the earth. The exchanges of mass and energy involved in biospheric processes—such as photosynthesis, the evaporation of water, and the circulation of winds and ocean currents—have inexorable entropic effects, which must be removed from the ecosystem. "Ecosystems favor species that, in funneling energy into their own production and reproduction, also increase the total energy flow through the system. The effect is to increase the dissipation of energy as entropy production to the surroundings."[23] The increase in energy flow is not "free"; some part of the terrestrial energy system "pays" what the ecosystem in question owes for its coherence.[24]

Systems of human economy entail similar transfers of cost for the reason that "[t]he world available to human society is *inescapably finite*," as Garrett Hardin emphasizes.[25] The planetary environment "has a limited *carrying capacity* for living things."[26] Though the capacity in question might continue to be increased with the advent of new technologies, the earth cannot sustain a limitless number of people, let alone a limitless quantity of life. The "finitude of resources" situates human existence this side of the thermodynamic horizon.[27] As Daniel A. Underwood and Paul G. King frame the matter, "production requires the economic process to receive a continuous flow of energy-matter obtained from the natural environment," and the "[e]xtraction, use, and discharge of this flow must conform to the immutable laws of thermodynamics and the conservation of matter." Those laws necessitate that "[a]ll production and consumption actions of homo economicus increase the entropy of the universe and diminish the future productive potential of the biosphere."[28] In particular, as Underwood and King explain, "the more society relies on an increase in material flows to satisfy an increasing demand for production, the greater will be the level of pollution and the disamenities associated with it; the greater will be the demand placed on the assimilative capacity of the biosphere; and finally, the smaller will be the productive potential of the biosphere in the future."[29] The consequences are inevitable: "a global society with an endlessly increasing thirst for material production dependent upon a coinciding flow of resources is doomed to extinction," for the laws of thermodynamics and conservation impose an absolute energy limit in the form of "absolute scarcity."[30] Through the advent of technological innovations, civilizations can divert the buildup of entropy. However, as Underwood and King emphasize, they cannot do so indefinitely: "Most major civilizations have had environmental weaknesses at the heart of their collapse. Technological fixes could not ward off the effects of entropy." There is no such instrumentality as "a technological perpetual motion machine" for sustaining economic growth.[31] The carrying capacity of the earth is not inexhaustible but thermodynamically bounded. In short, "[t]he fact that there are no known exceptions to the laws of thermodynamics should be incorporated into the axiomatic foundations of economics."[32]

THE EXTINCTIVE CHARACTER OF THE
EVOLUTIONARY ECONOMY

The laws of thermodynamics stipulate why the biochemistry of life is not infinitely self-perpetuating but self-annihilating in the long run and deathly to most of its organismic productions in the short run: the particular configurations of energy that support the advent of living things must inevitably dissipate. Circulations of energy preceded the rise of terrestrial life and likely will after the demise of the biosphere. Although the appearance and subsequent course of life, especially human life, has profoundly modified the energy patterns of the earth, life did not initiate the earthly flow of energy. Rather, particular patterns of energy gave rise to life. Those patterns were manifestly nonliving before they produced life, and nothing about their thermodynamic qualities will enable life to be eternal. No matter how intricately self-balancing the biosphere is, and no matter how apparently "endless" its "forms most beautiful and most wonderful" might appear,[33] the planet's biological dynamics will come to an end. What enables self-catalyzing chemicals to emerge from out of an inorganic environment, and what then permits self-replicating entities to arise from autocatalytic chemical cycles, do not attest to the necessity of life's advent but instead to its fortuitousness: "Luck was needed. . . . There were stringent geological requirements for the origin of life," and those requirements were not inevitable.[34] Life on earth could easily have never arisen. A corollary to the chanciness of life's emergence from the nonliving is the inevitable future cessation of life also as a result of nonliving chemical and nuclear processes—solar, galactic, or cosmic. The movement of energy that first propelled the inception of life, in other words, did so not as the consequence of the evolution it engendered, not as the result of some teleological reqirement, but as a consequence of thermodynamic constraints on the circulation of energy, constraints that will and must bring evolution to an end. In this regard the general flow of energy does not favor the perdurance of particular life forms nor of life itself, except momentarily. What is more, this momentariness is virtually instantaneous when the mortal tenure of individual creatures is measured against the span of life's appearance on earth, and all the more so when the biological era is gauged against the geological, the geological against the solar, the solar against the cosmic, and the cosmic against its universal entropic exhaustion.

The "moment" of life is not merely transitory, however, but also principally extinctive. It is so despite the reassuring image of evolution as a kind of "great Tree of Life,"[35] one that seems to encompass all living things in a single death-transcending unity. In his influential reassessment of evolutionary thought in 1966, George C. Williams emphasizes that the general "direction" of adaptation and natural selection is not toward more life or better life or more complex life but toward life's extinction: "In evolution it is easier to lose elaborate mechanisms" of adaptation "than to acquire them. . . . These losses would be examples of . . . evolutionary *black holes*. They are paths often taken in evolution, but once taken are largely irreversible."[36]

These losses can be biotically driven, as when a species outcompetes another. The losses can also be the consequence of abiotic events, as when an organism's habitat is subjected to significant alteration from fire, earthquake or volcanic irruption, bolide (large meteor) impact, glaciation or the recession of glaciers along with the concomitant changes in weather and sea level, and so on. Whereas Darwin surmised that the struggle for survival accounts for most extinction, and whereas many biologists continue to affirm various amended versions of Darwin's argument, some contemporary paleobiologists argue that abiotic processes are the chief cause. As Richard Leakey and Roger Irwin explain, the unpredictability of abiotic-driven changes in environments, especially during times of mass extinction, means that sheer luck, not superior adaptiveness, determines which organisms survive.[37] During times of relative habitat stability, natural selection enforces competitions that favor certain species and drive their less adapted competitors into nonexistence, contributing to the biosphere's low-level "background extinction" rate. During times of widespread ecological transformation, however, "species survive or succumb for reasons unrelated to their adaptations"—that is, unrelated to what had been their adaptiveness to their previous environments before those environments changed. "Here, bad luck is dominant in consigning species to evolutionary oblivion." Of the approximately one hundred basic body plans that arose during the Cambrian era, for example, most disappeared due to changes in environments that rendered them no longer adaptive. The thirty that did survive and that are the basis of modern life survived mostly by chance.[38]

Bad luck, chance, and randomness are other names for the dependency of the biological world on its nonbiological context, terrestrial as well as galactic. They are names for the contingent relation of the biosphere to those abiotic events and processes that underlie the kinds of environmental alterations that exceed the adaptive resources of the species and genera of organisms in question. Life is always adapted to local and only local ecological circumstances. Because these environments are dynamic and thus subject to change, and because no set of adaptation is able to fit a given species to all possible future environmental transformations, adaptations that were once survival positive often become

survival negative.[39] Indeed, since evolution does not and cannot antici-
pate new conditions, especially major climatic and geological changes,
survival, Williams emphasizes, "will always be largely a matter of historical accident."[40] An ineluctable consequence of the biosphere's vulnerability to various geophysical forces and events as well as to extraterrestrial impingements, extinction has never been able *not* to occur.
Massive extirpation of life—in relation to which previous adaptations of
dying lineages are no longer adaptive but are now Williams' evolutionary black holes—cannot not come to pass.

Just how often do species end up on a dead-ending evolutionary path?
In the long run, always.[41] In the short run, nearly always, since "[m]ore
than 99 percent of the species that have ever lived are extinct."[42] According to David M. Raup, "somewhere between five and fifty *billion*
species have existed at one time or another." The number of extant
species—"possibly as many as forty million"—represents less than 0.1
percent, perhaps less than 0.01 percent, of this total and "results from a
minor surplus of speciations over extinctions, accumulated over a long
time."[43] During each of five eras of mass extinction over the last 600 million years, perhaps between 76 percent of the, until then, extant species
disappeared.[44] These massive extinctions represent an extreme degree
of intensity in relation to the range of extinctive magnitudes. Thus, while
"mass killings," as Raup calls them, "are approximately 100-million-year
events," extinctions of less severity are frequent: "a species kill of about
5 percent occurs about every one million years."[45] If this figure is correct, then over a span of 20 million years most species will have disappeared. As Williams notes, "[o]f the systems of adaptations produced by
organic evolution during any given million years, only a small proportion
will still be present several million years later."[46] Moreover, their survival
will have been fortuitous, as has been the case with humans.

The evolutionary sequence that has produced humans has depended
upon the "sheer chance that finally shifted the balance of control of terrestrial ecosystems from reptiles to mammals" and later to humans.[47] Niles
Eldredge is here alluding to the cataclysmic environmental changes that
doomed the dinosaurs, which until then had been phenomenally well
adapted to their world for some 100 million years. Of course, without
their extinction, along with the dying out of countless other terrestrial as
well as marine species that eventually led to the formation of petroleum
and coal, mammalian evolution would almost certainly not have eventu-
ated in the appearance of the primate lineage that would then give rise
to a species able, after several million years, to convert certain consequences of mass extinction (fossil fuel) into the means of powering its
industrial inventions.

Thus, as numerous biologists have sought to make clear, the rise and continuation of human existence to the present has been utterly dependent upon forces that might just as easily have destroyed the species. As Williams notes, "we have no idea how many narrow escapes from extinction man's lineage *may have* experienced." The number of such escapes is finite: extinction "*is* the statistically most likely development."[48] The existence of *Homo sapiens sapiens* "was not inevitable," Leakey and Lewin avow: "we are a mere accident of history," and our species "is destined for extinction, just like other species in history."[49] Stephen Jay Gould affirms as well the transience of humankind, the existence of which is "not a predictable result of an inherently progressive process" but rather "a *momentary* cosmic accident."[50] The brief history of the human appearance on earth, Leakey and Lewin conclude, "involves a degree of randomness that many will find difficult to accept. But it's true."[51]

What accounts for the resistance to the contingent nature of humankind's origin? In Gould's view it is the mistaken idea that evolution is progressive, a notion he characterizes as "a delusion based on social prejudice and psychological hope."[52] Evolution does not nor cannot protect against extinction: "We have evolved. Our closest relatives are already extinct, and our species will, inevitably, also one day be extinct."[53] No biological adaptation or cultural enhancement can ensure that humankind will escape from some future macro-extinction. Though he has helped elucidate this inevitability, Williams himself resists it. Finessing the prospect of our eventual extinction, Williams imagines the demise of human lineages in terms of a hypothetical past that we have escaped: "the extinction of this lineage *would* . . . have provided the world today with a strikingly different biota." he avers.[54] And yet the present survival of this lineage has in fact resulted in the drastic modification of the world, both animate and inanimate, a fact that underscores the extinction-tradeoff implicit in any organism's successful reproductive continuance of its line.

Human-Driven Extinction of Nonhuman Life

Humankind has not merely altered the "balance of nature"; from the point of view of much of the ecosphere, the economizing interventions of humans have been catastrophically costly. As Leakey and Lewin explain, "human colonization of pristine lands is an extreme example of an invading species and the consequences of that invasion on existing communities"—that is, on the flora and fauna of the area in question. Whereas "mature, species-rich communities can often resist invasion attempts by most species," they almost never avoid succumbing to human encroachment: "*Homo sapiens* is no ordinary species, and its attempts at invasion are almost always successful and almost always devastating." For this reason humans "have a long history as an agent of extinction."[55] Paul S. Martin has argued that human exploitation is responsible for the dramatic reduction, over a relatively brief period of one or two millennia approximately eleven thousand years ago, in two-thirds of the larger mammals inhabiting North and South America.[56] Similarly, A. Hallam and P. B. Wignall affirm that "for more recent times . . . our species is believed to be responsible for most or nearly all recorded extinctions. Indeed, "[i]t is now clear that the first arrival of human inhabitants has always precipitated a mass extinction in the island biota."[57]

In the course of its preeminent success in outcompeting other creatures, humans have irrevocably reduced the world's previously evolved biodiversity. To this effect our species has exponentially multiplied the rate of the extinction it has so far avoided. David Steadman estimates that "the presence of humans in an environment . . . increases the [extinction] rate one hundred fold, which in terms of evolution," he declares, "is a disaster."[58]

Existence costs, and from the perspective of the life forms humans have eradicated or are on the verge of killing off, human existence costs disastrously. Leakey and Lewin identify three major threats posed by humans. "The first is through direct exploitation, such as hunting."[59] The development of "weapons and other harvesting tools, such as kilometer-long drift nets, have made humans such efficient hunters that many species have literally been hunted to extinction." In modern history such "anthropogenic extinction" has overtaken "the Steller's sea cow, great auk, passenger pigeon, and Labrador duck—all formerly abundant species, all prized for food, all vulnerable." In prehistoric times the first humans in Australia killed off every one of "several large marsupial mammals," several species of flightless birds, and one species of tortoise. "The advent of humans in the Americas about 12,000 years ago was accompanied by the rapid extinction of 56 species in 27 genera of large mammals, including horses, a giant ground sloth, camels, elephants, and saber-toothed tiger, a lion, and others." The arrival of humans in Madagascar 1,500 years ago "brought the demise of 14 of 24 species of lemurs . . . and between 6 and 12 species of elephant birds, flightless giants" found nowhere else.[60]

The second threat humans have posed is "the biological havoc that is occasionally wreaked following the introduction of alien species to new ecosystems, whether deliberately or accidentally."[61] The history of Europe's modernization illustrates this. Analyzing the impact, over the last five centuries, of a global transformation instigated by European development, Sheldon Watts has studied the creation of disease networks that were put in place by the spread of European economic, political, and social institutions and processes, such as industrialization, colonization, imperialism, and the like. Previously unknown to the New World, these diseases were, Watts says, "[a]mong the unintended consequences" of European expansion. Occurring in dynamic relation to European practices and policies, these diseases include bubonic plague, leprosy, smallpox, cholera, malaria, yellow fever and venereal syphilis.[62]

Finally, according to Leaky and Lewin "[t]he third, and by far the most important, mode of human-driven extinction is the destruction and fragmentation of habitat, especially the inexorable cutting of tropical rainforests."[63] Since the tropics are home to the greatest numbers of terrestrial species, the deracination of the forests bodes an incalculably negative environmental impact. The authors of *Life: The Science of Biology* report on the estimated future extent of species extinction from continued logging of tropical forests: "if we assume that about half of existing terrestrial species live in tropical forests, and that about one-third of the remaining tropical forests will be logged during the next few decades, the species-area relationship"—which says that the number of species increases with the size of an area—"suggests that about 1 million species will be extirpated during that period."[64]

The loss of forests of all kinds underscores the imminent danger of what many ecologists characterize as a perhaps irremediable human-induced biological crisis. Eight thousand years ago, forests covered more than twenty-five million square miles, approximately forty percent of the earth's land surface. At the end of the twentieth-century, forests covered only about half that many square miles.[65] Forests protect watersheds, they prevent flooding and soil erosion, and they stabilize climate.[66] Forests also produce and support biodiversity by sustaining key species, which in turn support countless other ecological relationships, and by contributing to the maintenance of species richness. Moreover, they provide sources of the active ingredients in many medical prescriptions.[67] Therefore, the losses from deforestation are incalculable.

The range of resources compromised by deforestation, as well as by other environmental transformations, provides an index of the ecological expense associated with human domination of the ecosphere. As their title suggests, Leakey and Lewin foresee a "sixth extinction" in the making: "Dominant as no other species has been in the history of life on Earth, *Homo sapiens* is in the throes of causing a major biological crisis, a mass extinction, the sixth such event to have occurred in the past half billion years."[68] Even the most cautious biologists predict that the human ecological impact will drive no less than 10 percent of the earth's species extinct by 2010; others foresee the extinction of 50 percent of the earth's species by mid-century.[69]

With the advent of farming, the human use of technology to modify the environment "began to mimic the effects that for all of the preceding eons of geological time had been primarily the province of climate change and the odd extraterrestrial collide."[70] With the introduction of modern industrial *technē* in particular, the losses humans have been imposing upon the world are continuing to diminish ever more rapidly the number not only of individual creatures but of *kinds* of creatures, flora as well as fauna. The result is to irreversibly narrow the compass of life, actual and potential. "For the first time we have a species on earth that has been altering habitat so pervasively that the effects even now border on true mass extinction."[71] "Evidently we are in the midst of a new phase of mass extinction, and only a panglossian optimist would believe that this is likely to be checked in the foreseeable future."[72] As John C. Briggs has summarized, humans have destroyed habitats with such virulent rapidity that by 2025 two million out of at least ten million animal species and approximately sixty-five thousand out of three-hundred thousand species of vascular plants will have disappeared. These losses, due to habitat destruction by humans, are occurring with a rapidity that is unprecedented in Phanerozoic time." Even if "[h]istoric extinction episodes were so gradual that many lineages were able to accommodate in an evolutionary and ecological sense," it is manifestly the case that "[t]he tempo of the current extinctions precludes any such adjustments."[73] Amy Coen, President of Population Action International, offers this perspective on human-driven decimation of the biosphere: "Every 20 minutes the world adds another 3,500 human lives but loses one or more entire species of animal or plant life — at least 27,000 species per year."[74]

HUMAN-DRIVEN EXTINCTION OF HUMAN LINEAGES

The extinctive price of humankind's destruction of other living things extends to intraspecific relations within and among human cultures. No human culture escapes the economically driven necessity of calculating and monitoring its distribution of resources, and this demand always entails a mortgaging of the health, welfare, reproductivity, and life of some individuals or groups. No society invests equally in all of its members, and every society derives some benefit from its differential allocation of resources. That advantage is paid for, as it must be, by one or another form of human sacrifice, as Mark Nathan Cohen recognizes in *Health and the Rise of Civilization*. Though he does not use the word "sacrifice," he invokes a version of the concept in describing how societies levy the cost of health against some but not others: "Societies have limited resources," he writes, and that fact determines not whether but how and to what extent humans will exploit or "eliminate outright" certain individuals among themselves for the sake of others, typically in the name of a good—health, for example—on behalf of the larger social group. This is Cohen's final point concerning the relation of health to social adaptation, namely "that individual well-being is *always* being traded against group success." Not surprisingly, this idea is "the one that seems hardest for us to recognize or accept," and even Cohen himself softens his otherwise unflinching ratification of it with an initial parenthetical qualification:

> competitive success by populations has often (*perhaps* always) been bought at the expense of the well-being of some individuals. Every human group known has some basis for excluding certain members from full participation in health benefits and has had mechanisms to decide who will enjoy scarce resources and who will be bypassed in times of scarcity. In fact, *all* known human groups have mechanisms by which they eliminate some individuals outright: exile, exclusion, or execution of adults; neglect, abortion, or infanticide of the young.[75]

As the catalog of "mechanisms" indicates, the life of the group is purchased by "bypassing," "eliminating," "excluding," and variously "executing"—in a word, sacrificing—those who will not be allowed to "enjoy scarce resources." The argument entails its correlative: insofar as anyone's health depends upon a system of differential resource allocation, this person's well-being costs. It is a cost the sacrificial nature of which is seldom immediately apparent precisely to the extent that it is embedded in the network of laws, policies, administrative procedures, and cultural practices that support a system of economic arrangements whereby some people enjoy a healthier standard of living than others. Those others may reside either within one's political community or outside its boundaries. Regardless, it is they who suffer the health of the favored.[76]

That suffering can be partially quantified in the widespread death that accompanies the appearance of new epidemic diseases before a population has managed to adapt, genetically or otherwise. Cohen explains: "A so-called virgin soil epidemic is one occurring in a population in which no one has had the disease before. Typically, many people of all ages are sick at once, and there is no one to provide food and basic hygiene. The death rate can be extremely high. . . . Once epidemic diseases become a common fact of life, as they do in civilized populations, however, the group can adjust. Genetically susceptible families have already been weeded out, and people may have learned important lessons about how to help the sick."[77] Over the course of centuries such genetic "weeding out" in conjunction with the prophylactic "lessons" learned by survivors has reduced the virulence of numerous diseases, at least for some inhabitants of the world today, that once decimated untold numbers. Here, the disease history of a population exemplifies the deathly economy within which biological characteristics (in the case at hand, resistance to one or another disease vector) arise and, if they manifest adaptive value, spread throughout a population. Increasing immunity might be understood as a measure of a population's "progress"; if so, it is progress only for those who do not pay its cost. Conversely, insofar as disease is a mechanism of "weeding out," it is a potential evolutionary opportunity for those who can escape its fatal effects relative to those who succumb. The relative health of a population is thus an index of the survival costs it has not yet had to pay for its present immunities. The advent of new virulent diseases will reacquaint a population with those costs, previously hidden insofar as they have been paid by others.

If the health of a population attests to the sacrificial nature of existence, so too does its very survival. In the competition among family lines, clans, tribes, city-states, nations, and so on for territory, food, and other resources, "success has meant the competitive displacement of rival groups or, at least, the ability to hold one's own. In fact, such competitive success has been the bottom line of cultural survival."[78] Viewed from the perspective of the losing cultures, however, the "bottom line" of the competition for survival is the non-survival that has always paid for it and that pays for it still, perhaps more self-evidently today than ever before.

The eradication of human languages provides a telling example. According to Michael Krauss, at least twelve hundred and perhaps as many as three thousand of the world's estimated 6,000 languages (between 20 and 50 percent) are no longer spoken by children and are thus doomed to extinction.[79] These numbers suggest that human linguistic diversity is disappearing at a rate even faster than the disappearance of animal species. In *Language Death*, David Crystal reports that nearly 26 percent of all languages have less than 1000 speakers, 55 percent have less than 10,000 speakers, and approximately 67 percent have less than 20,000, a possible "danger-level" for many of them. The small numbers of speakers of these languages should be measured against the 96 percent of the world's population — 5.76 billion out of an estimated 6 billion people — who speak 4 percent (240 out of 6,000) of the world's languages. "Turning this statistic on its head," Crystal notes that just 4 percent of the population speak 96 percent of the world's languages.[80] It is not likely that these populations will long be able to resist linguistic and other forms of takeover, assimilation, or annihilation by the mass cultures associated with the language groups that have incalculably greater numbers of speakers and that participate in world-reshaping political economies that utterly dominate the biosphere. Andrew Dalby predicts that "in the present century, 2,500 languages are likely to be lost . . . one language every two weeks."[81]

In many places, native cultures and their languages are imperiled by the same forces that threaten biodiversity, such as deforestation, a particularly relentless expression of the expense attaching to humankind's (industrial and now postindustrial) proliferation and intervention in the world. Because only about three hundred languages—a mere 5 percent—have sufficient numbers of speakers or government support to survive, over 90 percent of existing languages will be extinct or nearly so by the year 2100–a death-rate of 20 languages per year.[82] Summarizing the work of Krauss, Dalby predicts that only thirty-four of the indigenous languages of North America, and only twenty in the United States, will still be spoken by 2070. These languages represent a mere 20 percent of the languages spoken before European contact, and their continued existence will be tenuous.[83] Daniel Nettle and Suzanne Romaine report that eighty-six of the approximately 210 native languages still spoken in North America have fewer than 100 speakers.[84] According to Berkeley linguistics professor Leanne Hinton, in California alone "at least one native language . . . goes extinct every year." Such linguistic extinction proceeds infanticidally. That is, it occurs by way of the loss of the language's future speakers—the linguistic community's descendants, its children—who in effect "die" to their mother tongue.

What Michael Krauss calls the diminishing "logosphere"[85] represents but one measure of the disastrous costs of cultural survival—which is to say of one culture's ability to supplant another. A second measure is provided by the historical record of the deaths consequent upon European exploration and colonization, one of the major causes in western history of language eradication. In *American Holocaust: Columbus and the Conquest of the New World*, David E. Stannard characterizes the post-Columbian destruction of New World natives as "the most massive act of genocide in the history of the world."[86] He writes: From almost the instant of first human contact between Europe and the Americas firestorms of microbial pestilence *and* purposeful genocide began laying waste the American natives. Although at times operating independently, for most of the long centuries of devastation that followed 1492, disease and genocide were interdependent forces. . . ."[87] Together, these conjoined forces killed off ninety-five percent of the native inhabitants. In other words, "for every twenty natives alive at the moment of European contact . . . only one stood in their place when the bloodbath was over."[88]

The absolute numbers of dead expand the meaning of this percentage. Twenty-one years after Columbus arrived in the Caribbean, nearly eight million had died on the once populous island Columbus renamed Hispaniola.[89] By the end of the sixteenth century, between sixty and eighty million natives from the Indies, Mexico, and Central and South America were dead, displaced by the approximately 200,000 Spaniards who had arrived.[90] By all measures the Europeans decimated the inhabitants of the new world continents. They accomplished their fatal demographic takeover in large part through the introduction of new diseases, varmints, pathogens, and parasites. So massive was the scale of mortality that "the major initial effect of the Columbian voyages was the transformation of America into a charnel house."[91]

During his voyages aboard the *Beagle* Darwin himself came to recognize the fatal effects of European exploration upon indigenous populations: "Wherever the European has trod, death seems to pursue the aboriginal. We may look to the wide extent of the Americas, Polynesia, the Cape of Good Hope, and Australia, and we find the same result." Though he focuses on the vectors of European destructiveness — germs, alcohol, armed invasion, and the massive disruptions of native life brought on by colonialism — Darwin recognizes the problem of human-on-human, culture-on-culture violence to be universal: "The varieties of man," Darwin attests, "seem to act on each other in the same way as different species of animals — the stronger always extirpating the weaker." Such is the "more mysterious agency generally at work" behind the destructiveness of a particular era of human history.[92]

Throughout the nineteenth century some Europeans, like Charles Lyell in his revolutionary three-volume study of the earth in the early 1830s, *Principles of Geology,* equated the operations of this agency with those of culture, finding in the European "advance" an expression of nature's most basic truth: "Yet, if we wield the sword of extermination as we advance, we have no reason to repine the havoc committed. . . . We have only to reflect, that in thus obtaining possession of the earth by conquest, and defending our acquisitions by force, we exercise no exclusive prerogative," for "every species which has spread itself from a small point over a wide area, must, in like manner, have marked its progress by the diminution, or the entire extirpation, of some other, and must maintain its ground by a successful struggle against the encroachment of other plants and animals" (2:156).[93] Thus does Lyell interpret and justify the genocidal cost of (European) progress as an inevitable outcome of a teleological necessity immanent to both nature and culture. For Lyell, in the "struggle against encroachment" the *is* of existence coincides with its axiological *ought:* the acts of species success can and must be paid for by the "diminution" or "entire extirpation" of competing species. Thus the successful "spread" of European culture testifies to its ability to make other groups, other cultures, pay the cost of its evolutionarily rationalized "prerogative."

Lyell's "sword of extermination" has been unsheathed throughout the twentieth century. Continuing to be brandished at the end of one millennium and the beginning of another, it does not merely draw blood but does so, in one accounting, more and more: "never have violence, inequality, exclusion, famine, and thus economic oppression affected as many human beings in the history of the earth and of humanity" as they have today, Derrida declares in 1993, designating the sacrificial ground of what, following the presumptive end of the cold war, has been triumphantly announced as "the new world order."[94] In denouncing this order, Derrida attempts to name and account for the violence, which no arithmetic and no naming is adequate to represent, that is associated with the present state of geopolitical economy. Derrida analyzes this violence in relation to ten "plagues," above all "[t]he ruthless economic war among the countries of the European Community themselves, between them and the Eastern European countries, between Europe and the United States, and between Europe, the United States, and Japan. This war controls everything, beginning with the other wars, because it controls the practical interpretation and an inconsistent and unequal application of international law."[95] The conflict among economies drives "[t]he aggravation of the foreign debt and other connected mechanisms [which] are starving or driving to despair a large portion of humanity."[96] It governs the "gross imbalance" in the distribution and use of the world's resources, such that there is an "explosive increase in the consumption of non-renewable resources by the long-lived *few* living mostly in the North" at the expense of the "short-lived multitudes, living largely in the South."[97] It underwrites the massive trade in armaments as well as what Derrida characterizes as the "super-efficient and properly capitalist phantom-States that are the mafia and the drug cartels on every continent."[98] It includes the scourge of ethnic war and the bloodletting undertaken in the name of the dream of a homeland, itself "rooted first of all in the memory or the anxiety of a displaced—or displaceable—population."[99] Who can calculate the number of victims worldwide from ethnic cleansing? It is precisely this impossibility that moves Derrida to pray: "let us never forget this obvious macroscopic fact, made up of innumerable singular sites of suffering: no degree of progress allows one to ignore that never before, in absolute figures, never have so many men, women, and children been subjugated, starved, or exterminated on earth."[100] And yet it is impossible not to forget the reality this fact attempts to embrace, for the "singularity" of each person namelessly "subjugated, starved, or exterminated"—in a word, sacrificed—is beyond recall, let alone commemoration. The sites of suffering themselves defy summation. Their numbers unknowable, they signify that "the ground we live on is little other than a field of multiple destructions."[101]

Nevertheless, however avoidable these destructions might or should have been, they have produced a future—the future that is being lived out in the present in inextinguishable debt to the life that has been extinguished as well as to all the once possible futures that have been traded for and thus lost to this life. Such is the double bind of the sacrificial economization by which the living destroy the living.

The next chapter will demonstrate how the evolutionary basis of this economization is infanticidal through and through.

2

The Infanticidal Horizon of Biological Evolution

If we look back to an extremely remote epoch, before man had arrived at the dignity of manhood, he would have been guided more by instinct and less by reason than are the lowest savages at the present time. Our early semi-human progenitors would not have practiced infanticide . . . for the instincts of the lower animals are never so perverted as to lead them regularly to destroy their own offspring. . . .
—Charles Darwin, *The Descent of Man*, (430)

Let us guard against saying that death is opposed to life. The living being is only a species of what is dead, and a very rare species.
—Nietzsche, *The Gay Science* (3.109)

INFANTICIDE AS EVOLUTIONARILY COUNTERINTUITIVE

IN *THE DESCENT OF MAN* (1871) DARWIN EXPRESSES AN ATTITUDE that bespeaks the historical difficulty in arriving at an evolutionary understanding of infanticide. Without discussing why the evidence of infanticide among animals might be difficult to come by, he flatly denies that this form of behavior occurs throughout the animal world. And yet he is quick to acknowledge the prevalence of infanticide among humans. The "murder of infants" is a practice that "has prevailed on the largest scale throughout the world, and has met with no reproach."[1]

Why would infanticide suddenly appear among humans? Why would the destruction of offspring not have arisen among animals? Such questions are absolutely central to Darwin's entire project, which aims at explaining the evolutionary continuities between the human and the animal. However, Darwin does not raise these questions but forecloses them with a sententious, and explanatorily empty, insinuation that what is "never so perverted" about animal instinct has suddenly become so in humans.

Darwin here presupposes that the concept of animal infanticide would be in contradiction to the adaptive, survival-positive nature of instinct.

57

Until the 1970s such a perspective was common. Prior to that time animal infanticide had been ignored as a subject for active investigation because its seemingly maladaptive, survival-negative character made it a Darwinian abnormality that would eventually have to disappear.[2]

In *Of Time, Passion, and Knowledge* (1975), J. T. Fraser elaborates the reasoning behind this assumption. The "care and concern" for the young self-evidently enhance survival. Since "attitudes to children explicitly correlate with attitudes toward the future," Fraser concludes that "parental care is an example of evolutionary techniques where the future is favored over the present."[3] Generalizing this value across the animal kingdom, Fraser asserts that to protect the young, in whom "the future" is incarnated, is an absolute biological necessity: "To die while protecting an offspring amounts to a biological defense of a biological future," for "it is life protecting itself."[4] A metonymy of life, each altruistic act of parental nurturance not only promotes the survival of the offspring in question and of the genetic endowment those offspring share with their progenitors, it actualizes the very form, the very telos, of the evolutionary processes it transmits to the next generation. For Fraser, caring is inherent in evolution and delimits evolution's ontological economy, which predicates the metaphysical primacy of life over death.

If it is assumed that life necessarily protects itself and that it persists by virtue of such self-protectiveness, then any invocation of parental care to figure life's fundamental characteristic implies the converse for infanticide. Infanticide would have to represent something on the order of anti-life. It would signify a death threat not only to a specific genetic line but also to life itself. If the value of the care of the young were absolute, then to fail to protect one's offspring, and all the more so to succeed in any attempt to kill them, would be to imperil the "biological future" of the organism in question and, Fraser implies, its population group. Infanticide, therefore, would be absolutely inimical to life as such, to "life protecting itself." Thus, attributing an absolute positive value to the care of offspring, and by implication an absolute negative value to the failure to care, Fraser all but names infanticide an evolutionarily doomed strategy, a biological disaster, the threat of threats to life. If it were to occur, then according to the logic that governs Fraser's thinking it necessarily would be selected against. And yet it is demonstrably not the case that either infanticide or parental investment in offspring work this way. To the contrary, in the past three decades there has been amassed a significant body of evidence that infanticide occurs with a previously unimagined frequency among a previously unimagined range of animals. This evidence has supported the paradoxical hypothesis that infanticide has been positively selected for because of its reproductive benefits.

This hypothesis has two unexpected implications. The first is that the logic of infanticide is the logic of evolution in general, that in its most fundamental conceptualization evolution must be understood as being infanticidal through and through. Although evolutionary biologists have not drawn this conclusion, it is a logical entailment of the central concepts in contemporary evolutionary theory. The second unrecognized implication is that the logic of evolution is aporetic[5] and that evolutionary theory is bounded by a deconstructive horizon that neo-Darwinians have not seen nor wanted to see. The purpose of this chapter is to establish and discuss the significance of these implications. To that end this chapter will scrutinize the "sociobiological" approach to evolution in general and to infanticide in particular.

The Reproductive Value of Infanticide: Group Selection Theory

In order for infanticide to become the subject of field observation and theoretical explanation, evolutionary biologists had to abandon the idea that natural selection works "to produce adaptations 'for the good of the species.'"[6] Up into the 1960s advocates of group selection argued that natural selection favors the perpetuation of the fittest population groups rather than the fittest individuals.[7] However, evolutionary biologists now strongly agree, though not unanimously so, that natural selection not only favors the individual organism but may do so at the expense of the group.[8] Group selectionists tend to hypothesize otherwise, conceiving of adaptations as increasing the viability of the group at the expense of the individual members, who altruistically sacrifice their self-interest for group interests.

If altruism refers to behavior that may disadvantage the altruistic animal but benefit others of its kind, the ultimate biological cost for the altruist is lost or diminished reproductivity: "Biologists call a behavior pattern altruistic if it increases the number of offspring produced by the recipient and decreases that of the 'altruist.'"[9] Altruistic behavior, therefore, entails an explanatory challenge: if by virtue of being altruistic an animal reduces its reproductive success relative to the greater reproductive success of the non-altruistic cohort that does not sacrifice its reproductivity, how can the altruist not lose the reproductive game? Therefore, how can it not be selected out of existence within the very population it supposedly helps?

Group selection theory answers that altruism confers an adaptive advantage on the group. The argument is that a group whose members sacrifice themselves for the good of the other members will be more viable than a competing group whose members are not willing to do so.[10] Since the welfare of a group requires the survival and well-being of its offspring, the group selection argument requires that altruistic individuals invest more in the group's collective progeny than in their own.

Indeed, group selection theory also requires that under certain circumstances some of its altruistic individuals must be willing to commit infanticide, and not only of their own offspring but of their cohorts, for the sake of the group's survival. Those circumstances might include catastrophic weather, ecosystem collapse, or any other life-cycle interference that disrupts the food web, rendering the environment incapable of supporting the group's numbers. In times of meager food supply, infanticide would be an important adaptation enabling the group to modify its collective reproductivity. The theory of group selection not only does not exclude the possibility that infanticide could emerge as a response critical to the survival of the group, it requires this possibility. If parental investment in offspring signifies an altruistic commitment to the future, as Fraser holds, so too can the willingness to forego one's individual future for the sake of the group's.

Such altruism, therefore, might entail the curtailment of the individual organism's own reproductivity at any point in the reproductive cycle. It might also involve the willingness of the individual organism to kill any of its offspring that it brings to term and to do so in order to reduce the otherwise unsustainable size of the group's population. In such a scenario infanticide would represent, paradoxically, a better biological defense of the future than would be provided by unconditional nurturing. The further paradox is that the value of a group's parental care would be strikingly contingent upon the altruistic willingness of some individuals to forgo such care.

The major proponent of the principle of group selection has developed just this line of thought. In *Animal Dispersion in Relation to Social Behaviour* (1962) and more recently *Evolution Through Group Selection* (1986), V. C. Wynne-Edwards argues that evolution has favored the survival of population groups constituted by individuals able to altruistically check their reproductivity in response to their recognition of the resources available to the group as a whole. He suggests that group selection has led to social behavior as a mechanism by which groups limit their populations so as not to exhaust the available food supply and risk starvation. Among humans such adaptive social behavior has included various "traditions" of infanticide. Summarizing the findings of A. M. Carr-Saunders (1922), Wynne-Edwards concludes that "a good many primitive races of men . . . were adapted by tradition to practice infanticide as a means of family limitation. Primitive man, in fact, applied the brakes to his fecundity at every stage, though not all methods were customary in every tribe; the most important of these were the deferment of marriage, abstention from intercourse, abortion, and infanticide."[11]

Following Carr-Saunders, contemporary anthropologists have inferred that infanticide has been a prevalent, perhaps constitutive, feature of human sociality. Their ethnographic studies have repeatedly evinced the widespread occurrence of human infanticide throughout history and prehistory. According to Marvin Harris, "a substantial anthropological literature demonstrates that prehistoric peoples maintained very low rates of population increase by means of abstinence, abortion, prolonged nursing, and direct and indirect forms of infanticide."[12] Indeed, Harris believes that, from hunter-gatherer times to the recent past, female infanticide was very likely the most common means by which individuals limited the size of their families and groups controlled their numbers.[13] Because infanticidal methods of population control are often covert, indirect, or deferred rather than overt, direct, or immediate, the incidence of human infanticide has been difficult to ascertain, all the more so since anthropologists have not always been alert to the reality of its disguises: "anthropologists have only recently awakened to the likelihood that a large portion of infant and child deaths formerly attributed to unavoidable starvation and disease may actually represent subtle forms of de facto infanticide."[14]

For Wynne-Edwards human infanticide represents a self-conscious means of "braking" fecundity and limiting family size, an end that he understands as conducing to the survival and subsequent reproductive viability of a given human group. According to this view the uncontested fact of human infanticide can best be explained by regarding it as a cultural institution adapted to the reproductive aims of "tradition"—that is, of group norms and the social imperative those norms institutionalize, namely the urgency that the reproduction of group members be monitored and controlled. Suzanne Ripley has commented on this urgency for humankind during its existence, before the Neolithic transition, as an exclusively forager species—that is, during the first 99 percent of its existence. Evidently infanticide was a crucial population control mechanism; it was, Ripley deduces, an adaptation to the ecological scenarios humans had to confront as hunters and gatherers with a high rate of reproduction coupled with a low tolerance for living in densely populated groups. For this reason "the possibility of *adaptive infanticide* is an inevitable accompaniment of the status of an ecologically generalist species," such as humans, "and is *simply a price our species had to pay in the process of becoming, and remaining, human.*"[15] For Ripley, the human species appears to have thrived because of its infanticidism.

THE REPRODUCTIVE VALUE OF INFANTICIDE:
SOCIOBIOLOGICAL THEORY

Although group selection theory acknowledges the fact of infanticide and accepts its potential "adaptiveness" for the group, sociobiology yields a much more robust account of animal infanticide because it solves the paradox of altruism. Its approach is based on the firmly established premise that the strongest effects of natural selection occur not at the level of the group but at the level of the individual: infanticide is adaptive for individuals, not for groups.

In 1976 Dawkins set forth the reasoning that has led most biologists to discount the explanatory framework provided by models of group selection.[16] His explanation centers on the inevitable reproductive superiority of non-altruists over altruists. According to Dawkins, in a group of altruists any selfish individual will more likely survive than those who are self-sacrificing and will more likely have more children than they. Since these offspring will tend to inherit the selfish traits of the parent, the consequences are inexorable. Across several generations, the numbers of selfish individuals will increase as they supplant and perhaps drive into extinction the altrusitic individuals. This will be the case even if a group is initially constituted entirely of altruistic individuals, for it will most likely not be able to prevent the arrival of selfish individuals from outside the group.[17]

Dawkins illustrates his argument with an example of selfish behavior — it is the very first example of animal behavior in his book — that turns on an act of predatory infanticide, an ordinary enough event among animals. Infanticidal predation is a common occurrence among blackheaded gulls, the subject of Dawkins' exposition. These birds "nest in large colonies, the nests being only a few feet apart. When the chicks first hatch out they are small and defenceless and easy to swallow. It is quite common for a gull to wait until a neighbour's back is turned . . . and then pounce on one of the neighbor's chicks and swallow it whole. It thereby obtains a good nutritious meal, without having to go to the trouble of catching a fish, and without having to leave its own nest unprotected."[18] In addition, the gull reduces the future competition its own offspring will encounter. The infanticidal gull, then, by virtue of its predation on other gull offspring, immediately increases its own survivability; moreover, it enhances its reproductive success as well as the potential success of its offspring, and it does so at the expense of the reproductivity of its neighbors. Finally, if any of those neighbors were for their part to be disinclined to engage in such infanticidal predation, their "altruism" would quickly prove to be reproductively fatal. In a population of altruists, the payoffs from infanticide make infanticidal behavior extremely economical for the selfish individual and its genetic kin, both in the short run and in the long run, and fatally costly for any altruistic cohort and its genetic relatives. Infanticide is adaptive because it confers reproductive advantages upon the individual infanticidal organism, not upon the group.[19]

With gulls the adaptiveness of the intraspecific killing of unrelated infants is straightforward. More complicated is the adaptiveness, in the following case among mice, of the infanticidal "Bruce effect." This effect refers to the abortion-inducing properties of a certain chemical secreted by males. In the absence of the mate that has impregnated her, a female mouse aborts if the smell secreted by the new male differs from that of the former mate. She then becomes receptive to the new male. In addition to acquiring reproductive opportunities, the male capable of inducing the Bruce effect eliminates the competitors of his offspring in advance of their births.[20] An adaptation among male mice, the Bruce effect is thought to protect them from the efforts of females to trick them into investing in offspring they themselves have not sired. Thus the Bruce effect functions to maximize the individual male's reproductive success at the cost of the female's reproductive success. What complicates this scenario is that if selection pressures have favored male mice with the ability to secrete an abortifacient, those pressures evidently have also favored females with the ability to abort when they have lost their mates and are being courted by potential replacements and otherwise not to abort. Presumably over their lifetimes the reproductivity of these females is greater than that of their competitors who are not receptive to the abortifacient. By the same token, females who attempt to bring their pregnancies to term and then to tend their offspring without a mate, rather than to abort and mate anew with an aborticidal male, suffer lower reproductive success. That is, they suffer greater reproductive failure relative to those females that do abort.

That infanticide might be adaptive and hence selected for, runs counter to the predominant thinking among biologists up into the 1960s. Then, Dawkins writes, "'genteel' ideas of vaguely benevolent mutual cooperation" were supplanted "by an expectation of stark, ruthless, opportunistic mutual exploitation."[21] The advent of a new explanatory paradigm, one focusing on the exploitive nature of animal sociality, occurred at about the same time that the systematic tracking of the occurrence of infanticide began in earnest. In their preface to the proceedings of a 1982 international conference, *Infanticide: Comparative and Evolutionary Perspectives* (1984), Glen Hausfater and Sarah Blaffer Hrdy note that prior to the 1970s animal infanticide was discounted as "abnormal and maladaptive behavior"[22] and human infanticide dismissed as an abhorrent aberration.[23] In addition, researches "failed to realize how widespread infanticide is in the natural world" because there was little empirical data concerning its frequency and no framework for conceptualizing its role in natural selection. "Early field reports of infanticide among langur monkeys and lions were sketchy; data were even sparser for other wild mammals." Egg destruction and siblicide among birds "were generally considered to be isolated phenomena," their incidence unknown. When "detailed information" about infanticide finally emerged from laboratory studies of rodents, the results were "typically attributed to overcrowding or to other features of captivity itself" and hence interpreted as an artifact of non-natural conditions. Such interpretations depended upon classical ethological theory, according to which "animals (with the notable exception of humans) rarely kill members of their own species under natural conditions,"[24] and on group selection theory, which specified that infanticide was either "pathological" or, when not "maladaptive," an effect of group mechanisms for limiting overcrowding.[25]

Gradually, however, infanticide acquired a stronger evolutionary explanation than hitherto had been available. One reason was increasing documentation of intraspecific infanticide and other killings, often in the absence of crowding or other abnormal conditions not typically seen in the wild.[26] Another was the critique of group selection. A third was the rise of sociobiological models of sexual selection, kin selection, and inclusive fitness. The result of the new theoretical footing was that documented reports of mammalian infanticide rapidly increased.[27] By 1984 Hausfater and Hrdy could announce that "in many populations infanticide is a *normal* and *individually adaptive* activity."[28] Three years earlier, in a work that examines the evolutionary history of female primates, Hrdy had arrived at a similar conclusion: "for many primates" infanticide "is, and has been throughout a substantial portion of their evolutionary history, a recurrent hazard."[29] However, to be a *hazard* for the potential victim infanticide must be an *opportunity* for the aggressing animal. Hrdy's study of langurs, an animal group comprised of several species of long-tailed monkey, offers a case in point.

Most species of langurs are sexually dimorphic: males are larger and heavier and more aggressive than females and able to dominate them physically, as is the case among the majority of primates, in which "males can usually displace females for access to commodities they both want."[30] The physical asymmetry between langur males and females plays a key role in determining their polygynous social structure. Langur troops are composed of a number of females, who enforce a dominance hierarchy among themselves, and a single male, who typically acquires his "harem" by driving out the former male leader and any weaned male offspring and who, if challenged by nomadic males, keeps his position only if he can rebuff them. Not surprisingly, there is a rapid turnover of male leaders, most of whom maintain their dominance for only twenty-seven months, on average, before being supplanted by a new alpha male, who poses an infanticidal threat to unweaned offspring of the previous leader.[31] Since the threat of infanticide by males of her own species is, Hausfater and Hrdy emphasize, "one of the most serious recurrent hazards that a mother has to face, comparable to predation and starvation . . . why, then, has she not evolved to sufficient size or dominance . . . to protect her own interests"?[32]

The evolutionary answer comes from the constraints on langur reproductivity. Upon acquiring a harem, a male langur has a short reproductive career ahead of him. One limit is a function of the female's reproductive cycle in general and the presence of any unweaned infants in particular. The typical langur female bears its young for twenty-eight weeks and nurses its offspring for another twenty-six or more weeks. Once pregnant, therefore, she will not become receptive again for well over a year unless the newly dominant male kills her unweaned offspring, an action that quickly brings her into estrus. If he reigns for only a short period of time, he may never have the opportunity to conceive offspring of his own with any presently nursing female unless he were to commit infanticide. If he commits infanticide, however, he insures himself the opportunity of reproducing more quickly, at least on the female who is no longer nursing. He also destroys his genetic competition.[33] Moreover, he thereby reduces the competition of his offspring, most immediately for food, maternal nurturance, and more distantly for future mates. Hausfater has calculated that male langurs who commit infanticide can double their reproductive success. Under these circumstances not to commit infanticide would doom a male to absolute reproductive failure.[34]

At the time *The Woman That Never Evolved* was written, Hrdy's research team had recorded the disappearance of forty-six langur infants "just after a new male entered the troop." They also saw "hundreds of unsuccessful assaults on infants, including cases where the infant was wounded but did not die . . . when new males usurped troops. In thousands of hours of observation," they never saw "normally tolerant male langurs . . . attack an infant under any other circumstance."[35] Infanticide on the part of males against unrelated offspring "provides a classic example," Hrdy notes, "of reproductive exploitation of one sex by another. In this instance, males compete with other males and pursue genetically selfish strategies at the expense of females and their offspring."[36]

Such "sexual selection"[37] —in this case of males able to commit infanticide under certain circumstances and of females able to be receptive to such males—operates in other primates. According to Carolyn M. Crockett and Ranka Sekulic, infanticide enables male red howler monkeys to "sire more offspring and do so sooner after infanticide since interbirth intervals are shortened." Infanticide may also "increase the likelihood

of a male's breeding in the first place by provoking male-male confronta-
tions necessary for the resolution of status."[38] In a report on "Infanticide
by Adult Males in Three Primate Species of the Kibale Forest, Uganda,"
Lysa Leland, Thomas T. Struhsaker, and Thomas M. Butynski conclude
that infanticide among males is sexually selected for: "an infanticidal male
will, with a few minor exceptions, gain a reproductive advantage over
a noninfanticidal male by bringing more females into estrus within a
shorter period of time."[39] Along with her collaborators, Anthony D.
Collins and Curt D. Busse, Jane Goodall has concluded that among
savanna baboons infanticide, observed and inferred, clearly contributes
to the reproductive advantage of immigrant males. . . ."[40] Christian Vogel
and Hartmut Loch note that infanticide by male langurs is almost always
reported as occurring only when an incoming male replaces an established dominant male.[41] Finally, Dian Fossey speculates that all male
mountain gorillas probably commit infanticide: "Given the long period
of dependency of the gorilla infant upon its mother and the violent means
by which silverbacks acquire their harems, it seems likely that all sexually mature males at some time in their lives carry out infanticide, and
that most females probably have at least one infant that falls victim to the
attack of a silverback."[42]

If sexual selection favors infanticidal males, their reproductive strategies doubtless are affected by the reproductive strategies of their female
counterparts. And yet, as Hrdy remarks, seldom noticed "is the necessary underpinning for the evolution of this system: competition between
females themselves."[43] Paradoxically, this competition enhances the reproductive success of the female that mates with infanticidal males. Why
would selection not favor females that avoid infanticidal males?

At first sight it would appear that no mother gains from losing her
infant regardless of who its father is. Nevertheless, female langurs do
not resist the infanticidal aggression of males nor cooperate with other
females to defend one another's offspring. In addition, they do not refuse
to mate with infanticidal males. These facts, together with their smaller
musculature and tooth size, shorter reach, and lighter weight, are evidence of counter-selection: sexual selection favors females that do not
grow significantly larger than other females and that do not form alliances against infanticidal males but rather mate readily with such
males. In bearing the offspring of infanticidal males that seek infanticide-
tolerant mates, these females contribute to the persistence of infanticidal
tendencies in their male offspring and of infanticide-tolerance in their
female offspring; the male selections of these offspring in turn reinforce
the presence of infanticidal traits among the population.[44]

Hrdy offers three reasons in support of this "counter-selectionist" contention. First, a female that grew larger than other females would have

to expend more time and energy foraging and eating to sustain her greater size than would other females and would have less time and energy available for reproduction and then caring for her offspring. She would be at a marked survival and reproductive disadvantage, therefore, during times of drought or other environmentally exigent periods. In addition, unless she were as large as a male, she would not be able to fight off an infanticidal threat in any case. For this reason, Hrdy concludes, "the advantage to self-defense of growing bigger would be nonexistent in the short run," for "the disadvantage to reproduction would soon be overwhelming."[45]

Second, if infanticide is both advantageous for males and an inherited tendency, then "any female who sexually boycotted infanticidal males would do so to the detriment of her own male progeny."[46] Presumably she would have fewer reproductive opportunities. If she were to bear the same number of male offspring as her competitors, "her sons would inevitably suffer in the ruthless competition with the sons of less discriminating mothers."[47] The sons of those males that are able to kill unrelated offspring will have a survival advantage over the sons of non-infanticidal males: they will be relatively less subject to infanticide than will the sons of the females that mate only with non-infanticidal males.

Finally, any female in her reproductive prime who actively resisted the infanticidal attacks of males against her offspring or those of a relative, let alone those of a stranger, would put herself in physical jeopardy and lessen her reproductive opportunities with this male.[48] Such altruistic behavior would represent an evolutionarily *un*stable strategy, one easily bettered by any competing female who did not expend energy and risk injury for the sake of another female. Over time such an altruistic strategy would be, Hrdy says, "selected right out of the genetic repertoire of the population."[49] Hausfater underscores Hrdy's contention: "females can, in theory, prevent the spread of infanticidal behavior among males by cooperatively or individually penalizing infanticidal individuals. However, any female who did not participate in this counterstrategy would, in the long run, have higher reproductive success than participatory females. . . ."[50]

Once infanticide arises within a population, it will be selected for, even if the presence of infanticidal reproductive strategies lowers the overall reproductivity of the population. In this regard the adaptiveness of infanticide may lead to a variation on the "tragedy of the commons," Hardin's name for a class of problems having "no technical solutions."[51] One such problem concerns the relation between individual reproductivity and a group's optimum size. In *The Wealth of Nations* (1776), Adam Smith imagines that the individual, "intend[ing] only his own gain," is "led by an invisible hand to promote an end which was not part of his intention," namely "the public interest."[52] The tragedy of the commons suggests otherwise.

The tragedy takes shape as a double bind, which confronts communities on the verge of over-exploiting some finite resource hitherto available to all members of the group. If each member seeks to maximize his or her self-interest, then as the resource becomes scarcer, each individual stands to gain more from any act of acquisitiveness than this individual stands to lose. The reason why is that the cost of overusing the resource is suffered by all whereas any gain is enjoyed more or less by the individual alone. Were the members to cooperate, they might collectively optimize the use of the resource; they would be able to protect its sustainability, however, only by curtailing their individual gains. The larger the difference between the cost of cooperating and the gain from not cooperating, the greater the temptation not to cooperate. Once even a few individuals refuse to cooperate, cooperation rapidly becomes a losing strategy for any other individual in the population.

Infanticide is a stark example of how group members that seek to maximize their respective individual reproductivity can wind up compromising their collective reproduction. Once introduced into a population, infanticidal behavior quickly becomes selected for, since infanticidal males achieve a reproductive advantage over those males who do not kill the unweaned offspring of their competitors. Infanticide thus illustrates the following evolutionary paradox: a trait that "produces a short-term increase in reproductive success for some individuals of one sex" simultaneously "locks adults of both sexes into patterns of behavior that ultimately result in a decreased rate of reproduction for themselves and for their population as a whole."[53]

ADAPTATIONS AS EVOLUTIONARY TRAPS

The selective pressures for and the adaptive advantages of infanticide thus yield a deeply problematic phylogenetic legacy that is representative of a recurrent evolutionary phenomenon: "In case after case throughout the natural world, animals are caught in similar evolutionary traps: selection favoring individual gain detracts from the fitness of others, from the general viability or survival of the species, and from what humans might call 'quality of life.' Infanticide simply happens to be a particularly striking and well-documented example of this larger phenomenon."[54]

Hrdy's description of evolutionary traps is suggestive of the prisoner's dilemma, one version of which is the "tragedy of the commons." The prisoner's dilemma refers to competitive interactions in which the aggregate payoff is not the highest or greatest of the available outcomes. In these scenarios, as competitors try to maximize their own outcomes and minimize the outcomes of their opponents, they wind up selecting noncooperative strategies the payoffs of which are lower for them together than are the payoffs they would receive were they to select strategies of cooperation. Indeed, the structure of the payoffs in the prisoner's dilemma is able to result in the competitors choosing strategies that produce negative outcomes not only for their opponents but for themselves as well.

Dawkins gives a hypothetical example concerning a population of "suckers," who groom others indiscriminately and thereby rid them of parasites such as ticks, and of "cheats," who accept being groomed but do not reciprocate. "If the incidence of parasites is high, any individual sucker *in a population of suckers* can reckon on being groomed about as often as he grooms. The average pay-off for a sucker among suckers is therefore positive." If a cheat appears on the scene, however, this individual will receive a significantly higher payoff than will the suckers. "Being the only cheat, he can count on being groomed by everybody else, but he pays nothing in return. His average pay-off is better than the average for a sucker. Cheat genes will therefore start to spread through the population. Sucker genes will soon be driven to extinction." Why? Because "no matter what the ratio in the population, cheats will always do better than suckers" since they do not reciprocate the grooming they receive. For this reason "the average pay-off for both suckers and cheats will be less than that for any individual in a population of 100 per cent suckers" where all individuals groom one another in turn.

> When the proportion of cheats reaches 90 per cent, the average pay-off for all individuals will be very low: many of both types may by now be dying of the infection carried by the ticks. But still the cheats will be doing better than the suckers. *Even if the whole population declines toward extinction,* there will never be any time when suckers do better than cheats. Therefore, as long as we consider only these two strategies, *nothing can stop the extinction of the suckers and, very probably, the extinction of the whole population too.*[55]

Infanticide, like other non-cooperative strategies, may produce similar consequences. It may be selected for against non-infanticidal strategies and yet "trap" the infanticidal animals in an evolutionary dead end.

Imagine two evenly matched animals of the same population group, each of which opts either to attempt to kill the opponent's offspring or to forgo such attempts. In the following table, the upper left cell stipulates the outcome if neither engages in infanticide: both produce the same number of offspring (four) and neither has an advantage over the other. This non-infanticidal strategy (live and let live) is not stable, however. In a world previously devoid of infanticide, the individual that discovers this behavior comes out significantly ahead of its cohorts (the outcomes

Table 1
Hypothetical Payoffs for Infanticidal versus Non-Infanticidal Strategies

	Non-Infanticidal Strategy B does not kill its competitors' offspring	Infanticidal Strategy B kills some of its competitors' offspring
Non-Infanticidal Strategy A does not kill its opponents' offspring	B: 4 offspring. No advantage A: 4 offspring. No advantage	B: 6 offspring. Advantage +5 A: 1 offspring. Disadvantage –5
Infanticidal Strategy A kills some of its opponents' offspring	B: 1 offspring. Disadvantage –5 A: 6 offspring. Advantage +5	B: 1 offspring. No advantage A: 1 offspring. No advantage

represented by the upper right and lower left cells). Choosing to kill the opponent's offspring lowers the total reproductivity of both individuals (from 8 to 7) but dramatically increases the difference (from zero to +5) in reproductive success between them. The infanticidal individual wins a huge reproductive payoff. Its lineage will quickly drive any non-infanticidal lineage into extinction. When both competitors engage in infanticide, neither achieves an advantage or suffers a disadvantage. Nevertheless each reproduces at a lower rate than they would if neither committed infanticide. If the rate is insufficient to sustain the population, the resulting extinction will have been a consequence of a behavior—infanticide—that was nevertheless selected for. Many noncooperative strategies are extinctive even though they are evolutionarily stable—that is, "cannot be bettered by an alternative" strategy "if most members of a population adopt it."[56] An evolutionarily stable strategy (ESS) will not necessarily prevent a group from oblivion. "If a population arrives at an ESS that drives it extinct, then it goes extinct, and that is just too bad."[57]

Insofar as an adaptation confers a survival or reproductive advantage, however, it is always able to set an evolutionary trap for the individual that does not have it. Here, the adaptiveness of infanticide is no different from the adaptiveness of any trait, including non-infanticidal ones: it is adaptive to the extent that it facilitates the organism's differential, not its absolute, reproductive success, its success relative to that of its competitors; alternatively, it is adaptive insofar as it contributes to lowering the reproductivity of competitors. Any and all adaptations must therefore be understood from two points of view—the perspective of the individual that possesses the adaptation and that outreproduces its competitors in consequence and the perspective of the individual that does not possess the adaptation and that therefore reproduces less successfully. In other words, any and all adaptations are simultaneously life-enhancing and life-reducing.

Moreover, adaptations are not purely adaptive but only contingently and relatively so: they are adaptive only in relation to a certain history, a certain context. Because no adaptation can guarantee the stability of the environmental context in which it arose, any adaptation is able to become non- or maladaptive—an evolutionary trap—under the right set of environmental changes. During periods of mass extinction nearly all adaptations cease to be adaptive. No adaptation can contribute to an organism's survival under all possible environmental conditions. In addition, no adaptation can halt all the mutagenic and other processes by which organismic variation occurs; hence no adaptation can immunize itself to the selection by which superior adaptations occur relative to previous adaptations. The consequence, again, is that the relativity of any adaptation implies its *potential* nonadaptiveness. Any adaptation is in its very structure able to become nonadaptive. It is in this sense that every adaptation is afflicted by what is able in principle to destroy and what in fact eventually undermines its adaptiveness—namely, its relative or differential nature. Coming into existence within a certain environmental niche, any and every adaptation supercedes previously selected but now inferior adaptations and in turn is subjectable in principle and sooner or later subjected in fact to such supercession by differentially favored new adaptations. The result is that any and every adaptation remains bound to an evolutionary process that is deathly at every instance of the "life" that evolution selects for. "Life" is within quotation marks because of its ability to become extinct not merely in spite of its evolutionary stability but because of that very stability. The critical issue is not that organisms sometimes adopt strategies that lead to the extinction of the population; it is that natural selection results in adaptations that are adaptive to the extent that they reduce the viability of other adaptations and often drive them out of existence. Selection processes do not select for life as such or for what promotes life in general, only for those traits that promote the differential viability of the bodily vehicle which carries them relative to the lesser viability of some other body—all within a certain environmental context. It is for this reason that infanticide can represent the inner dynamic of evolution. The general form of infanticide—and thus of the class of evolutionary death traps—is the general form of evolution itself.

This conclusion is implicit in the various definitions of infanticide. It is also implicit in the infanticidal consequences of all parental investment.

INFANTICIDE AND THE INFANTICIDAL

Some definitions restrict infanticide to "the destruction of young per se" between the time of their birth and weaning.[58] In his historical survey William L. Langer limits the scope of infanticide to "the willful destruction *of newborn babies* through exposure, starvation, strangulation, smothering, poisoning, or through the use of some lethal weapons."[59] Langer's definition, however, "represents only the extreme end of a continuum of behaviors which function to reduce the costs (in terms of time, energy, risk, and resources) that offspring impose upon parents."[60] In order to take into account the entire continuum of the means by which organisms try to lower the cost of their parental investment relative to the reproductive gain that such investment brings, others have expanded the meaning of infanticide in either or both of two ways.

In the first, infanticide is generalized to include intrauterine processes that destroy incipient offspring or that even block conception. For example, according to Dickemann if "within the category 'young,' morphologically discriminable stages in development (egg, larva, embryo, foetus, nestling, infant, weanling) may or may not be relevant to the infanticidal behaviour of adults," then intrauterine mortality may very well be not fundamentally different from extrauterine mortality but rather continuous with it."[61] Virginia D. Hayssen supports this view when she extends the category of infanticide to include resorption of the zygote, embryo death, miscarriage, and abortion. In each case the process of destruction obeys the same evolutionary law, the same principle of differential reproductive investment and its curtailment, that governs extrauterine destruction or support of offspring. For example, embryo resorption, a common effect of normal reproductive biochemistry, occurs in various mammals under conditions of "physical or biotic stress" when there is insufficient energy available to sustain gestation at that time.[62] In response, the animal's pregnancy is terminated almost as soon as it begins and the incipient life resorbed.

The category of infanticide can be enlarged further still to include not only those biochemical processes that destroy the zygote but those that destroy the male gamete—for example by chemically decapacitating the sperm deposited within the female reproductive tract before conception has taken place. By Hayssen's definition infanticide can occur before conception. It can also occur by means of conception itself, since every conception suppresses the possible conceptions that otherwise could have taken place. In other words, the life-forming event of conception is simultaneously contraceptive.

The second way of conceptualizing the infanticidal has been to include fatal aggressions against offspring long after infancy. Dickemann, for example, sees no essential difference between the killing of offspring after or before weaning in "some species, though not in others." For Dickemann pedicide, "the destruction of the offspring (not necessarily young) of self or others," is a form of infanticide.[63]

Hrdy and Hausfater advocate a broader rather than narrower definition, one that refers to "any form of lethal curtailment of parental investment in offspring brought about by conspecifics. Included in this definition would be the termination," just-mentioned, "of parental investment through destruction of gametes . . . or reabsorption of a foetus." Also included would be the abandonment or killing of offspring, in which case gameticide and feticide would join infanticide and pedicide as different expressions of the same underlying phenomenon of reproductive curtailment. Siblicide, the killing of offspring by related offspring, would also qualify under this general heading.[64] So too, in fact, would any reduction in parental investment, the infanticidal effects of which would be deferred rather than immediate, cumulative rather than instantaneous, nonfatal rather than death-dealing. In this regard Hrdy and Hausfater accept as examples of infanticide any parental behavior that reduces the chances of survival for their children—not just such extreme forms of abuse as starvation, beatings, and malnourishment but the scarcely noticeable forms of unwitting disfavoritism or underinvestment.[65] The results of the more indirect, covert, passive, unconscious, and deferred forms of infanticidal attitudes and behaviors might not show up for years or might manifest in ways that cannot be readily traced back to any recoverable act or sequence of parental neglect during infancy and childhood.[66]

Writing of the human capacity for inventing ways of denying nurturance to their children, and also of disavowing the denials, Harris evokes the possibility of forms of infanticide virtually impossible to verify: "I want to stress the fact that infanticides are not merely committed by direct means such as strangulation, drowning, exposure, and head bashing, but *more commonly by indirect means* such as slow starvation, physical and psychological neglect, and 'accidents,'" especially in countries that condemn infanticide on the one hand and birth control, including abortion, on the other. These two proscriptions would confront child-bearing women who find themselves in dire economic straits with a stark necessity: "Under these circumstances, mothers may be motivated to unburden themselves of unwanted children, but may find it necessary to hide their intentions not only to others but to themselves as well."[67]

Such concealment may take advantage of institutionalized permissions for the disposal of children before the performance of identity-conferring rituals: "it should be pointed out that many cultures do not regard children as human until certain ceremonies, such as naming or hair cutting, are performed. Infanticide and the induced death of small children seldom take place *after* such ceremonies have been performed. Hence, in the emic perspective, such deaths are rarely seen as homicides."[68] In such cases the cultural legitimation of the child's death may free the individual parent from having to conceal the desire and what would otherwise be a covert effort to get rid of the child.

Those efforts sometimes take considerable time, even years, to accomplish. The more encompassing conceptions of infanticide acknowledge this possibility by redefining infanticide less as a definitive event than as a process of accumulated effects across extended periods of reduced nurturance and care. These definitions recognize that "in some species (such as humans) . . . the decision by a parent to terminate investment may occasionally take place late in the overall reproductive process." If infanticide can occur not only at any time "throughout the period of offspring dependence," including by degrees, or even before that period, then "at this level of generality, contraception, abortion, direct killing of an infant, or nutritional neglect of a child are seen as related phenomena, differing only in the stage of the reproductive continuum at which curtailment of parental investment occurs."[69]

And yet the scope of the infanticidal is broader still. Once indirect, surreptitious, and otherwise delayed forms of infanticide are admitted into the category at hand, the boundaries of infanticidal phenomena come to extend indefinitely, their compass no longer subject to empirical delimitation. Why? The answer follows from the fact that reduced nurturance can lead to infanticide under circumstances where the intentionality behind such an outcome is either hidden or repressed and thus not available to public acknowledgment. Since an unverifiable number of children will have survived long enough to escape the fatal consequences of (intentional or unintentional) infanticidal strategies, the incidence of these strategies of diminished care in fact and in principle can never be known. Infanticidal efforts may fail; the child may live in spite of its care-givers' neglect; this person may survive but fail to reproduce in turn, or may reproduce but then neglect his or her children. In consequence, no child's survival can attest to parental motivation. Any child's survival may reflect the life-affirming investment of the parents in their offspring; however, the child's survival may also disguise the nature of the upbringing the child has received and betoken a more ambiguous or even utterly negative parental "investment." In sum, the child's survival in and of itself does not necessarily testify to the child's having been wanted, let alone having been responsibly cared for. The child's survival constitutes no guarantee that its parents did not decrease their investment, and did not engage in forms of indirect infanticide.

Despite their manifest differences, both direct infant killing and deferred infanticide are forms of curtailed reproductive investment. Such (infanticidal) curtailment, however, is not something that happens on rare occasions but all the time, for in a Darwinian economy any act of parental investment is simultaneously an act of disinvestment and for that reason infanticidal in its logical entailments.

THE INFANTICIDAL NATURE OF PARENTAL INVESTMENT AS SUCH

At issue in parental investment is the inescapability of opportunity costs. To invest in x is to not invest in y. To invest parental time and energy is to allocate finite resources one way and not another. To attend to one offspring (for example, by feeding it, grooming it, watching after it) is to withhold that attention from another offspring. This principle obtains between as well as within reproductive units. To distribute resources to one's own offspring is to not distribute those resources to the offspring of others.

One may or may not acknowledge the cost. Indeed, one may or may not recognize, understand, or experience the cost as a cost. Nevertheless, because every act of parental investment involves deciding who gets what portion of the resource in question and who does not get that portion, the payoff of that decision is relative to a possible payoff that is forgone, sacrificed. So acknowledges one of the early researchers into the nature of parental investment (P.I.). According to Robert L. Trivers the concept of parental investment refers to *"any investment by the parent in an individual offspring that increases the offspring's chance of surviving (and hence reproductive success) at the cost of the parent's ability to invest in other offspring."*[70] The payoff for parental investment is inseparable from its cost: the increased survival and reproductivity of the one offspring is purchased at the cost of the reduced survivability and reproductivity of "other offspring." That reduction is the infanticidal disinvestment that accompanies every act of investment, and it is structured into the very nature of parental care.

Dawkins suggests as much in the following illustration of Trivers' concept.

When a child uses up some of its mother's milk, the amount of milk consumed is measured not in pints, nor in calories, but in units of detriment to other children of the same mother. For instance, if a mother has two babies, X and Y, and X drinks one pint of milk, a major part of the P.I. that this pint represents is measured in units of decreased probability that Y will die because he did not drink that pint. P.I. is measured in units of decrease in life expectancy of other children, born or yet to be born.[71]

To mete out resources is to affect the probability not only of increased life expectancy but also of decreased life expectancy—that is, it is to affect the chances of an infanticidal outcome, however indirect or deferred this non-survival result might be. In addition, to allot resources to an existing child is to divert those same resources from the begetting of other potential offspring. It is, therefore, to lose other reproductive opportunities. Standing in for parental care in general, nursing exemplifies how any life-giving investment is simultaneously a life-subtracting (infanticidal) disinvestment.

To describe parental investment from the perspective not of the recipient of the resources but from the perspective of those who do not receive them is to describe the infanticidal meaning—the infanticidism, infanticidality, or infanticity—that attaches to evolution in general. The non-recipient is not necessarily a child that has been born into the world; it may be a future child that has yet to be or never will be conceived. If an individual's life expectancy is a probability function of parental investments that antedate this offspring's conception and birth, if the resources that a prior offspring consumes effect what Dawkins notes is a "decrease in life expectancy of other children, born or *yet to be born*," then even before a new life is conceived there is a sense in which it is already dying.

This alreadiness stipulates the infanticidal character not only of every act of nurturance but of every step in the reproductive process. Because the reproductive process occurs in the context of an organism's economizing effort to transfer more of its survival costs onto others or the environment than competitors are able to transfer, reproductive success for the one organism is a measure of its anti-reproductive—that is, infanticidal—consequences for its competitors. Differential reproductive success for the positively selected individual implies differential reproductive failure for the unselected individual. Infanticide is merely the most immediate expression of the more general infanticidism inherent in natural and sexual selection. The *selection for* that enables life to evolve is, in effect, always equivalent to infanticidal *selection against*. If evolution is a theory of life, it is perforce a theory of life's inscription—which is to say its evolutionary entrapment—within processes that are ineluctably sacrificial, infanticidal.

Earlier Hrdy was quoted to the effect that infanticide exemplifies the paradoxical structure of the evolutionary trap. The trap occurs when "selection favoring individual gain detracts from the fitness of others, from the general viability or survival of the species," and thus ensnares a population in an intraspecific competitive regime that debilitates it, eventually driving it to extinction. However, since all adaptations arise in relation to existing ecological circumstances, not to environments that have not yet appeared, no adaptation can protect an organism or its species against all possible ecosystem transformations. Because adaptations fit organisms to particular circumstances, they do not provide infinite adaptability. All adaptations, therefore, must eventually become evolutionary traps. The kind of technical evolutionary trap Hrdy analyzes—in which infanticidal behavior is adaptive for the individual but potentially disastrous for the group—is but a specific form of the trap constituted by all adaptations, including those that comprise parental investment. Thus does Hrdy assimilate the fact of evolutionary double binds to the inexorability of extinction in general: "Anyone who for even a moment thinks that what is natural is necessarily desirable has only to remember that 90 percent of all species that ever evolved are now extinct—through natural processes."[72] An outcome of those "natural processes," extinction is infanticide writ large; it is the wholesale expression of the infanticidism not only of infanticide but of all adaptations, of adaptivity as such.[73]

Infanticide and extinction, then, constitute two modes of the same evolutionary necessity, which is to say the same evolutionary trap. And that trap's catch is always being sprung.[74] No organism can escape this necessity, not even those organisms that have been selected for, the felicity of their present adaptations being utterly contingent upon unanticipatable futures. Thus, when Hausfater notes that evolution favors behavior that is good not for the species but rather for the individual, and that is "'good' only in the short run," he is defining the radical provisionality of any and all adaptation. He is also alluding to the principle of loss—not an actual loss but the logically necessary possibility of loss even when there is (for the moment) an evolutionary gain —that structures all selection by virtue of selection's differential nature. The loss in question is a form of the deathliness in every instance of selection against as well as in every instance of selection for. Therefore, the infanticidal is not an empirical phenomenon that emerges in the course of evolution; it is the nonempirical condition of the possibility of evolution. It is that which renders death and extinction immanent to the very form and structure of the biological order.[75]

THE INFANTICIDALITY OF GENES

The infanticidal operates at the level of the individual organism. It also operates at the level of the gene, the focus of theoretical approaches to evolution that seek to describe the diversity of life not in terms of successful species or of successful individuals within a population group but of the successful "germ-line replicator" or "replicating molecules" of heredity, the "replicating fragments of DNA."[76] The evolutionary story of the gene or gene segment is the narrative neither of an immortal hereditary substance or vehicle nor of an immortal molecular form; it is the account of a replicability or iterability that is inseparable from the way death at the organismic level functions as the infanticidal condition of life. The version of the genetic story to be examined is supplied by Dawkins, whose expositions lead him to the threshold of a deconstructive notion of death distributed throughout every moment of life, every moment of adaptation, every moment of evolutionary selection.

In *The Extended Phenotype* (1982), the book he considers his most important contribution to evolutionary biology, Dawkins reexamines the "central theorem" of the modern Darwinian paradigm, the "dogma of individual organisms working to maximize their own reproductive success, the paradigm of the 'selfish *organism*.'"[77] He wishes to amend this view by specifying its genetic basis. "It is legitimate to speak of adaptations as being 'for the benefit of' something, but that something is best not seen as the individual organism. It is a smaller unit which I call the active, germline replicator"—the selfish gene. "The most important kind of replicator is the 'gene' or small genetic fragment. Replicators are not, of course, selected directly, but by proxy; they are judged by their phenotypic effects."[78] A phenotype is "the manifested attributes of an organism, the joint product of its genes and their environment during ontogeny."[79] Phenotypic effects are usually thought of "as being packaged together in discrete 'vehicles' such as individual organisms," but such parceling "is not fundamentally necessary. Rather, the replicator should be thought of as having *extended* phenotypic effects, consisting of all its effects on the world at large, not just its effects on the individual body in which it happens to be sitting."[80]

The concept of the extended phenotype decenters the place of the individual organism as the unit of selection in several ways. Most immediately it represents the organismic body as one among an array of the gene's effects, and these effects reach well beyond that body. As an instrumentality of the gene, the body is part of a larger constellation of genetic manifestations that includes the organism's behavior and its consequences; body and behavior along with their impacts on the environment, then, are the gene's phenotypic means of ensuring its survival and chances of replication. They are vehicles of genetic replication.

"The obvious and archetypal vehicle is the individual organism," Dawkins writes.[81] If a "body is the genes' way of preserving the genes unaltered,"[82] so, too, is behavior and its impact. Thus, any animal artifact, indeed any behavioral outcome, functions as a genetic vehicle: "A nest, like a bird, is a gene's way of making another gene."[83] In this view the individual physical organism—the body—is an adventitious arrangement within the total field of the gene's operations. The relation of organismic body to its genetic endowment, then, is not the relation of a superordinate whole to one of its elements, for genes do not belong to the individual that is their conveyance. It would be more accurate to suggest that the body belongs to the genes that inhabit it.

Even that formulation would be misleading, however. It is rather that the body is part of a contested field, serving as a target of genetic appropriations in the course of the natural selection of replicators, which may be situated within the body but, just as well, outside it. Thus the organism does not constitute a locus of integration and unity, for genes do not necessarily work in concert with one another. They may, but they also may not. On the one hand "selection favours those genes which succeed *in the presence of other genes, which in turn succeed in the presence of them.* Therefore mutually compatible sets of genes arise in gene-pools. This is more subtle and more useful than to say that 'we call the resultant object a body."[84] Why? Because the sets of genes in question may or may not reside within the same bodily housing.

On the other hand, however, replicators may be in conflict not only with replicators in other bodies but with those in the same body. "The idea of a discrete vehicle maximizing a unitary quantity— fitness— depends on the assumption that the replicators that it serves all stand to gain from the same properties and behaviour of their shared vehicle. If some replicators would benefit from the vehicle's doing act X, while other replicators would benefit from its doing act Y, that vehicle is correspondingly less likely to behave as a coherent unit."[85] Dawkins here challenges an assumption that is part of what Donna Haraway has termed the "techno-organicist or holistic ontology." In accord with a philosophical tradition going back to Aristotle and Plato, this ontology posits the organic unity and self-identity of the individual "cybernetic" or self-steering— that is, autonomous—organism.[86] Dawkins implicitly and Haraway explicitly challenge this ontological view of the organism. If we have come to "treat groups and ecosystems as collections of warring, or uneasily cohabiting, organisms," we remain largely bound to a view of the body as an integrated entity: "we treat legs, kidneys, and cells as cooperating components of a single organism" rather than as aspects of a nonunitary biological assemblage.[87] By relocating the object of the effective action of natural selection from the organism to the replicator, Dawkins not only decenters the concept of the organism, he reconceptualizes it in non-identitarian terms.[88] Thus arises the possibility of the "outlaw" gene, a class of gene that works "to promote its own survival while harming the survival chances of most of the rest of the genome" and that is in conflict with genes that would neutralize or otherwise modify its injuri-ousness. Dawkins believes that "we should expect selection to favour genes that happen to have the effect of neutralizing the outlaw's delete-rious effects on the body as a whole"; at the same time we should antici-pate that "if outlaws do, in general, call forth the selection of suppressing modifiers, there will presumably be an arms race between each outlaw and its modifiers."[89]

The metaphor of an escalating conflict anticipates the evolutionary stakes of within-body competition among genes. Not only can outlaw genes threaten the rest of an individual organism's genome with replicative death, they can also subject "the whole population" to the risk of extinction. Such an outcome is a theoretical possibility that has been demonstrated in a computer simulation. When a male with a gene on a Y chromosome that caused him to have only sons was introduced into a population of one thousand males and one thousand females, in only fifteen generations the number of females declined to zero and the pop-ulation became extinct.[90] As Dawkins all but declares in the ensuing dis-cussion, the gene in question (a driving Y chromosome) is equivalent to a gene that "makes its possessor kill his daughters and feed them to his sons. This is clearly a behavioural version of a driving Y-chromosome effect."[91] It is also an explicit illustration of how the logic of infanticid-ity is implicit in Dawkins' conception of the selfish gene. If Dawkins can entertain this imaginary biocontest in which simulated extinction has been replaced by simulated infanticide, it is because natural selection at the genetic level produces effects that are necessarily infanticidal in their logical form. Dawkins' thought experiment makes this logical necessity explicit by representing an immediate and direct form of the possible be-havioral or organismic outcome of a sex-linked genetic outlaw—namely infanticide. The extinction to which this infanticidal outcome leads makes readily apparent what in fact are nothing other than the normal consequences of the otherwise indirect, deferred, and scarcely visible in-fanticidal differentialization that governs all of natural selection. "Nat-ural selection is differential survival of genes,"[92] and differential survival necessitates the differential death or destruction of those other genes. In not being destroyed outright, these other genes do not simply survive, they survive less frequently. Their differentially reduced survival is marked by their lower replicative success relative to some other gene's higher replicative success. Their relative replicative failure, then, is an expression of the differential destruction that is dramatically accelerated and foregrounded in the conventionally understood act of infanticide. In other words, as the site of intracorporal genetic competition, the decen-tered organism is subject in principle as well as in fact to the infanticidal force of selection operating among the genes housed within its body.

At the same time, the organismic body, its erstwhile unity displaced by the structural possibility of internal division, is also always subject to the infanticidal force of selection among genes located outside it and acting upon it at a distance. Although "[m]ost serious field biologists now subscribe to the theorem . . . that animals are expected to behave as if maximizing the survival chances of all the genes inside them," the location of these genes "inside" the individual body is merely fortuitous. They can just as well be located elsewhere. In taking this possibility into account, Dawkins proposes an amended version of the traditional theorem, which he calls the "new central theorem of the extended phenotype": "An animal's behaviour tends to maximize the survival of the genes 'for' that behaviour, whether or not those genes happen to be in the body of the particular animal performing the behaviour." Sometimes the control of an animal's phenotype is exerted by genes housed in other organisms. Thus, "the behaviour we are looking at *may* be, at least partly, an adaptation for the preservation of *some other* animal's or plant's genes. It may therefore be positively *maladaptive* for the organism performing the behaviour."[93]

When Dawkins asserts that some animal's behavior *may* be an adaptation that subserves the genes not of that animal but of some other living entity, he is specifying a possibility that is immanent to the structure of any and every adaptation. The reason, again, is that adaptations occur only within a system of differential exchanges, tradeoffs, or sacrifices: one organism's adaptations often impose maladaptive effects — costs — on other organisms and always impose a cost on some facet of the biosphere. The example Dawkins returns to is the aforementioned Bruce effect. In the language of individual reproductivity, a male mouse increases its Darwinian fitness if it can cause a female, pregnant by another male, to abort and thus to come into estrus again, this time to be impregnated by himself. In "the language of the extended phenotype," which is the language of "genetic action at a distance," the Bruce effect registers the "phenotypic expression in female bodies" of the genes in the male body that produce their aborticidal effect by means of a scent secreted in the urine.[94] For Dawkins the precise chain of causation leading from gene to phenotype is not confined by the seemingly discrete boundaries of the individual male and female organisms; those boundaries are a strictly "incidental" effect,[95] Dawkins says, of the struggle for survival of the genes in question. As Dawkins' example evinces, that struggle is infanticidal. And it is so whether selection is understood in terms of the differential reproductive success of the individual or the differential replicative success of a gene fragment.

This infanticidality affects the entire class of adaptations that enable one organism, to the replicative advantage of its own genes, to exploit the nervous system of another organism. This class includes "all of animal communication as manipulation of signal-receiver by signal-sender."[96] Dawkins devotes an entire chapter, "Arms Races and Manipulation," to a review of behaviors by which "an individual induces the effectors of another individual to work against its own best interests, and in favour of the interests of the manipulator."[97] Such phenomena as brood parasitism and egg mimicry are flagrant examples, since the connection between manipulation and differential reproductive success is immediate. Immediate or deferred, however, the effect of such manipulation is inexorably infanticidal. Not only does the logic of the infanticidal characterize the competitive interactions of genes, it also inheres in the structure of replication.

REPLICABILITY VERSUS REPLICATION— A DERRIDEAN VIEW OF MUTABILITY

In a chapter entitled "Immortal Coils" in *The Selfish Gene*, Dawkins defines the gene as "a unit [of DNA] that survives through a *large*" but not infinite "number of successive individual bodies."[98] Genes are not immortal: "the gene is a long-lived replicator, existing in the form of many duplicate copies," but "it is not infinitely long-lived."[99] However, even as it is replicating successfully, and thus long before all its copies finally disappear, it can be in the process of dying out insofar as it replicates less frequently than its competitors.

A gene dies in a second way as well—that is, through its ability to undergo and survive mutation. Under normal circumstances a replicator duplicates itself, preserving its identity in the process. However, it is always possible that the identity of any molecular sequencing will be transmuted—altered, lost, destroyed—for under any number of other circumstances the copying process is beset with errors: "mistakes *will* happen," Dawkins notes, and this eventuality constitutes "an important *property* of any copying process."[100] As Dawkins emphasizes, "erratic copying in biological replicators," no matter how infrequent, is "*essential* for the progressive evolution of life." Although the modern genetic descendants of the original replicator molecules are, Dawkins says, "astonishingly faithful," they nevertheless "occasionally make mistakes, and *it is ultimately these mistakes that make evolution possible.*"[101] If genes were not able to be inaccurate, however slight the difference, then their self-replication would not produce the variant genetic forms which, competing to survive and reduplicate themselves, generate the processes of evolutionary selection.[102]

If replication can still be said to occur even when copying errors change (however minimally) that which is identified as having been replicated, then replication does not so much reproduce any supposed identity of the gene segment as it replicates the gene's replicability. Replication typically copies exactly the pattern of one DNA sequence, in the process constructing an identical molecular twin. And yet the twin need not be identical so long as its differences do not interfere with its ability to replicate in turn. In this case the altered or mutated sequence is not the same as the original sequence: the new sequence preserves the replicability of the old sequence even as it does not preserve the identity of that sequence.

Replicability, then, is not the same as replication; replicability is different from and logically prior to its empirical instantiations in the form of actual replications, actual duplications. If replication can be either exact or inexact and still be replication, then that is because there is something more fundamental than replication, something that facilitates the transfer not primarily of the (exact) copy but of this copy's copyability, something that thereby is always able in principle to interfere with the transfer of the (exact) copy. That something is the DNA sequence's replicability, the mistake-inducing copying and copyable "property" Dawkins has identified as rendering the sequence susceptible to alteration.

It is just this replicability, not the replicator "itself," that makes evolution possible. It is not in its replication that the replicator is able to be the unit of selection but in its replicability upon the occasion of its mutation, of an alteration or transformation that, by definition, must make it other than it was. That a gene is able to duplicate itself exactly is a contingent and not a necessary feature of its ability to transfer the power of transfer, to transfer transference, to transmit its transmissibility, even when "copying errors" are interposed upon the previous identity of the replicating molecule. Indeed, only because the replicator is able to be so modified has (terrestrial) life been able to arise and evolve.[103] It therefore would be precisely in its immortality—that is, in its eternal and unmutated or otherwise unaltered duplication of itself—that a replicator would not be alive. Unable to undergo mutagenesis, a replicator would be dead every time it copied itself perfectly. Only if it is not immortal, only if it is susceptible to alteration, to the possibility of alteration, can its replicability become the condition of life.

The gene's mutability, not the fact of any specific alteration but the structural possibility of erroneous copying, is its evolution-driving divisibility. "It was the great achievement of Gregor Mendel to show that hereditary units can be treated in practice as indivisible and independent particles. Nowadays we know that this is a little too simple. Even a cistron[104] is occasionally divisible and any two genes on the same chromosome are not wholly independent," Dawkins acknowledges. "What I have done is to define a gene as a unit which, to a high degree, *approaches* the ideal of indivisible particulateness. A gene is not indivisible, but it is seldom divided."[105] Only when it is divided, however, does evolution have an opportunity to occur; without the replicator's divisibility—its susceptibility to alteration, to mutation—there would be no evolutionary selection. Even if it is but seldom or even rarely subject to division, the replicator must be divisible for it to function as the so-called "unit"— more accurately, the non-unitary site—of evolution. To assert the ideality of the replicator's indivisibility, therefore, is to retreat from the divisibility that is the mark of the "death" already at work, and necessarily so, in the "life" of life's molecular instantiation.

The argument here rests on the Derridean logic of iterability as opposed to iteration, repeatability as opposed to repetition. In its conventional meaning the concept of repetition designates an operation that applies to something that already exists or that has already happened and that is then copied, multiplied, or otherwise reproduced. According to this view repetition is always a secondary process, one that occurs after the first appearance of whatever is then repeated. In the case at hand the empirical duplication of a gene requires that there be a gene in the first place, its replication occurring subsequently. This conception of repetition, however, fails to account for the repeatability that is logically prior to any and every repetition. What Derrida explains about the difference between the repetition and repeatability of signs applies to the difference between the replication and replicability of genes, between their mutation and their mutability. In order for a sign to be a sign and to function— to be sent and received—it must be repeatable. "A sign which would take place but 'once,'" Derrida writes, "would not be a sign."[106] "Once" is within quotation marks because a single occurrence of the sign is not possible. In consequence, there can never have been a pure "first" appearance of the sign: any sign must appear from out of a repeatability that in some sense precedes any actual repetition, indeed that precedes the sign's very first appearance.

This repeatability is independent of what the sign designates, of what it is intended to mean or is believed to refer to. Neither the sign's link to some referent—for example, to some concept—nor its employment to convey the sender's intention, nor its reception determines its repeatability. What is sent and what is received by way of the sign is first and foremost not the sender's intention. Even when signs are successfully sent and received, nevertheless they are always able in principle to be separated from the sender's intention and therefore are always able in principle to lose their original meaning in the course of their sending. "A written sign . . . can give rise to an iteration both in the absence of and beyond the presence of the empirically determined subject who, in a given context, has emitted or produced it," Derrida notes. "By all rights, it belongs to the sign to be legible, even if the moment of its production is irremediably lost, and even if I do not know what its alleged author-scriptor meant consciously and intentionally at the moment he wrote it."[107]

Not only can the subject's meaning be lost but the context in which the transmission has occurred can be destroyed: "a written sign carries with it a force of breaking with its context, that is, the set of presences which organize the moment of its inscription. This force of breaking is not an accidental predicate, but the very structure of the written." Thus, a sign can always be cited in terms of a new context that breaks with the context in which it was produced: "one can always lift a written syntagma from the interlocking chain in which it is caught or given without making it lose every possibility of functioning, if not every possibility of 'communicating,' precisely. Eventually, one may recognize other such possibilities in it by inscribing or *grafting* it into other chains." The ability of the sign to be cited—to be removed from the context of its earlier use, to be "grafted" onto a new context—means that "no context can enclose it."[108] There is no ultimate context that would limit the movement of additional graftings.

What is sent and what is received, then, is not just a particular meaning but the sign's ability to be sent and to be received even if in its transmission the sign's intended meaning is lost. In Derrida's famous observation, "a letter does *not always* arrive at its destination, and from the moment that this possibility belongs to its structure one can say that it never truly arrives, that when it does arrive its capacity not to arrive torments it with an internal drifting."[109] The possibility of erroneous arrival, of what Derrida calls "destinerrance," belongs to the structure of the genetic replicator. The gene's mutability "precedes" and makes possible its actual alteration, so that even when it remains unaltered in fact, it nevertheless transfers in the course of its replication its ability to be altered in principle. This is why even the most faithful genetic copying is something of an oxymoron: genetic replication always includes the replication of the genetic sequence's structural susceptibility to changes—its structural mutability—which might destroy its previous identity.

And yet the destructibility of this identity—not its actual destruction but its ability to be destroyed—is the very condition of its possibility, for if it could not be destroyed, if it could not be altered or mutated, it would not have its quintessential evolutionary characteristic. Of necessity genetic copying remains subject to alteration, to the production of non-identical genetic variants, to inexact replication, which is to say to a kind of replication without replication, once again to the replication of a replicability that is able to be transferred without this transference preserving the identity of the replicator. Although replication may transfer intact the identity of the replicating genetic sequence, it is always able not to; it is always able to be modified, whether or not it does in fact undergo any mutagenesis.

The divisibility, that is, the alterability, mutability, or modifiability of any replicator is tantamount to its "death"—not its empirical disappearance but the destructibility that structures its replicability. Why formulate the issue in this extreme way? In order to draw attention to the teleological assumption that remains embedded in the concept of the evolution of life. This assumption has prevented neo-Darwinian formulations of this concept from distinguishing replication, which is always presented as the replication of living entities, from replicability, which is independent of any particular form of replication, hence which is not limited to biological replication.

EVOLABILITY VERSUS EVOLUTION

Natural selection has produced an astonishing array of DNA-based entities—genetic replicators—the collective natural histories of which constitute the genealogy of earthly life. As biological entities, genetic replicators represent a particular kind of replicable or replicative instantiation. That is to say, on earth replicability has been biochemically incarnated. As a logical form, however, replicability depends upon no such living materialization; replicability is in principle independent of the particular life forms to which replication, under the pressure of selection processes, has given rise. That is why Dawkins can envision nongenetic replicators— for example the so-called meme, a whole new kind of replicator—in potentially deadly competition with its genetic precursors.

Here Dawkins' notion of a nonbiological replicating entity, memic or otherwise, begins to recognize the living-dead character of replicability, though once again his language falls back on a concept of life that his logic contests. "We must begin," Dawkins says, "by throwing out the gene as the sole basis of our ideas on evolution."[110] Why? Because the gene is only one kind of replicator, and it gives rise to only one kind of evolution. Other kinds of replicators are possible; and if they are not DNA-based, then they will give rise to non-DNA-based forms of evolution: "a new kind of replicator," Dawkins avers, can "start a new kind of evolution. . . . Once this new evolution begins, it will in no necessary sense be subservient to the old" form of "genetic evolution."[111]

Although there is no logical necessity to assume that the "new kind of replicator" is alive or would be a living entity, Dawkins introduces just this presupposition when he poses the following question concerning alternative evolutions: "is there anything that must be true of all life, wherever it is found, and whatever the basis of its chemistry? If forms of life exist whose chemistry is based on silicon rather than carbon, or ammonia rather than water, if creatures are discovered that boil to death at −100 degrees centigrade, if a form of life is found that is not based on chemistry at all but on electronic reverberating circuits, will there still be any general principle that is true of all life?"[112] Dawkins does not know but wagers that the principle in question is "the law that all life evolves by the differential survival of replicating entities."[113]

Even if it were to be the case that all life evolved in this way, would it also be the case that all replicating entities were alive? That is, does the differential survival of replicating entities produce only the evolution of life, or is it also able to produce another kind of evolution, the evolution of something else, something that would not be life, that would be better called non-life? Dawkins comes close to acknowledging this possibility when he speculates on the "evolution of evolvability" as separate from the evolution of survivability. However, because he envisions evolvability in terms of the living entity, he is not able to formulate the logical independence of evolvability as such from its manifestation in biological evolution.

In "The Evolution of Evolvability," Dawkins distinguishes between three different orders of change.[114] The first two are common. One, which occurs within an already existing genetic system, involves the replacement of one allele by another at the same locus. In the textbook example of peppered moths during the industrialization of Great Britain, a gene for blackness that replaced a gene for grayness spread among this species. Such allelic changes within a genetic system are common throughout evolutionary history. Although changes to genetic systems themselves occur much less frequently than do changes within genetic systems, nevertheless these sorts of changes are also widespread across evolutionary time. These changes, the second of the first two to which Dawkins alludes, account for the differentiation among the variety of living things of the same class—mammals, for example—such that they have different numbers of chromosomes and thus different genetic systems but trace their evolution back to a common ancestor from which they have inherited the same basic kind of genetic system. Dawkins suggests that the number of changes to different genetic systems is probably on the order of hundreds of millions.[115]

There is, Dawkins observes, a third kind of genetic change, which is much rarer than the first two. It entails a kind of mutation that promotes yet further mutation. Such genetic developments—for example, the advent of segmentation—are "watershed events" because they open the floodgates to future evolution."[116] They have the unusual characteristic of being both first-order and second-order evolutionary adaptations. That is, they are specific changes that transfer the capacity to undergo further genetic alteration in a way that capitalizes on and generalizes the adaptability of the initial change. This third kind of genetic mutation is an example of the evolution of the trait of evolvability.

The genetic transmission of this higher-order trait—namely, of the capacity (to transmit the capacity) to undergo mutagenesis—is paradoxical. In the case at hand the paradox is that segmentation may or may not have provided an initial adaptive advantage to the segmented entity. In fact Dawkins thinks the survivability of any particular segmented entity in the midst of a population of its unsegmented genetic kin might have been at the outset problematic. "I suspect that the first segmented animal was not a dramatically successful individual. It was a freak, with a double (or multiple) body where its parents had a single body. Its parents' single body plan was at least fairly well adapted to the species' way of life; otherwise they would not have been parents. It is not, on the face of it, likely that a double body would have been better adapted. Quite the contrary. Nevertheless," as the contemporary existence of its segmented descendants evinces, "it survived."[117] However, the ability of this mutated organism to reproduce itself and its mutation is less important than its ability to pass on its mutability, its susceptibility to further mutation. The first segmented entities survived long enough to reproduce not so much exact copies as mutated and, what is more, mutable versions of themselves. The reproductive success of these segmented creatures, then, has inhered not in any particular segmentation but in a kind of general segmentability—that is, in the ability of segmented creatures to undergo further mutagenic segmentation and in consequence to produce "descendant lineages" that have "radiated, speciated, and [given] rise to whole new phyla":

> the individual success, or otherwise, of the first segmented animal during its own lifetime is relatively unimportant. No doubt many other new mutants have been more successful as individuals. What is important about the first segmented animal is that its descendant lineages were champion *evolvors*. They radiated, speciated, and gave rise to whole new phyla. Whether or not segmentation was a beneficial adaptation during the individual lifetime of the first segmented animal, segmentation represented a change in embryology that was pregnant with evolutionary potential.[118]

To be a "champion evolvor" is not first and foremost to be successful at reproducing viable self-copies that reproduce in turn; rather it is to be successful at producing mutated offspring whose offspring too are able to produce yet other successful mutagenic deviations from themselves.

It is this transferable mutability that underlies the evolutionary potential of what Dawkins calls segmentation but what would be better termed segmentability. More generally, such transferable mutability enables Dawkins to distinguish between two orders of embryological selection—a lower-level selection of particular embryologies and a higher-level selection of embryological evolvability:

> New embryologies that are evolutionarily fertile tend to be the embryologies that characterize the forms of life that we actually see. As the ages go by, changes in embryology that increase evolutionary richness tend to be self-perpetuating. Notice that this is not the same thing as saying that embryologies that give rise to good, healthy individual organisms tend to be the embryologies that are still with us, although that, too, is no doubt true. I am talking about a kind of higher-level selection, a selection not for survivability but for evolvability.[119]

Survivability is emphatically not the same as evolvability. To the contrary, survivability is what evolvability is not, especially in the case when new genetic lines replace rather than coexist with the parent lines from which the new lines have evolved. Their evolvability implies the nonsurvivability of the parent form. If the mutant offspring form entails the death of the parent form, however, it signifies the living on of the parent form's ability to have transferred its own mutability.

This transference has not always been and will not always be genetic, for genetic transference is itself a consequence of some nongenetic transference and its mutagenesis. The capacity to transfer information genetically arose from some nongenetic context. For this reason evolvability in general, evolvability as such, must not be confused with genetic evolvability. The difference is categorical: genetic evolvability is a subset of general evolvability. If the relation were the reverse, if evolvability were an instance of genetic transferability, then Dawkins would not be able to endorse the possibility that genetic replicators evolved out of nongenetic replicators based on inorganic crystals;[120] nor would he have been able to imagine genetic replicators giving rise to a new kind of non-genetic replicator, the memic cultural replicator. The logical form of replicability, then, provides for the possibility of but does not require living, biological, genetic replication. What is logically necessary is not that replicability would take on the characteristics of life but that replicability entails the death of life—not merely the death of individual lives, not merely the extinction of genetic lines, but the annihilation of the biological itself. Life is a contingent, not teleological, outcome of the evolvability that mutability together with replicability make possible. For this reason evolvability is able to lead to an evolution that will destroy the biological.

Wherever there is replication there is (differential) death. And if a new kind of replicator can arise, a nonbiological replicator that might out-replicate its biological competitor and drive it into extinction, then the replicability of this new kind of replicator can no longer be adequately described in terms of the life that characterizes biological entities. Thus, Dawkins' inquiry—"is there anything that must be true of all life," whether its chemistry "is based on silicon rather than carbon, or ammonia rather than water?"—should be turned around. The question is not whether all life has something in common, namely evolution by means of "the differential survival of replicating entities," but whether all replicating entities must be conceived of as living.

Memes, as Dawkins conceives them, illustrate why the answer is no. Memes are alive only metaphorically, only by virtue of the analogy between their structure and the structure of the replicator that is considered to be alive—the gene. The success of memes is not the success of a new life form but the success of a nonbiological replication that is differentially fatal for life-based replication. Dawkins all but admits as much when he concludes that once such an evolutionary sequence begins, the new kind of replicator will dominate and eventually replace the older kind, which will die out differentially. The advent of self replicating molecules eventually led to the rise of DNA. DNA, however, is not the telos of evolution. Just as DNA differs from an earlier replicating predecessor molecule, another kind of replicator may arise at some future point. If that were to happen, it would, Dawkins insists, proliferate: "Whenever conditions arise in which a new kind of replicator can make copies of itself, the new replicators will tend to take over, and start a new kind of evolution of their own."[121] No doubt natural selection will continue to operate on genetic replicators; and yet it is manifestly the case that human culture—Dawkins' example of an evolutionary scenario in which selection operates on nonbiological memic replicators—is obliterating one gene pool after another throughout the "natural" world. Although it is possible that the two evolutions, genetic and cultural, will coexist or co-occur for some undeterminable length of time, the force of Dawkins' argument is that the newer kind of evolution can and will, in fact must, supplant the older. It can and must do so, however, only because selection does not favor this or that replicating entity, living or otherwise, but rather its replicability. Certain conditions will allow for this replicability to take on a biological or, if it can be said without contradiction that not all life is biological, some other living form; other conditions will allow for replicability to take on a nonbiological, and more generally a non-living, form.

As long as the new form is said to be living, then evolution continues to be the evolution of life. Once again, however, it is not the case that life makes replicability possible but that replicability allows for the advent of life. It does so by simultaneously necessitating its disappearance. According to the logic of Dawkins' argument, it is not the case that the replicator is the vehicle or engine of life's evolution but that living replicators are one set of vehicles for a general replicability that can always proceed in a way that destroys those vehicles, and that destroys life. In its very structure, then, replicability entails the possibility that one form of replication, biological for example, can come into unsuccessful competition with a different form of replication to which it itself has given rise, just as the hypothesized early form of inorganic crystalline replication is said to have come into unsuccessful competition with the biological copying of which it was the precursor form. In this case replicability "survives" even if one manner of replication, bioreplication, and hence one mode of evolution, the evolution of life, dies out.[122] The logical form of replicability as such, of replicability in general, is not the logical form of (biological) life, as this life has been traditionally understood, but of a "survival" that can outlive life. Such survival is a kind of death; more accurately it is a repeatability that defies the categorical distinction between life and death, that is therefore both living and dead, neither living nor dead, at one and the same time.

For this reason replicability must not be equated with the concept of life or of the living entity. Replicability is not in its essence alive; it "is," rather, that without which life cannot arise. At the same time, however, by being the condition of the advent of nonbiological, or rather nonliving, replication, replicability "is" the death of life; it is a deathliness that is the condition of the possibility of life's replication of itself. This "death" happens to the replicator even before it replicates; it is what enables any replicator to copy itself in the first place. This deathliness is the necessity that the replicator be able to lose its identity, and it precedes every replication whether or not the replication process goes without a hitch. The defining characteristic of a replicator, then, is the expression of the "death" that inhabits living things, that enables them to come into and go out of empirical, material, biological existence. If the replicator can transfer the power of transference even as the genetic sequence in question is modified, is so altered that it is no longer the same, is subject to a loss or destruction of its previous identity, then the logical form of genetic replicability is the expression at the genetic level of the infanticidal at the organismic level.[123] To read the evolutionary tree as a tree of life rather than of death or of life-death is to miss this infanticidality-cum-genicidality. It is therefore to accede, however unwittingly, to an overdetermined cultural metaphor and to participate in the wish fulfillment this metaphor puts into effect. For the image of the tree of life transforms the deadliness of natural selection— extinctive at the level of the species, differentially fatal at the level of the individual, mutagenic at the level of the gene, supercessive at the level of general replicability—into a reassuring image of biological continuity and near-immortality vis-à-vis an ongoing progenerativity into the future.

That image is false. Life is not self-originating, and it is not self-perpetuating. To the contrary, its apparent self-production depends upon a supplementary force that is neither simply internal nor external to evolution and that in either case is not equatable with life. According to the synthetic theory of evolutionary biology—of Darwinian selection and of the differential death that is the other side of differential reproduction and replicator survival—life does not and cannot commence by virtue of some transcendental creator, some *deus ex machina*, what Daniel Dennett calls the mechanism of a "skyhook."[124] At the same time, however, it does not and cannot begin with some primal "autopoiesis" or self-making, as Steven Rose claims: "The central property of all life is the capacity and necessity to build, maintain and preserve itself, a process known as *autopoiesis*."[125] To the contrary, the central property of life is its capacity and necessity to evolve out of itself—to generate the multiplicity of its forms by means of a replicability that entails the supercession of its signal biological property of being alive. To this end life arises and evolves from out of the same replicability that in principle allows for other kinds of replicators—not just other kinds of living replicators but *wholly other, nonliving, alien* kinds of replicativity. Life arises and evolves from out of an infanticidal-cum-extinctive replicability, which makes of humans in principle a dead species living on the borrowed time that constitutes the temporal horizon of evolution.

One might imagine that the earliest, prehistoric intimations of this (infanticidal, extinctive) horizon were unspeakable. In any event, such recognition has been recorded in historical times but only in the most indirect, carefully shrouded manner, for the knowledge in question is so troubling that its articulation and announcement have been repeatedly blocked. And yet, in some of the West's greatest works the very tradition that has resisted the thought of the infanticidal has produced narratives that have, in fact, identified and transmitted, however covertly, this culturally forbidden knowledge. The dominant tradition has worked very hard to interpret these texts—for example, the book of Genesis, the Gospel of John, the *Odyssey*, Sophocles' *Oedipus the King*—in ways that preserve the dream of an escape from the costs of existence. Nevertheless, as the next eight chapters will show, these texts recognize that the costs in question are, finally, inescapably infanticidal and that the dream of transcending the world's infanticidity increases the risk of infanticide.

Just as a "war against terrorism" can increase the threat of the very terrorism the war is intended to stop, so too can certain attitudes about the infanticidal precipitate more virulent forms of it. The texts this study investigates in the following chapters understand and seek to work through the existential challenges this paradox embodies.

II
Infanticide and the Infanticidity of Being in Genesis

3

Infanticide and Reproduction in Genesis

Myth proper lacks a chronology in any strict sense, for the beginning
and the end must be apprehended simultaneously. . . .
                    —Edmund Leach, *Genesis as Myth and Other Essays* (28)

"I am the Alpha and the Omega, the first and the last, the beginning
and the end."
                    —Revelation 22:13 (cf. 1:8 and 21:6 and Isaiah 44:6)

INFANTICIDE VEILED, INFANTICIDE UNVEILED

IN THE OPENING CHAPTER OF THE LAST BOOK OF THE BIBLE, JOHN
announces that God has given Jesus a "revelation . . . to show his servants what must soon take place" (1:1).[1] Twelve chapters later John
describes this revelation:

> And a great portent appeared in heaven: a woman clothed with the sun, with
> the moon under her feet, and on her head a crown of twelve stars. She was
> pregnant and was crying out in birth pangs, in the agony of giving birth. Then
> another portent appeared in heaven: a great red dragon. . . . His tail swept
> down a third of the stars of heaven and threw them to the earth. Then the
> dragon stood before the woman who was about to bear a child, that he might
> devour her child as soon as it was born (12:1–4).

John accepts that Jesus is "the beginning and the end"; midway through
his apocalyptic prophecy, in one of the most taxing scenes of the Bible,
he recasts the meaning of Jesus' momentous double nature in terms of
the most gruesome of infanticides. What does the appalling picture of a
neonate's beginning as its end, its first breath being its last, its new life
expiring in the mouth of a ravening dragon, suggest about the Alpha and
the Omega? Is John indeed bringing forbidden knowledge into the
light? About to be born of the stars and about to die by what destroys
the stars, the infant's fatal jeopardy signifies nothing less than the Word
itself and what its incarnation reveals about the infanticidal meaning of
the beginning and the end.

97

"What must soon take place" has already taken place in the first book of the Bible, for the story of the Fall is the veiled story of the same infanticidal horizon to human existence that is unveiled in the Bible's concluding book. In Genesis as in Revelation, the story involves a scene of appetite, of a desire figured literally as a hunger for the forbidden fruit and metaphorically as a yearning to be "like God, knowing good and evil" (3:5). Adam and Eve eat from the prohibited Tree of Knowledge, the Hebrew word for which, *∂ha'ath*, derives from the root *yâda'*, "to perceive, understand, acquire knowledge, know, discern" and also to "be acquainted with a woman (in a sexual way, i.e., sexual intercourse)."[2] Immediately after the fall, "knowing" explicitly takes on a sexual meaning when "the man knew [*yâda'*] his wife Eve, and she conceived and bore Cain" (4:1).[3] Since both the Old and New Testaments refer to the fetus as "the fruit of the womb,"[4] the first sin would be infanticidal, as David Bakan notes. "When I was a child," he writes, "I was told that the story of the fall of man had a hidden secret: the fruit of the tree of knowledge which Adam and Eve ate was a baby." He then hypothesizes that the "biblical writers . . . may indeed have intended to tell us that the fruit of knowledge is an infant"[5] and that "the sin of eating the produce from [the tree of knowledge] was the eating of one's own children."[6] The book of Revelation supports Bakan's supposition—not, however, in order to name infanticide as the original sin but in order to signify the infanticidality of sin and salvation alike.

Two acts of eating—one human, the other monstrous; one completed, the other impending; one inaugurating the beginning of evil, the other announcing the time of evil's defeat; one specifying the infanticidism of the human, the other pointing to the infanticidism of the sacred—frame the Bible. And between the two is the account of how Jesus institutes the mediating ritual of the Last Supper in which he offers himself to be eaten. He offers himself as the world-creating Word; he accepts his incarnation to become, at his birth, the target of an infanticidal king[7] and then, in his adulthood, the champion of children, to whom he attributes an unspecified revelation. Thus does he thank his "Father, Lord of heaven and earth, because you have hidden these things from the wise and intelligent and have *revealed* them to infants" (Luke 10:21; my emphasis). Associating himself repeatedly with the innocence of children, Jesus institutes a salvific meal during Passover.

The ritual focus of Passover, of course, is the remembrance of infanticide averted. The infanticide in question is God's massive extermination of the firstborn children and animals of the Israelites' captors, the Egyptians: "'I will pass through the land of Egypt . . . and I will strike down every firstborn" (Exodus 12:12). Instructing Moses on how the Israelites were to safeguard their children, God tells him that his people must properly slaughter a lamb and sprinkle its blood "on the two doorposts and the lintel of the houses in which they eat it," for "[t]he blood shall be a sign for you on the houses where you live: when I see the blood, I will pass over you, and no plague shall destroy you when I strike the land of Egypt" (12:7 and 13).

The paschal lamb of the Passover (the Sparing) becomes in Revelation a figure of Christ, "the Lamb that was slaughtered" (5:12), "the Lamb at the center of the throne" who is the "guide . . . to springs of the water of life" (7:17), the Lamb whose blood is the ink used, during the time of "the foundation of the world," to write the names of the saved "in the book of life" (13:8), and so on. This Lamb presides over the Last Supper, serving up his body and blood to the apostles, the first of his "flock" (Luke 12:32), substituting himself for the animal meat they would have expected. Through the meal that is the basis of the Pauline Eucharist, then, Jesus reenacts the infanticidal hunger that is veiled in the story of Adam and Eve's fall from grace and acts out in advance the same hunger that is unveiled in Revelation. He does more: he performs its greatest, deepest, most far-reaching implication, which is that the infanticidal upsets the distinction between good and evil, sacred and profane, the beginning and the end.[8]

The book of Genesis attempts to name the infanticidism that cuts across all such conceptual oppositions, beginning with the opposition between the seemingly perfect creation of the world and the (infanticidal) fall of this world into its decreating violence. On the one hand, God makes a world that then continues the inaugural act of making. Having given form to the void, having lighted the universe, and having separated the terrestrial elements, God directs the earth to continue the work of creation by producing what will produce in turn: "Let the earth put forth vegetation: plants yielding seed, and fruit trees of every kind on earth that bear fruit with the seed in it" (1:11). Thus too does God command the earth to "bring forth swarms of living creatures" that will "be fruitful and multiply" (1:20 and 22). Finally, God commands humans in similar terms. Even before announcing the first proscription, God delivers humans to the reproductive imperative that governs all living things: "Be fruitful and multiply, and fill the earth and subdue it" (1:28). The progenerativity of humans—the last named manifestation of the divine fecundity that gives the world an earth and then the earth its teeming life—reproduces the incarnate productivity of God himself.

On the other hand, God immediately imperils the world's procreativity. Hard upon the narrative of creation he condemns Eve to "bring forth children in pain" and Adam to "toil" upon the "cursed ground" (3:16 and 17 RSV); as if no time had elapsed, Adam and Eve have two grown children, one of whom, a "tiller" (4:2) like his father, kills the other. In the next major narrative sequence God sends the flood that "blot[s] out every living thing that was on the face of the ground" (7:23). These and other uncreations culminate with God's call to Abraham to take the son he "dearly loves" and "offer him . . . as a burnt offering" (22:2). In other words, when God expels Adam and Eve, it is into an infanticidal world that he himself "creates" in the very act of sentencing to death the first of his human "children," their violently afflicted world thereby coming into its paradoxical being through God's essentially infanticidal act.[9]

Genesis thus intimates what the two portents of Revelation unveil about the world's infanticidity. As it moves from reproduction to the specter of infanticide, Genesis announces its implicit reading rule: the juxtapositioning of new life begotten with new life imperiled organizes the Genesis narration of primeval events—creation, the expulsion from Eden, the story of Cain and Abel, the Babel disaster, and the Flood. Accumulating and intensifying from one episode to the next in the era of prehistory, the ramifications of this juxtapositioning achieve their most perspicuous dramatization with the onset of historical times, in particular with the life of the first patriarch. An examination of reproduction and infanticide in Genesis anticipates the decisive event when Abraham agrees to slay his son.

THE THEME OF *TOLEDOT*

According to J. P. Fokkelman, Genesis signals its "characteristic contribution . . . to the Torah and to subsequent books . . . by its own key word *toledot*, literally, 'begettings,' from the root *yld*, which is used for mothers (*yaldah*, 'she gave birth'), fathers (*holid*, 'he begot'), and children (*nolad*, 'he was born')."[10] The narrative voice of Genesis uses its allusions to conception and birth to unify its narrative, thematic, hermeneutic, and other textual strands into a single coherent pattern. Thus, as Fokkelman points out, Genesis begins each of its five genealogies (at 5:1, 10:1, 11:10, 25:12, and 36:1) and the narrative units they introduce with references to the *toledot* of the fathers.[11] These naming rituals "reveal the *toledot* as a genre in its own right and function as a conclusion; they complete two acts (chaps. 1–4 and 6–9) and two cycles (those of Abraham and Jacob)." In addition, they underscore the paternal inheritance of three major protagonists—Abraham, Jacob, and Joseph. The result is that the recurrent story of patriarchal transmission produces an "image of concatenation" that "reveals the overriding concern of the entire book: life-survival-offspring-fertility-continuity."[12]

Perhaps because human reproductivity can be problematic, Genesis uses a verb that carries no procreative connotations and no suggestions of paternity to describe the unproblematic act by which God "created [*bârâ*]" (1:1)[13] the world from nothing (1:1). And yet at the end of the opening account of the creation, "the heavens and the earth" produce, as if from a sexual union, what is specifically represented as their offspring, their *toleḏot*: "These are the generations [*toleḏot*] of the heavens and the earth when they were created" (2:4). Fokkelman is uneasy about the implications of this verse. "Everywhere else" in Genesis, Fokkelman writes, "'the *toleḏot* of X' refers to human beings as fathers and as subjects of begetting, but 2:4a raises the radical question whether heaven and earth may be the objects of God's begetting."[14] In their other appearances in Genesis the various cognates of *toleḏot* retain their literal meaning— "generations," "begettings," or perhaps "childings." In the verses concerning the creation, however, the term functions as "a metaphor." Even so, Fokkelman admits that the figurative meaning of the term "approach[es] the boundaries of the taboo in Israel's strict sexual morals" and "carries the oblique suggestion that the cosmos may have originated in a sexual act of God."[15] Such a possibility accords with the first command to humankind to reproduce, especially since this directive "both prepares for the Genesis genealogies," which Kselman interprets as "the continuation of God's initial act of creation," and "reaches its climax in the fruitfulness of Israel in Egypt (Exod. 1:7, 12)."[16]

If the world-begetting generativity of the divine father is perfect, the culture-shaping progenerativity of the mortal father, bound to that of the mortal mother, is correspondingly imperfect—subject to compromise and vulnerable to nullification. Preoccupied with issues of patriarchal governance and authority, and thus with the need to secure patrilineal descent,[17] Genesis nevertheless repeatedly represents progenerativity as contaminated. It does so, first, to indicate the infanticidity of all being, sacred or profane, and, second, to show the crisis of infanticide that invariably erupts whenever a people forget, deny, presume to transcend, or otherwise try to escape this existential horizon.

THE REPRODUCTIVE LEGACY OF ADAM AND EVE

What Adam and Eve suffer after eating the forbidden fruit is appropriate not to an act of disobedience but to a productivity-reproductivity crime. First, "the eyes of both were opened, and they knew that they were naked" (3:7). Henceforth ashamed, they twice conceal themselves—by covering themselves and then by hiding "because" they are "afraid," Adam says, of their "nakedness" (3:7 and 10). Second, both must endure lives of labor. "Cursed is the ground [*'aḏāmāh*] because of you," God says to the earthborn Adam; "thorns and thistles it shall bring forth to you; and you shall eat the plants of the field. In the sweat of your face you shall eat bread till you return to the ground, for out of it you were taken; you are dust [*'âphār*], and to dust you shall return" (3:17–19).[18] To similar life-encumbering effect, God condemns Eve to reproductive "sorrow [*'etsev*]": "To the woman he said, 'I will greatly multiply your pain [*'it-stāvōn*] in childbearing; in pain you shall bring forth children'" (3:16). In exiling Adam and Eve from Eden, God delivers humans into a self-consciousness that begins with an awareness of an absolute cost to reproduction. Since Eve's name (*Chavvâh*, from *châvah*, "to live")—means "life,"[19] the pain of her birthings signifies the primal harm that besets human life from within its reproductive onset. Eve's difficult labor, like Adam's, represents a constant reminder that they have been cut off from the Tree of Life to which they never had access. The Tree of Life thus stands for what is possible only in fantasy—namely, a cost-free existence. In sum, in relation to its immediate consequences, "knowing" is disastrous not because it is disobedient but because it raises to consciousness a danger inherent to the nature of existence.

The third consequence Adam and Eve undergo—the loss of their second-born at the hands of their firstborn—once again embodies this danger. Having inherited a cursed patrimonial legacy, Cain tills the earth as did his father. When he offers as tribute to God "the fruit of the ground [*'adāmāh*]" (4:4)—the very ground Adam first walked, the father's ground—he does so in implied identification with his fallen father, whose sin also involves fruit. Therefore, when Cain murders his brother, his paternal identification renders his siblicide a surrogate form of infanticide. So Hertz suggests when he explains why the word for the blood Cain spills, which God hears "crying out to me from the ground" (4:10), is plural: "In slaying Abel, Cain slew also Abel's unborn descendants"[20]—that is, his future descendants, including those as yet not conceived. In other words, Cain's crime is not merely an empirical violence—one infanticide—but a limitless (infanticidal) loss of opportunity, for according to the Talmud, "he who destroys a single human life is as if he destroyed a whole world."[21] No wonder that God has "no regard" (4:5) for Cain's offering.

That the word for tiller or laborer of the earth, *'avad*, is also used to designate serving God, *avoda* (as in Exodus 20:5), intensifies the force of God's rejection of Cain and links that rejection to God's exilic repudiation of the first parents. Here, the narrative anticipates the contaminated generational relation of father to son and brother to brother that will occur in the primogenitary defeats of Ishmael and later of Esau, each of whom loses the father's blessing. God's repudiation of Cain's offering, then, could not be more consequential in its symbolic reach. And when Cain responds by spilling his brother's blood, thereby despoiling the same earth from which he had gathered his unacceptable, inefficacious, unproductive—in short, "fruitless"—offering, he acts out the uncreating infanticidality associated with the ground (*'adāmāh*) of the father (Adam). In punishment Cain is fated "to be hidden from [God's] face" and to be "a fugitive and a wanderer on the earth" (Genesis 4:12), the uprooted son of Adam and Eve taking on the sin of the father and mother. Exiled by God in a repetition of the banishment imposed on his parents, Cain has engaged in a genesis-nullifying violence.

The speed and radical compression of the narrative sequence—from the Fall to the imposition of the (re)productive punishments to the birth of Cain and Abel, the intervening years of their childhood development elided, to the fraternal murder—reinforce Cain's role as a stand-in for both his parents. The text could not more blatantly move from conception to violent death. It collapses several predications—to know and to lie, to beget, to kill—into a single predication, for which there is no word, about the infanticidality of existence after the Fall.[22] When Cain reenacts the violence of the Fall in his fatal aggression against his brother, the narrative foregrounds the injuriousness which God forewarns Adam and Eve will be an inescapable aspect of the labor of all subsequent reproduction and production.

THE EXAMPLE OF CAIN

The rest of the Cain narrative will indicate that this (infanticidal) inescapability is to be understood as both a curse and a blessing—that is, as a mark of the cost attaching to all mortal existence. On the one hand, the Genesis narrative calls Cain a murderer. On the other hand, the narrative sacralizes this outcast. In joining these antithetical characterizations, the narrative condemns Cain's empirical violence but simultaneously sees through it to another kind or order of violence—to the infanticidal as such, which cannot be eluded no matter how effectively the forms of empirical violence might be prohibited.

The double marking of Cain begins when God curses him (for his infanticidal murder of his brother) but then protects him (by threatening what is in effect an infanticidal fate for anyone who would avenge the killing of Abel): "Whoever kills Cain will suffer a sevenfold vengeance" (4:15). God here interdicts the possibility of vengeance avenged, the consequences of which would be genealogically disastrous, by threatening precisely those consequences. In other words, he warns not only that the avenger will be destroyed but that his kin will be as well, including the kin of this kin through the seventh generation—that is, as far into the future as can be imagined.[23] In this way God asks humans to envision what they will never survive to witness—namely, the incalculable future costs of the present reprisal, of the series of retaliations that must be retaliated against in turn, and thus of the expanding losses that are the invisible meaning of the present violence. Economizing on the escalating nature of vengeance, God announces his curse in order to evacuate any possible gain for those who would attempt to get even. In consequence, God would immunize future generations to the reproduction-compromising contagion of vengeance; he would shield reproductive increase from the cross-generational—which is to say infanticidal—vitiation that is here the meaning of vengeance.[24]

What, then, is Cain's ultimate legacy? It is the paradoxical sacredness of the curse— legible, hence knowable, in the mark upon the murderer's body—by which God safeguards this man's future progeny at the cost of the non-progeny of Abel. God speaks to ensure the one son's future children but remains silent to mark the invisible loss of the other son's future children. The narrative thematizes this invisible consequence of Cain's violence—the lineage that will never descend from Abel—in the way Cain "shall be hidden from [God's] face" (4:1) but expressly visible to the world. Bearing the mark of God,[25] Cain will embody the blessing (he will be fruitful) of the curse (when he "till[s] the ground, it will no longer yield . . . its strength" and he "will be a fugitive and a wanderer on the earth" [4:12]). Thus does God punish while yet rewarding him for having destroyed the bloodline of his brother, and thus does God indicate the infanticidism attaching to all reproductive success.[26]

THE INFANTICIDISM OF THE FLOOD

At the end of the Cain narrative, Genesis appears to recuperate the reproductivity of Adam and Eve in the begetting of Seth and then of Seth's son (4:25–26). At this moment chapter 4 ends and chapter 5 begins with "the generations [toledot] of Adam" (5:1) down to Noah and his sons, those who will be the only ones to survive the world-destroying Flood. In other words, chapter 5 opens with a patrilineal registry the continuation of which through Noah's generativity will be purchased with an unimaginable loss of life and the future lineages the survival of this life would have produced.

The account of the Flood expands to the last degree the peril associated with God's condemnation of Adam and Eve to lives of hardship ending in death. The Flood, then, will cover the entirety of the very earth ('erets) out of which God created Adam and Eve in the second account of creation—that is, the very ground of humankind's autochthonous origin and the very soil ('aḏāmāḥ) or dust ('âpḥār) that, at the expulsion of Adam and Eve from the garden, God names as the cursed site of human existence. Covering the earth, the Flood immerses the world in the death that is first figured as Adam and Eve's passage from "dust to dust" (3:19). But why does God send the Flood?

By the time of Noah, humans have begun "to multiply on the face of the ground" (6:1) according to God's initial reproductive imperative at the time of the creation. The results, however, are disastrous; something terribly amiss happens when "the sons of God came in to the daughters of men, and they bore children to them" (6:4).[27] Their reproductivity is part of an unspecified "wickedness" so "great" that "the Lord was sorry that he had made man" (6:5–6). One tradition of midrashic commentary "speculates that it was unbounded affluence that caused men to become depraved . . . and to commit sexual aberrations"; another postulates that "the chief sin of the generation of the Flood lay in their refusal to beget children."[28] The two traditions identify adjacent facets of a single underlying concern, namely a turn away from progenerative responsibilities toward a lawlessness the violence of which arouses God to his uncreating violence: "I will blot out man whom I have created from the face of the ground" (6:7). God will spare only Noah and his "generations" (6:9) — once again, toledot — this infanticidal annihilation (7:4 and 7:23) of life because "I have seen that you are righteous before me in this generation [ðōr]"[29] (7:1). And yet just before it affirms Noah's righteousness and immediately after it mentions that "Noah begot three sons, Shem, Ham, and Japheth" (6:10), the narrative announces, "And the earth was corrupt before God, and the earth ['eret͜s] was filled with violence" (6:11). Whether or not this juxtaposition assimilates Noah's reproductivity to the earth's corruption or, to the contrary, heightens the contrast between Noah and the world, the movement of the verses establishes a reproductive frame of reference for comprehending the nature, meaning, and extent of the human evil God cleanses by subjecting virtually all of humankind to violent erasure.

The focus on generation recurs throughout the subsequent narrative, most obviously in God's directive to Noah to take by twos, male and female, the animals of the world into the ark (7:2–3 and 8–9). It occurs less obviously in the terrible inversion of meaning in the use of the language of conception and parturition to designate the coming of the Flood: "all the fountains of the great deep burst forth [nivqa'u, split or burst open, from bâqa', cleave, breach], and the windows of the heavens were opened [niphta'u, a verb able to be used of parturition, as in Genesis 29:31 and 30:32, though not restricted to childbirth, from pâthach]" (7:11), as if the flood were the birth or rebirth of the world rather than its (infanticidal) obliteration.

The focus on generation also determines the details of the story's end. When the waters finally recede, Noah and his wife, along with his sons and their wives, together, in an action of symbolic parturition, "bring forth" (from *yâtsâ*) from out of the ark the creatures they have saved "that they may breed abundantly on the earth, and be fruitful and multiply upon the earth" (8:17; cf. 9:1 and 9:7). Their act is doubly generative: first because the command to be fruitful recalls the rejected fruitfulness of Cain and the disastrous fruit of the Tree of Knowledge; and second because the command to multiply (from *râbâh*, to increase, to make more in number, to make great or greater) plays off of the cognate term (*rab*) used earlier of the "great" evil that prompted God to send the life-destroying Flood to begin with. Twice over the generative commandment, which repeats the blessing bestowed on Adam (1:28), brings death in its wake.

It does so a third time as well, for the future, which it brings forth or opens up through reproduction, apparently requires a mediating act of sacrifice. "Then Noah built an altar to the Lord, and took of every clean animal and of every clean bird and offered burnt offerings on the altar" (8:20). God accepts the sacrifice not despite but because of the evil inclination at the center of the human person: "I will never again curse the ground because of man, for the imagination of man's heart is evil [*ra'*] from his youth" (8:21). Moreover, "neither will I ever again destroy every living creature as I have done" (8:21). He then pledges: "Behold, I establish my covenant with you and your descendants" (9:9).[30] This covenant repeats but infinitizes the reproductive blessing that arises from the curse laid upon Cain. Whereas Cain kills one man, God kills numberless men, women, and children. Whereas God protects Cain's lineage at the cost of one man's potential generativity, he ensures Noah's heritage at the cost of countless other—indeed, all other—genealogical futures. That is, God explicitly measures the line of descendants that he promises Noah against both the innumerable dead and the numberless offspring these dead will now never conceive.

This tradeoff is absolute. Paradoxically, when he promises never again to subject the world to such destruction, God memorializes the irreversibility of his massively –cidal violence and binds the future that will transpire to the futurity that will now never come to pass. Indeed, God destroys an infinite number of futures with the respective deaths of the Flood's victims, for whom the waters of the Flood will never stop flooding, never cease obliterating the future.[31] When he ratifies his promise in the covenant with Noah and his descendants, God inscribes the future reproductivity of the Noahic lineage in the limitless infanticidism of the Flood.

THE INFANTICIDAL CONTAMINATION OF NOAH'S PATERNITY

Warranting the future against a future act of obliteration, but simultaneously indebting the future to the endless loss of the future, God binds himself through the covenant to the offspring of the biblical fathers and imposes a reciprocal obligation on the part of humans. The difficulties of honoring that responsibility are nowhere more apparent for the mortal father than when it comes to his *toleḏot*. For example, the covenant produces a split legacy when Noah, another "first tiller of the soil ['*aḏāmāh*]" (9:20), succumbs to a temptation that reverses and yet renews the epistemological seduction in Eden. "He planted a vineyard" and later "drank of the wine, and became drunk, and lay uncovered in his tent. And Ham, the father of Canaan, saw the nakedness of his father and told his two brothers [Japheth and Shem] outside," who cover him with eyes averted: "their faces were turned away, and they did not see their father's nakedness [*erwāh*, shameful nakedness]" (9:20–23). As is the case in the story of Adam and Eve, so in the story of Noah's drunkenness: self-consciousness is above all consciousness of the naked body and its problematic sexuality. Whereas Adam and Eve sought to clothe and hide themselves, Noah exposes himself without the slightest indication of the shame that characterizes the first parents.

To some commentators Noah's sexuality appears to be "perverted." According to Plaut, for example, "uncovering a relative's nakedness was a biblical euphemism for sexual relations (see Lev. 18). The story of Ham and Noah should be read, therefore, as one of sexual perversion," thereby bringing home "the theme of sexuality in the stories of both the first antediluvians (Adam and Eve) and the first postdiluvians (Noah and his offspring)" and anticipating "the motif of sexual aberration linked to drunkenness . . . in the story of Lot and his daughters."[32]

Mirrored in Plaut's reluctance to name Noah's homosexual incestuousness, the narrative's ambivalent technique is one of indirection—that is, attempted concealment and partial uncovering. The narrative's duplicity parallels the psychological transference at work in Noah's reaction to having been seen or "known," to having been caught in the euphemistic act of illicitly "knowing." Thus the narrative does not say who uncovered Noah—Ham, Noah himself, or an unnamed party; the narrative nevertheless goes on to record Noah's unattested accusation of Ham: "Noah awoke from his wine and knew what his youngest son had done to him" (9:24)—not what he had done to his youngest son, but what his youngest son had done to him.[33] His putative knowledge coming after the fact of the defiling event, Noah projects his vengeance into the distant future. To this end he does not curse his son Ham but damns the son of his son— "Cursed be Canaan, a slave of slaves shall he be to his brothers" (9:25)[34]— in a displacement of wrath that is overtly sacrificial and covertly infanticidal. The infanticidal nature of the curse is implied by its contrast to the blessing Noah simultaneously bestows upon his other son when he calls upon God to "enlarge" Japheth—that is, to cause him to have many descendants (9:26–27).

The duplicity of Noah's curse-blessing, like the narrative indirection in which it is embedded, all but calls out for the kind of interrogative uncovering God engages in when he demands the truth of Adam and Eve after they have deliberately—knowingly—hidden from him. Here, the story of Noah rationalizes the father's differential investment in his sons, which is to say his infanticidal disinvestment in the one son and his offspring in preference to the other. The account of Noah's besottedness and subsequent angry consciousness attempts to represent, however indirectly, the sacrificial tradeoff between reproductive blessing and infanticidal curse. For the framework of Noah's curse and blessing is the prospect of reproduction twice ruined, unhallowed, in short undone, first by the "sexual perversion" between father and son and then by the father's repudiation of his son's paternity.

Like Cain, then, Noah is caught up in the infanticidal costliness of all generativity, including God's. In genealogically execrating Ham, Noah succumbs to a violent paternal temptation that echoes the extraordinary violence of God in bringing the world's life to the edge of extinction during the Flood. The conclusion to the Noah episodes covers up this violence in its ritual listing of his descendants: "These are the generations [*toledot*] of the sons of Noah" (10:1). If the catalog names the future that comes to pass, it cannot narrate the no longer possible future of the descendants who have been "blotted out," liquidated before they have been born, their conceptions, births, and lives aborted by the infanticidal deluge God sends against the primeval "*generations* of the heavens and the earth" (2:4). The Genesis account of these generations imposes a looming reproductive shadow over the subsequent era of the first patriarchs.

THE TOWER OF DISSEMINATION

The transition from primeval to patriarchal history occurs by way of the ethnographic "table of nations" begun in chapter 10 but then interrupted by the story of the tower, the project by which the Babylonians seek to "make a name [*shēm*] for ourselves, lest we be scattered abroad upon the face of the whole earth" (11:2–4). Before the narrative returns to the table of nations, it records God's displeasure at "the continuing sin of humanity,"[35] which leads him to interrupt the construction of the great tower, to "scatter" humankind, and to "confuse the language of all the earth" (11:8 and 9). At this point the narrative interrupts the (interruptive) story of dissemination to continue the table of nations with a listing of the "descendants [*toledot*] of *Shem*" (11:10). Bearing the same name in the name of which the Babylonians attempt to reach the "Gate of God" (the meaning of *Babel*) only to be blocked in their efforts, Shem is the son who participates in covering up Noah but who is not mentioned, who is not named, when in the aftermath Noah curses and blesses his other two sons.

The founder of the lineage that nine generations later produces Abraham, Shem thus has a name the unspoken meaning of which interprets and is interpreted by the story of Babel. With regard to the episode of his father's "shameful nakedness," Shem is neither cursed nor blessed because he is both, a circumstance for which Genesis has no name. The interdicted completion of the phallic Babylonian tower translates, in the image of a heaven-breaching phallicism that becomes an earth-bound dissemination, the nameless doubleness of Noah's reproductive blessing and infanticidal curse.

In other words, *shēm* attempts to name what cannot be directly named — the disseminal, infanticidal consequences of the seminal dream of an absolute, pure, total, transcendental, in other words non-infanticidal, generativity. *Shem* — proper name and common noun — performs what this name cannot otherwise say, which is that the empirical future (embodied in a genealogy) must be understood in relation to the nonempirical futures (the nonexistent genealogies that, perforce, have no names), that are lost, that must be lost, in the lineages that do come to pass. For this reason, the empirical future is internally divided by the non-presentable losses that are its condition of possibility. As the Babelite dispersal indicates, the seminal nature of the future entails a radical dissemination or "scattering," for reproductivity is not a force of life but of life and death; it is not a source of genealogical continuity but of a limitless genealogical discontinuity within any such continuity; it is not what secures the future but what secures one future by sacrificing countless others; it is an expression of the anti- or un-conceptive within any conception. It is, in short, infanticidal.

REPRODUCTIVE BLESSING AND COVENANT PROMISE

The Abraham cycle begins under a heavy reproductive shadow as Abram (not yet renamed) and the childless Sarai (later Sarah) seek just the kind of homeland that God denies the Babelites. At the outset God gives Abram, as he did Noah upon emerging from the ark, his (parturitional) command to "go forth": "Go from your country and your kindred and your father's house to the land that I will show you. And I will make of you a great nation, and I will bless you, and make your name great, so that you will be a blessing" (12:1–2). The blessing is all-encompassing, extending into the earth-bound future of every family of the world: "and by you all the families of the earth will bless themselves" (12:3). After Abram leaves,

God promises that he "will make your descendants as the dust of the earth; so that if one can count the dust of the earth, your descendants also can be counted" (13:14–16). If at the time of the expulsion from Eden "dust" signifies death, it now bears the meaning of life, the collective vitality of a people who claim the land as "given" to them by God "for ever." When God appears yet again to Abram to renew his covenant, he further infinitizes the image of the descendant as the dust of the earth becomes the stars of the firmament, seminal signs of the light by which God beckons Abram to glimpse the otherwise unseeable future of his lineage: "Look toward heaven and number the stars, if you are able to number them. . . . So shall your descendants be" (15:5).

Abram responds to God's astral promise by sacrificing three animals, which he "cuts" (from *bathâr*, to split or cut evenly) in two to confirm the covenant (*berîyth*, literally a cutting) (15:9–11).[36] God countersigns the sacrifice: he "makes," literally he "cuts,"[37] the covenant, saying, "To your descendants I give this land" (15:18). In doing so God offers the future fulfillment of his promise as an already accomplished fact. At the same time he warns that Abram's descendants will have to undergo a time of exile. By this warning he converts the eventuality of being cut off from the land, a condition that would threaten the covenant, into a sign of its future fulfillment.[38] Having encouraged Abram to see in the dust the genealogical light of the stars, God asks the patriarch-to-be to act out, through the sacrificial cutting, his deepest existential anxiety—being reproductively cut off from the future.

For the covenant to be fulfilled, of course, Abram must become a father; he must be "blessed" with *toledot* by a wife who is barren. When he receives this blessing, however, he must come to terms with the God who demands his son's sacrifice. Mediating between the condition of being reproductively cut off from the future and reproductively connected to it, the "cut" of the covenant opens onto the logic of the infanticidal.

THE THREAT OF BARRENNESS

Given to Abram in a dream, the covenant expresses the fulfillment of his wish for continued life through offspring and thereby mitigates his anxiety of a life that, without children, would be tantamount to a living death. According to rabbinical tradition, a man who is unable "to fulfill the commandment of propagation, and leave pious offspring behind him," writes Judith R. Baskin, is "reckoned as 'cut off' (*menuddeh*) from all communion with God, like one who has deliberately disregarded divine commands."[39] Indeed, based in part "on Rachel's plaint in Gen 30:1," he is as if "*already dead*" and thereby isolated from the future.[40]

The power of the covenantal "cut" is, paradoxically, to join—humans to God, one generation to the next, the past to the present, the present to the future—by "opening" the otherwise closed or sealed off womb of the childless woman. "When the Lord saw that Leah was hated, he opened [*pathach*] her womb; but Rachel was barren. And Leah conceived and bore a son" (29:31–32). When "God remembered Rachel," he "hearkened to her and opened her womb. She conceived and bore a son" (30:22–23). As Baskin demonstrates, the exegetical tradition affirms that "conception is granted by the grace of God," who "may open the womb whenever he wills it" (110 and 111).

However, all reproductive success is deeply problematic (as intra-familial contestation among brothers over patrimony and warfare between opposing groups over land illustrate) and ultimately infanticidal. Struggling to negotiate this infanticidism, the Genesis narrators envision the "blessing" of the opened, henceforth fruitful, womb. On the one hand, then, the Israelites sought to purify the value of reproduction by seeing in it the miraculous working of God. The stories of the once-barren Sarah, Rebekah, and Rachel, illustrate. According to Fokkelman:

> In the stories themselves, the births of Isaac, Jacob, Esau, Joseph, and Benjamin are never described in terms of a begetting (*holîd*) by the father; only afterward is such paternity indicated in the concluding *toledot* lists. The conception is always represented by God's opening the womb of the barren woman, after which she can give birth (*yaldah*). Thus the birth achieves the status of a miracle, foreseen and effected by God alone. Only he can enable and guarantee continuity.[41]

Barbara L. Estrin seconds this view: "For the Hebrews, then, the truth of God's presence is manifested in the human power of perpetuation," which they receive as a gift from God. "Without that gift, rendered throughout the Old Testament as miraculous, there can be no miracle in the miracle story."[42] The truth of such miracles, by which the Israelites interpreted their progenerativity as continuing the work of the creation, protects them from the counter-truth of the infanticidism at the center of life. Precisely because the miraculous conception attests to the divine "blessing" of progeny, however, it necessarily preserves the fear of progeny lost.[43] This prospect opens onto a radical ambiguity that divides God's potency as well as the mortal father's.

If it takes God to open the woman's womb, then "[t]ry as he might," Eilberg-Schwartz writes, "the man cannot impregnate his wife without the blessing of God. Like Jacob, the men can only throw up their hands when their barren wives ask them for children. The human male, therefore, can never really control the womb of his wife. Virginity may be proof that he has been the first to possess her (Deut. 22:13), but only the father God possesses her womb."[44] The result is that "the divine male can be seen to compete with and threaten the role of human males."[45] Even if "the father God and son jointly participate in procreation," even if the "Father must open the womb and the son must plant the seed," nevertheless "the son's virility is very much threatened by the Father's control. It is the Father who dispenses the rights of reproduction to the son."[46] And it is the human father who dispenses these rights to his son or withholds them. As the disputes over primogeniture in Genesis reveal, the father's control of the birthright can threaten not just the manliness but the very life of his offspring, and with it the temporal arc of God's blessing.

The major social, political, and economic function of circumcision is to convert the father's control over the son into the safeguarding of the son's own reproductivity. Its religious function is to inscribe the covenantal blessing on the body of the male. These uses notwithstanding, its most radical function is to acknowledge and respond to the infanticidism that makes reproductivity a force of life and death, hence to the infanticidism of the reproductive blessing itself.

INFANTICIDE, CIRCUMCISION, INFANTICIDITY

The immediate meaning of the *berîyth mûlâh*, the cutting off of a piece of the son's body, is clear: "This is my covenant, which you shall keep, between me and you and your descendants after you: Every male among you shall be circumcised [from *mûl*, to cut]"[47] (17:10), marked by "the fruitful cut," in Eilberg-Schwartz's phrase.[48] According to Hoffman, this indelible sign is the "sine qua non of Jewish identity throughout time."[49] What makes it so "fruitful," however, is partly the way it embodies the very reproductive threats against which it protects—principally the threat of being cut off from the land (identified in Genesis 15 by the so-called J author) and the threat of being cut off from one's descendants and from God (elaborated in Genesis 17:13–14 by the P author).[50] The power of the covenantal cut, literalized in the bodily incision and generalized in the condition of temporary exile, is thus apotropaic: it guards against a more dangerous form of cut—the condition of being permanently cut off, either from the land or from one's people.[51] The "fruitfulness" of circumcision also derives from the way it symbolizes a complex set of social practices through which the male is rendered open to "the divine speech and vision of God."[52] Hovering over these practices, however, is the shadow of infanticide.

In the traditional ritual, the rabbi, citing God's life-bestowing command in Ezekial 16:6, says to the circumcised child, "live." This citation is part of Ezekiel's extended allegory of Jerusalem as an adulteress, whose inhabitants in the immediately preceding verses are represented collectively as a female infant abandoned to an infanticidal fate. "As for your birth, on the day you were born your navel cord was not cut, nor were you washed with water to cleanse you, nor rubbed with salt, nor wrapped in clothes. No eye pitied you, to do any of these things for you out of compassion for you; but you were thrown out on the open field, for you were abhorred on the day you were born" (16:4–5). Having evoked a scene of pitiless violence toward the newborn, Ezekiel then speaks the excerpted words included in the rite of circumcision: "I passed by you, and saw you flailing about in your blood. As you lay in your blood, I said to you, 'Live! and grow up like a plant in the field.' You grew up and became tall and arrived at full womanhood; your breasts were formed, and your hair had grown; yet you were naked and bare" (16:6–7). God's maternal care makes this growth possible. The allegorical meaning of God's actions is that they prepare the young woman for marriage to him; their literal meaning is that they save the infant from infanticide. Despite God's protection, formalized in the marriage and covenantal relation God establishes with his bride (16:8), Jerusalem will become an infanticidal harlot whose "abominations" repeat the metaphor of her abhorrent birth. "You took your sons and your daughters, whom you had borne to me, and these you sacrificed to them to be devoured. As if your whorings were not enough! You slaughtered my children and delivered them up as an offering to them. And in all your abominations and your whorings you did not remember the days of your youth, when you were naked and bare, flailing about in your blood" (16:20–22). Ezekiel could not be more explicit: he wants his audience to acknowledge not merely the general name of their wrongdoing ("your abominations and your whorings") but its specifically reproductive consequence (the "slaughter" of "my children"). To this end he models the self-understanding he wants his auditors to have by imagining them as helpless, vulnerable, blood-smeared newborns.

Ezekiel's rhetorical strategy is to remember for his listeners what they cannot recover of their own advent into the world. In this regard his text accomplishes precisely what the circumcision does: it celebrates the infant's advent and initiates a lifelong commitment on the part of the parents and community to the child's well-being.[53] What Ezekiel knows is that the covenantal cut of circumcision requires a recognition of every infant's potential jeopardy at the hands of a pitiless adult.[54] David Bakan emphasizes this meaning of circumcision by which the covenantal tie between God and humans is transferred to the relation between mortal father and son: "In the circumcision ceremony the father essentially claims and recognizes the child as his own, and binds himself to provide maintenance, protection, and education for the child."[55] Bakan believes that such recognition constitutes a crucial psychosocial turning point in the evolving Judaic attitude toward paternity. If Abraham, "presented as the father of nations, is a paradigmatic figure in whom is formed a transgenerational ego identity," Bakan writes, this father's achievement occurs in the context of "a document [the Torah] which tells of the crisis involved in becoming a good father to children."[56]

Bakan reads this crisis through the infanticidal violence of the circumcision. If, as Freud asserted, "circumcision . . . is an equivalent and substitute for castration,"[57] it is also a mechanism for sublimating the father's aggressions against his son and redirecting them toward the son's care and well-being. Commenting on the fact that circumcision takes place on the eighth day, the day when the firstborn was to be sacrificially offered to God, Bakan remarks that "the circumcision may be interpreted as a symbolic infanticide, whereby, instead of putting the child to death by the knife, only the foreskin is removed." By this ritual, then, the father both "mak[es] the child 'his'" and "symbolically expresses the infanticidal impulse in a partial 'acting out.'"[58] Like the covenant of which it is the seal, circumcision cuts several ways: it is a sign of the anti-generative injury that it heals in advance of such harm coming to pass. It is therefore not sufficient to note only that circumcision "signifies the Father's blessing of the son's reproduction,"[59] for this practice also signifies the death-delivering power of the father (human or divine) to withhold this blessing—to let the knife slip, for example, and to cut too much.

In *The Politics of Reproductive Ritual* Karen Ericksen Paige and Jeffery M. Paige interpret circumcision as a socially promulgated ritual symbol of (attempted) paternal control over reproductivity. One danger internal to reproductively successful lineages is that they may "fission"—split off into warring factions. On the one hand, "the faster a lineage segment multiplies, the greater the number of its male offspring; the greater its generational depth and military power and wealth, the greater the rewards for fissioning." On the other hand, in a splintering lineage "every man is a potential lineage head and, therefore, also a potential traitor to his lineage."[60] Circumcision mitigates this predicament, the Paiges argue, by "demonstrate[ing] loyalty to agnatic kin in general and to village elders in particular." Despite the fact that circumcisions "are often brutal and sometimes result in castration or death," the father "is forced to permit his son to participate in the ceremony." The compulsion comes in the form of "direct orders (in centralized political systems)" or "social pressure—the stigma attached to an uncircumcised son and the social prohibition against his marrying. This prohibition means that a father who wishes to expand his family power base must have his son submit to the operation or forfeit the son's assistance in continuing his line."[61] Nevertheless, circumcision "does not provide a certain solution to the problem of fission since insofar as the operation is a success and the patient and his penis survive intact, he can continue building a line of sons powerful enough to defect in a lineage fission."[62]

A highly ambiguous cultural practice, the public performance of the "dangerous operation"[63] of circumcision establishes paternal control over reproduction by withholding, substituting for, and symbolizing the castration that might have occurred. Circumcision, in other words, is a shorthand for the father's (potentially death-dealing) control over the son's (potentially death-dealing) reproductive competitiveness.[64] It responds to a danger at the very center of human reproductivity—that the reproductivity of one person, one family, or one lineage is always capable of threatening the reproductivity of another. For this reason circumcision signifies the reproductivity of the male both in relation to reproductivity jeopardized and in relation to that reproductivity as itself a menace.

In trying to turn this reproductive threat into the source of covenantal blessing and protection, the Judaic tradition sometimes assimilates circumcision to other religious rituals, including the burnt offering. According to one rabbinical source, "If I [God] appear to the one who sacrifices an ox or ram for My name's sake, how much more so to Abraham who has circumcised himself for My name's sake."[65] More emphatically, Wolfson notes that "some scholars have even suggested that infantile circumcision in ancient Israel on the eighth day must be seen as a replacement for child sacrifice."[66] Other commentary associates Abraham's circumcision with the Passover, the commemoration of the culminating plague sent against the Egyptians. Whereas God destroyed all the firstborn children of the Egyptian captors, he spared the Israelite children, passing over their parents' houses where the sacrificial blood of a lamb had been sprinkled. According to Bakan, "tradition modified the story of the Passover by adding the blood of the circumcision to the blood of the lamb." He then cites from *Pirke De Rabbi Eliezer:* "The Israelites took the blood of the covenant of circumcision, and they put it upon the lintel of their houses, and when the Holy One, blessed be He, passed over to plague the Egyptians, He saw the blood of the covenant of circumcision upon the lintel of their houses and the blood of the Paschal lamb, He was filled with compassion on Israel."[67] That the blood of the surrogate victim is to be placed over the architectural threshold—the opening—of the home reinforces the rite's meaning as a reproductive antidote to an infanticidal threat.

One of the texts used in American Orthodox synagogues, the *Daily Prayer Book,* includes a ceremony that commemorates just that deflection of infanticide. Philip Birnbaum explains the origin of the ritual observance of the "Redemption of the First-Born Son" in two injunctions from Exodus. The first prescribes that "when the Lord brings you into the land of the Canaanites . . . you shall set apart to the Lord all that first opens the womb. All the firstlings of your cattle that are males shall be the Lord's. Every firstling of an ass you shall redeem with a lamb, or if you will not redeem it you shall break its neck. Every first-born of man among your sons you shall redeem" (Exodus 13:11–13).

Why? Why does God tell Moses that it is just this particular sacrifice that he wants?

> And when in time to come your son asks you, "What does this mean?" you shall say to him, "By strength of hand the Lord brought us out of Egypt, from the house of bondage. For when Pharaoh stubbornly refused to let us go, the Lord slew all the first-born in the land of Egypt, both the first-born of man and the first-born of cattle. Therefore I sacrifice to the Lord all the males that first open the womb; but all the first-born of my sons I redeem." It shall be as a mark on your hand or frontlets between your eyes; for by a strong hand the Lord brought us out of Egypt. (Exodus 13:14–16)

The second injunction, given to Aaron, repeats the infanticidal terms of redemption withheld: "the firstling of a cow, or the firstling of a sheep, or the firstling of a goat, you shall not redeem," but rather "you shall sprinkle their blood upon the altar, and shall burn their fat as an offering by fire" (Numbers 18:15). In both passages the act of redemption saves the firstborn from sacrificial slaughter.[68]

Although Eilberg-Schwartz does not discuss infanticide, his remarks on the symbolism of the Passover suggest that circumcision preserves the memory of while protecting the son against the infanticidal death visited upon the Egyptian firstborns. The Passover symbolism does so by acting out an encoded or displaced version of the son's killing. Circumcision, Eilberg-Schwartz says, "is described as an 'ot [or 'ôwth] of the covenant (Gen. 17:11)."[69] This sign, he explains, is not an arbitrary sign but a motivated symbol, like a rainbow, which, because it sometimes appears after a storm, can serve as an appropriate seal of the divine covenant with Noah. This kind of symbol "has an intimate association with the content of the divine promise and thereby serves to remind God of the obligation undertaken to humankind (Gen. 9:15–16)"—the obligation not to commit biocide, not to uncreate his creation. "The priestly writer also used the term 'symbol' ('ot) to describe the blood Israelites purportedly put on their doorposts before their departure from Egypt (Exod. 12:13). This blood, which was taken from a slaughtered lamb or kid, indicated that God should pass over the home and slay only firstborn Egyptians. The blood of the animal serves as a symbol because it metaphorically parallels the blood of the Israelite child which God has chosen not to shed."[70]

The bloody *'ôwth* of circumcision marks the spiritual identity of the Jewish male child who has a right to life. But it also marks the pagan identity of the Egyptian child who did not have this right. Like the rainbow following the Flood, the *'ôwth* of circumcision symbolizes life only in simultaneous relation to its (infanticidal) cost. The covenantal symbol here arises not from infanticide withheld but from the contrast between infanticide forborne and infanticide carried out.[71]

THE INFANTICIDAL DESTRUCTION OF SODOM AND GOMORRAH

Genesis enacts this contrast in the sequence of events that immediately follows upon Abraham's institution of circumcision. After Abraham circumcises Ishmael "and all the slaves born in his house or bought with his money" (17:23) as well as himself, he learns that he and Sarah shall beget a child (18:1–15). Before that conception occurs, however, Abraham must first journey to Sodom and Gomorrah, which he hopes to save from destruction in the name of "what is just" (18:25), a "justice" that posits the absolute injustice of killing the righteous: "Will you indeed sweep away the righteous with the wicked?" he asks God. "Far be it from you to do such a thing, to slay the righteous with the wicked" (18:23–25). Abraham negotiates with God to spare the cities should he find first fifty then forty, thirty, twenty, and finally ten righteous individuals: "For the sake of ten I will not destroy it" (18:32). But God's response is ambiguous. On the one hand, he accepts Abraham's plea to distinguish between the two categories of humans—those who have committed sins of an appalling nature (18:20–21) and those "doing righteousness and justice" (18:19), as Abraham has. On the other hand, he plays the numbers game that Abraham introduces, and its consequences are momentous. As Leo Strauss points out, God "did not promise that He would spare it if nine righteous men were found in it." Evoking the infanticidal consequences, Strauss asks rhetorically: "would those nine be destroyed together with the wicked? And even if all Sodomites were wicked and hence justly destroyed, did their infants who were destroyed with them deserve their destruction?"[72] Unreported in the narrative, the deaths of the infants and unborn compound the ruination of what is supposedly the punishment's moral coherence. In this respect the impending destruction of Sodom and Gomorrah entails the same massive destruction not only of the present but of the multiple futures that occur with the Flood.

The imagery of the holocaust underscores God's uncreating violence as a repetition of the Flood: "Then the Lord rained on Sodom and Gomorrah sulfur and fire from the Lord out of heaven; and he *overthrew*[73] those cities, and all the Plain, and all the inhabitants of the cities, and what grew on the ground" (19:24–25).[74] Like the Flood, which indiscriminately kills all living things and which God promises never again to send, the divine voice that "rains" down is here indifferent to the category of life that it destroys, "overthrowing" alike the (large number of) bad and the (small number of) good, the human (already born or still gestating) and the nonhuman (existing or coming into existence), "the inhabitants of the cities" as well as "what grew on the ground"—all the life of these two cities, life that ultimately traces back to the creation. If, as Eilberg-Schwartz explains, the (Priestly) account of creation is also an account of classification, if cosmogony simultaneously establishes the categories proper to the world's divine origin,[75] then God's categorical violence at the time of Sodom and Gomorrah, as at the time of the Flood, is doubly uncreating. He destroys both a particular people (a destruction that includes the possibility of literal infanticide), and through them part of his own creation.

The antidote to this infanticidal violence is Abraham, whose own "righteousness and justice" are specific manifestations of his care-giving identity as "the 'good father,'" according to Bakan.[76] God "has chosen" Abraham as emissary to Sodom and Gomorrah "that he may charge his children and his household after him to keep the way of the Lord by doing righteousness and justice so that the Lord may bring about for Abraham what he has promised him" (18:19). The word translated as "chosen" is *yâða,'* "to know," the same word that names the forbidden Tree of Knowledge. God chooses Abraham *that he may be* a good father because he wishes him to be known *as* the good father, the paternal model that is missing in Sodom and Gomorrah, the figure who knows right from wrong, above all the person who understands both the problem of infanticide and the immeasurably greater problem of the infanticidal. Abraham accepts God's choice, returns the call, and then demonstrates his knowledge when he asks the divine father to "do right" and curb the (infanticidal) violence by which Abraham is afraid God would "sweep away the righteous with the wicked."

ISHMAEL'S JEOPARDY AND THE INFANTICIDISM OF THE FATHER

Because Abraham has demonstrated his paternity-affirming readiness to "charge his children" and set an example for Sodom and Gomorrah, it is all the more surprising when he reveals his paternity-negating tendency to imperil his children. Having circumcised himself and Ishmael to witness God's covenantal protection of his descendants, he then cuts Ishmael off when he sends him into life-threatening exile. Having circumcised Isaac, he later submits without objection when God calls him to cut up his son in an egregious rite of human sacrifice. Together, Abraham's relations to his two sons bring the Genesis concern with the empirical threat of infanticide into the starkest possible relief. Abraham's treatment of his sons does more: it foregrounds the deeper problem of the world's infanticidity.

In Abraham's repudiation of Ishmael, Genesis all but names the infanticidal ramifications of paternal control over reproductivity. That repudiation begins almost immediately after Abraham (then Abram) impregnates the servant Hagar, evidently with the consent of Sarah (then Sarai) in compensation for her barrenness. But then, ostensibly in response to Hagar's "contempt" (16:4) for Sarai's childless condition, Sarai harasses the gravid woman. When Hagar flees into the wilderness to escape this mistreatment (16:6–7), she enacts the genealogical cutting-off implicit in Sarai's abuse and in the previous reproduction-compromising exiles of Genesis. At the mercy of the world, the vulnerable mother-to-be is visited by an angel who instructs her to "[r]eturn to your mistress, and submit to her," for God promises to "so greatly multiply your descendants that they cannot be numbered for multitude" (16:9–10). Assured of a hereditary future by this covenant with God, Hagar goes back to deliver her child to its father (16:16), the problem of Sarai's aggression (toward either Hagar or her child) thereafter omitted from the narrative until years later.[77]

Thirteen years after the covenant with Hagar and the birth of Ishmael, but immediately after in the narrative sequence, God makes a second covenant with Abram, promising to "multiply you exceedingly" and to make him "the father of a multitude of nations" (17:2 and 4). He seals the promise by changing Abram's name to Abraham and repeating the vision of this man's limitless paternity-to-come (17:5–7). God endorses this covenant a second time by changing Sarai's name to Sarah and promising her a son (17:15–16). There follows yet another repetition of the covenantal promise, this time between God and Isaac (17:19), and then another, between God and Ishmael (17:20).

In Abraham's two sons by two different women, however, God opens not a unitary but a divided genealogical future for the patriarch. This division does not double the genealogical blessing; rather, it sets it in opposition to itself. It thus constitutes a specific empirical manifestation of the deeper (infanticidal) division within any single lineage between the children who have been conceived and those who might have been but for those who actually are. In the story of Abraham and Ishmael, when Genesis explains the consequences of the empirical division, it broaches the meaning of the infanticidism within each and every line of descent—

indeed, within each and every conception. Because it represents Sarah and Abraham's violence toward Ishmael as occurring after the various covenants have been established and after the names of the lineage-founding parents changed, the narrative establishes not that their aggression is in contradiction to the covenant but that it is an inevitable consequence of trying to actualize the covenantal blessing. The narrative in effect explains their aggression as the genealogical cost that must be paid for the genealogical vision Abraham has received. Sarah understands perfectly when she insists that her husband "cast out this slave woman [Hagar] with her son; for the son of this slave woman shall not be heir with my son Isaac" (21:10). Abraham balks until God removes the cost: "through Isaac shall your descendants be named. And I will make a nation of the son of the slave woman *also,* because he is your offspring" (21:12–13; my emphasis). Evidently believing that Ishmael will survive and assured of credit for the divine blessing Ishmael will receive, Abraham can with impunity expose his son to death and cut him off from the possibility of any human blessing.

When he does so, he provisions Hagar and Ishmael in an action that mimes the initial steps of a burnt offering. According to Kselman, "Abraham places (Heb. *sam*) bread and water on Hagar's back" just as he later "places (Heb. *yasem*) the wood for the holocaust upon Isaac."[78] Ambivalent about acceding to Sarah's demand, Abraham acts out the sacrificial meaning of abandoning his child and its mother. When he sends them forth into the wilderness, he nearly kills them, for they are dying of thirst until God intervenes. God's deliverance of Ishmael and Hagar testifies to the otherwise fatal aggression of Abraham's act. That divine rescue occurs when God hears Ishmael crying at the moment when Hagar is dying of thirst, the son's tears brimming with the water that Abraham has denied the mother and child when he sent them into exile:[79] "When the water in the skin was gone, she cast the child under one of the bushes. Then . . . she said, 'Let me not look upon the death of the child.' And as she sat over against him, the child lifted up his voice and wept" (21:15–16). This passage anticipates Exodus 3:2, which records God's appearance to Moses "in a flame of fire out of the midst of a bush" in order to announce that he has "seen the affliction of my people who are in Egypt, and have heard their cry . . . I know their sufferings, and I have come down to deliver them out of the hand of the Egyptians, and to bring them . . . to a good and broad land, a land flowing with milk and honey" (3:7–8). The divine voice from the burning bush translates the cry of the dying child Hagar has cast under a bush in an arid land, a land devoid of the milk and honey that will be promised to the descendants of Abraham's other son on condition that these people protect their children when the angel of death passes over and kills all the Egyptian firstborns.

Having heard the voice of Ishmael, not the prayers of Abraham, God sends an angel to Hagar with the command to retrieve her child: "Fear not; for God has heard the voice of the lad where he is. Arise, lift up the lad, and hold him fast with your hand; for I will make him a great nation." Hearing that God has heard her child's crying, Hagar's eyes are "opened" to the identity of God and the waters of life: "Then God opened her eyes, and she saw a well of water . . . and gave the lad a drink" (21:17–19). The opening of the mother's eyes saves the child whose eyes are closed with tears. Those tears incarnate the life-saving compassion of God—"God was with the boy, and he grew up" (21:20)—and underscore the pitilessness of the mortal father. In fact, the pattern of covenant, near-death, and subsequent rescue following upon the opening of Hagar's eyes to the vision of God heightens Abraham's guilt: he is a father who has subjected his firstborn son, in whose life he refuses to invest himself, to a potentially deadly act of repudiation.

And yet perhaps the father saves the son after all, since it seems Abraham himself has dug the well—that is, "opened" the earth to its generative waters—from which Hagar and Ishmael drink. In the ensuing verses, Abraham petitions Abimelech for the return of the well this king's people have seized. Abimelech agrees, "and the two men made a covenant." Abraham gives Abimelech "seven ewe lambs . . . that you may be a witness for me that I dug this well," the site of which is then consecrated and called Beer-sheba ("Well of seven" or "Well of oath") "because there both of them swore an oath" (21: 30–31).

In relation to Abraham's repudiation of Ishmael, the history of the well is ironic. Though the episode of the well comes after the account of Hagar and Ishmael's expulsion and salvation, the narrative begins long before, when Sarah is still barren and the two of them, identifying themselves as brother and sister,[80] enter the territory ruled by Abimelech, who takes Sarah just as his kinsmen will have appropriated the well. Told by God in a dream to "restore the man's wife," Abimelech obeys. In response Abraham "prayed to God; and God healed Abimelech, and also healed his wife and female slaves so that they bore children. For the Lord had closed all the wombs of the house of Abimelech because of Sarah" (Genesis 20:1–18). At this point the account of the circumstances surrounding the well is interrupted as the narrative reports that God visits Sarah, who conceives and gives birth to Isaac and then demands that Abraham exile Hagar and Ishmael. Not until after Hagar has discovered the well does the narrative return to continue the story of its origin.

The inverted ordering of episodes thus enacts the ironic reversal within the story of Ishmael: God rescues Ishmael from the boy's father by means of the boy's father, who "preserves his son unawares." He has done so "by making peace in the presumably hostile territory, by bringing water to the desert and by keeping his faith."[81] That is, he saves his son by virtue of the very actions he withholds from his son (making peace with him, or making peace between his mother and Sarah) but has directed toward Abimelech, the king whom God had previously afflicted with the curse of childlessness.[82]

Anticipating and repeating one another, the two episodes relate versions of a single overriding concern with the reproductive crisis that organizes their respective individual elements. When Abimelech takes the barren Sarah, God closes the wombs of the women of this ruler's household, the curse of an individual woman now generalized. When Abimelech returns Sarah to Abraham, God opens or heals the wombs he had closed, including Sarah's, her fertility particularizing the political achievement of previously aggressive relations between strangers now "righted" (20:16), now made productive. This productivity, however, is immediately compromised when the subsequent conception and birthing of Isaac, just three or four verses later, arouses Sarah's envy of Ishmael's claim to the birthright.[83] When she urges Abraham to get rid of Hagar and her son, in effect she is attempting retroactively to close the servant woman's womb. God for his part reopens it and assures that it will have been wondrously fertile when he saves the outcasts and confers upon Hagar's son the promise of lineage-cum-nation-founding reproductive success. There follows the story of the peace accord between Abraham and Abimelech, which ends with the consecration of the well and an act—the planting of a tamarisk tree in the name of the "Everlasting God" (21:31–33)—that looks forward to a time of literal and symbolic fruitfulness.[84] A formulaic, single-verse allusion to Abraham's subsequent "days of sojourning" (21:34) anticipates what occurs next, the call to Abraham to make the journey to Moriah.

The pattern of the Ishmael narrative rehearses the narrative progression that will structure the story of Abraham and Isaac. In that story the patriarch's willingness to abandon his first son returns to haunt him in the form of the command to kill with his own hand his second son. The larger sequence of episodes enacts and reenacts just this reproductive threat. For this reason, in the story of Ishmael as in virtually every other Genesis episode, toleḋot and the home that the blessing of children will make of the covenanted land are not only the heart of God's consecration of the Jewish people, they are also the source of the deepest of conflicts.

Just how deep is suggested by the compensatory tendency of the Genesis narrations and the commentaries on them to idealize their value. When Rebekah is married to Isaac, she is regaled with hyperbolic wishes of unlimited fertility: "And they blessed Rebekah, and said to her, 'Our sister, be the mother of thousands of ten thousands; and may your de-

scendants possess the gate of those who hate them'" (24:60). The reproductive terms of this blessing recur in Jacob's dream of a ladder reaching to the very heavens; it is an image that redeems the failure of the
Babylonian tower and the subsequent confusion of tongues, for in speaking to Jacob God promises him that "your descendants shall be like the
dust of the earth, and you shall spread abroad to the west and to the east
and to the north and to the south; and by you and your descendants shall
all the families of the earth bless themselves" (28:14). Estrin draws the
ontological consequences of this glorious dispersion: "Earthly perpetuation opens the way to the skies, a horizontal extension in time leading
to a vertical ascension in space."[85] Such miraculous generativity, denied
to the Babylonians but promised to the Israelites, comes only from God's
world-inaugurating paternity. "For while man's seed is to emerge as co-
pious as the dust of the earth," Estrin comments, "that same dust is linked
to man's beginnings in God." The result is a return to the beginning. "The
way forward in the text reiterates the original creation referring through
its images of plenitude back to the passage in Genesis where man was
made: 'And the Lord God formed man of the dust of the ground.'"[86]

Virtually all the commentaries on Genesis mime the text's overt celebrations of generativity. They thereby miss the text's allusions to the infanticidal backdrop of these celebrations. Fokkelman, for example, idealizes the value of children and in the end dissociates their presence from
the manifold social, economic, political, religious, and other conflicts that
throughout Genesis are acted out over their bodies and persons. Focusing on *toledot* as the covenant made incarnate, Fokkelman suggests that
God's promises of a sanctified genealogical futurity establish not only
the social and political but nothing less than the metaphysical center post
of the Israelite nation to come. In particular, he writes that the promises
of offspring and homeland "thematize and explicate space and time, the
fundamental coordinates of life and narrative, at the highest level of meaning. Space in Genesis is divided, ordered, and sanctified by the divine
promise and is also promoted to the status of a theme: the origin, wanderings, and sojourns of the forefathers. Time, too, is ordered and, because
of the promise, stands under a sign of expectation and fulfillment."[87]

Investing the birth, survival, and belovedness of the child with the
meaning of God's promise to Abraham, Fokkelman might have asked
why the promise would require that Abraham refuse a birthright to his
one son, Ishmael, or that he undergo the terror of an infanticidal testing.
Fokkelman does not. And yet if *toledot* are to affirm the furthest metaphysical reach of God's covenant—the space and time of the genealogical
future that the covenant guards—would the story of the *akedah*, the binding of Isaac, not threaten the very "coordinates" of the world? Would not

the call to Abraham to sacrifice his son indicate the infanticidism of God himself, hence the infanticidism of the life he has created? Why must Abraham submit not just to a test but to an infanticidal trial?

Moreover, what can it mean to test the father by forcing him to terrorize his son? Why would God so use the son as to reduce him—without comment, without any address to the boy—to being an instrumentality of the father's testing? Why is the narrative silent about the boy's awareness, the boy's emotionality, the boy's fear and trembling, perhaps his desolation or his hatred, perhaps his faith, in the story of the father's? What are the metaphysical coordinates of Isaac's being when he is bound upon the altar, supine beneath the looming shadow of his father and his father's upraised arm? Where does Isaac look, or are his eyes closed? Does he cry out to his father, or is he silent? What is each thinking as the fatal moment nears? What passes between them? Does the father apologize? The father is to be tested. But why in this particular way? Why by means of such a hopelessly cruel exposure of the child, to which the narrative itself and virtually the entire history of commentary on it seem to consent? Why has the child been forced into the role of victim, and why is his involuntary participation not remarked upon in the narrative, the apparent narratorial indifference reflecting and being reflected by God's seeming callousness? If in the time and space of God's call the child is an adjunct to the divine will, is he no more than a means by which God would achieve his inscrutable ends, here a brutal evaluation of the son's father? Is there no moment and place of Isaac's appearance as a person in his own right? Where and when is Isaac Isaac? What would be the psychological fallout of surviving the ordeal? What would such survival signify about the time and space of the creation, about existence under the aegis of a covenant punctuated by the threat of infanticide?

4

Refusing the Infanticidal:
Interpretive Closure in Teleological Readings
of Abraham's Sacrifice

We are crushed by the deity.
— Edmond Jabes, *The Book of Questions* (I:85)

INFANTICIDE AND AUERBACH'S *MIMESIS*

ERICH AUERBACH BEGINS HIS MAGISTERIAL STUDY, *MIMESIS: THE Representation of Reality in Western Literature,* by distinguishing between the stylistic features of the *Odyssey* and those of the Bible in order to illustrate how two fundamental modes of mimesis have governed the representation of reality in European literature.[1] In particular, he contrasts the famous recognition scene of the *Odyssey,* when the hero's childhood nurse touches the scar he received in adolescence, with the shocking account of Abraham's near sacrifice of Isaac in Genesis. As will be made clear in chapter 7, the Homeric sequence links Odysseus' present circumstances back to a rite of passage when he is gored by a wild boar, and further back to his birth and the meaning of his name. In each case the narrative characterizes Odysseus' identity and kingdom-defining destiny in terms of indirect, glancing, or otherwise shrouded references to an infanticidal jeopardy, references that recur at many of the epic's decisive turning points. These infanticidal motifs implicit in the Homeric story are, of course, explicit in the biblical narrative. In other words, despite the manifest differences in mimetic technique, which otherwise set the two episodes radically apart stylistically, both incorporate a pattern of infanticidal allusion — obvious in the one work, less so in the other, but in either case unremarked by Auerbach. Nevertheless, the threat of infanticide is so basic to the representation of reality in Western literature that it appears in the very first texts in which Auerbach locates the initial "full development" of the Western world's double mimetic tradition.[2]

Basically, the threat of the child's death focuses awareness not only on the possible futures that will be lost through the child's death but on the corollary that lost opportunities are the backdrop of every moment of time. As the *akeðah* endeavors to indicate, these losses are non-presentable; were they imaginable, they would trace the general infanticidism of being. Whereas chapters 6 through 9 will demonstrate the difficulty the Greeks had in moving from the thought of infanticide to the thought of the world's infanticidality, this and the next chapter will show how the story of Abraham and Isaac attempts this very hermeneutic leap.

THE INFANTICIDISM OF THE CALL TO SACRIFICE

The nineteen verses of Genesis 22 begin out of the blue. God "appears" with the inscrutable order for Abraham to make his son disappear on a mountain that overlooks a valley associated with infanticidal slaughter.[3] With no explanation of divine motivation, the narrative simply declares: "After these things 'God tested Abraham, and said to him, 'Abraham!' And he said, 'Here am I.' He said, 'Take your son, your only son Isaac, whom you love, and go to the land of Moriah, and offer him there as a burnt offering. . . .'"[4] The mortal father is not just in the uncomprehending position of having to accede to God's seeming revocation of the covenant, and not just in the agonizing position of having to renounce his claim to the future previously promised to him through the birth of Isaac, but in the impossible position of having to kill his son. According to Fokkelman the voice that calls Abraham knows the unendurable demand it is placing upon the father, whom he has "*cruelly* ordered . . . to sacrifice his son, the bearer of the promise, whose coming he has awaited a lifetime."[5] Three times over God emphasizes Isaac's identity—as Abraham's son, then as his "only" son, and finally as his "beloved" son. The climactic redundancy establishes the greatest possible tension between the intimacy of father and son and the violation of that intimacy by means of the forthcoming sacrificial bloodletting. Before saying anything else, before specifying Abraham's obligation to sacrifice Isaac, the voice insists on marking and remarking and marking yet again not merely the general relation of father and son but that relation particularized: this father and this, his only and beloved, son. If Abraham believes in the divine imperative to be fruitful and multiply, the loss of the son must be unbearable.

Twice more does God refer to Isaac as "thy son, thine only one" (22:12 and 16). The thrice-emphasized singularity of the son who is "thine *only one*" (*yāchîð*, from the root *yâchað*, to be or become one, to join, to unite) is contrasted with three references (6, 8, and 19) to Abraham and Isaac as "they went both of them *together*" (*yachdôw*, also from the root *yâchað*),[6] as if "father and son were alike condemned."[7] Economizing on Hebrew etymology, the narrator's technique, Fokkelman infers, is "to set us thinking of the *unity* of father and son, now being threatened"[8] by the directive that will turn the former into the murderer of the latter and both into victims of their God.

God's demand that Abraham by his own hands destroy the "unity of father and son" identifies the time of Abraham's call and response not merely as one among other moments of violent cross-generational encounter. It focuses the manifestation of God's voice as the disastrous moment when the Jewish calendar would itself begin to be self-erased by the very "testing" that marks its origin were it not for the mystery of the way God converts his infanticidal command into a generative blessing and Abraham's infanticidal obedience into the condition of his identity as the symbolic father of his people. "Because you have done this, and have not withheld your son, your only son, I will indeed bless you, and I will make your offspring as numerous as the stars of heaven and as the sand that is on the seashore" (22:17). God's infanticidal call and Abraham's infanticidal response lead to a vision of a universal blessing, fabulously reflexive and reciprocating, that is promised to everyone through the Jew: "And your offspring shall possess the gate of their enemies, and by your offspring shall all the nations of the earth gain blessing for themselves, because you have obeyed my voice" (22:17–18). In possessing the gate of their foes, the threshold to their adversaries' homes, Abraham's descendants will "open" the future to what has been "sealed shut" in the relation of enemy to enemy—a community of "all the nations of the earth."

And yet, because any future that does come to pass is purchased at the cost of all other possible futures, not even the most robust genealogical future can escape being sacrificial; not even a lineage that bears God's imprimatur can escape from the limitless infanticidism that it necessarily entails. The blessing to Noah's descendents does not undo the obliteration that precedes it, an annihilation that continues to unfold throughout all possible futures. For this reason the blessing by which God projects the world's future—after the destruction of the multitudinous in the Flood, after the last-second salvation of the one in the *akeðah*— thus implicates "all the nations of the earth" in the same general infanticidity that this blessing brings to the fore in the promise of Abraham's future line of descent.

As the next chapter will make clear, all of the *akeðah*'s narrative's elements indicate how infanticide is but a specific manifestation of the infanticidal horizon of being. In this regard the narrative's manifest contradictions and interpretive conundrums are intended to overcome resistance to the thought of the infanticidal as an irreducible condition of existence. That resistance is evident in the history of *akedah*-interpreta-tion — in particular, in the insistence that the *akedah* should be read for its moral instruction concerning the self-evident evil of infanticide.

Such insistence yields to an interpretative temptation — namely, the desire to find in the Abraham narrative an ethical exoneration of God for calling Abraham to an infanticidal sacrifice, the very call that sets the nar-rative in motion and that is seemingly but only seemingly revoked at the end. Indeed, the temptation is to read into the beginning of the story the apparent meaning of its subsequent climactic reversal, when an angel stops Abraham, who then slaughters a ram instead of his son. Such "tele-ological" interpretations miss the radical paradox that Abraham is in-fanticidal whether he kills or saves his son; they miss how the narrative recognizes the patriarch's infanticidity as the inescapable burden of mor-tal existence; and thus they miss the meaning of Abraham's blessing, which is not an escape from but an encounter with the infanticidism of God's creation, an encounter that is the very possibility of ethics, as the next chapter will show. The *akedah*, then, is a test not of Abraham's un-wavering faith in a non-infanticidal God but of his steadfastness before the revelation of God's infanticidity.

Because the history of *akedah*-interpretation is so deeply committed to rationalizing God's initial infanticidal call in the name of an anti-infanti-cidal outcome, above all to seeing in the opening command a means of achieving a divine economization without (infanticidal) loss, it is critical to understand the interpretive violence this history has directed against the text. This hermeneutical aggression signals the anxiety associated with the struggle against becoming aware that the infanticidal is not the same as infanticide, that the absence of infanticide does not and cannot denote freedom from the infanticidal, and that finding infanticide ab-horrent is insufficient for comprehending how all existence is indelibly marked by the infanticidal. The rest of this chapter will explicate the cog-nitive blockage at work in this violence to see how the *akedah* arrives at its paradoxical blessing.

THE *AKEDAH*'S CHALLENGE TO ETHICS

The key difficulty with the *akedah* is the apparent moral contradictori-ness of God's unexplained demand that Abraham sacrifice his son. Why does God direct Abraham to undertake an action that in the future will have been in violation of nothing less than one of the ten command-ments (Exodus 10:13 and Deuteronomy 5:17)? Is God's command not also in clear contradiction to the warning he has given following the Flood: "Whoever sheds the blood of a human, by a human shall that person's blood be shed; for in his own image God made humankind" (Genesis 9:6)?

Moreover, since the Bible repeatedly condemns child sacrifice as an "abomination" that "profanes the name of your God" (Leviticus 18:21), "How could God have ordered a man to murder his son?"[9] For that matter, "How could Abraham have been so sure that God had, indeed, commanded him to kill his innocent child? Even if he was convinced that God had so commanded him," Louis Jacobs asks, "was it his duty to obey? Is obedience to God's will so supreme an obligation that it can override man's moral sense, demanding of him that he commit a criminal act of the very worst kind for the greater glory of God? Can or should one worship a being who wishes to be served by an act of murder?"[10] Why does the narrative not allow Abraham to challenge the injustice of God's demand for the life of Isaac, as he had when he contested God's demand for the complete obliteration of Sodom and Gomorrah?[11]

Kierkegaard presses the ethical question to the extreme. For Kierkegaard "Abraham's relation to Isaac, ethically speaking, is quite simply expressed by saying that a father shall love his son more dearly than himself."[12] Shall he love his God more dearly than his son? Not as a matter of ethical obligation. According to Kierkegaard, faith, not ethics, binds the individual to God; ethics, not faith, binds the individual to other humans. To be ethical, therefore, Abraham must disobey God. Insofar as "the ethical as such is the universal," insofar as it "applies to everyone" and "applies every instant," then, Kierkegaard concludes, Abraham condemns himself to murder in accepting God's call and preparing to sacrifice his son: "The ethical expression for what Abraham did is, that he would murder Isaac."[13] By Kierkegaard's logic God must share Abraham's culpability: the ethical expression for what God does is that he would murder a son through the intermediary of the son's father.[14]

An initial hermeneutic challenge, then, is why Abraham must obey a call—heinous, terrifying, monstrous—to kill from the same God who has already prohibited killing and who will later incorporate that prohibition into the governing law of his chosen people. Why does God appear to call out against himself, to oppose his own covenant-granting authority in soliciting the violence he has tabooed and will taboo yet again? Why does he put Abraham in an analogous position of absolute self-contradiction, with a manifestly immoral demand for the father to take the life of one he loves and thereby to abolish his paternity and deny his very name (the root of *Abraham*, *'âb* means "father")?

TELEOLOGY AND THE PUTATIVE ETHICAL COHERENCE
OF THE *AKEDAH*

According to the ethical reading of the *akedah*, God's initial call "was only a 'test,' a divine vindication of Abraham's absolute trust in God. There was never any divine intention for Abraham to kill Isaac. God, being God, could never so deny his own nature as to wish a man to commit a murder in obedience to him."[15] If so, how can a reader of the narrative know that God does not harbor the intention that his call to Abraham would seem to announce? The simple answer is that in his second command, given by his surrogate, an "angel of the Lord" (22:11), he reveals his real meaning: "Do not lay your hand on the boy or do anything to him; for now I know that you fear God, since you have not withheld your son, your only son, from me" (22:12).

All ethical interpretations of the *akeдah* read the meaning of the narrative in terms of this presumptively happy ending. That is, they construe God's first directive as a pretext for the second. In doing so, they presume that the ethical content of the second command exerts narrative control over the first. For example, according to Milton Steinberg: "From the Jewish viewpoint—and this is one of its highest dignities —the ethical is never suspended, not under any circumstances and not for anyone, not even for God. *Especially not for God*. . . . While it was a merit in Abraham to be willing to sacrifice his only son to his God, it was God's nature and merit that He would not accept an immoral tribute. And it was His purpose, among other things, to establish that truth."[16] However, if at the end God will not accept "an immoral tribute," what can it mean to denote as "a merit in Abraham" his "willing[ness] to sacrifice his only son to his God" according to the demand at the narrative's beginning? If the *akeдah* expresses an attitude of "natural recoil" against a "monstrous idea,"[17] why does the narrative not inculpate Abraham for his initial obedience? Why does it represent God as rewarding Abraham with an outcome more appropriate to having resisted the call to human sacrifice? If such pagan sacrifice is a heinous practice, what is the status of God's request for precisely that ritual undertaking? Moreover, if God abhors human sacrifice, why the pretense of calling for just that act? In his book on child sacrifice in Judaism and Christianity, Jon D. Levenson finds it "passing strange" that the *akeдah* should begin with God demanding the very action he is thought to detest,[18] the very action that, both earlier and later in the course of Jewish history, God condemns directly and unambiguously, that is, without recourse to any testing or other form of indirection. Here, the presumptive ethical content of the *akeдah* does not and cannot account for the narrative staging of that ostensible content. What the narrative discloses at its supposedly ethical climax (the call for no sacrifice) does not explain the unethical nature of the call for sacrifice that sets the narrative in motion. Again, the ethical moment does not explain the sum of the narrative's other moments or their temporal sequence in the movement from one call to its abrogation in a second call.

One response to the flagitious nature of the first command has been to distinguish between the generic "elohim," who calls for a burnt offering of human flesh at the beginning, and the highly specific YHWH (Yehôwâh, also Adonai),[19] who intervenes at the end. Abraham himself might seem to make just this discrimination, for after he sacrifices a ram instead of his son, he renames the site "Yehôvâh-yireh," which means "the Lord will see," not "elohim-yireh."[20] This discrimination enables readers to posit the singleness of the narrative's ethical meaning but only at the interpretive cost of an unexplained doubleness to God. Erich Wellisch, for examples, agrees with others that the "Elohim, who tempted Abraham, was only a servant of God and not the real God Himself" but does not ask why such a "servant" would pronounce a command that God himself would subsequently abolish, why God would speak through such an immoral servant, nor why Abraham would obey its voice. Wellisch also declares that when Abraham "heard God's real voice," he recognized it immediately and "no longer obeyed the inferior Elohim but God Himself";[21] but Wellisch does not pursue the resulting implication that prior to his testing Abraham had been unable to distinguish the "real" God from his "servants." Such a possibility does not arise for Wellisch, who concludes that after God reveals himself to Abraham the patriarch "exchanged the Elohim for Him. And therefore 'Abraham called the name of that place Jehovah-jireh,' because he saw Him on the mount, the Holy Hill of the psalm."[22]

The "exchange" of the lesser for the greater god, however, either voids the testing of its moral challenge or renders it incoherent. Abraham can heed neither of the voices he hears over the other unless he can differentiate the "inferior Elohim" from "God Himself." What enables Abraham to decide that the second voice comes from "the real God" rather than from yet another of his delegates? The answer is the ethical superiority of the second voice's command. Its self-evident morality is the source of its preemptive force. Accordingly, Abraham must obey the second voice not because it demands obedience as such but because it does so in the name of a moral principle. If Abraham can differentiate between the two voices, it must be because he understands the immorality of the one and the morality of the other.[23] As his earlier encounters with God illustrate, Abraham is acutely aware of the injustice in killing the righteous along with the iniquitous. For this reason he must know that the first directive cannot be what "God Himself" wants of him. And yet if that is the case, why does Abraham not repudiate the initial summons as a moral temptation to which he has no intention of yielding? Why does he not announce his intention of waiting for the real God to manifest himself, of obeying not the false but the true voice, whose ethical demand he will be able to follow as a matter of course?

A response related to the substitution of YHWH (Adonai) for Elohim has been to interpret the narrative as an anthropological allegory of the Israelite achievement in repudiating the Near Eastern practice of human sacrifice. Elohim might demand such rituals, but not "Abraham's God, Adonai, who stays his hand. Elohim might ask him to proceed, but Adonai says 'No.' He, too, will ask extreme devotion, but it will never again take this form," for "Abraham's religion not only rejects the sacrifice of a son by a father but rejects, as well, its use as a theological theme."[24] Hertz argues for a similar conclusion: "a primary purpose" of God's test, he writes, "was to demonstrate to Abraham and his descendants after him that God abhorred human sacrifice with an infinite abhorrence."[25] Nahum M. Sarna goes further, believing that the *akedah* is "a product of a religious attitude that recoils naturally from associating God with human sacrifice and which felt the need to explain the ancient tradition as an unprecedented and unrepeatable event, as a test of faith." Abraham, in this view, understands from the outset the execrable nature of sacrifice and, in obeying the call to kill his son, mimes the pagan acceptance of a ritual practice he and his people detest: "That God rejected the practice as utterly abhorrent was taken for granted."[26]

Shalom Spiegel finds in the *akedah* an etiological account of a "daring innovation" in religious attitude and practice:

> It may well be that in the narrative of the ram which Abraham sacrificed as a burnt offering in place of his son, there is historical remembrance of the transition to animal sacrifice from human sacrifice — a religious and moral achievement which in the folk memory was associated with Abraham's name, the father of the new faith. . . . And quite possibly the primary purpose of the Akedah story may have been only this: to attach to a real pillar of the folk and a revered reputation the new norm — abolish human sacrifice, substitute animals instead.[27]

Although Spiegel offers this interpretation as if it were an empirically driven hypothesis about a shift in Canaanite religious practices, his qualifying remarks ("may well be," "quite possibly," "may have been") indicate the desire-driven nature of his speculation: he wants the "father of the new faith" to be associated with the "new norm." By the end of the paragraph his wish has been fulfilled: the "only" purpose of the *akedah* was to record the moral advance of a people relinquishing a primitive and brutal cultural practice. To this end "the Akedah story declared war on *the remnants of idolatry in Israel* and undertook to remove root and branch the whole long, terror-laden inheritance from idolatrous generations."[28] Paul G. Mosca repeats Spiegel's ambivalence when he, too, substitutes his certainty about the narrative's ethical meaning for his uncertainty about the akedah's "original purpose," which "*may* have been," he surmises, "to explain why YHWH no longer—or ever—*demanded* the sacrifice of the first-born son."[29]

Levenson argues that archeological findings do not substantiate such anthropological speculations.[30] In addition to lacking empirical support, these readings rest on an unquestioned premise, which is that the *akedah* presents an unambiguous ethical imperative, one that evinces the immediate intelligibility and coherence of God's intention. Sarna, for example, insists that "[t]he narrative as it now stands is almost impatiently insistent upon removing any possibility of misunderstanding that God had *really* intended Abraham to sacrifice his son. To make sure that the reader has advance knowledge of God's purposes, the story begins with a declaration that 'God put Abraham to the test.'"[31] How does knowing that God is testing Abraham signal that God does not really mean for Abraham to kill his son? If the narrative did not include the framing remark, addressed to the reader but not to Abraham, would the reader be more inclined to believe that God really did intend Abraham to go through with the sacrifice? Does Abraham really not know that he is being tested? Would being suspicious or ignorant render his initial obedience any less ethically repugnant? Why does the narrative reveal God's true purposes to the reader before it reveals them to Abraham, and why to Abraham only after he has fully committed himself to acting on what in Sarna's interpretation clearly is not God's aim and cannot possibly be understood to be his aim?[32]

Like Sarna, Hertz takes for granted that God would not have required what he seems to demand: "A test is never employed for the purpose of injury, but to certify the power of resistance. All [Abraham's] other trials of faith were to be crowned by [his] willingness to sacrifice his dearest hope to the will of God. The Rabbis speak of it as the tenth and the greatest of the trials to which he was exposed."[33] When Hertz then reads that willingness in Abraham's "complete moral surrender" to God's first command (75n12), however, he opposes Abraham's faith to the ethical: Abraham's "moral surrender" effectively "certifies" God's moral incoherence, in which case his obedience is merely to the unpredictable, indeed unintelligible, will of a willful God. If Abraham accedes to God's will as (inexplicable) will, as force, not to God's will as (explicable) moral imperative, as existential ought, then how can Abraham's victimization of his son signify a "crowning" act of faith? What interpretive principle licenses the idealization of the father to the neglect of the son and what he must be going through? Doesn't the focus on Abraham's dilemma ignore the barbaric treatment—the torture—of the boy? Doesn't it reduce Isaac to a mere prop in the father's drama of faith? Doesn't it turn him into an instrument of the father's testing? Doesn't it thereby misuse the son, sacrifice his well-being in order to establish the exemplarity of his father? Echoing God's silence toward Isaac, doesn't it violate what Kant will formalize as each person's categorical right to life as "a Citizen of the world"?[34]

DOES ABRAHAM BELIEVE GOD MEANS WHAT HE SAYS?

Ethical readings of the *akedah* do not resolve its hermeneutic difficulties, they reproduce them. They do so, however, in ironic non-recognition that they are unable to provide a noncontradictory motivation for and meaning of God's test, and that they fail to establish God's intelligibility. Such readings, in other words, defend themselves against the text's representational crisis by repeating it. That mimetic impasse can be specified in the form of two questions about God's self-representation. If he does not really want Abraham to sacrifice, then is he not pretending at the outset that he does? If God can feign his meaning, by what principles of interpretation can one be certain of understanding his real meaning?

Since God withholds his reasons and plans, Abraham does not know what the ultimate outcome of the testing will be. Nevertheless, it is certain that Abraham cannot believe God will halt the test. The only way the story can be a record of Abraham's faith is if he does not know God's intentions. For the trial to be a test of faith rather than of cognition, a test of commitment to God in the absence of knowledge, a test of fidelity despite the threatened catastrophic consequences, Abraham must experience the first command as a literal injunction, not a figurative expression of God's will. He must be overwhelmed by its absolutely peremptory force — "you will kill your son" — with no hope of escape.

If Abraham knew, as Sarna claims, that he would "not really" have to immolate his son, then he would be merely miming the ritual action God demands. He would not really be offering his son but only seeming to. He would be participating in a charade or masquerade. If God did not mean what he says, then God too would be engaged in a pretense. If Abraham knew he would not have to eviscerate Isaac, then the action of taking his son on the pilgrimage to Moriah would be an ironic performance based upon the equally ironic intentionality of God. If Abraham knew from the outset that God would stay the execution, he could obey without dread; indeed, he could pretend to obey, and even pretend to be terrified, in which case he would be doubling the feint by which God himself only seemed to be asking for a blood sacrifice. How would a reader be able to tell the difference between appearance and the supposed reality behind appearances, between intention and intention feigned, between obedience and the pretense of obedience? Moreover, when God says he blesses Abraham "because you have done this, and have not withheld your son" (22:15), can he really be rewarding Abraham for merely affecting a willingness to go through with the sacrifice?

The consequence of all ethical readings of the *akedah* is the very possibility that God does not mean what he says, that his literal statements are dissimulations the communicative intent of which is not only to mislead but to erase the traces of his misdirections. So argues Franz Rosenzweig. Jacobs summarizes Rosenzweig's explanation: "God must, at times, conceal his true purpose. He must mislead man (as he misled Abraham into thinking that he was the kind of God who demanded that a murder be committed for his glorification) because if everything were clear men would become automatons."[35] The most immediate difficulty with this speculation is one of self-reference: Rosenzweig claims to know what Abraham does not about the possibility that God would conceal himself; that is, he denies Abraham the acumen he grants himself and the reader — namely, the perceptiveness to see through God's artifice. How else can it be suggested that Abraham mistakenly believes God to demand a murder and that God deliberately misleads his servant?

In substituting the reader's knowledge for Abraham's befuddlement, Rosenzweig eliminates the radical uncertainty he evokes concerning God's communications with humans. According to Rosenzweig, God withholds just those unambiguous, certifying signs that would remove any doubt about his divine intention: "God does not deal in such signs." Why not? "Apparently he dreads the inevitable consequence: in that case precisely those least free, those most fearful and miserable, would become the most 'pious.' Evidently God wants for his own only those who are free."[36] In consequence, God must lead humans toward temptation, must himself harm them, must "hide his way from man" and "deceive him" about such hiding so as to elicit their greatest trust. "God must not alone not help, he must actually harm. And so there remains nothing for him but to tempt man. Not only must he hide his way from man: he must deceive him about it. He must make it difficult, yea impossible, for man to see it, so that the latter have the possibility of believing him and trusting him in truth, that is to say in freedom" (*Star of Redemption*).[37] If God not only withdraws into hiding but conceals his concealments, then any and every manifestation of God would be caught up in the deception Rosenzweig here attributes to him. Not only would God's first call to Abraham be suspect, but so would the second. Indeed, a divine communication that contradicted another such communication would precipitate humans into an interpretive abyss concerning all communications — past, present, and future — with God. In the case at hand, on what basis could Abraham know that the second call were the trial's end rather than another turn of the screw? Under circumstances of such doubt, would God himself not become indistinguishable from his satanic counterpart, the "father of lies" (John 8:44)? Would "God" not be the ultimate deception, resistant to every demystification?

The interpretive knots that result from the possibility of God's radical duplicity double back on Rosenzweig's own insight. For example, how can Rosenzweig know that God "must deceive" humans without being able to see through God's misdirections? If God does misrepresent himself, how would anyone have access to the fact of this deception and the sacredness of human freedom that this deception's harm apparently ensures? If it is "impossible for man to see [God's] way," would this blindness not require that it be impossible for humans to recognize this impossibility? Here, Rosenzweig claims precisely the (meta-level) knowledge that God's deceptiveness would undermine. In other words, as is the case with all ethical readings of the *akeдah*, Rosenzweig seeks to economize on the *akeдah*'s interpretive binds by converting an irrecoverable cognitive loss (humankind's susceptibility to God's radical deception) into an absolute moral gain (the sign of our ethical freedom). The result is that Rosenzweig seems to remove the possibility of knowing God only to reintroduce such knowledge in the "truth" of humankind's freedom—its escape from the temptation and falsity of a slavish piety. This truth is, for Rosenzweig, both immanent to God's deceptions and transcendent of them and for this reason enables humans to name, know, and follow God's way after all, to discover in his "harm" the ultimate existential blessing.[38]

The test of such an interpretation is to grant Abraham the same self-consciousness as the reader—to treat Abraham not only as a participant in the drama of the *akeдah* but as a reflexive interpreter of it—and then to ask: what would be the interpretive consequences for Abraham were he to attempt to employ Rosenzweig's logic? Would Abraham be able to determine, as Rosenzweig is able to do, that the command to sacrifice is one of God's tricks? Would he be able to infer that the command not to follow through on the sacrifice is to be taken at face value? Would not Abraham have to be able to discern when God were concealing his intentions and when revealing them, when he were speaking duplicitously and when not? How can Abraham achieve this power of discrimination? How can Abraham know that God does not really mean what he says upon the occasion of the first call but that he does when he breaks in on the sacrifice with his second command? Confronted with antithetical commandments, how can Abraham know which to trust and which to distrust? On what basis can he decide? How would belief and trust in God assist him in his deliberations? Has Abraham in fact decided that the two commands are essentially different? Has he reasoned that the first is ethically insupportable? That it is a coded communication not to be taken literally? That it is a message about the primitive nature of a cultural practice—sacrifice—that God wishes his people to repudiate? That it is, therefore, a test? Has he also recognized that the second command is morally axiomatic? That it communicates what God literally means? That it bespeaks a truth that evacuates the non-truth of the first command? That it provides the entire episode with a retrospective, teleological coherence?

As has been indicated, many readings of the *akedah* presuppose that the second command, being ethically superior, abrogates the first. Accordingly, then, if Abraham submits to the second request, it is because of his ethical relation—his caring for and duty to his beloved son—which the first call had compelled him to abandon. Emmanuel Levinas has written that "the attention Abraham pays to the voice that brings him back to the ethical order by forbidding him to carry out the human sacrifice, is the most intense moment of the drama."[39] Such a reading implies that the first call takes Abraham away from the ethical order. If so, why did Abraham obey it? What was the force of this call that Abraham would be susceptible to its allure? Moreover, what in the second call enables it to overcome the first? If Abraham finds the first command compelling, what makes the second call more so? If the second call "brings him *back* to the ethical order," then presumably Abraham abided there before the first command. If so, then prior to the first command Abraham had already heard and obeyed the second. Under this circumstance, however, the first command would be manifestly superior to the ethical force of the second, since the first command would have been powerful enough to tempt Abraham away from his moral obligation. In consequence, when the second command returns Abraham to the ethical, it cannot immunize him to a future call that would demand yet another turning away. The return to the ethical does not protect the ethical; to the contrary, it opens the ethical to infinite jeopardy. Either the second command institutes the ethical for the first time or it condemns the ethical to endless subversion.

Perhaps, however, Abraham obeys the second command irrespective of its content. Perhaps he heeds it merely because it comes after the first and is, as it happens, the latest of God's dicta, its ethical content being incidental to its demand primarily for obedience as such and only secondarily for obedience to its particular directive? Perhaps Abraham has intuited that God is beyond all human understanding and that, therefore, the only option is to obey him unconditionally, without trying to divine his intentions, without trying to extract a moral. If God issues contradictory commands, how can their respective content provide the means for evaluating them? If the ethical content of the second command ultimately claims Abraham's attention, then, once again, would Abraham not have failed his testing from the outset in obeying the first command? Would God, too, not have failed in his testing of his steward?

If the testing had proceeded in reverse—if the order to sacrifice the son had come at the last moment rather than at the beginning of the trial—and if under those circumstances Abraham were to be as firm in his faith as he appears to be in the extant story, and if he were therefore to consummate the ritual, then the contradiction within God's two commands would not be open to the apparent ethical resolution so favored by most readers. If the "tempting" of Abraham is to pivot on both his and God's adherence to an ethical imperative, then the most intense moment of the drama does not occur with the second command and the attention he pays to it. No, it occurs with the attention this mortal pays to the voice that first calls him away from the ethical sphere. Any reading that insists on construing the second call as the occasion for Abraham's ethical homecoming must account for the fact that God's first call inflicts an irreparable ethical exile. What child, having once been tied and readied for sacrificial slaughter by his or her father, having once seen the father's knife-wielding hand raised and about to plunge, could ever trust this person again? If the point of the *akeдah* narrative is to dramatize Abraham's ethical homecoming, what of its inattention to the voice and suffering of the son? In the story of Ishmael and Hagar's wandering, God hears and responds to the boy's weeping; he takes pity on him and his mother and rescues them from their straits. It is just such an act of listening to the child—of registering and responding to the child's vulnerability, the child's desperate condition, the child's terror—that goes utterly unremarked during "the most intense moment of the [*akeдah*] drama." Abraham's readiness not to sacrifice the child after he had been absolutely ready to destroy him is no evidence of a moral transformation—either in terms of achieving a new sense of the ethical or of returning to the ethicality that has guided him in previous encounters with God but that inexplicably has disappeared at the outset of his present testing. Indeed, the *akeдah* records nothing about what transpires between Abraham and Isaac either during the sacrifice (as Abraham binds his son and steels himself to kill his child) or after. It gives no indication of Isaac's emotionality—paralyzing dread? enraged sense of betrayal? depression?—nor of Abraham's response.[40] In fact, Isaac disappears at the end as Abraham appears to return alone to his retinue, the boy unmentioned: "So Abraham returned to his young men, and they arose and went together to Beer-sheba; and Abraham lived" there (22:19). The "beloved son" is not included—neither by name nor by attribution—in the father's literal return home.

THE DISAPPEARANCE OF ISAAC

What might Isaac's disappearance signify? "Even the ancients, long ago, were surprised that immediately after the Akedah . . . all traces of Isaac son of Father Abraham disappear." So Spiegel begins his book-length study, *The Last Trial,*[41] of the "legends and lore of the command to Abraham to offer Isaac as a sacrifice." According to one rabbinical exegesis, "Although Isaac did not die, Scripture regards him as though he had died and his ashes lay piled on the altar. That is why it is said, 'So Abraham returned unto his young men.'" According to another, God "sent him to Paradise, as a reward for all he had suffered when about to be slain." Other commentaries are more explicit: Abraham killed Isaac, whom God takes to paradise "to recover from the effects on his neck of what his father did to him."[42] According to the Tanhuma, a collection of rabbinical commentaries (midrashim) on the Pentateuch, "if it were not for" the angel's interposition at the last minute, Isaac "would *already* have been slaughtered."[43] The adverbial qualification, of course, is blatantly contradictory: how can the angel's intercession at a later point in time prevent Abraham from killing his son at an earlier point in time? Whether or not the Tanhuma hints that the angel spoke too late, it insinuates that, in his readiness to obey the first command, Abraham mentally or psychologically has already carried out the act, and that Abraham is guilty of the intention to kill his son even if he is stopped short of doing so.

Various midrashim construe Sarah's death as a reaction to news of the *akedah,* as if she knew her husband were entirely capable of sacrificing their son. According to one interpretation, Satan lies to Sarah: "Your old husband has taken the boy Isaac and sacrificed him as a burnt offering, while the boy cried and wailed in his helplessness [lit., for he could not be saved]. Immediately, she began to cry and wail. She cried three sobs, corresponding to the three *Teki'ah* notes of the Shofar, and she wailed (Yelalot) three times, corresponding to the *Yevava,* staccato notes of the Shofar. Then, she gave up the ghost and died."[44] The wailing of the Shofar, the ram's horn used in ritual celebrations, echoes Sarah's sobs and perhaps Isaac's as well. In the midrash at hand, the Shofar originates in commemoration of a mother's dying grief upon hearing the report of her husband's infanticidal ritual, completed or not. The midrash's inclusion of Satan's lie displaces the agency of infanticide from the person of Abraham to the figure of the Deceiver himself, thereby protecting the motivation of the mortal father. However, the great medieval commentator on the Torah, Rashi, removes Satan from the scene of Sarah's demise, thus all but naming Abraham's infanticidal intent: "The death of Sarah is narrated directly after the Akedah . . . because, as a result of the tidings of the Akedah—that her son had been fated for slaughter, and had been all-but-slaughtered—she gave up the ghost and died."[45] Although he accepts that Abraham stays his hand, Rashi implies either that Sarah does not believe Abraham held back or that she sees little difference between her husband's sacrificial intentions and his final inhibition.[46]

Such speculations baffle Spiegel, who wonders at their persistence throughout the Middle Ages:

> In a milieu so totally committed to the inherited, clinging to the old and ha-bitually devoted to its traditions, how could there have arisen, and then even have been disseminated, such paradoxical haggadic lore? What compelled the faithful of Israel to depart from the clear statement of Scripture and from what was public knowledge among this people and every other people? The story of the Akedah—is it possible that these pious generations failed to be affected by the plain meaning of the words of Scripture?"[47]

The answer is that the "plain meaning" of the narrative centers on pre-cisely the recognition—and its affective roots—that the absence of in-fanticide does not mean the absence of the infanticidal. The ambiguities of Abraham's blessing reinforce this meaning against the temptation of believing in a test, a faith, a love, and a God free of (infanticidal) cost.

THE ENIGMA OF ABRAHAM'S BLESSING

At the end, Abraham is blessed with a promise of a progenerative future beyond measure: "'Because you have done this, and have not withheld your son, your only son, I will indeed bless you, and I will make your offspring as numerous as the stars of heaven and as the sand that is on the seashore'" (22:16–17). Why is he rewarded in this particular way? Such a blessing might be understood as making the entire narrative ironic. God repays Abraham for his willingness to disinvest in his single son with numberless sons—sons of the sons of the sons (and so on) of this "only son." The inflationary genealogical return on Abraham's infanti-cidal sacrifice would compensate for the absolute reproductive cost of killing off one's offspring—the loss of the future, a loss that, from the perspective of his genealogical hope, would render the rest of Abraham's days a living death. In these terms the narrative trades the inscrutability of the command to destroy the son for the presumptive intelligibility of the command not to.

The narrative irony of this hermeneutic substitution militates against the ethical reading, for the blessing Abraham receives is not at all ap-propriate to obeying an immoral command. If it is linked to Abraham's actions, perhaps it is to his ability to desist from the sacrifice. The nar-rative raises this possibility when God says that he is blessing Abraham because Abraham has done "this" (in Hebrew, *ha ∂hāvār haze*, "the thing this"—that is, "this thing," "this matter") before specifying the referent in question (not withholding his son). Since *∂hāvār* can also signify *word*, the angel affirms that Abraham has done God's word.[48] But what is revealed in doing God's word if that word is double? After all, God has given two commandments. When the angel refers to "this thing" that Abraham has accomplished, the referent can refer to either of the two things Abraham has been willing to do—sacrifice his son but also stop himself from sacrificing his son. Although Abraham has obeyed two words, he is told his reward, which could not have occurred had he not done the second thing (hold his hand and his son back), is because he has done "this" other "thing" (not hold his hand and son back). Why does the text itself "hold back" from naming the other thing Abraham did, especially when the issue in question is a matter of "not withholding" in a matter that involves the very word of God, the divine *dhavar*, the very "thing" in question? In other words, if Isaac is to be the medium of Abraham's paternal legacy, then his life and person must be guaranteed. And yet it appears to be precisely the willingness to take the son's life and thus abolish his own fatherhood for which Abraham is blessed by a God who is indifferent to the very son in whom Abraham stakes his hopes to an ongoing line of descent.

What explanatory principle links the blessing to Abraham's sacrificial (that is, infanticidal) behavior? Exegetes typically do not say; rather, they merely assert that there is a causal connection. For example, Fokkelman asserts that "by showing his willingness to give up his only son, Abraham gets him back," but he does not explain why he gets his son back just because he has been willing to give him up. Nor does he explain why or how "a much deepened togetherness begins, both between father and son and between the Lord and his obedient follower," only that it does.[49] Estrin offers a similar causally empty "explanation": "Because he listened to his divine Father, Abraham regains the human potential"—paternal generativity—"which earlier he believed to have been gone forever. . . . By 'obeying' God, Abraham repossesses his fatherhood and is blessed."[50] Neither Fokkelman nor Estrin explain why God excuses Abraham from completing his sacrifice just because Abraham was willing to go through with it. The narrative supplies no *because*. Why, just because he is willing to destroy his son, should he be granted his son's life and be restored to a paternity greater, far greater, than the fatherhood he was willing to relinquish? What transforms his literal act of obedience into the "obedience" that Estrin puts within quotations marks? What makes Abraham's violent adherence to God's word an act deserving of infinite blessing? And what is the evidence that the physical "binding" of Isaac becomes transmuted into a deepened psychological "bond" of togetherness between father and son, especially in view of the fact that Abraham and Isaac have ventured forth "together," the narrating voice says three different times, while at the end of the ritual Abraham alone is remarked as returning, the "togetherness" of father and son now conspicuously missing from the narrative? And what of the possibility that either the father or the son might suffer a reaction of delayed stress and disturbed affect—anxiety and depression, bewildered longing, resentful or even poisonous disillusionment and ineradicable suspicion, perhaps as well as loathing, terror, dreadful aversion, and so on? Might not son or father at some point respond with rage?

"The Akedah story itself," Wellisch admits, "does not give a clear indication of what follows." And yet he believes that readers can nevertheless "draw the conclusion that it marked the beginning of a new relationship between father and son which initiated a new era in the family relationships of man." For Wellisch this "new relationship can be described as *a covenant between parent and child* which inaugurated a new era of moral code," an era the "realization [of which] depends on a situation in which selfish aims are abandoned and real personal love and dedication to God's call"—God's real call, the second and not the first—"are possible."[51] The terrible irony of Wellisch's hope is that it rests on a tacit indictment of the father. Refusing to name the son's trauma at the hands of the father, Wellisch euphemistically alludes to certain "selfish aims" that are to be given up. One can draw conclusions such as Wellisch's only by imposing on the text a coherence it does not have—which is to say, only by sacrificing the text's contradictions. To remove the text's contradictions is to provide interpretive closure and emotional resolution to an otherwise scandalous narration. To insist that the text offers a form of solace—either cognitive or affective —is to rationalize its message. It is to convert it into a precept, a rule, even a promise: by doing what one is called to do, the tested individual receives God's blessing.

The story of Abraham and Isaac cannot offer such assurance. If Abraham makes a leap of faith, he can do so only if he does not know that the sacrificial offering will not have to be completed, only if he does not know that it will be redeemed with the return of the victim's life. Such knowledge would nullify the test. Moreover, such knowledge would prevent it from serving as the very example it is held up to be. In knowing what Abraham did not know, no subsequent reader could recover Abraham's terror, the abyss before which he stands. For this reason the testing, as such, of Abraham cannot occur *and* be narrated, told, or received without such narrative repetition bringing to an end the possibility of the test's repetition. The very retelling of the story supplies the outcome that must be missing for the test to be experienced as a test.

If the first "command to Abraham was, on any showing, a once-and-for-all matter, never to be repeated and not carried out in practice even in the instance of Abraham himself,"[52] what, then, is being narrated? That the demand of Abraham was not what it seemed? That God did not and never will call for human sacrifice? That were such an impossible call to be placed, we could be assured of not having to defile ourselves with the blood of a victim? To the contrary, what is being narrated is precisely that the *akeðah* can never not be repeated. That it takes place all the time and everywhere, even when it does not take place as such. That it is testimony to the infanticidal as an inescapable feature of existence, one that cannot be reduced to the act of infanticide. And that the prospect of the world's general infanticidism affirms the ethical even as it opens the ethical to the greatest contamination.[53]

How is this possible?

5

"The Most Common Event in the World": Abraham's Sacrifice and the Infanticidity of Being

> . . . a price must be paid for being human.
> —Martin Buber, "The Tree of Knowledge:
> Genesis 3," in Harold Bloom, ed. *Genesis* (48)

> Kierkegaard wants to drive the cost of faith impossibly high. . . .
> Abraham is the father of faith because he is willing to pay the cost. . . .
> —John D. Caputo, *The Prayers and Tears of Jacques Derrida* (200)

THE PRICE OF THE ONE

THE PRICE THAT MUST BE PAID FOR BEING HUMAN IS "IMPOSSIBLY high": the giving of life is simultaneously a taking of life. The taking does not have to be an overt exchange of one life for another; more typically it transpires as the loss of potential life, an insight elliptically commemorated in the rabbinic aphorism: "To kill one human being means to kill all humanity."[1] If the crime against "one" is a crime against "all," that is because one and all share the same irreplaceability, the same absolutely singular value, the same sacredness. To kill the one, therefore, is not merely to destroy a life that was in any case finite but to destroy the infinitude of being that belongs in principle to any person. If the infinitude of the one life is equivalent to the sum of all other infinitudes of being, then the snuffing out of the one is tantamount to the death of humankind. If the loss is (spiritually) infinite, humankind never survives the killing of the one. Accordingly, the collective, ongoing, empirical existence of the human species notwithstanding, the possibility of saying "we" is lost at the outset. The first murder merely personifies the infinite loss in the death of the one.

To kill the one is to kill all of humanity. The converse, however, does not hold. To save the one is not to save all of humanity. If saving the one means choosing the one rather than the other—Sophie's unbearable choice in Styron's novel—then to save the one is still to kill all of humanity in the infinite sacrifice of the other that occurs on behalf of the one. Such is Kierkegaard's insight regarding Abraham and Isaac. So argues Derrida in *The Gift of Death*, in which he examines the double-binding, aporetic economy of ethics. The *akedah*, however, does not merely provide the occasion for Kierkegaard's meditation on and Derrida's elaboration of the impossible logic of ethical obligation; the biblical narrative itself anticipates these two commentaries. Through its imagery of ascent it performs what Kierkegaard and Derrida deduce from its moral content, while at the same time it hides in the open what the Western world has not wanted to admit, concerning the infinitely sacrificial cost of existence.

INFANTICIDISM AND THE LEAP OF FAITH

In the third chapter of *The Gift of Death*, an exacting work the logic of which this chapter will try to summarize as clearly as possible, Derrida analyzes Kierkegaard's reflections in *Fear and Trembling* on Abraham's obedience. Derrida does so in order to draw out the implication of Kierkegaard's double-faceted judgment of Abraham—that from the perspective of ethics "he is and remains a murderer," but that from the viewpoint of faith he is the exemplary believer, the "knight" and "father" of faith, the very model of the fidelity and trust that are achievable only by harkening, as he did, to a call that is infanticidal.[2]

From an ethical point of view the story is, Derrida writes, "monstrous, outrageous, barely conceivable: a father is ready to put to death his beloved son, his irreplaceable loved one, and that because the Other, the great Other asks him or orders him without giving the slightest explanation."[3] About "[a]n infanticide father who hides what he is going to do from his son and from his family without knowing why," Derrida asks, rhetorically, "what mystery could be more abominable what mystery could be more frightful (*tremendum*) vis-à-vis love, humanity, the family, or morality?" (*GD*, 67). Moreover, this frightfulness must not be rationalized, justified, or in any way explained away. It must be kept clearly in the fore and felt full force: "the sacrifice of Isaac is an abomination in the eyes of all, and it should continue to be seen for what it is—atrocious, criminal, unforgivable; Kierkegaard insists on that. The ethical point of view must remain valid: Abraham is a murderer" (*GD*, 85). And yet at the same time Kierkegaard discerns in the *akedah* something else, something in contradictory addition to the ethical fault that must be condemned—namely the achievement of an incomprehensible faith, a commitment to God that transforms Abraham's action into an absolute affirmation. "By his act he overstepped the ethical entirely and possessed a higher *telos* outside of it, in relation to which he suspended the former" (*FT,* 69). By his call God demands an action that falls "outside" of ethical categories.

Insofar as Abraham's sacrificial obedience defines another and "higher" order of answerability, his behavior is all the more terrifying for emanating from a love that is equivalent to hate, from a distressed and dreadful love that renders this man "unable to make himself intelligible" to his son and perhaps also to himself. On the one hand, Kierkegaard infers from Abraham's obedience that "[t]he instant [Abraham] is ready to sacrifice Isaac the ethical expression of what he does is this: he hates Isaac" (*FT,* 84). From an ethical point of view, Kierkegaard maintains, there is no difference between sacrificing, for whatever reason, and hating one's child. The abominable nature of the command Abraham is willing to obey bespeaks his hatred of the son whose life he would trade for relation to God. Abraham detests his child.

On the other hand, Abraham must love his son "with his whole soul." As Kierkegaard argues, "when God requires Isaac" be sacrificed, Abraham "must love [his son] if possible even more dearly, and only on this condition can he *sacrifice* him; for in fact it is this love for Isaac which, by its paradoxical opposition to his love for God, makes his act a sacrifice. But the distress and dread in this paradox is that, humanly speaking, he is entirely unable to make himself intelligible" (*FT,* 84). Once again, on the one hand Abraham must love, not hate, his son. If Abraham hated Isaac, Isaac's death would not count as a sacrifice, for Abraham would have given up nothing in giving over a detested son. For this reason God makes clear from the outset that Abraham must sacrifice what is dearest, most beloved. If he loves his son, however, such sacrifice must be hateful to him—appalling, frightful. His love must tempt him to denounce his God, a temptation to which Job's wife yields when she demands that her husband "curse God, and die" (Job 2:10). On the other hand, Abraham loves the God he hates, and all the more so for demanding the terrible sacrifice, for making of it the opportunity of a lifetime. His love of God, however, must tempt him to detest the son he loves; it must tempt him for just the reason that Isaac is his beloved child and for thereby making the choice of fidelity to God infinitely costly.[4]

At this point "Kierkegaard rejects the common distinction between love and hate; he finds it egotistical and without interest. He reinterprets it as a paradox. God wouldn't have asked Abraham to put Isaac to death, that is, to make a gift of death as a sacrificial offering to himself, to God, unless Abraham had an absolute, unique, and incommensurable love for his son" (*GD,* 65). Derrida does not say a pure love, in the sense of an unconflicted devotion, but rather a measureless or incomparable love, a love for the one that cannot be rendered in terms of a love for the other, any other, including God. And yet if the love for the other is also absolute, singular, and incommensurable, then it is like the love for the one at the very moment it is unlike it. In either case it is also a love that is afflicted with what jeopardizes, compromises, contaminates, and contradicts it by virtue of the way this love is open to what it must hate in loving, and therefore to what it must love all the more in hating.

Abraham knows that he cannot communicate this paradoxical love/hate. And yet he can attest to his faith, Kierkegaard says, only if he honors this violent conjunction within his passion for his son and for his God: "Only at the moment when his act is in absolute contradiction to his feeling is his act a sacrifice" (*FT,* 84). For the contradiction to be absolute, Abraham must not feel only one way and act another, love his child but nevertheless set out to kill him. He must love and hate loving, love and fear loving, love and tremble at the thought of loving. He must apprehend in the sacrifice both the fulfillment and the destruction of his love, by which he loves and hates what he is called upon to perform. He must feel this way toward his son and all the more so toward his God.

Every human generation, Kierkegaard says, must discover for itself and repeat anew precisely this sacrificial task. Every generation is bound to this duty, which involves an unintelligible and incommunicable passion for and from the other. Every generation must undertake this ethically execrable sacrifice without possibility of passing beyond it; it is what makes humans most human, most authentically who they are. *The* "authentically human factor is passion," he says, the "highest form of which is the faith exemplified by Abraham (*FT,* 130 and 131). This faith is untransmissible in the sense that it cannot be taught, though it can be learned: "that which is genuinely human no generation learns from the foregoing. In this respect every generation begins primitively, has no different task from that of every previous generation, nor does it get further, except in so far as the preceding generation shirked its task and deluded itself" (*FT,* 130).

No generation can learn from Abraham because it cannot put itself in the position he is in at the outset of his testing—the position of not knowing the outcome, the very position which the narrative recounting of Abraham's testing removes. To know the ending of the story is to be separated from Abraham's position of believing that he will have to go through with the sacrifice. Such knowledge excludes all readers of the *akedah* from repeating Abraham's trial. In other words, the Genesis narrative cannot record Abraham's reward without relieving its readers of the very doubt that makes Abraham's actions a leap of faith. One cannot turn the story of a man who has no precedent, no precursor narrative to rely on, into a precedent. In consequence, Abraham cannot be a model, and his obedience cannot be the paradigm of faith.

And yet, Kierkegaard insists, to attain the highest belief each generation must undergo (something like) Abraham's probation. Since we cannot have the historical knowledge of Abraham's encounter with God and recapitulate the patriarch's uncertainty concerning God's intentions, we must repeat without repeating Abraham's tribulation.[5] We must hear Abraham's call for the first time, be the first one to have been commanded to take one's child to Moriah, as if the demand for the sacrifice of one's own flesh and blood had never before been made. Only then, Kierkegaard says, can we become human.

How can we follow Abraham's impossible example? The first requirement would be to recognize that Abraham sacrifices his son in principle even if he stops the sacrifice in fact. God only stops Abraham's arm, not the intention that has led Abraham to embark on the journey, build the altar, bind his son, grasp the knife, and raise his arm. God can direct Abraham to interrupt the action of killing; he can bring the empirical destruction of the boy to a halt. He cannot, however, return Abraham or Isaac to the time before the testing, to the time before the father has entertained the sacrificial intentions God has mandated. From this point of view neither Abraham nor Isaac survives the otherwise interdicted sacrifice. In that case the Kierkegaardian event of becoming human comes to pass at the instant when, the infanticide averted, Abraham apprehends the limitlessness of the world's infanticidism.

The second requirement for following Abraham's inimitable example derives from the first. It is to comprehend how the essence of the Abrahamic test could occur anew—that is, in the absence of the specific form it takes in the Genesis narrative. When and where does each individual of each generation encounter the same testing—which means the same double bind—that Abraham did? When and where does each individual take on the sacrificial task that Kierkegaard says makes us human? If every generation learns without being able to be taught the sacrificial nature of love, the paradoxical hatred within love, including love at its purest, then the *akedah* would be occurring everywhere every day. Isn't Abraham's sacrifice of his son, Derrida asks, "also the most common thing? What the most cursory examination of the concept of responsibility cannot fail to affirm?" (*GD*, 67–68). Again, "is it not true that the spectacle of this murder . . . is at the same time the most common event in the world? Is it not inscribed in the structure of our existence to the extent of no longer constituting an event?" (*GD*, 85).

"The most common event in the world" is, strictly speaking, not an event in itself but rather the condition of any event. Worse, it is the condition of any event's ruination, for it afflicts every event with an irreducible infanticidality. How is this possible? How can the sacrifice of one's child— infanticide—be at the heart of the concept of responsibility? How can it be the basis of absolute faith? How can it be inscribed in the very "structure of our existence"? The answer is that Abraham's suspended infanticide is a sign of the general infanticidity within being, sacred and profane alike.

THE ECONOMY OF SACRIFICIAL SUBSTITUTION

The content of the *akedah* concerns a mystery—why God would demand "the most cruel, impossible and untenable gesture" (*GD*, 58). In withholding any explanation either of God's reasons or of Abraham's for accepting his terrible duty instantly and without question, the narrative mimetically doubles the mystery. The narrative redoubles the mystery when it recounts the climax of the sacrificial ritual. An angel interrupts Abraham at the last possible second and commands Abraham to "lay not your hand on the lad or do anything to him" (22:12). In response, Abraham "looked up and saw a ram, caught in a thicket by its horns" (22:13). At this point, in the absence of any directive to sacrifice it in place of Isaac, Abraham "offered it up as a burnt offering instead of his son" (22:13). Why? Why does the son live and the ram die? Why does the narrative remain silent about why Abraham, no longer under divine direction, seeks out a replacement for his son? Why does the narrative not allow Abraham to drop the knife and lower his hand altogether? In the absence of a command from God or his emissary either to kill or not to kill something else in place of the human victim, why does Abraham elect on his own, of his own will, to look for a surrogate target? He has the opportunity to choose otherwise but does not. Why not? And why does the narrative repeat Abraham's gesture? Why does it turn, without comment and seemingly as a matter of course, from the angel's disruption of the sacrifice to Abraham's discovery of another way to complete the ritual?

The answer is that sacrifice is unavoidable, that there must be some sacrifice of the living—not a vegetarian offering (Cain's mistake), but the slaying of an animal. What the narrative does not explicitly say, what it does not put into words, but what all of its features dramatize, is that there is no escape from sacrifice. At the climax of the drama, blood must and will be spilled. The narrative provides no reason why because the spilling of blood is self-explanatory: human life costs, Isaac's life costs. The exchange of animal life for human life in the story of Isaac's survival indicates the deathliness that is the condition of living on; the death of the ram establishes that there is an irreducible ontological price to be paid for the person who lives in its stead.

One of the most influential rabbinical commentators is unequivocal in identifying the ram as a substitute for Isaac, a substitution that renders the nonhuman sacrifice the symbolic enactment of a human sacrifice. According to Avivah Gottlieb Zornberg: "The climax of the Akedah is the displacement of Isaac by the ram: 'He went and took the ram and offered it up as a burnt offering in place of his son' (22:13). Rashi comments on the redundant 'in place of his son': Over every part of the ritual that he performed with the ram, he prayed, 'May it be Your will that this act should be *as though* [*ke'eelu*] it were done to my son—as though my son were slaughtered, as though his blood were sprinkled, as though he were flayed.'"[6] Zornberg believes that "Abraham has earned the right to metaphoric substitution," which is the right to pray to God to receive the sacrifice of the ram "as though" it were the sacrifice of his son.[7] The substitution, however, proceeds in two directions, not one: animal for the human child, human child for the animal. As Rashi grasps, the substitution does not signify Abraham's refusal to kill his son but the patriarch's awareness of the displaced infanticidal meaning attaching to every sacrifice. Three times seeing the death of the son in the death of the ram, Rashi reads the infanticidism of infanticide withheld.

Zornberg then universalizes the infanticidism of Abraham's substitution when she invokes the midrash that stipulates how the ram was "created at twilight on the last day of Creation."[8] The last creature to appear in the last hour of light on the last day of creation before God rests, the ram in this midrashic tradition is a metonymical figure of the world's formation—not merely a sign of the creation but the part that incarnates the whole. And if the ram "has been waiting in the wings for the moment at which it *becomes* Abraham's son,"[9] then Zornberg's "metaphorical substitution" of ram for the boy is suddenly an infanticidal identity, and the sacrifice of the ram not only the destruction of Isaac but nothing less than the infanticidal unmaking of creation itself.

Zornberg wants to find in Abraham's sacrifice the "capacity [of love] to confront fears of all kinds, to absorb them in a kind of joy at the survival of lover and beloved."[10] So be it. But if the ram is the sign that stands in for the boy, then its death is the paradoxical disappearance of the beloved in the survival of the beloved. In a simple way, for example, the son will never be the same. He is no longer the Isaac he was. That boy is dead to his father and to himself. In this boy's place is another version of the "same" boy who through his harrowing must thereafter live in the shadow of what might have happened. Having survived at the expense of the ram, which substitutes for him, (one) Isaac lives in place of (another) Isaac (who is yet the same Isaac). In other words, Isaac does not live simply and solely in his own person but in the death of the other, a death that is symbolically equivalent to the destruction of God's entire creation. If the death of the one is the death of the many, the death of all humanity, the death of all the life-worlds that might have been, then henceforth Isaac must live in the consciousness of the limitless, creation-subtracting, infanticidal cost of his survival, which is the cost of anyone's survival.[11] Thus, the presence of the ram in the *akeðah* narrative underscores how every human life, the life of every Isaac, costs, not only in its continued existence but in its very advent; and how the costs are paid for by others, not only other people but also other creatures in general, other life, other embodiments of God's world-inaugurating action. Substituting for Isaac, the sacrificed ram signals the infanticidity within the creation itself.

THE INFANTICIDITY OF THE ETHICAL

Infanticidism is the very condition of the world's possibility. There is no political economy in which the distribution of resources is not exclusionary, hence is not irremediably sacrificial. This economic principle afflicts the most conscientious act, the most responsible act, the most just act, as well as the most nurturing and loving act—if not in the intention that instigates it, nevertheless in the act's structure. One cannot, for example, love all the children that need and deserve to be loved: to love this child and to act on this love, to direct one's time and energy and devotion to its well-being, is perforce not to act on the love one feels or ought to feel for other children. No child comes into the world without making demands upon the world's resources, and yet to satisfy those demands is to direct resources to one person rather than to another, to the countless others already born or not yet born or not ever to be or to have been born. "We are reluctant, of course, to treat birth as a scourge . . . source of . . . every disaster."[12]

That "source" precedes birth. Conception too, so often idealized in terms of an imagined purity attaching to the beginning of new life, is tied to sacrifice, to absolute injustice. For no conception can occur except in relation to the simultaneous blocking of all the other possible conceptions that might otherwise come to pass: every conception is simultaneously an incalculable contraception. A common reproductive sequence illustrates. A woman miscarries but then conceives again soon after, this subsequent pregnancy successfully coming to term. The completion of the first pregnancy would have eliminated the possibility of the second, the birth of the one infant entailing the non-conception, nonexistence, and "death" of the other. However, one need not have been conceived in the aftermath of the mother's previously terminated pregnancy to recognize the sacrificial cost of all conception. Because every conception is simultaneously an infinite contraception, each person receives the gift of life as a gift of death. Irreplaceable, each person's life, each person's conception, nevertheless already replaces the irreplaceable conceptions of those countless others who will never have been.

The otherness of these others, however, is no different from the otherness of the person who is least other, one's own child. This fact undercuts any assumption of responsibility by dissolving the difference between one's own and those not one's own at the very moment the singularity of each, or the uniqueness of one in contrast to the generality of others, is the most keenly felt. Even those whom one calls "my own" remain absolutely other, all the more so when one experiences them, insofar as this is possible, as belonging exclusively to themselves, but no less so even when one claims them in any way as somehow same (of the same family, gender, or culture, for example). In his or her absolute singularity, as a unique and irreplaceable being, no child of mine is my own or the same as I; no child of mine is any the less other, any the less not mine, than all the other children that are not mine.

Conversely, no child not my own is any the less my responsibility than my own child is—if responsibility means answering to the individuality of the child, for that individuality arises and perdures independently of any biological relatedness and, more generally, beyond any other determinable relatedness. Neither nature nor culture can delimit the otherness of the other, which must always surpass every conceptual category, every means of apprehending the other on this side of its boundaries. The other is not other if it can be said to be mine or in any other way can be classified, sorted, grouped. It must remain singular and unique. The other as other, uniquely and wholly other, thus produces an insurmountable dilemma: responsibility to the other entails a responsibility to all the other others, to all other otherness, and therefore is impossible, unjust from the outset, in a word, sacrificial. Within the framework of ethics as universal responsibility, to take responsibility for the life of this priceless child is perforce to neglect taking responsibility for the well-being of all the other priceless children whose rights to life, to a certain minimal level of care, and to freedom of person cannot be less than that of the one child. The dependence of an individual's life on the more or less felicitous circumstances of his or her advent into the world at this time and in this place rather than at some other time and in some other place means that the gift of life is never equal but differential, unjust, favoring some over others. And yet the singularity of any child gives it not merely an equal but an absolute claim to life, which is to say an absolute claim to the sacrifice—the death—of the others that their claims to life also entail.

To respond to the singularity of one's own child, then, precipitates the individual into the abyss of an infinite responsibility the structure of which is irreducibly sacrificial: "what binds me thus in my singularity to the absolute singularity of the other," Derrida explains, "immediately propels me into the space or risk of absolute sacrifice." Why? Once again because "there are also others, an infinite number of them, the innumerable generality of others to whom I should be bound by the same responsibility, a general and universal responsibility (what Kierkegaard calls the ethical order). I cannot respond to the call, the request, the obligation, or even the love of another without sacrificing the other, the other others" (*GD*, 68). If in offering Isaac Abraham yields an irreplaceable life, then in the moment of staying the hand that would kill his son he does not avoid sacrificing. His hand nonetheless descends, and not only upon the throat of the ram; it falls as well, invisibly and inaudibly, upon all the throats of all the others he sacrifices to his son and to himself in his devotion to his son. "As soon as I enter into a relation with the other . . . I know that I can respond only by sacrificing ethics, that is, by sacrificing whatever obliges me to also respond, in the same way, in the same instant, to all the others. I offer a gift of death, I betray, I don't need to raise my knife over my son on Mount Moriah for that. Day and night, at every instant, on all the Mount Moriahs of this world, I am doing that, raising my knife over what I love and must love, over those to whom I owe absolute fidelity, incommensurably" (*GD*, 68).

Within the Western world's deconstructive counter-tradition, God's call to Abraham attempts to measure the immeasurability of this bind. The predicament is that "Je ne peux repondre a l'un (ou a l'Un), c'est-a-dire a l'autre qu'en lui sacrifiant l'autre." In David Wills' translation of Derrida's French: "I can respond only to the one (or to the One), that is, to the other, by sacrificing that one to the other" (*GD*, 70). Derek Attridge believes Wills "gets it the wrong way round," reversing the direct and indirect objects of the subject's sacrificial act, and so he offers this "paraphrase": "I can respond to the one (or to the One), that is, to the other, only by sacrificing the other—the other other—to it."[13] Who or what sacrifices, who or what is sacrificed, and to whom or what? In either case it is the one or the other—the one as other and as one of the other others. Both translations of Derrida are correct: before sacrifice can be divided into subject and object, the sacrificer and the sacrificed, there is—sacrifice. Why the dash after the ontological predicate? In order to indicate the sacrificial erasure that constitutes and destroys the condition of "isness," of the being that is purchased at the cost of (infanticidal) loss of being. Every individual being bears the trace of what it is not, of what is other to it, of the not-being that it both shares and cannot share with the other others. To be is to sacrifice, hence to be suffered for the non-being that one's existence imposes on others, on the world. It is also to be sacrificed in turn, to be the target, by design or not by design, of the sacrificiality that underwrites the other's existence.

What does this ethical bind mean for Abraham? According to Derrida's logic, Abraham is not asked to choose between faithfulness in his responsibilities toward his son and obedience toward his God. Rather,

Abraham is given the opportunity to recognize that fidelity toward either Isaac or God, each in his otherness, necessitates an infinite sacrifice of the other one as other, hence, of all the "other others." Isaac as well as the ram—indeed, all others, including God[14] —are already dead the moment Abraham answers the first call, in fact the moment Abraham is ready to answer the call should it occur. Regardless of its empirical interruption, the sacrifice—of the son, of the ram, of all the other others, of God—has already taken place. And yet there is no indictment of the father here. In question is not Abraham's particular motivation—whether or not he wants to kill his son or some surrogate victim. At issue is not the "psychology of any *psyche*," Derrida says in another context,[15] but rather the logical form of a responsibility, of an answerability, that is prior to every psychological determination.

The sacrifice takes place in principle even if it is avoided in fact. This nonempirical sacrificiality in the absence of an empirical sacrifice has an enormous interpretive consequence. If Isaac both dies (in principle) and lives (in fact), he does so not simply as Abraham's son but as other, as one of the other others, whom Abraham sacrifices when he devotes himself to his son and not to those who are not his sons. Isaac dies (in principle) and lives (in fact) as a personification of all the other others whose empirical lives and deaths will be affected—immediately, as is the case with Ishmael, or distantly, as is the case with nameless others—by Abraham's investment in the one and not in the other; more radically, Isaac dies and lives as a personification of all the other others who will never exist as a result of the untraceable opportunities that are foreclosed when anyone passes on a legacy to the one and not to the other.

That is why Abraham's testing must follow his exile of Ishmael, the child whose name means "God hears." When Ishmael cries in the wilderness, God, not Abraham, hears. However, he hears Ishmael in two different ways. He hears the wailing of the empirical child—the child who, along with his mother, will die of thirst unless someone intervenes. What are readers to hear when Abraham hears God hearing? To hear the other (the wholly other, God) answering the inarticulate crying of the child (also other) is to behold, through the imagined omniscience of the wholly other the infanticidal jeopardy that is, might be, and will have been happening but that is otherwise inapprehensible. Part of Abraham's test, then, is to "hear" what God hears—the Ishmael whom Abraham has repudiated, but also all the other Ishmaels he cannot hear, all the other Ishmaels he has indirectly, accidentally, or involuntarily repudiated. In other words, it is to "hear" God hearing in the crying out of the empirical child all the cries that have gone unheard, including all the "cries" of those who will never have come into existence. In this regard it is to "hear" the infinite infanticidity that God hears.

God hears in the cries of those who are on the verge of losing their existence not only their imperilment but the loss of all the other existences that have been foreclosed in order for this particular world, this particular people, this particular person to come to pass. In being called by a God who responds to an infanticidity without limit, Abraham comes to apprehend that, whenever he answers the summons of the other in the name of his faith, he cannot not sacrifice. Abraham's challenge is to grasp Isaac as other, even wholly other, which is to say to apprehend the sacrifice he makes of other children as a consequence of fidelity to his own, here his only beloved son. It is, then, to love Isaac as other. For this reason Abraham's "reward" is not merely the return of "his" son, not merely the safeguarding of his paternity, and not merely a symbolic paternity, but "the gate of the enemy"—that is, the necessity of living in relation to the enemy other, whose existence makes explicit the sacrificial context of all survival.

"THE GATE OF THE ENEMY"

Abraham is rewarded with a "vision" of his "descendants" [zera', seed or semen; *HGSB*,1610] who, according to a metaphor that is both military and sexual, "shall possess the gate of their enemies" (22:17). To possess the gate is to conquer the enemy—to kill or enslave the enemy man, for example, and to seize the enemy woman, appropriating her reproductivity.

But why in the course of unfolding the future perfect moment of Abraham's triumph does the text employ this particular trope, especially if to have an enemy is to be an enemy? In relation to the specter of reciprocal enmity, the evocation of enemies is not to designate antagonists who are to be defeated, for such a prospect would threaten not a future blessing but the eventual return of violence against Abraham's people according to the principle, announced over and over in the story of Cain and his descendants, of vengeance avenged. Rather, the evocation of enemies is to designate others, the most alien and threatening others whose otherness is to be recognized as blessed: "by your descendants shall all the nations of the earth bless themselves, because you have obeyed my voice" (22:18). God's promise of a universal blessing is to announce something on the order of a universal reciprocal dependency of all people. In relation to this promise, to possess the single gate is not to crush the multiple enemies into submission. It is to stand at the threshold to their homes, to the house of their being, welcomed as blessed into their blessedness. And yet such reception cannot be given or received except sacrificially. The gate denotes the inevitable exclusion that occurs whenever the one is admitted and not the others, including all those who are never able to arrive, those whom the gatekeeper will never be able to greet.

The passage to the blessing of all the other "nations of the earth" is through this gate, which at the end of the *akedah* becomes the architectural counterpart to the circumcisional "opening" that signals a God-ensured reproductivity, which is to say a God-protected future.[16] How does Abraham's sacrificial obedience to God effect the generative passage, how does it open the gate, to this temporal horizon? It does so by compelling the father, who would love his son, to recognize within every blessing the face of the other caught in the same sacrificial bind that Abraham is—the face of the other as beloved but also as enemy, the beloved enemy. Abraham must behold and affirm in this face the divinity of the other. He must say yes, *ja*, to the neighbor who is, Derrida avers, just "as . . . transcendent as *Jaweh*": "God, as the wholly other, is to be found everywhere there is something of the wholly other. And since each of us, everyone else, each other is infinitely other in its absolute singularity . . . then what can be said about Abraham's relation to God can be said about my relation without relation to *every other (one) as every (bit) other [tout autre comme tout autre]*, in particular my relation to my neighbor or my loved ones who are as inaccessible to me, as secret and transcendent as Jahweh" (*GD*, 78). So, too, is my enemy as inaccessible, secret, and transcendent. The otherness as such even of one's enemy, an otherness that resides in this person's identity as another singular being, is an otherness that belongs to God as the wholly other. God's otherness thus announces both the otherness of everyone in their otherness and the above-cited "infinite sacrifice" that Derrida discovers is attendant upon every effort to respond to the otherness of others as well as of oneself. "I can respond only to the one . . . that is, to the other, by sacrificing that one to the other"; alternatively, I can respond to the one "only by sacrificing the other—the other other—to it."[17] One way or another there will be sacrifice.

> I am responsible to any one (that is to say to any other) only by failing in my responsibilities to all the others, to the ethical or political generality. And I can never justify this sacrifice, I must always hold my peace about it. Whether I want to or not, I can never justify the fact that I prefer or sacrifice any one (any other) to the other. . . . What binds me to singularities, to this one or that one, male or female, rather than that one or this one, remains finally unjustifiable (this is Abraham's hyper-ethical sacrifice), as unjustifiable as the infinite sacrifice I make at each moment. (*GD*, 70–71)

There is no non-sacrificial position available; there is nothing outside of sacrifice: "At the instant of every decision and through the relation to *every other (one) as every (bit) other,* every one else asks us at every moment to behave like knights of faith" (*GD*, 78–79). To behave like such a knight is to de*cide,* which is to engage in a *-cidal*—an infanticidal—cut. "At the instant of every decision," one cannot not sacrifice. Every singular act of responsibility bears the trace of all the other singular acts that the performance of this particular one requires be abandoned. One cannot work on behalf of one's own without withdrawing one's labor from the behalf of those not one's own. One must and yet one cannot love one's neighbor as oneself. In general one cannot act in the name of without sacrificing the other names in which one can and should act. Not even a universal name would solve the problem, for to act in the name of the all-encompassing name would be to sacrifice the individual name—indeed, the infinite number of individual names. "And this name which must always be singular is here none other than the name of God as completely other, the nameless name of God, the unpronounceable name of God as other to which I am bound by an absolute, unconditional obligation, by an incomparable, nonnegotiable duty" (*GD*, 67). This duty cannot, finally, be rationalized. "There is no language, no reason, no generality or mediation to justify this ultimate responsibility which leads me to absolute sacrifice; absolute sacrifice that is not the sacrifice of irresponsibility on the altar of responsibility, but the sacrifice of the most imperative duty (that which binds me to the other as a singularity in general) in favor of another absolutely imperative duty binding me to every other."[18] In consequence, "Isaac's sacrifice continues every day" for "this land of Moriah . . . is our habitat every second of every day" (*GD*, 71, 70, and 69).

"Every second of every day" and "Moriah, our habitat" are no ordinary tropes. On the one hand they function as metonymies, representing the specific time and place—the four dimensional coordinates—of each and every empirical sacrifice, each and every literal infanticide. On the other hand they also operate as figures, for which there is no name, of the nonempirical "location" of the infanticidism that afflicts the spatio-temporality of all living things and their evolution. What is more, "every second of every day" simultaneously universalizes and particularizes the time of human sacrifice, "just as Moriah, our habitat" simultaneously particularizes and universalizes the site where such infanticidal violence comes to pass. Time becomes space and space becomes time—not through the empirical infanticide of the dearly beloved son Isaac, which never occurs as such, but through the infanticidality to which his contravened sacrifice points. The two figures—"every second of every day" and "Moriah, our habitat"—attempt to indicate the infanticidality that is neither universal nor particular but the condition of both.

As the Smoke Rises

The *akedah* acts out this recognition in its imagery of verticality within which the movements of ascent and descent, of rising and falling, of living and dying, occur the one within the other. Through the motif of verticality, each of the narrative actions repeats the *akedah*'s overarching infanticidal predication.

In addition to meaning "the father of multitudes," Abraham's name is suggestive of upward movement. As has been noted, *Abraham* derives from *'âb*, father, and *râ'mâh*, sacred height or elevation, and perhaps also from *'abr*, to fly up or soar. *Abraham* thus means literally that "the father is high" and metaphorically that "the father is exalted."[19] The narrative underscores both meanings when it ends with the sacred blessing that exalts the first patriarch, elevating him from the biological father (of one) to the position of the political father (of innumerable many). Abraham's name, and the generativity with which it is associated, thus signifies the very meaning of being itself, the Hebrew word for which, *kiyyum*, means "to rise up (*la-koom*), to be tall (*koma zekufa*) in the presence of God."[20] Insofar as the letter *h* (by which Abram becomes Abraham) links the patriarch's name to the name of God (Y*H*WH),[21] it further reinforces this meaning.

The *akedah*'s imagery of verticality, however, reveals the infanticidal implications of this meaning. The imagery of the blessing itself—the stars of heaven and the sand of the shore—establishes the endpoints of a vertical continuum between God and Abraham, the firmament and the ground, the heavens and the earth, and ultimately the hand upraised in obedience to God and the hand coming down to slit the throat if not of the son then of the animal that is substituted for the son. This vertical linkage commemorates the sacrificial violence that is inherent in Abraham's obedience to the will of God and that the patriarch's name translates: he who would be exalted, lifted up, granted standing in the presence of God, must raise a sacrificial hand according to an imperative that comes from the sacred itself. Interrupted as he is about to consummate the slaughter of Isaac, Abraham is captured in a tableau that for an instant freezes his upraised arm. In this moment the narrative transforms the slaughter of Isaac into its endless rehearsal; it memorializes in the threat here averted what in another world, another time, another future has already happened, is happening, or is about to happen.

Since what has happened, is happening, or will happen is the illimitable sacrificiality that pays for the sacrifice withheld here and now at this moment in this world, the narrative focus on Abraham's upraised arm explicates the meaning of his name, which for its part translates the meaning of God's call. Modeled upon and reflecting God's transcendental elevation, the name *Abraham* duplicates the infanticidism of God's call. Abraham's name thus dictates the obedience that guides the mortal father in moving—upward—toward the place of sacrifice where God will grant him the full scope of his generativity and its infanticidal cost. Every aspect of the narrative's movement inflects Abraham's ascent toward the sacrificial implications of his name, of his being, of his virility, of his leadership, of his nation-founding authority, and of its divine source.

Repeated either literally throughout the episode's course of events or inscribed symbolically in them, the movement of ascent defines the terms of Abraham's testing and punctuates his ritual preparations. God calls to the father who is high and instructs him to go to Mount Moriah, the place of sacred elevation, where he confronts the infanticidism of the world, the infanticidism that previous sacrificial practices would try to reduce to infanticide. Thus, he is instructed to ascend a mountain that overlooks Hinnom, which God condemns for the infanticide-evil that comes with the raising of sacrificial altars. The people of Judah, God warns through Jeremiah, "go on building the high place of Topheth . . . to burn their sons and daughters in the fire—which I did not command" (7:21). Again, they have "gone on building the high places of Baal to burn their children in the fire as burnt offerings . . . which I did not decree" (19:6). God here objects unequivocally to the very sacrifice that he calls Abraham to perform. He objects because the people of Judah are not prepared for Abraham's discovery that ritual sacrifice is abominable not only because it is an infanticide but because it conceals the (infanticidal) sacrificiality behind or within all acts. God repudiates Judean sacrifice because the people of Judah intend their practice to be a pure means of signifying the will of God. To the contrary, one can live in the name of God only on condition that one recognizes the infanticidism of all life, of the very creation, hence of God himself and his blessing. Rising above Hinnom and the altars erected to Baal and Molech (cf. Jeremiah 32:35), Moriah raises into view not only the sacrificial rites that have been carried out in the valley of infanticide, but the meaning of those rites as a paradoxical denial of what Abraham faces atop the mountain—the limitless infanticidity that the specific infanticide ritual seeks to control.

God's initial instruction to Abraham joins the act of ritual slaughter to the action of rising. Abraham is to seek out Mount Moriah and to "*offer* [Isaac] there as a *burnt offering* ['ôlāh, what goes up in smoke; *HGSB*, 1644]" (22:2). Grammatically, the verb ('*âlāh*) and object ('*ôlāh*) are reduplicative, deriving from the same root, '*âlāh*, to ascend, mount up, go up, rise, be led up, be offered, travel from a lower to a higher elevation, and so on (cf. *HGSB*, 1644). To offer up a victim as a burnt offering is to make it go up in smoke. The same terms are used a second time to describe the burnt offering Abraham makes of the ram instead of his son (22:13). Over and over the story's principal actions repeat in their spatial directionality the divine directive that elicits Abraham's obedience.

Having been called by God to his ritual task, Abraham "rose [*yâshkem*, from *shâkam; HGSB*, 116] early in the morning" to begin the acclivitous journey up Mount Moriah (22:3). Drawing on the relation between human consciousness, the action of standing up, and the condition of walking upright, the Hebrew verb *v'yashkem* means to be early to rise. Having arisen early in the morning, Abraham then "saddled his ass, and took two of his young men with him, and his son Isaac; and he cut the wood for the burnt offering, and arose [*yâshkem*] and went to the place of which God had told him" (22:3). The verb *yakam*, orthographically and semantically akin to *yâshkem* if etymologically distinct, derives from the root *qûun* and denotes the physical act of standing, rising, getting up, and by extension the taking place of an action or event. This same verb reappears at the end of the narrative, when "Abraham returned to his young men, and they arose [*yâshkem*] and went together to Beer-sheba" (22:19).

The two appearances of the verb echo the two appearances of the sacrificial predication, to offer up a burnt offering. As particular actions within the overall sacrificial sequence, the two instances of rising and going—first "to the place of which God had told him" and then to Beer-sheba—together act out the form and essence of the sacrifice that the one instance anticipates at the beginning of the narrative and the other recollects at the end. In other words, they function as metonymies for the complete ritual: call, departure, sacrificial preparation, holocaust averted, substitute sacrifice, and return. Abraham's double action of rising thus mirrors from within the sacrificial journey the entirety of the sacrificial process.

The verticality implicit in Abraham's initial response to God and then explicit in his preparations for the journey to and from Moriah orients all of his other actions. Approaching the mountains after three days, "Abraham *lifted up* [*yisa*] his eyes and saw the place from afar off" (22:4). Once again announcing the onset of the ritual sacrifice that has already begun, this same action will enable Abraham to discover the ram, which he then sacrifices in his son's stead: "And Abraham *lifted up* [*yisa*] his eyes and looked, and behold, behind him was a ram . . . and Abraham went and took the ram, and offered it up as a burnt offering instead of his son" (22:13). *Yisa*, from the root *nâsâ'*, means to carry, bear, lift, or raise; its use to characterize Abraham's act of looking upward to God repeats the action of carrying the fuel for the sacrificial fire.[22] The narrative does not say who bears the burden—father, son, servant, or pack animal. Regardless, the action anticipates the holocaust to come when, arriving at the place of sacred elevation, Abraham erects an altar upon which he places his son. At the climax of the drama, Abraham lifts his arm and knife-wielding hand before they are suddenly arrested by the call of the angel from heaven (22:11).[23] Having perhaps pricked up his ears, Abraham at this point "lifted up his eyes and looked" (22:13), an action suggestive of how, in the text's silence on the matter, he might have responded to God's initial call. In his omniscience, invisible to the human eye, God himself could be characterized as overseeing the entire scene from on high, the traditional location of the Jewish God. Although God inhibits Abraham from killing his son, God permits a substitute sacrifice. Thus, Abraham does not come down from the mountain until after he raises his arm one final time in order to lower it in the act of ritual slaughter. Even Abraham's return from Moriah, however, is framed in terms of the rising that initiates the sacrificial process: "So Abraham returned to his young men, and they *arose* and went together to Beer-sheba; and Abraham lived at Beer-sheba" (22:19). Abraham arose, and Abraham lived. If the conjunction transfers the meaning of "he lived" to its metonymical instance, "he arose," it also transfers the sacrificial meaning the *akedah* has encrypted in the action of rising to the entirety of Abraham's life and through him to the lives of everyone among "all the nations of the earth."

Over and over repeating its principal predication, the entire narrative spells out the sacrificiality that is embedded in the father's name: the father is he who sacrifices; more accurately, the father is he who recognizes the infanticidal sacrificiality of his actions at the very moment that he withholds his violence. In the *akedah*, the father who is held in high regard rises with the sun, ascending the mountain to an elevated and exalted place, a sacred site, where he begins to offer up to God the rising smoke of the holocaust, the burnt flesh of his son, but then destroys a substitute instead. The father who is highly esteemed raises his arm in infanticidal obedience before he can receive the blessing that exalts him. Through God's directive to the father to sacrifice his child and give up his reproductivity, the narrative forces the name *Abraham* to speak its infanticidal meaning. Abraham the particular historical individual may or may not be infanticidal in the sense of harboring violent impulses toward his second son. But because existence costs, Abraham cannot avoid being infanticidal. His infanticidality does not belong to him as a personal attribute, it inheres in existence in general. The narrative tries to say this through the root meaning of Abraham's name—father. It endeavors to specify how being alive—particularized throughout Genesis in terms of being a father, being a begetter of new life—means being implicated in the infanticidality of existence.

At the outset of the narrative God names both a person and a name. The rest of the narrative impels "Abraham," the person and the name, to take on the infanticidality of the divine call in response to which the father affirms his existence. "Here am I," Abraham declares three times—

to God, who calls out "Abraham!" (22:1), then to Isaac, who calls out "Father!" (22:7), and yet again to God through God's angel, who calls out "Abraham, Abraham!" (22:11). Answering the first address, Abraham responds to his God-acknowledged name; answering the next address, Abraham responds to his child-acknowledged role; answering the angel, he responds once again to his God-acknowledged name, doubly invoked as if to underscore the convergence of the previous two calls, as if to indicate the identity of God and child, the voice of the one and of the other. For Abraham, to be is to be *Abraham,* a father who has no choice but to accept the consequences of the reproductive success that establishes his paternity—namely an infinite loss, an infinite sacrifice, which transpires even when the ritual slaughter is diverted from child to animal.

According to the Talmud, "No man stands on [i.e., can rightly understand] the words of Torah, unless he has stumbled over them."[24] As Zornberg explains, "To discover firm standing ground, it is necessary to explore, to stumble, even to fall, certainly to survive the chaotic vibrations of a world that refuses to *be.*"[25] This "refusal to be" represents the world's rejection of the infanticidal cost of existence. "The price to be paid for a *tzaddik*—a righteous man—is creation," Zornberg comments in explicating Rashi's question of God: "Why create man at all, why create a problem?"[26] The price to be paid for the one is equivalent to the creation—the sum of all that is other to this one. That is why the *akedah* endeavors to enable its readers to hear in Abraham's response to God, "Here am I," the unvoiced infanticidality within the ontological predication "I am." Abraham perceives this infanticidism—the infanticidism of his own existence, of his ability to stand upright and say "I am here"—and therefore it is to him that God entrusts responsibility for the universal blessing. The enigma of this blessing, however, is that it embodies the father's generativity only by virtue of the infanticidism that makes this embodiment possible. For this reason God gives his blessing to one who becomes an Abraham, a father of a people, and who lives out the meaning of his name only by working through the temptation of infanticide to an intimation of the infanticidal.

III

Counter-conceiving the Symbolic Order — Infanticide and the Name of the Father

6
Counter-conceiving the Law of the Father

Metaphor, from the Greek *meta* + *pherein,* to carry, bring forth, bear, beget.
Concept, from the Latin *conceptum,* something conceived, from *concipere,* conceive.
— Adapted from *The Oxford Dictionary of English Etymology*

. . . a contradictory conception, a thwarted conception, or a contraception . . . .
— Jacques Derrida, "Hostipitality" (359)

. . . it seems necessary here to . . . recognize what I have elsewhere proposed to call . . . the "metaphoric catastrophe" . . . .
— Jacques Derrida, "Des Tours de Babel" (113)

Now all these tales [from Greek and German myth] are inspired by the same preoccupation. Cronos and Tantalus are fathers intent on destroying their offspring. The wicked queen, the hag, the giant and the giantess too are adults who try to destroy children, but in the end are destroyed by them. The common theme is generational conflict, between those who at present hold power and those who are destined to inherit it. And the means by which the adults try to retain power is, precisely, cannibalistic infanticide.
— Norman Cohn. *Europe's Inner Demons* (260).

INTERPELLATION AND THE INFANTICIDISM OF THE SYMBOLIC ORDER

THE *AKEDAH* BEGINS WHEN GOD CALLS ABRAHAM. IT CONTINUES when Abraham directs his servants and son to undertake a journey with him — that is, when he calls them in turn. It ends when the angel calls Abraham not to sacrifice his son after all. Three times over the storyline is punctuated by a call. The narrative itself — the telling of the story — produces a fourth call, one that asks its readers to hear the sequence of hailings as the same hailing, as the call that simultaneously includes a vision of blessing and a vision of this blessing's infanticidal loss — the loss

165

that might have occurred, and thereby the unimaginable losses of all that in effect goes up in smoke because of what does not go up in smoke. The narrative, then, announces what cannot be announced—what cannot be made present, what cannot come to pass—in what is announced as the future that will be realized. In a sense, it signals that there is something to be apprehended that cannot be directly represented in concepts.

In his famous disquisition on how humans are "interpellated" into being, Louis Althusser reformulates this basic apprehension when he all but identifies the cost, the violence, and finally the infanticidal implication of just the kind of hailing that occurs in the *akedah*. This is the hailing that produces a genealogy and through it one future rather than another, indeed one world rather than any other world. In explaining the structure of this hailing, Althusser has recourse to the reproductive example of the child conceived but not yet born. Because the child-to-be is *subjected to* the hopes, fears, and other desires of its parents, this child-to-come "is always-already a subject, even before he is born."[1] By virtue of being expected, the gestating child is hailed or "interpellated" into or inscribed within a network of relations governed by the symbolic order. "Everyone knows how much and in what way an unborn child is expected," Althusser notes. They often take for granted, for example, that the child "will bear its Father's Name, and will therefore have an identity and be irreplaceable. Before its birth, the child is therefore always-already a subject, appointed as a subject in and by the specific familial ideological configuration in which it is 'expected' once it has been conceived."[2] These expectations, which may begin not only before the child is conceived but even if the child is not, are forms of address by which the subject is welcomed into the world.

Clearly, however, a child can be ushered out of the world not only before it is born but before it is conceived. It can be hailed into being or just as easily hailed out of being. If Althusser considers the decision to bear a child to term as a form of address to the future child, the decision not to complete a pregnancy and even earlier a decision not to conceive must also constitute an address to the child—not a child-to-be but a child who might have been. Rather than leading to the conception and birth of this child, the counter-conceptive decision abolishes the (future) subject even before this subject has begun to materialize, to be incarnated in a body.

It does not, however, abolish the subject-ness of this (non-existing) child (who will never be). Since a subject is always addressed before it exists, since being subjected to interpellation is the condition of the possibility of coming into existence, then being *subject to* is independent of being born. In other words, the example of a negative, life-withdrawing, or contraceptive interpellation demonstrates that the *subjectivity* of a person is a contingent and not a necessary feature of *subject-ness* (which does not depend on the life of the subject). Before the subject is a person, it is a subject-to-be or not-to-be. In other words, there is subjection, which is either into life or into not-existence, before there is a living subject; *subjection to* must precede the life or death of any individual.[3] We are not subjects because we are conceived and born; we are conceived (or not) and born (or not) because we are subjected to an address by the other, an address that can, once again, subject us to life or to non-existence. In order for there to be being, there must be "subjection"— a being subjected to—which may or may not eventuate in the subject's biological conception and birth and entry into an embodied existence as a living person.

What Althusser explains about interpellation and subjection applies more generally to the symbolic order—the sum of the signifying processes that mediate the affective, cognitive, and behavioral life of the person already born or yet to be. Every child comes into a particular world— a particular society at a particular time in history. In other words, every person comes into a world as this world is constituted by and inscribed in the symbolic order. If one understands God as the source of the symbolic order, as the guarantor of the system within which humans must make decisions that are intrinsically sacrificial; and if, as the *akedah* and other Genesis narratives indicate, God bestows life only against the backdrop of a universal infanticidism; then the symbolic order is inseparable from the infanticidal, and so too is the life of each person, whose conception and birth the symbolic order mediates.

In this regard all humans are descendants of Cain. Having killed his brother, Cain bears a "mark" or "token" (the Hebrew word for which is the same *'ôwth* that names the mark of circumcision, but the physical appearance of which remains unspecified in Genesis 4:15). This sign both condemns him as a murderer and protects him from being murdered in turn; it blesses him with freedom from the very aggression he has directed against his brother. By virtue of the sign God places over Cain's being, Cain lives as a witness to the fact that the gift of life is, in Derrida's terms, a gift of death. In his person he embodies the message that there can be no pure blessing, no pure birthright, that there can be no life that does not entail the sacrifice of other life, and that whatever blessing can come to pass must be measured against the lost futures which, by definition, are beyond imagination. In short, he incarnates twice over the divided nature of all hailing: the hailing by which a (potential) subject is interpellated either into or out of existence; and the hailing by which each living person nevertheless bears the trace of the other life or lives that might have been interpellated into being if this person had not.

Cain has a mark but it is undescribed.[4] Because this strange marking is to indicate the paradox that the gift of life is the gift of death, the marking is equivalent to Cain's very person. But this is the case with anyone.

Every person is born not only with the mark of Cain but, according to the logic of interpellation, as the mark of Cain, as what exists only by virtue of the (infanticidal) cost of any person's existence. The nonempirical *'ôwth* of Cain anticipates the empirical *'ôwth* of the circumcision. As has been indicated in chapter 2, both marks specify the infanticidism within all reproductivity. Both marks hail the arrival of someone whose life attests to the existential cost inherent in all reproductive success, a cost the starkest form of which is infanticide. More importantly, both inscriptions announce what cannot be represented as such—namely, the infanticidism that is the interpellative horizon (theological and evolutionary alike) of human existence. In the form of either the undescribed mark over Cain or the cut of circumcision, the symbol-driven process of being named, addressed, called, or interpellated into being retains an explicit, evocative allusion to the infanticidal cost of coming into existence.

Throughout its history, the Western world has endeavored to escape this economy. To this end it has endeavored to think its way toward a cost-free mode of being. It has attempted to discover in thought itself a means of apprehending the world that would not participate in but transcend the world's infanticidism. It has striven, in short, to discern in thought a principle of absolute generativity, and in the symbolic order a medium for translating thought's life-begetting power into communicative, expressive, and other symbolic form. In this effort Western culture has undertaken to produce and reproduce itself in its own image and in consequence to generate an archive of itself—indeed, what Derrida calls a "patriarchive,"[5] an ontotheological record of its putative self-begetting. Western culture has carried out this project as a praxis of "consignation," a "gathering together" of signs "in a system or a synchrony in which all the elements articulate the unity of an ideal configuration." This unity would seem to protect the archive of Western conceptuality from destruction, for "in an archive, there should not be any absolute dissociation, any heterogeneity or *secret* which could separate (*scernere*), or partition, in an absolute manner."[6]

However, the infanticidism that makes life possible—which is to say that makes life impossible as pure life, that cuts off endless potentialities of life in the making of any and every life, that thereby inscribes the living in a process of an infinite deathliness—does just that. It divides the patriarchive from within. By registering the fact that the lost futures—the lost possibilities of life, the potential lives lost in the life that comes to pass—cannot be registered, let alone mourned and laid to rest, the infanticidity of being haunts the archive of Western conceptuality, which has repressed those modes of thinking that do not posit thought as conceptive in general and paternally conceptive in particular. That repression occurs at the outset of the philosophical tradition and is evident in the work of Plato and Aristotle.

THOUGHT AS (PATERNAL) GENERATIVITY: PLATO

In *Metaphors We Live By*, George Lakoff and Mark Johnson observe that "metaphor is pervasive in everyday life, not just in language but in thought and action. Our ordinary conceptual system, in terms of which we both think and act, is fundamentally metaphorical in nature."[7] As they underscore in propounding the theme of their title, we conceive of things in terms of metaphor and then act—live—according to these conceptions.[8] If so, however, then the idea of "conceptual system" too would be metaphorical, as would the concept of conceptuality. The very concept of concept would be metaphorical through and through, as Derrida has elucidated throughout his work. In "White Mythology," for example, Derrida examines how philosophy's "'founding' concepts" have been developed and articulated in terms of certain "'archaic' tropes."[9] One of the most pervasive and least analyzed of these arche-tropes is the metaphor, literalized centuries ago, of (thought as) conception, a trope that likens (self-reflexive) acts of consciousness to (heterosexual) acts of reproduction.[10]

The analogy between thinking and conceiving is such a commonplace that its underlying metaphorical character has been forgotten. As Page duBois has demonstrated in her analysis of "The Platonic Appropriation of Reproduction," at the outset of the philosophical tradition Plato propounds and Aristotle literalizes the analogy.[11] How they do so is crucial to understanding the cultural work this metaphor continues to perform. The work is ideological—it rationalizes the sacrificial and ultimately infanticidal consequences of a society's responses to the Darwinian exigencies of existence. Insofar as culture answers to the infanticidity of the (evolutionary) world, and specifically to the infanticidity of reproduction, the literalized metaphor of thought as conception helps promote a view of the mind as quintessentially life-promoting. The literalized metaphor thereby becomes a means of refusing the infanticidal as a constitutive feature of thought itself.

Plato's *Phaedrus* provides a first step in the construction of thinking as conceiving. There, Plato explicitly opposes the love of knowledge to the carnal passions of the person who has not been "initiated" into philosophical reflection. This person "does not quickly make the transition from beauty on earth to absolute beauty; so when he sees its namesake here he feels no reverence for it, but surrenders himself to sensuality and is eager like a four-footed beast to mate and beget children."[12] In being released from such reproductive "eagerness," the philosophically initiated is freed to participate in another kind of intercourse the conceptual generativity of which infinitely surpasses the biological. Socrates establishes the fructifying power of thought by suggesting that "the man with real knowledge of right and beauty and good will treat what we may by analogy call his seed [*sperma*]" by "plant[ing] and sow[ing]" in a "suitable soul" "truths accompanied by knowledge." The result is that "such truths . . . are not sterile, but contain a seed from which fresh truths spring up in other minds; in this way they secure immortality for it."[13] Here, the philosopher's metaphorical virility imparts to him epistemological rather than reproductive generativity.

In order for the virility of the mind to be transcendent, however, Socrates must attribute to it both the power to beget new life and a corresponding power to destroy the life of which it is the source. On the one hand, then, Socrates invokes the sacredness of the "midwife's art" as a model of the still greater divinity of thought. The art of the midwife is, he says, "a gift from heaven; my mother had it for women, and I for young men of a generous spirit and for all in whom beauty dwells." Blessed by this heaven-sent donation, Socrates becomes the spiritual midwife who presides over the self-gestation of one who would "know himself" and be philosophically reborn. As he asks of Theaetetus: "Are we in labor, then, with any further child, my friend, or have we brought to birth all we have to say about knowledge?" Theaetetus agrees that the birthing is complete.[14]

The parturition in question, however, is infanticidal, for on the other hand, Socrates must attribute to thought the power to clear away what is either lifeless or "not worth the rearing" because untrue:

> *Theaetetus.* . . . I have already, thanks to you, given utterance to more than I had in me.
> *Socrates.* All of which our midwife's skill pronounces to be mere wind eggs and not worth the rearing?
> *Theaetetus.* Undoubtedly.
> *Socrates.* Then supposing you should ever henceforth try to conceive afresh, Theaetetus, if you succeed, your embryo thoughts will be the better as a consequence of today's scrutiny, and if you remain barren, you will be gentler and more agreeable to your companions, having the good sense not to fancy you know what you do not know. For that, and no more, is all that my art can effect. . . .[15]

Here, Socrates inverts the terms of the analogy between physical and mental conception. Physical reproduction is a debased form of mental reproduction and produces a less viable form of life than does the seeding (spermatic) activity of the mind. At this point Socrates must exclude the physical reproductivity that is the very basis on which he conceives of the mind's generativity. He does so by means of his dialectic, which effects a metaphorical infanticide of false thought in the name of the true thought that is a higher form of life. If this life transcends the weak, inferior, pseudo-life of "mere wind eggs," all the more does it transcend the life of the body. In this way Socrates tacitly refigures the body's reproductivity as analogous to the mind's. The body's generativity is no longer literal but metaphorical, and the mind's no longer metaphorical but literal.

In other words, when Socrates adverts to infanticide as a way of positing the mind as self-begetting, he enacts an inaugural version of the "conceptual" moves by which Western thinking paternalizes and transcendentalizes the symbolic order. In the process, he reduces infanticidality to infanticide, the power of which he vests in the authority of the philosopher, whose negative dialectic he nevertheless interprets as an affirmation of life. First, he employs his dialectic in the paradoxical name of "conceiving afresh" or remaining intellectually "barren," but in either case of nurturing those "embryonic thoughts" that are better off destroyed. Second, he evokes the analogy between abandoning newborns to death and giving up false notions in order both to shatter the sophist's pretensions to a merely positive, non-dialectical knowledge and to assert the potency of his meta-knowledge, his knowledge about the limits of knowledge, what Theaetetus "does not know." Third, at this point he introduces a metaphorical infanticide as the very figure of his dialectic. Fourth, he immediately converts this figurative destruction into a transcendent generativity, since if the philosopher is willing to undertake an infanticidal questioning of what he thinks he knows, an infanticidal clearing away of what he does not know, he has a chance of achieving an intuition of the Forms (the true, the good, the beautiful, the just, the eternal—in short, that which is, Being itself).

No wonder, then, that Socrates listens attentively when Diotima tells him, "All men are pregnant [kuousi]."[16] Shortly thereafter she urges Socrates to consider how "those whose procreancy is of the body turn to woman as the object of their love, and raise a family. . . . But those whose procreancy is of the spirit rather than of the flesh . . . conceive and bear the things of the spirit."[17] The medium of this transcendental conception is philosophical friendship: those bound in such amity "will help each other rear the issue of their friendship—and so the bond between them will be more binding, and their communion even more complete, than that which comes of bringing children up, because they have created something lovelier and less mortal than human seed."[18] Although the philosopher appears to mime the woman as mother, in fact he achieves through philosophical reflection a generativity infinitely greater than that of sexual reproduction.

Having ascertained the life-begetting power of thought, Plato then codifies this thinking in the form of a law that would ensure the reproductivity of sexual intercourse—specifically, that would prevent it from being followed by infanticide. This is the law "of restricting procreative intercourse to its natural function by abstention from congress with our own sex, with its deliberate murder of the race and its wasting of the seed of life on a stony and rocky soil, where it will never take root and bear its natural fruit, and equal abstention from any female field whence you would desire no harvest."[19]

Such a law results in "untold good":

> Once suppose this law perpetual and effective—let it be, as it ought to be, no less effective in the remaining cases than it actually is against incest with parents—and the result will be untold good. It is dictated, to begin with, by nature's own voice, leads to the suppression of the mad frenzy of sex, as well as marriage breach of all kinds, and all manner of excess in meats and drinks, and wins men to the affection of their wedded wives. There are also numerous other blessings which will follow, if one can only compass the establishment of such a law.[20]

Plato "supposes" that "nature's own voice" unifies the ought and the is, and that it does so by "dictating" the law that rectifies any deviation from the "natural function" of "procreative intercourse." The result is that Plato here joins the Logos, incarnate as the (paternal) "seed of life," to *nomos*, to the normativity of the law. In consequence, he determines the law as self-producing: the law establishes itself as the pure (reproductive) generativity that it guarantees.

In other words, he invests the value of thought with a pure generativity based on its analogy to the lesser generativity of procreation. He then institutionalizes this value of thought as a law that safeguards the "natural" procreativity of sex. That is, to understand understanding, he has recourse to a figure of speech that makes thought appear to be purely conceptive. The difficulty is that the figure of speech is based on a biological act that can always be counter-conceptive. He must guard against infanticide in the biological sphere to make sure his conception of thought as conceptive holds true.

The paternal nature of the law protects the "seed of life" from ruining itself in nonreproductive "frenzies" in particular and in marital "breaches" as well as other "excesses" more generally. As Derrida has demonstrated, this paternal function of the symbolic order, which Plato interprets in logos-centered terms, is to protect against the effects of the *pharmakon* (either a disease-remedying medicine or a poisonous drug) "which can *equally well* serve the seed of life and the seed of death, childbirth and abortion," Derrida writes.[21] As Socrates acknowledges, "with the drugs (*pharmakia*) and incantations they administer, midwives can either bring on the pains of labor or allay them at their will, make a difficult labor easy, and at an early stage cause a miscarriage if they so decide."[22] In its contradictory potency, the *pharmakon* can either facilitate birth or destroy it.

The *pharmakon* thus overlaps with what this study calls infanticidality, the general infanticidism the effects of which can be expressed more directly (in infanticide, for example) or more indirectly (in the conception and birth of a new life). There is no outside-the-text, Derrida writes. But "text" does not mean the empirical forms of written language. It means, among other things, the deathliness that is within, and not simply opposed by, the conceptive; hence, too, it means the generativity of the contraceptive. For this reason there can be no outside-the-*pharmakon* (no outside-the-remedy-that-is-simultaneously-poisonous), no outside-the-infanticidal.

THOUGHT AS (PATERNAL) GENERATIVITY: ARISTOTLE

When Aristotle systematizes his logical procedures, however, he posits precisely such an outside, which he locates in the paternal generativity of thought. As Robert Con Davis has demonstrated, Aristotle founds reason on "the nature of being male and the male ability to father." In his detailed examination of "Aristotle and the Gendered Subject," Davis shows how Aristotle superimposes the opposition between male and female on the opposition of form (*eidos*) and matter. Once he determines form to be essentially male, he then "silently institutes that notion of form in his canons of logic."[23]

Aristotle begins by opposing form, which imparts a teleological development to living things, to mere matter. He then identifies the soul as the form of the body. And finally he locates the heart of the "principle of form" — that which "is able to act thus in itself or in something else" — in the male seed, in *sperma*. Since it is the male body, Aristotle says, that "is able to concoct, to cause to take shape, and to discharge, semen possessing the 'principle' of the 'form,'"[24] *eidos* becomes, in Davis' words, "a natural and intrinsic expression of maleness."[25] Indeed, maleness forms the very principle of form insofar as *sperma* "causes [it] to take shape."[26] Maleness thereby informs that which informs every substance. Since maleness is one of these substances, it informs itself. The result is that form is a necessarily self-informing feature of maleness. In consequence, if "the logos of the movement"[27] of gestational growth is "derived from . . . the male 'principle,'"[28] and if this self-informing principle informs every substance, then "the generative parent" not only is but has to be male."[29] Case closed.[30]

When Aristotle puts forward the logical foundation of his epistemology, he affirms its metaphysical nature as the source of (masculine) form, for "it is according to the form that we know all things."[31] However, according to Davis his logic is also the consequence of this very form: logic and form engender each other in a self-generating spermatic circularity. How it is involves the technical details of the logical procedures Aristotle develops for answering the questions: What is the essence of some entity? What kind of thing is it? What is the nature of its substance (*ousia*)? The key to Aristotle's approach is to determine a proposition's deductive entailments—the "oppositional" propositions that can be logically derived from an initial (categorical) proposition.[32] For example, from the proposition, "all *eidos* is masculine and generative," can be deduced a "contrary" proposition, "no *eidos* is masculine and generative," a "contradictory" proposition, "some *eidos* is not masculine and generative," and a "subaltern" proposition, "some *eidos* is masculine and generative." In most of its applications this deductive procedure is unaffected by the content of the propositions it is used to examine. But when the initial categorical proposition concerns the self-reflexive principle of form itself, the character of form as masculine and generative transfers to Aristotle's logical procedure itself. How so?

Briefly, according to Aristotle: (1) as noted, things are knowable by their form; (2) insofar as *sperma* is the quintessential "motive principle" of form, form is male; (3) an argument must begin with "the first principles belonging to the particular subject";[33] and (4) "contraries are first principles of entities."[34] If so, then the principle of all first principles must necessarily be the generative principle of (male) form, which makes deductive knowledge possible. Once Aristotle affirms the truth of the above-listed four propositions, logic itself becomes spermatic. Form as masculine and generative, then, is not a particular subject of knowledge but the very condition of knowledge: the male principle grounds any and every act of knowing; it is the source of the very logic that validates its entailments.

At this point the relation between form (as masculine and generative) and logic (as masculine and generative) becomes circular or recursive, as Aristotle's argument about the nature of sexual difference evinces. The spermatogenic nature of form not only determines the maleness of the male, it also establishes the male as the source of sexual difference. Thus, rather than male and female being logically equal contraries, the male is endowed with an ontological fullness from which his ontologically subordinate contrary, the female, is derived. In other words, the contrary of maleness is no longer simply a matter of logic but of ontology. The ontological difference between the male and the female absorbs the logical difference (their relation of logical contrariety). Indeed, the "first principle" of (male) form absorbs not only the specific contrariety between male and female but contrariety as such, contrariety in general. The generative form of the male insinuates itself into the most basic formal constraint (the relation of contrariety) on thought. Logic itself—the logicality of logic, the logical foundations of the act of understanding—issues from the spermatic.

In consequence, the male is the superordinate subject, the (meta-) subject behind all other subjects of propositional discourse. Form as male and generative appropriates all propositions and inscribes them within a meta-propositional frame such that any universal affirmative proposition, All S is P, becomes "it is knowable, by virtue of the principle of (male) form, that all S is P." Translated into the first person, the linguistic *I* that knows "all S is P" is an *I* that takes on the nature of the male's generativity. Authorizing what can be known, the "male principle" transforms every proposition into the object of an act of a paternalized consciousness.[35]

THE PATERNAL FUNCTION GENERALIZED

Consciousness paternalized is perhaps the signal achievement of "patriarchy," of the cultural construction Davis calls "the paternal romance." In this master narrative, the concept of the father is not one concept among others but the very source and telos of conceptuality in general, including the concept of value. Not only does Aristotle place the father in the grammatically originary position of the first subject, he also establishes "a homology between the idea of a first position or foundation in logic and the ontological foundation of the 'good' in the world," for both "the 'good' and the *hupokeimenon*" are "logical representations of ontological and epistemological firstness."[36]

In this regard Aristotle follows Plato, for whom, Derrida writes, "the figure of the father . . . is also that of the good (*agathan*). Logos *represents* what it is indebted to: the father who is also chief, capital, and good(s). Or rather *the* chief, *the* capital, *the* good(s). *Patēr* in Greek means all that at once."[37] In other words, as the concept of value is paternalized, the figure of the father is transvalued. The result is that Plato writes of the double (productive and reproductive) generativity of the Good and its material economic manifestation as goods: the Good is able to generate "offspring," a "son" (*ekgonos*).[38] This "offspring" includes *tokos*, which includes progeny as well as monetary interest.[39] As Derrida remarks, the reproductivity of the pater guarantees all forms of social, political, economic—in sum, cultural—productivity: "Tokos, which is here associated with ekgonos, signifies production and the product, birth and the child, etc." *Tokos* "functions with this meaning in the domains of agriculture, of kinship relations, and of fiduciary operations."[40]

The source of this fabulous generativity is not available to the senses but only to the mind. In the following passage from the *Republic*, Plato likens this source to an invisible sun but then literalizes the analogy. In the process, the sun that can be seen becomes the "offspring" of its "father," the Good, which is the invisible sun that can be grasped only in thought:

"It was the sun, then, that I meant when I spoke of that offspring of the Good (*ton tou agathou ekgonon*), which the Good has created in its own image (*hon tagathon egennēsen analogon heautōi*), and which stands in the visible world in the same relation to vision and visible things as that which the good itself bears in the intelligible world to intelligence and to intelligible objects."[41] "The Good," Derrida concludes, "in the visible-invisible figure of the father, the sun, or capital, is the origin of all *onta*, responsible for their appearing and their coming into *logos*, which both assembles and distinguishes them." For this reason "the good (father, sun, capital) is thus the hidden illuminating, blinding source of *logos*," the animated and animating speech of the humankind.[42] As the Good, the father occupies the place of—he *is*—the transcendental signified, the thematic center and circumference of the paternal romance, that which imparts intelligibility to the world.[43] According to Derrida, in his being, the father poses and answers the question that launches Greek philosophy, the very question of being itself, "what is. . . ?" And this question, Derrida says, "is always, tautologically, the question 'what is the father?' and the reply 'the father is what is.'"[44] Since thinking is, in Plato and Aristotle, a paternal function, the result is a "fusion of Western reason with images and various cultural constructions of paternity" such that thought takes on the self-propagating characteristic of the paternalized sun's seminal being.[45]

When the Latin-speaking world translates the Greek philosophical vocabulary, the concept of conceptuality etymologically captures the generativity associated with biological conception and reinforces the literalization of thought as (paternally) self-engendering. What is more, it brings the entire range of what can be thought within the literalized metaphor of thinking as conceiving, as a force of life. That is, once the conceptive power of thinking has been literalized, thinking appears to be self-ontologizing; it seems to impart being to itself and to the world. In consequence, the concept of mental conception posits itself as equivalent to the begetting of new life. Insofar as thought is conceptive, then, it produces itself as a force of life—indeed, as the force of life that begets itself.

The idea that thought is conceptive is most clearly manifest in the conception of God as self-creating and, in consequence, the conception of thinking as God-like in being self-generating. Thus, regardless of how the Western conceptual system develops historically, once it names itself as conceptive, it is immediately manifest as its own source. Once the name "concept" arises, it is as if thought reaches back behind itself to produce its very advent and subsequent history. Thought as conception is thus no longer a consequence of some prior worldly condition but is the origin of all being, including its own. Thereafter, every concept as concept, regardless of its specific meaning, affirms the conceptive power of thinking.

The apparent self-genesis of thought, Derrida has shown, is the cornerstone of the "structured genealogy of philosophy's concepts." It is, for example, the basis of the traditionally conceived unity of being and *logos*, of ontology and speech, in the "auto-affective" experience of being present to oneself. "The experience of 'being,'" Derrida says in *Of Grammatology*, derives from the experience of seeming to be present to oneself, particularly in the moment of speaking.[46] As he explains in *Speech and Phenomena*, "When I speak, it belongs to the phenomenological essence of this operation that *I hear myself at the same time* that I speak," there seeming to be no delay, no interval or gap, between one's intentions and one's words, one's thought and one's means of expression.[47] "My words are 'alive' because they seem not to leave me; not to fall outside me, outside my breath, at a visible distance; not to cease to belong to me, to be at my disposition."[48] In the experience of hearing oneself speak, then, what one means to say appears to be transparently present, "immediately present," in the act of expressing this intention. "This immediate presence results from the fact that the phenomenological 'body' of the signifier seems to fade away at the very moment it is produced," as if the signifier, "animated by my breath and by the meaning-intention" that I want to express when I speak, were "in absolute proximity to me." Effaced of its "sensible body," the signifier appears to be drawn up into the meaning-intention, appears to become identical with the thought it signifies, appears to incarnate this thought's immediate presence to consciousness. "This effacement of the sensible body and its exteriority is *for consciousness* the very form of the immediate presence of the signified."[49] The experience of intending to say and simultaneously hearing and understanding what one intends to say constitutes thought's "auto-affection," which "is the unique experience of the signified *producing itself spontaneously*."[50] In other words, the experience of intending to say reinforces the etymological determination of the concept as living and even as self-begotten.

When Derrida writes of the "structured genealogy" of any concept—in fact, of conceptuality as a whole—he is identifying the foundational conceit of the concept's self-animation, the way it assimilates life and thought to one another in the self-production of the voice. Enlivening every concept, the voice bespeaks thought's self-conception, that which is "lived as the elementary undecomposable unity of the signified and the voice, of the concept and a transparent substance of expression."[51] With Plato and Aristotle, this voice is exclusively paternal.

INFANTICIDE AS CONSEQUENCE OF INFANTICIDITY REPRESSED

As a form of conception, thought appears to be the antithesis of that which injures, violates, or terminates life. By categorically locating this destructiveness outside of itself, conceptuality is able to represent its

operations as fundamentally life-giving or life-disclosing. For this reason conceptuality does not readily lend itself to formulating that which
within thought is not conceptive. To be sure, some philosophers have
characterized the inner force of thinking itself in terms of a disturbing
negativity. Wittgenstein, for example, alludes to philosophy "as a source
of 'deep disquietude,' of vague mental 'uneasiness,' 'mental cramps,'
and even 'torments,' and as an illness in need of cure"; and he wondered
"whether thinking should be considered the most vibrant expression or
the most profound depletion of the vitality of human condition."[52] Hannah Arendt suggests that philosophical thought is "unnatural" and "out
of order and notes that it has been described as "a kind of dying."[53] Such
remarks are more occasional than they are rigorous philosophical formulations. Even when the negativity to which they point is systematized,
however, the resulting perspective on the limits of knowing remains
bound to the metaphor of thought as conception. In *Against Method*, for
example, Paul Feyerabend lists "forms of life *and* thought" as a single
subject entry in his index, even though he repeatedly demonstrates these
"forms" to be "incompatible" or in "rivalry" with one another.[54]

However, if thinking arises only within the infanticidal, it can "conceive" of itself (as a "form of life") only at the risk of repressing that which
escapes the metaphorical reach of philosophy's conceptuality. A system
of thought that admitted its infanticidal condition of possibility would no
longer appear to itself as a form of generativity, as Wittgenstein alludes:
"My thoughts rarely come into the world unmutilated," he bemoans.
"Either some part of them gets twisted at birth or broken off. Or the
thought is a premature birth altogether and not yet viable in the language
of words. Then a small foetus of a sentence is born that still lacks the most
important limbs."[55] Unlike Wordsworth's intimations, which he associates with the image of the infant "trailing clouds of glory," Wittgenstein's
intuitions come to him as unviable fetuses, mutilated, twisted, broken.
Whereas he here characterizes thought as subject to an infanticidal threat,
elsewhere he insinuates that thought itself may have an infanticidal force.
When he evokes the image of a hatchling, it is in reference to "old"
thoughts, thoughts that must be discarded or supplanted. "It will be difficult to follow my presentation: because it says something new, but to
which still cling the egg-shells of the old." Again: "To this remark, as
to many others, cling the egg-shells of former views."[56]

A conceptuality that named its infanticidism would no longer "be"
what the metaphor of thought as conceptive suggests it "is." It would be
unable to situate the generative and the anti-generative, life and death,
conception and contraception, the care of children and infanticide in
simple oppositions. Confronted with the collapse of the difference between
the conceptive and the anti-conceptive, a conceptuality that accounted

for an infanticidality coinciding with the limits of the world—with the very "motion of thought and of the universe"[57]—would be opened up to the radical impurity of its categories.[58]

The contamination in question derives in part from the relational dependence of any category on the other categories from which it is differentiated. In its differential relation to what it is not, any single conceptual category bears the trace of what it is differentiated from. So, too, does any set of conceptual categories. Indeed, so, too, does the set of these sets—the entirety of conceptuality. Paradoxically, the conceptual order must include its other—the anti-conceptive, the inconceivable, the infanticidal—as what it cannot include, as what it excludes, as what is alien to and even inconceivable within the conceptual.

If the conceptual coincides with the thinkable, then insofar as the other is regarded as a concept, this concept must be thinkable. But this means that this otherness is not thinkable as radically other. This other otherness requires a different "thought." Within a system of thought that defines itself as a conceptuality, a different or radically "other" kind of "thought," a "thought" as non-, anti-, counter-, or contra-conceptive, cannot arise. If the conceptive were produced from out of its relation to what is counter-conceptive, then it would no longer be purely generative. In other words, thought as conceptive cannot "be" in relation to the counter-conceptive without succumbing to that which undermines its seeming production of itself from out of itself. From the point of view of thought as conception, there is no relation to something else that is exterior to conceptuality; to the contrary, all relationality appears to arise from within the conceptual order.

The infanticidal gives the lie to this (conceptive) understanding of the conceptual order. The infanticidal—not infanticide, but the logical necessity of inferring the effects or force of the infanticidal in the absence of infanticide—shadows the conceptual as its (inconceivable) trace or, once again, as what the conceptual order excludes but simultaneously includes as excluded. The Western world has tried to reduce this "exinclusion" to a simple exclusion. All such reductions repress the infanticidal at the cost of precipitating an infanticide crisis. Whenever the relational dependence of one category on another is reinterpreted as the one category's categorical mastery of otherness, there is a (violent, sacrificial, infanticidal) repression of the infanticidal and, sooner or later, its haunting return in the form of infanticide.

The concept of the father illustrates this infanticide-provoking feature of conceptuality. The concept of the father does not derive from some putative inner essence but from this figure's position in a structure of relationality mediated by acts of naming. A male becomes a father by virtue of a performative speech act, and that act may or may not be based on any supposed consanguineous relation between father and child. The father "is" father not by virtue of some ontological quality but because he is so denominated in a social context that authorizes the attribution of paternal status to him. If the denominating speech act conforms to the normative regulations governing it, then it is "felicitous," and the father "is" he who is so named. For this reason the "social father" is not necessarily the biological "genitor." To impregnate a woman may be sufficient, but it is not necessary, in order to be designated the child's father.

Even when the father is (recognized as) the sire, the purported establishment of his paternity always occurs in the context of some performative utterance of one kind or another—claims, attestations, wishes, blessings, curses, and so on—not on constative or fact-stating utterances. As Marc Shell observes, although it is a "commonplace . . . that kinship by consanguinity is primary, or real kinship," and although "[w]e like to think that consanguinity is easy to determine," in fact "nothing is harder than to make verifiable public assignations of biological parenthood. The possibility of being a bastard casts doubt on one's assigned father; the possibility of being a changeling casts doubt on both father and mother. Bastards and changelings indicate the indeterminability of biological parenthood; they suggest its fictional aspects.[59] Not even a DNA test can provide absolute but only relative assurance. The possibility of measurement mistakes and other forms of procedural error cannot be reduced to zero, and the possibility of communicative error in the relay of information cannot be eliminated. More fundamentally, the data in question must be "read," and no "reading" can be free from all contextuality. Not even the most empirically based assertions are entirely, exclusively empirical. The fact that males have a biological role in conception does not secure the empirical foundation for any individual male's paternity but merely provides a potential motif in the "figurative, fictive, artificial, and ritual" means by which a male becomes a father.[60] His paternity, like the family scene in which it is embedded, is a social construction.

A male becomes a father only in relation to a set of family relations that are logically independent of biology. A father is a father, a mother a mother, a son a son, a daughter a daughter not because each "is" such according to some ontological necessity, but because each has acquired that nomination in relation to a system of differentiation. A child is son or daughter only in relation to the father and mother; father and mother are such only in relation to the child.[61] Fathers and mothers never beget as fathers and mothers, and no son or daughter is ever begotten as son or daughter; to the contrary, the position of the child creates the position of the parent just as the position of the parent creates the position of the child. Parent and child reciprocally constitute and are constituted by one another, and that constitution constructs the family from out of a network of differential relations that have the same logical status.

Since no position can exist independently of the other positions, no position has an essential nature. Moreover, no position has ontological precedence. The positions are equally "empty" since each element "is" only as it remains in differential relation to what it is not. All the positions come into being together, simultaneously with the entire system of differentiations. On the one hand, this system makes possible the advent of its individual elements, the differentiated kinship positions, which for their part make the system possible. Thus, on the other hand, the system does not preexist its elements. The result is that the different kinship positions are as much causes as they are effects of the differentiations that produce them. There is, therefore, no outside of differentiability. Since there is no origin or no telos that anchors the play of these differences in a transcendental point of reference, the father cannot be what the tradition conceives him as being—the fountainhead of conceptuality, the transcendental that is independent of the system of differential relations within which it arises and operates. In order to claim such ontological status, it must erase all trace of the differentiated otherness through which it is constituted. It cannot do so without violence.

Since the person of the child is a literal embodiment of this otherness, the father cannot be self-existing unless he can eliminate the child's being. In the realm of practical social relations, the paternal position must be invested with the right of life and death over the child in order to be regarded as self-sufficient. The act of infanticide is required in order for the paternal position to cover up this position's logical dependency on the other (here the child) that prevents it from being what it "conceives" itself as being—namely, self-generating and self-sufficient. Even this act is not sufficient, however. Not only is the literal destruction of the child necessary, but so too is a supplementary act by which the empirical infanticide is also erased. A father who acknowledges (even only to himself) his dead child as his, who keeps faith with the memory of his child, remains in relation to the child. A father must therefore have an absolute right, beyond any law, to dictate that the child be killed and forgotten altogether.

For the father to destroy his child, however, would be for him categorically to destroy himself as father. Infanticide, therefore, implies both suicide and patricide. It also implies matricide, for to kill the child is to remove the relation that constitutes the mother as mother. What is more, in any tradition that represents the divine as a father (or as a mother), infanticide is deicide. Why? In destroying the child, the father removes the same relationality between himself and his child that must be in place between his father and himself, between this father and his father in turn, all the way back to God-the-Father. As Davis explains, "without the mediation through sonship as a concept," the father "loses the relation to the divine father." For this reason "[i]n killing his son, the father kills himself as a 'son' and destroys his own father's fatherhood."[62] Davis draws the necessary infanticide-consequences of the logic of the father's status as conceptive source: "In this cycle, because he loses his children, even god himself is destroyed *as a father*—in effect, [he] loses his own subject relations to the world. In thus seeking the role of preeminent son to god-the-father, without mediation, the father usurps (or attempts to usurp) god's position and ends up negating paternity over three generations, culminating in an act of theocide."[63] Conceived as self-conceiving, the figure of the father asserts the right to initiate an anti-reproductive violence that nevertheless abolishes his very nature.

Annihilating the parent-child relation, however, infanticide destroys the differentiated positions that comprise a family. In their logical form, neither the family (which is not an entity in and of itself but an effect of differential relations) nor the component social roles that make up the family survive the death of the parent-child relation. The power to commit infanticide, then, is necessary to establish the father's generativity at the same time that it abrogates it. The father must be able to destroy his offspring in order to be what the tradition has conceived him to be. And yet if he is able to destroy his offspring, he perforce is not the conceptive figure the tradition has represented him as being.

This contradiction is a symptomatic expression of the attempt to submit the world's infanticidity to paternal control, to restrict and channel the (infanticidal) costs of existence while remaining free of the (infanticidal) implications such efforts entail. The infanticidal horizon of the zoosphere puts humans in the position of having to economize—for example, of having to deflect more of the costs of their existence onto their competitors than these competitors are able to deflect onto them—of having to sacrifice. The concept of the father performs this sacrificial economization, the (infanticidal) costs of which the concept of the father's generativity appears to dissolve in the (illusory) prospect of worldly transcendence. Indeed, the very concept of conceptuality, which predicates and is predicated on the transcendental generativity of the father, enables the very activity of thinking itself, in all of the modes of reflection, to participate in while concealing this violent economization.

In the centuries before Greek philosophy institutionalizes the father's (infanticidal) self-capitalization, before Plato and Aristotle attempt to subsume the infanticidal within the generativity of the Logos, Greek literature for its part is burdened with its glimpses of the world's infanticidity. Two works in particular—the *Odyssey* and *Oedipus the King*—are especially helpful in dramatizing the difficulties involved in accepting the perception in question. Both works are concerned with a violence that occurs at home—Odysseus' massive slaughter of the suitors, sons of his Ithakan peers, and Laius and Jocasta's attempted murder of their newborn. The *Odyssey* attempts to reduce the infanticidal to infanticide; it then justifies infanticide-violence in the name of the father-god and institutionalizes the mortal father's violence as the founding principle of the *socius*. Seeking to expose this principle, *Oedipus the King* attempts to identify and work through the implications of the difference between infanticide and the infanticidal so as to rethink the possibility of the polis.

7

Sacrifice, Revenge, and a Justice Beyond Justice: The *Odyssey*

> ... the Homeric poems conceal nothing, they contain no teaching and
> no secret second meaning.
>   — Auerbach, *Mimesis: The Representation of Reality*
>   *in Western Literature* (13)

> The great achievement of the *Odyssey* resides in its narrative of *appar-*
> *ent* paternal inevitability and inflexibility, an economy of patriarchal
> values that seems to encompass all possibilities within culture.
>   — Davis, *The Paternal Romance: Reading God-the-Father*
>   *in Early Western Culture* (71)

REVENGE, JUSTICE, AND THE DENIAL OF THE INFANTICIDAL

BECAUSE BIOLOGICAL EXISTENCE ARISES WITHIN A UNIVERSE THAT
is constrained by the laws of thermodynamics, because living things
depend on energy transfers that deplete or destroy the sources of the energy they are able to capture, the concept of life cannot be a pure category. In evolutionary theory, the concept of life includes the manifest
ways living things live off of their environments as well as of the death
they impose on other living things, especially their offspring. The biological concept of life is therefore profoundly ambiguous. The classical
conception of life underscores its generativity, not its simultaneous anti-
generativity. This conception does not tend to recognize the empirical
deathliness at the heart of the production of new life. Nor does it recognize the structural deathliness—the lost opportunities to produce new life.

The Western cultural tradition has no simple name for this counter-
conceptive deathliness at the heart of the living. Because this deathliness
not only happens to the life that has been produced but overtakes the
possible futures that might have come to pass, I have proposed to call this
Darwinian feature of the world its infanticidism in order to underscore
the life-subtracting implications of the economization that governs animal and human existence. This economization is sacrificial. But the word

184

sacrifice does not sufficiently capture the negation of conception, the negation of birth, the negation of new life at the heart of the economization that occurs in the production of any life. Economization means that life is not simply and purely life but what simultaneously threatens life from within itself—in other words, that life is (infanticidally) vulnerable to life.[1]

For a species whose members know they will die, the sense of vulnerability can always arouse anxieties about the potential threats to one's well-being and thus about the potential loss of the future (for example, one's own and, even more, the generational future that comes through one's children). This sense of vulnerability is also linked to another order of anxiety that the Western cultural tradition has largely succeeded in repressing and thus that is difficult to recognize in one's own first-person experience. This would be an anxiety about the already lost futures that are the invisible condition of any first-person experience—indeed, any present moment of life. These anxieties are not an incidental but a constitutive experience of human existence, and all cultures must negotiate them.

The dominant interpretive traditions of the West have been extremely successful in diverting attention away from the insoluble nature of this order of anxiety. They have done so by developing an overarching cultural narrative—Davis' "paternal romance"—in tandem with an "ontotheological" conception of being that together attempt to purify individual and social existence of their contamination by the infanticidism that renders the category of life impure. To this end the paternal romance has promulgated dreams of transcendence all the while including anxious reminders that the promised deliverance is impossible—that any coming into being is simultaneous with the destruction not only of other life but of other potentialities of life. The paternal romance responds to two kinds of violence, then, one more restricted and determinable in its manifestations, the other more general and finally non- or supra-empirical. The former is evidenced in the costs of existence—for example, in the deaths that sustain the lives of survivors. The latter is inferable from the logical implications of such cost—for example, from the infinitude of futures lost,[2] thus from the incalculable deathliness, that is immanent to all life. Backed by its ontotheological investments, the paternal romance refuses or rationalizes the radical injustice inherent in this (infanticidal) economy of being.

At certain moments, however, some texts overcome the resistances programmed by the paternal romance. As chapters 4 and 5 have proposed, the *akedah* dramatizes the culturally transforming crisis that occurs when God demands that Abraham's people base their collective identity on an acceptance, not a denial, of the infanticidism that is coextensive with life.

Specifically, the *akeḋah* forces the mortal father to behold in the face of the son, whom he finally does not kill, a personification of the innumerable faceless lives of those he will never love, care for, protect from violence, stop from being killed, or mourn. The *akeḋah* thus binds Abraham and his people to the task of rethinking their survival in terms of the ethico-political responsibilities that Abraham confronts in the testing by which he is saved from committing a specific act of infanticide only to tremble in fear at the immeasurably greater infanticidism attaching to all life, including his and his son's.

At the beginning of the heritage that provides one of the foundations for European culture, the *Odyssey* acts out another version of this crisis. Unlike the *akeḋah*, however, the *Odyssey*, for all but about twenty-five of its twelve-thousand-plus lines, avoids the signs of the world's infanticidity, including that of the paternal function, signs the poem hides in its sacralization of the hero's suffering and the violence he inflicts on others. Many scholars approve this sacralization. Hugh Lloyd-Jones, for example, exculpates Odysseus for mutilating the son of Poseidon, the Kyklops Polyphemos, who "has ignored the *themistes* [the laws or rightful ways] and scorned the gods" by violating the protocols of guest-friendship. Lloyd-Jones emphasizes that in "persecuting" Odysseus for blinding his son "Poseidon is not punishing the guilty, but pursuing a private feud." Lloyd-Jones concludes that "Odysseus enjoys the special protection of Athene, the closest of the gods to Zeus," because "he has made regular sacrifices to the gods, he is as kind as a father to the people they have given him to rule, and with consistent good sense he has avoided overstepping the bounds which the gods set to human action." Unlike Odysseus, the Ithakan suitors who are seeking Penelope's hand in marriage violate these principles of virtue "and so they pay the penalty."[3]

George C. Dimock agrees: as an "agent" of the gods, Odysseus punishes the suitors "in an act of justice."[4] According to Seth L. Schein, Odysseus' "restoration as husband, father, and king" signals "the renewal of social and political order." His violence against the Suitors is a "justified vengeance"; his "defeat of their families" is condign "punishment of evildoers and the triumph of those who deserve and receive the gods' aid." For this reason, Schein writes, the *Odyssey* "invites readers to view Ithaca (with the restored Odysseus as king) as the locus of morally sound, human reality in the poem and Odysseus himself as the human hero par excellence." Contrasting the hero to Nestor, Menalaos, Agamemnon, and others, the poem, Schein affirms, "clarifies . . . the moral health of rocky Ithaca and the household of Odysseus" as the "quintessentially human community . . . in which Odysseus is able to be fully himself."[5]

Interpretations of this sort assign an absolute moral value to Odysseus' vengeance, attribute the political, social, and other costs of Odysseus' violence to his enemies, and free the hero of responsibility for the dev-astation he wreaks. They treat the hero's behavior as an expression not of self-interest but of the justice that imparts to the real world the moral coherence the epic supposedly reflects. In other words, they spiritualize Odysseus' violence as well as their own hermeneutic reception of it.[6] In doing so, however, they repeat the poem's indifference to the grievous losses the relatives of the Suitors suffer, massive losses which the poem — and many interpretations — refuse to mourn. This refusal underscores the contradiction at the heart of the Homeric world's principal social and re-ligious tenets concerning reciprocity, when the demand for retaliation is not the solution to the loss of social harmony but a cause of it. As Richard Seaford suggests, the *Odyssey* dramatizes a "crisis of reciprocity" in which revenge does not restore order but further shatters it.[7]

This crisis brings the Homeric world to the point of recognizing that its conception of the sacred as a transcendental force — personified as Zeus and partially available to those who worship him — must be rethought. Whereas the *akedah* records Abraham's acceptance of the infanticidism paradox — that the sacred does not and cannot offer a way of passing beyond the infanticidity of being, beyond the fact that there is no life except through the loss of life, including the infinite loss of possible life — the *Odyssey* largely refuses it. For most of its verses the poem is utterly invested in its vision of a transcendent god-force and therefore fails to recognize the infanticidity of this very force. It thereby blinds itself when it rationalizes the hero's violence as a god-sanctioned revenge and ignores the outpouring of grief among the other Ithakan households that Odysseus' vengeance unleashes.

In two ways, however, the poem hints that the idealization of Odysseus' revenge (as the justice of Zeus) reproduces the injustice that this ide-alization is meant to overcome and includes an inchoate critique of this idealization. It does so in Zeus's brief appearance near the beginning of book 1 and then again at the end of book 24, when Zeus appears to countersign Odysseus' revenge but in fact repudiates it. Through Zeus's tacit criticism, the poem points toward the infanticidism that its concep-tion of justice as revenge sacralized covers up.

It does so in a first way when, between the two brief moments of its incipient counter-conception, the poem seems to affirm the moral, polit-ical, and economic consequences of Odysseus' revenge-based heroism. However, the poem also hints at the internal contradictions of such seem-ingly heroic vengeance when it alludes to the infanticidal meaning of Odysseus' life (his birth, his accession to manhood, his identity-defining resourcefulness, the pain he suffers and causes others to suffer) as well as of the religious practice by which Odysseus would receive divine sanction for his life (the offering of meat sacrifices).

The second way in which the poem signals its anxiety about and critique of Odysseus' otherwise idealized violence, then, is by its infanticide imagery, which shows the hero to be a mimetic double of his enemies. The poem thereby highlights the social crisis of reciprocal violence into which the ethic of revenge plunges Odysseus and the other Ithakan households at the end of the poem. More fundamentally, it underscores how the symbolic order of the Homeric universe—manifested in the political economy and conditions of identity on Ithaka—entails infanticidism denied, a denial that prevents Odysseus and his world from rethinking the conditions of social life and identity in the knowledge that there is no existence outside of the infanticidal.

COUNTER-CONCEIVING THE JUSTICE OF ZEUS

At the poem's beginning Zeus invokes the presumptive ethical basis of the Odyssean universe—the spiritualization of revenge as divine justice— when he brings up the just punishment, meted out by Orestes, of Aigisthos, who "has paid the reckoning in full"[8] for his murder of Agamemnon and his adultery with Klytemnestra. However, Zeus undercuts this moral program and makes its economy of self-interest explicit when he accepts Athena's petition on Odysseus' behalf but not her characterization of the "justness" she believes he has been making Odysseus endure. When Athena beseeches Zeus to free Odysseus from Kalypso, she first acknowledges that this mortal deserves to die: "O Father of us all, that man is in the dust indeed, *and justly*. So perish all who do what he had done" (1.64–66). She then recalls Zeus's "pleasures" in "Odysseus' [sacrificial] offerings" (82). In response, Zeus declares that he will not permit Odysseus to perish, evidently because "There is no mortal half so wise; no mortal gave so much to the lords of open sky" (88–89).

Zeus here defines the fundamental meaning of Odysseus' vaunted resourcefulness when he specifies the moral-economic terms of the hero's wisdom (it is proportional to the plenitude of sacrifices he makes to the gods). Zeus then blames not Odysseus himself but Poseidon—who "bears the fighter an old grudge" ever since Odysseus "poked out the eye of Polyphemos"—for the hero's travails (91–92) and declares that Poseidon must give up his desire for revenge. In stipulating the demand that "Poseidon must relent" (102), Zeus himself gives up the desire for revenge he has moments earlier sanctioned in Orestes. Poseidon for his part is absent when Zeus passes his judgment: he is "at earth's two verges, in sunset lands and lands of the rising sun," where, receiving the sacrifices of the Ethiopians, he is "regaled by smoke of thighbones burning" (37–39). In other words the poem introduces sacrifice as an act that repeats the inaugural metaphysical categories of the world—as marking nothing less than the (sacrificial) advent and (sacrificial) structure of space (the edges of the earth) and time (the rhythm of the setting and rising sun).

In repudiating the revenge of Poseidon, with whom the poem first associates the practice of sacrifice, Zeus challenges the central ritual by which the Greeks—including Odysseus himself, the hero who ostensibly has Zeus's blessing—sought to legitimize the affective basis of their political economy and the metaphysical order they wanted it to mirror. Zeus redoubles this challenge when he exempts Odysseus from paying the price that Athena acknowledges this mortal ought to pay for his transgressions, a price that Zeus himself has required of Aigisthos and that Odysseus for his part will levy against the Suitors. In his contradictory judgment, Zeus anticipates the command he will deliver in the final lines of the poem when he interdicts the pursuit of vengeance and rejects the morality that directs the entire narrative trajectory of the poem.

When the hero massacres the Suitors, he incites the rage of his countrymen, who retaliate in order to "avenge our son's blood, and our brothers'" (24.477). In the battle that follows, Odysseus and Telemakhos "would have cut the enemy down to the last man, leaving not one survivor, had not Athena raised a shout that stopped all fighters in their tracks" (589–91). Why does she intervene? Because she heeds Zeus's thunderous warning that the violence of the protagonists is no different from that of their enemies and, unchecked, will subject father and son to the same holocaust to which they are furious enough to deliver their compatriots, now enemies: "With a cry to freeze their hearts and ruffling like an eagle on the pounce, the lord Odysseus reared himself to follow" the fleeing Ithakans, "at which the son of Kronos dropped a thunderbolt smoking at his daughter's feet" (599–603). In other words, at the very moment the poem would characterize Odysseus as divinely sanctioned, as appearing to his enemies in the form of a god-sign (the eagle) that Zeus elsewhere sends as an omen to the suitors, Zeus signals Athena who then signals Odysseus to stop. This transitive series extends to the poem's readers, who are thereby cautioned against the interpretive temptation of assimilating Odysseus' violence to Zeus's. As Athena admonishes: "Son of Laertes and the *gods of old*, Odysseus, master of land ways and sea ways, command yourself. Call off this battle now, or Zeus who views the wide world may be angry" (606–9). In addressing her charge, Athena reduces Odysseus' pious genealogical claim of godliness to a conventional, self-interested, and ethically empty self-designation, she underscores the anachronism of Odysseus' nominal inheritance from "the gods *of old*," and she ironizes the poem's initial praise of Odysseus' sacrificial displays. In other words, when Athena obeys "the father of gods and men" (1.44), she imposes an end to the deathliness of the collective Ithakan anger by evoking Zeus's immeasurably greater anger. By implication, the anger of this god is a new kind of anger, or the anger of a new kind of god: through his remarked passion, Zeus would visit on both sides a violence that up until this point Odysseus thinks he can level against his enemies, and that they think they can level against him, without being destroyed in turn.[9] If the parties were to have continued to fight, Zeus evidently would have made no distinction between Odysseus and the other Ithakans but have obliterated them all alike.

What is utterly different at the end of the poem, then, is the manifestation of the father-god as a force ready to personally destroy the poem's hero. Not once during the previous twelve-thousand-plus lines of the poem has Zeus been angry with Odysseus—not until the end, when Odysseus would claim the field for himself.

The last fifteen lines reverse the direction of the poem's seemingly ineluctable narrative movement: the hero who kills, ostensibly in the name of justice, but who evinces a desire to keep on killing his foes rather than to seek peace with them—this hero no longer acts with divine sanction. At the moment before the hero's triumph would become absolute, the god blocks him off from satisfying his desire, a desire the god countermands as itself a form of the evil it seeks to eliminate. Zeus does not want to become angry. He does not want to subject Odysseus to an Olympian violence this mortal cannot survive. He does not want to put Odysseus in the position in which Odysseus has put the leaders of the other families. Threatening his divine violence to quell the hero's mortal violence, Zeus announces that the hero's point of view cannot be the basis for determining the meaning of his actions. Zeus hurls his thunderbolt to stop Odysseus from hurling his spear: enacting the meaning of his justice, Zeus reveals the absolute injustice of the hero's violence and the fury that motivates it. Again, Zeus manifests his power in the name of holding himself back from a more extreme manifestation of himself. He checks Odysseus' violence so as to check his own. He binds himself and the hero, whose homecoming occurs under this god's aegis, to a new consideration of what constitutes justice. In his double interdiction—of Odysseus and of himself through his interdiction of Odysseus—Zeus redefines justice not as revenge or punishment but as revenge or punishment suspended at its most devastating pitch of intensity, when the avenger is entirely caught up in a killing frenzy. This new justice, to which I shall return, requires that the person not kill precisely when he feels most justified in killing.

The intervention of the god at this precise moment could not be more wrenching. It could not be more shocking. It could not be more unforeseen. Hence it could not be more indelibly impressed on the contestants.

At the height of the killing, the god inscribes his "no" across the entirety of their minds and bodies. No one must forget the interdiction nor the interdicted passion—the perfervid, self-inflating experience of fatally imposing one's will on others. No one must cease to feel the judgment against the primitivity of revenge the desire for which must be converted into a permanent, indeed perpetual, memory.

When God holds back Abraham's arm at the culminating moment of Abraham's passion, this man must live for the rest of his life in ceaseless recollection of and mourning over the call to kill and his willingness to do so. When Zeus arrests Odysseus, this Greek hero must also live for the rest of his life recalling the arousal, focus, emotional rush, and explosion of murderous aggression on the one hand and their god-decreed interruption at their climax on the other. At the moment Zeus manifests himself, a new conception of justice irrupts on the scene. Justice is no longer a revenge that can claim divine sanction. It is suddenly revealed to require the abandonment of that claim precisely when that claim is felt most intensely. Zeus gives the last emphasis to this requirement. Justice must not be defined from the point of view of the victor, who invariably sacralizes his violence. To the contrary, such self-sanctification must be refused in order to achieve a justice that predicates the renunciation of revenge as the basis of the law and the religious practices it prescribes.[10]

The *Odyssey* intuits but does not analyze the severe psychic burden of this new sense of justice. At the start of the poem the justice of Zeus signifies revenge; at the end it stands for a critique of the affect that is the engine of vengeful action and reaction throughout the poem—the venom of Poseidon, the wrath of Athena, the righteous resentment of Telemakhos, the indignation and acrimony of the Suitors themselves, and so on. On the one hand, the murderous animosity between the Ithakans and Odysseus arouses the counter-vehemence of Zeus, who threatens to unleash an indiscriminate holocaust on everyone. Zeus, in other words, acts out the meaning of their anger: left unchecked, it can become so virulent that it results in a non-survivable, community-wide bloodbath. Zeus does not merely double the fury of Odysseus and the Ithakans, however, but brings it to a halt. On the other hand, then, his divine rage marks the incipient recognition of a need for a justice beyond anger and beyond the desire for and violence of revenge, a justice that paradoxically would be initiated by and yet would be beyond the sovereignty of even Zeus's irresistible might, a justice that would be beyond Zeus's justice.

The poem does not anticipate how warring parties would ever achieve the transformation of consciousness necessary to lay down arms and enter into negotiations. It does, however, insist on this necessity, the secret mystery of which gives the lie to Odysseus' furious desire for revenge. "What is your secret will?" Athena asks Zeus when confronted with the prospect of "war and battle, worse and more of it." At first glance, Zeus appears to endorse Athena's wish that Odysseus should annihilate not only the Suitors but their relatives, that he "should have their blood," to satisfy his honor. Zeus, however, immediately insists that if Odysseus is to regain his rule, it must not be by unilateral victory but by a truce signed under oath by all parties, including the aggrieved survivors of the Suitors. Because these Ithakans will be tempted for their part to seek revenge against Odysseus, Zeus promises to "blot out the memory of [their] sons and brothers slain." The result will be to "let men of Ithaka henceforth be friends," the condition of "prosperity enough and peace" (24.523–39).

If a letting-go of anger, if a forgetfulness of the demand for revenge, is necessary to the justice of Zeus, then this is a new kind of justice predicated on a consciousness different from that which has propelled the narrative. This consciousness and the justice it makes possible requires internalizing the example of Zeus's self-checking in order to release the culturally transformative force of the verbal exchanges by which enemies can "swear to terms of peace" (24.611). This justice requires that humans substitute diplomacy for brute force in an inoculating mimesis of the way Athena translates Zeus's irresistible violence and the anger that motivates it into the protocols of arbitration. In this way the *Odyssey* stages its wholly unexpected critique of revenge as a mirror scene, in which Athena interprets the meaning of Zeus's intervention as a new paradigm of reflexivity. That is, she instructs each of the opposing sides how to transform its consciousness of having been wronged into a consciousness of Zeus's grievances against both groups, and through this intermediary awareness into a consciousness of the enemy's consciousness of its sense of being a victim who must retaliate in order to achieve justice. The poem does not dramatize the process whereby the recognition that the god has held back his anger becomes the occasion for empathizing with the enemy. Nevertheless, the poem points toward the consequences of this second-order consciousness—this consciousness of the other's consciousness of his deep grievances—namely, the renunciation of revenge, the sublimation of rage into an energy available for cooperation, and thus a previously unachievable peace.

This new sense of justice means giving up the sacrificial mentality according to which one can win, through the proper ritual observances (propitiation, atonement, and supplication), the favor of the gods at the expense of one's enemies. The implications are enormous. It means accepting the economy of infinite loss as the condition of the possibility of being. It means counter-conceiving the sacred as the Derridean gift of death. It means understanding how subjectivity is inscribed in an infanticidal structure. It means, in sum, opening oneself to rather than hiding from the infanticidal horizon of life. Two episodes in particular illustrate how difficult this challenge is for the Homeric world.

THE INFANTICIDAL INSCRIPTION OF THE NAME "ODYSSEUS"

In the famous digression surrounding Eurykleia's recognition of Odysseus by the scar on his thigh, the poem broaches the infanticidal horizon of the symbolic order. It links together the circumstances and meaning of Odysseus' naming to his adolescent wounding during a boar hunt, his disguised return as the adult warrior to Ithaka, and his impending attack against the Suitors. The result is that the poem thereby tells an allegorical story of the potentially infanticidal hailing that precedes the human subject as its condition of possibility.

When Autolykos visits Ithaka "just after his daughter's boy was born" (19.469), he is asked to name his grandson. Autolykos, whose name means "the wolf himself" or "the very wolf," is a cattle thief who, in one tradition, relies on a characteristic "trick of changing the animals' brands so as to deceive their owners."[11] Because he steals the very animals his victims might have used for sacrifice, because he compromises their ability to "give to the lords of open sky" (1.89) as much as they ought (as much, for example, as the adult Odysseus will), because he imposes both a material and a spiritual loss on others, therefore Autolykos elicits the "odium" of his victims for having "odysseused" them (19.480) and risks being the target of their revenge.[12]

When Autolykos names his grandson for the victimizing effect on others of his predatory thievery and deception, he effectively "brands" Odysseus with the most primitive of paternal imperatives: live up to one's name by economizing at the expense of others. Not surprisingly, according to Dimock the epic's orienting predication, *odussasthai*, (to will pain to) is echoed in Odysseus' name, which can mean Hater on the one hand and Hated, Man of Suffering, or Child of Woe on the other.[13] When he names the newborn, then, Autolykos links its identity to the "pain" this future hero will cause others and himself be subjected to as he lives out the interpellative legacy that gives him his right to life. This is the profane legacy of the grandfather's shameless resourcefulness at sacrificial economization, at deflecting the cost of his existence onto those from whom he steals while endeavoring to avoid being victimized in turn.

Odysseus' name symbolizes the infanticidal force of this legacy — indeed, of the interpellation by which any child is hailed into or out of existence. The scarring Odysseus undergoes in adolescence repeats this infanticidal inscription. In a boar hunt organized by Autolykos to mark Odysseus' passage from boyhood to manhood, the hero-to-be receives a scar that imprints the violence of the symbolic order—the violence of the hailing that threatens as much as it confers the possibility of recognition, existence, identity, and destiny—on his body. The hunt reaches its climax when Odysseus suddenly comes upon a great boar that has just awakened and emerged from beneath a dense cover of undergrowth (19.515–16).[14] Although Odysseus "lung[es] to stick him . . . the boar had already charged under the long spear. He hooked aslant with one white tusk and ripped out flesh above the knee but missed the bone. Odysseus' second thrust went home by luck, his bright spear passing through the shoulder joint; and the beast fell, moaning as life pulsed away" (522–28). The result of Odysseus' injury, a permanent scar on his thigh, consolidates the violent destiny encoded in his name. Just as his naming commemorates the infanticidal peril that he has escaped in being cared for in his infancy, so too does his scar attest to the similar danger he avoids in being nursed back to health in the days following his wounding, when the sons of Autolykos "bound his gash," "stanched the dark flow of blood" with a "rune" or incantation,[15] "tended him well," and sent him home to his father and mother "with Grandfather Autolykos' magnificent gifts" (529–37). Narrowly surviving the boar hunt with his reproductive organs intact, Odysseus "comes of age," Hexter writes, "but not without a cost": he bears a scar in which can be read the genealogical dead end had he not received both the care lavished on him as an infant and later as the victim of the boar.[16]

Appropriately, Odysseus is first recognized by his childhood nurse, Eurykleia. Her name means "broad or far fame," and it mirrors his status as a chieftain or king of wide renown. But it also reflects the contingency of his identity, which requires the recognizing gaze of the other, beginning with the parents or caretakers and the paternal authority who, in Greek culture, conferred the right to life. Eurykleia, then, is the one who takes Odysseus "into her arms the hour his mother bore him," places the infant Odysseus in the lap of Autolykos, and petitions him to warrant the child's existence: "It is for you, now, to choose a name for him, your child's dear baby; the answer to her [mother's] prayers," she says to Autolykos (19.414–15 and 473–75). Eurykleia here asserts as fact what she knows is socially produced when she pleads with Autolykos to recognize the sacredness of the child's life. That the sacredness must be countersigned by the mortal paternal authority underscores the child's interpellative vulnerability to being hailed out of being.

The recognition scene reenacts the infanticidal implications of the jeopardy inherent in interpellation. When she washes the feet of Odysseus, who is disguised as a beggar, she recognizes his scar, whispers his name, and addresses him as "dear child" (19.550). Having "traced" (543) his

wound during her ablutions, she regains her own identity as Odysseus'
childhood nurse. The narrative transition from her memory to the present
superimposes the images of Odysseus' helplessness as an infant, his near-
death from the hunt, and his present straits. When Odysseus warns
Eurykleia, who is about to relay her joyous news to Penelope, to keep
quiet, he alludes to the infanticidal terms of his vulnerability. Murray and
Dimock's translation underscores the maternal surrogacy of Eurykleia's
nursing, hence the infanticidal extremity of his danger: "Mother, why
will you destroy me? You yourself nursed me at this your own breast."[17]
Odysseus is afraid that if the news of his identity gets out, the Suitors
will arm themselves and destroy him before he can destroy them. The
present risk of exposure thus repeats the earlier (infanticidal) risk within
the first days of his life of being exposed had Autolykos refused to name
him. The childhood scene of public or published naming, which authorizes Eurykleia's life-giving care to the infant, is inverted in the adulthood
scene of naming silenced, which enables Eurykleia once again to protect
his life. The recognition scene, then, foregrounds the infanticidal nature
of the threat to identity not just from not being named but also, in fact,
from receiving a name and the right to life that the naming guarantees.

   One of the poem's principal metaphors conveys the infanticidal destiny
of the hero, who on the one hand suffers Poseidon's efforts to *odysseus* —
"will pain" to—him by "sow[ing] for you the seeds of so many evils" and
who on the other hand will himself *odysseus* his enemies by "planting"
such evil for them (Murray and Dimock, vol. 1, 207; Fitzgerald, 5.352).
The oxymoronic trope of "sowing seeds of doom" is, Dimock notes, "a
translation of Odysseus' name."[18] Indeed, the naming of Odysseus is
itself an instance of such violent productivity, as Autolykos' invocation
of the "fruitfulness" of his aggression indicates: "'Inasmuch as I have come
here,'" Autolykos says upon the occasion of Odysseus' birth, "'as one that
has willed pain to many, both men and women, over the *fruitful earth*,
therefore let the name by which the child is named be Odysseus'" (Murray and Dimock, vol. 2, 265).

   "Odysseus" must therefore be read as a name that signifies the (infanticidal) deathliness that is the economic-cum-sacrificial condition of
the possibility of being hailed into an existence. However, apart from the
two moments when it permits Zeus to intervene, each time to prevent
the further pursuit of vengeance, the poem treats this cost not as an irreducible structural feature of existence but as a punishment deserved
by its victims. It thereby attempts to convert Odysseus' violence into a
moral force that levies revenge as a price the wicked could have avoided
by not being wicked. To the extent that the poem tries to "conceive" of
Odysseus' violence as just and therefore as generative, it misunderstands

the counter-conceptive meaning of his name and the implications of this meaning for the new sense of justice that Zeus introduces.

Nevertheless, the poem announces this meaning whenever it adverts to the metaphor of "planting" or "sowing" trouble, evil, doom, or death. For example, early on, when Halitherses interprets the meaning of two eagles "wielding their talons, tearing cheeks and throats" (2.163), he concludes that this "deathly omen" (161) is a "sign sent by Zeus" (155) and that it announces Odysseus' imminent return to Ithaka, "carrying in him a bloody doom for all these men" (2.174–75), or "sowing slaughter and death for these men, one and all" (Murray and Dimock, vol. 1, 59). Both translations retain the oxymoronic force of the Greek: Odysseus will make a killing, beget a slaughter, or harvest a death; alternatively, he will bear his deathly revenge to term, giving birth to a slaughter

Helen's interpretation of the omen of the eagle and the goose—which follows Telemakhos' wish that he were able to tell his father of the friendship he has received from Menelaos—underscores the paradox of Odysseus' homecoming and the justice he seeks: his revenge will be violent *and* generative. Indeed, it will be productive by virtue of being infanticidal. "Even as this eagle came from the mountain, where are his kin, and where he was born, and snatched up the goose that was bred in the house, even so shall Odysseus return to his home after many toils and many wanderings, and shall take vengeance; or even now he is at home, and is sowing the seeds of evil for all the suitors" (Murray and Dimock, vol. 2, 89; Fitzgerald, 15.214–18). The final metaphor of sowing evil and harvesting death identifies the infanticidal implications of the economic tradeoff by which Odysseus will regain his household: the deaths of the sons and brothers of the Ithakan patriarchs, the destruction of the present and future generations of this city-state's households, is the cost of Odysseus' justice.

This constellation of motifs recurs throughout the poem. When it does, Fitzgerald substitutes various tropes for the Homeric formula, which Murray and Dimock retain. When "inwardly [Odysseus'] thought shaped woe and ruin for the suitors" (14.132–33), he is thinking ahead to "sowing the seeds of evil" for them (vol. 2, 45). When Odysseus describes how he "set a trap . . . for my enemies" (14.257), he is recalling how he "'picked the best warriors for an ambush, sowing the seeds of evil for the foe'" (vol. 2, 52). When Menelaos interprets the flight of an eagle to be an omen of how "Odysseus, back from his hard trials and wandering, will soon come down in fury on his house" (15.217–18), he is imagining how "even so shall Odysseus return to his home after many toils and many wanderings, and shall take vengeance; or even now he is at home, and is sowing the seeds of evil for all the suitors" (vol. 2, 89). When Theoklymenos tells Penelope that Odysseus "knows what evil is afoot" and that her husband "has it in him to bring a black hour on the suitors" (17.198–200), he, too, employs the metaphor of "sowing the seeds of evil" (vol. 2, 167). Telemakhos as well relies on the same trope (once at 17.33 and then again at 17.104–5; vol. 2, 157 and 161).

Homer literalizes the metaphor when Odysseus reveals his identity to his father following the destruction of the Suitors. With a view of the "revetted plot of orchard," Odysseus addresses Laertes and recalls a scene of idyllic paternal instruction when he had been "a small boy at your heels, wheedling amid the young trees, while you named each one. You gave me thirteen pear, ten apple trees, and forty fig trees. Fifty rows of vines were promised too, each one to bear in turn. Bunches of every hue would hang there ripening, weighed down by the god of summer days" (24.372–79). In the fabulous productivity of the cultivated garden, the poem seeks to purify Odysseus' genealogical inheritance of the infanticidism on which his name and his victorious homecoming turn.

Anticipating Odysseus' homecoming, Menelaos invokes the infanticidal basis of all economy, which the father's agricultural legacy denies, when he tells Telemakhos: "Out upon them! For truly it was in the bed of a man of valiant heart they undertook to lie, who are themselves of little prowess. Just as when in the thicket lair of a powerful lion a doe has laid to sleep her newborn suckling fawns, and roams over the mountain slopes and grassy vales seeking pasture, and then the lion comes to his lair and upon her two fawns lets loose a cruel doom, so will Odysseus let loose a cruel doom upon these men" (Murray and Dimock, vol. 2, 163–65; Fitzgerald, 17.157–64). These "men" are first and foremost "sons," as Halistherses calls them when he attempts to calm the Ithakans who are enraged at the deaths of their kinsmen: "Friends, by your own fault these deaths came to pass. You would not . . . put down the riot of your sons" (24.503–5). Precisely because they are sons, bearers of now lost futures, their (infanticidal) deaths are all the more grievous for signifying what cannot properly be signified—namely, irretrievably lost futures.[19] Since these futures are potential, not actual, since they cannot be addressed except as what escapes interpellation, what is lost is, finally, indeterminable. The prospect of incalculable loss blocks consciousness from being able, on the one hand, to fix the limits to grief and, on the other, to deduce what a satisfactory recompense could possibly be. Faced with this double impasse, the kinsmen of the Suitors cannot abide the economizing morality of Halistherses and his advice to cut their losses. Enraged at the absolute injustice they believe themselves to have suffered, they become enraged and retaliate, seeking the same oblivion for Odysseus to which he has consigned their genealogical prospects.

"OUTIS," INTERPELLATIVE ANNIHILATION, AND THE INFANTICIDISM OF THE SYMBOLIC ORDER

Each of Odysseus' adventures, none more blatantly than his deliberate encounter with the Kyklops, dramatizes the (infanticidal) threat of the interpellative annihilation that was discussed in the previous chapter. According to Karl Reinhardt, "In no other case does he feel himself so attracted by danger." Odysseus "wishes to 'test' and 'find out' what kind of people the Cyclopes are, 'whether they are savage and violent, and without justice or hospitable to strangers and with minds that are godly.'"[20] In discovering that Polyphemos has no regard for the principle of *xenia* — of the guest friendship that is to be extended to another, of the civilizing potential of hospitality as a means of establishing reciprocity and friendship between strangers — Odysseus has recourse to an extended interpellation of the Kyklops. In the course of this deceptive address, he acknowledges his vulnerability before the giant, petitions to enter into a relation of friendly reciprocity, and, when Polyphemos imprisons him and begins to eat his crew, reciprocates this savage violence with an immeasurably more sophisticated destructiveness. His response is a lesson in –cidal, specifically infanticidal, economics. Odysseus repays his host with physical force in conjunction with a deceptive act of linguistic self-representation (when he calls himself "Outis," no one, nobody, no man). The result is that Odysseus acts out the injuriousness of any subject's inscription within the symbolic order, the cost of any subject's hailing, even as he imposes that very injuriousness on his auditor when he declares triumphantly who he is. To this end he is caught up in an infanticidal scenario, which functions as a symptom of the general infanticidism (to which the poem for the most part turns a narrative blind eye) of even, perhaps especially, the most heroic life.

The entire Kyklops episode expands this lesson concerning infanticidal economics. The Kyklopes are, Odysseus recounts, "without a law to bless them." Their lawlessness, a metonymy of their cultural rawness,[21] anticipates how Polyphemos will misunderstand Odysseus' name as the "planter of evil," for "in ignorance leaving the fruitage of the earth in mystery," the Kyklopes "neither plow nor sow by hand, nor till the ground" (9.114–17). Odysseus will inseminate this "unplanted and untilled . . . wilderness" with his name and its meaning (133). Through his name Odysseus will make explicit the infanticidal basis of the symbolic order, metonymically figured in the anti-name, the un-naming name, the infanticidal name (*Outis*) that he adopts in anticipation of a deadly (interpellative) reception from Polyphemos. Having passed himself off to the giant as "no one," Odysseus eventually gets the monster drunk and then blinds him. He sharpens a "pike" or "stake" of olive wood (410), an olive tree that "was like a mast" (348), heats it, and then bores into the Kyklops' eye in a phallic gesture, which repeats the thrust of the boar that had impaled him in adolescence.[22] He then manages to escape from the cave where the Kyklops had imprisoned him and cannibalized his men. The terms of that cannibalism echo the predatory imagery Menalaos employs to figure the revenge he hopes Odysseus will exact against the Suitors: the Kyklops "dismembered [two of Odysseus' crew] and made his meal, gaping and crunching like a mountain lion," Odysseus recalls (316–17). The sociality of humans means nothing to Polyphemos, who represents them only as "good to eat."[23]

Polyphemos disregards the twin categories of the Homeric world — reciprocity and ritual[24] — which Odysseus invokes when he answers the Kyklops' demand that he identify himself. Odysseus explains that he and his men are "homeward bound, but taking routes and ways uncommon; so the will of Zeus would have it." He then recalls the Greek custom of giving "honor to strangers. We would entreat you, great Sir, have a care for the gods' courtesy; Zeus will avenge the unoffending guest" (9.281–84 and 290–93). The "pitiless" Kyklops dismisses Odysseus' invocation: "We Kyklopes care not a whistle for your thundering Zeus or all the gods in bliss; we have more force by far" (295 and 298–300), as if force were independent of its symbolic articulations, which for Odysseus are governed by the sacred name of Zeus, a name he believes demands reciprocity. Responding to the Kyklops' own "thundering," Odysseus engages in a deceptive speech-act, one that reveals Polyphemos' inability to recognize that another mind might know what he does not about himself. When Polyphemos asks where Odysseus' ship is anchored, Odysseus "answered with a ready lie," saying that it has been destroyed in a storm and that "We are survivors, these good men and I" (311). At this point "Neither reply nor pity came from him, but in one stride he clutched at my companions and caught two in his hands like squirming puppies to beat their brains out, spattering the floor," and proceeds to dismember and consume them (312–15). Because Polyphemos cannot represent himself beyond his own immediate appetite, because he cannot hear the words of others as markers of their like desire, because he cannot translate his needs into the symbols that could then be exchanged in a process of mutual recognition, Polyphemos is limited to cannibalistically incorporating rather than symbolically introjecting the world.

As the subsequent narrative evinces, Odysseus, in contrast, represents a consciousness that has undergone the social disciplining of appetite, which turns the mouth from an organ of literal incorporation into an organ of symbolic reference. Clinging to the bellies of the giant's sheep to escape his detection when he lets his animals out of his cave in the morning, Odysseus and his men steal the animals, which they herd toward their ship. As his crew rows their captain and their plunder out to sea, Odysseus sacralizes his identity by linking his violence to the retributive justice of Zeus when he taunts the Kyklops: "Puny, am I, in a Caveman's hands? How do you like the beating that we gave you, you damned cannibal? Eater of guests under your roof! Zeus and the gods have paid [literally, taken vengeance on] you!" (9.520–23). Speaking in the name of the symbolic economy to which the Kyklops is blind, Odysseus avenges himself by asserting the superiority of "Odysseus" and its place in a genealogy of names: "Kyklops, if ever mortal man inquire how you were put to shame and blinded, tell him Odysseus, raider of cities, took your eye: Laertes' son, whose home's on Ithaka!" (548–552).[25]

According to Dimock, Odysseus' self-declaration is the final expression of the symbolic parturition that he undergoes in the Kyklops episode: Odysseus' escape is "an analogue to human birth: the stake in the eye suggest[s] the sexual act; the cave, a womb; and receiving a name upon issuing from it, the birth of a child. The text itself," Dimock notes, "alludes to the pain of childbirth when Odysseus speaks of Polyphemos as 'travailing with pains [ōdinōn odynēsi]' as he himself is about to escape from the cave." Dimock concludes: "The inference that, from the biological point of view, at least, we owe our existence to pain, is obvious, together with the secondary implication that not to inflict pain is not to be born and therefore to be nobody."[26] If so, however, then to be somebody is to be a bearer of potentially fatal injuriousness to others who have come into being and to be a bearer of an infinite deathliness to those whose existence one's own being forecloses. For this reason any birthing is a passage not into life but into lifedeath—that is, into a life that brings death, that is deathly.

Odysseus' near death following his initial escape from the Kyklops delimits the infanticidal meaning of this injuriousness yet again. When he proclaims his name to the Kyklops, Odysseus provides his nemesis with a final opportunity to destroy him (by estimating his range and hurling a boulder his way), to render him *outis*. In inviting yet another threat to his identity, a threat he mocks after Polyphemos first misses the boat, Odysseus declares himself "Laertes' *son*" (9.552). In doing so he announces his identification with the parental interpellation by which he has been given his claim to life the violent and ultimately infanticidal cost of which he will impose on others. In surviving the Kyklops' wrath, then, Odysseus the son stages the infanticidal threat that haunts every child's birth, a threat institutionalized in Greece in the practice of exposing unwanted children and commemorated in his own name. Like all so-called proper names, his memorializes the nonbeing the infant escapes by virtue of being named. In reenacting the scene of his symbolic rebirthing (his emergence from the cave) as a drama of self-renaming, Odysseus prevents the Kyklops from ever forgetting the identity of the one who has repaid his violence with a new kind of violence. Ironically, he tempts the Kyklops to try once more to destroy him. In this way he symbolically anticipates what will be described later, when the poem recalls the postpartum scene of Odysseus' naming. In that scene he is given the right to life by his grandfather, not by the fact he was born but by the fact of receiving a name—that is, of being interpellated in a certain way.

Figuratively returning to this scene of his inscription in the symbolic order prior to the advent of his self-consciousness, Odysseus purposefully provokes an experience of the vulnerability to annihilation that is the (infanticidal) context of the subject's interpellation into life. At the end of his experience he attributes his survival to the will, law, and justice of the gods.[27] He thus internalizes the contradictory meaning of the fundamental Greek religious practice—the burnt offering—which defends against while commemorating the possibility of annihilation that is a structural feature of all interpellation.

SACRIFICE, INFANTICIDAL INSCRIPTION, AND THE BODY OF ODYSSEUS

According to Walter Burkert, at "the center of Greek sacrificial practice" is the procedure of "burning *thighbones* on the altar, *meria kaiein*, and setting up *boukrania* [skulls] to mark a sanctuary or an altar."[28] In relation to this practice, Odysseus' thigh wound is not merely a mark of the physical danger he escaped during the hunting trip that was his rite of passage into manhood. It is the writing of sacrifice across the body of the hero. Bearing a scar that stands in for the slaughter of the sacrificial animal and the offering of its thighbone to the gods, Odysseus is the living embodiment of the sacrificial impulse and its ritual sanctification. Scarred with the symbol of the principal religious ceremony of his culture, Odysseus lives out the (infanticidally) economizing function of sacrifice—which is to deflect the costs of one's existence onto others. He sacrifices better than anyone else and therefore escapes becoming the sacrificial offering of others. He is, therefore, the figure who represents his world's ideological commitment to a political economy based on retributive justice. And yet it is just this commitment, along with the ritual which supposedly guarantees it, that the poem covertly criticizes through its allusions to the infanticidal meaning of Odysseus' identity.

When Eurykleia recognizes Odysseus, the poem twice draws attention to the practice of ritually offering thighbones to Zeus. The first allusion connects sacrifice to the reproductive success of the hero. When Eurykleia bathes the seeming stranger in front of her, she weeps in frustration that the will of the gods has turned against Odysseus, whom she apostrophizes in his apparent absence: "Oh, my child! I can do nothing for you! How Zeus hated you, no other man so much! No use, great heart, O faithful heart, the rich thighbones [*meira*] you burnt to Zeus who plays in lightning — and no man ever gave more to Zeus — with all your prayers for a green age, a tall son reared to manhood" (19.425–31). The second allusion links sacrifice to the productive success of the hero's grandfather, "a great thief and swindler by Hermes' favor, for Autolykos pleased [the god] with burnt offerings [*meira*] of sheep and kids" (464–66).

The two references reinforce the meaning of the boar hunt as an extension of Greek religious observance. Reflecting the meaning of Odysseus' name — once again, to "give pain to" or "plant evil for" — the injury to his thigh signifies the paternal inscription of his culture's most fundamental religious practice upon his person.[29] That inscription consecrates Odysseus' survival and yet perpetually recalls its sacrificial costs. It immunizes Odysseus from the various (infanticidal) menaces others direct against him and legitimizes the similar violence he himself engages in. The result is that it translates the force of the (paternal) law as a potential source of Odysseus' death in infancy into a resource of his survival and subsequent heroic triumph in adulthood. In sum, the wound to the thigh figures the infanticidal economization of the rite by which Odysseus acquires his adult identity, an economization the poem mystifies by sacralizing on the one hand but, in its rudimentary counter-conception of Zeus's justice, begins to demystify by desacralizing on the other.

Sophocles' *Oedipus the King* radicalizes the Greek effort to rethink the sacred — that is, to counter-conceive the gods not as those who have the power to deliver one from the world's infanticidism but as those who embody the infanticidity that gives the possibility of life, including human consciousness.

8

The Wounded Infant and the Infanticidism of the Gods: Oedipus' Cultural Critique

> . . . the initial helplessness of human beings is the primal source of all moral motives.
> —Freud, *Project for a Scientific Psychology* (318)

> The worst image of . . . self-damage is the most unimaginable act of all: killing your own child, a murder that is the prototype of horror in Greek imagination.
> —Ruth Padel, *Whom Gods Destroy* (207)

> Imagine having a father that wanted to kill you. That's the part they all leave out of the Oedipus story.
> —Joseph Heller, *Something Happened* (315)

> In some versions [Laius] is actually the *cause* of Thebes' troubles, not the victim whose death must be avenged.
> —Frederick Ahl, *Sophocles' Oedipus: Evidence and Self-Conviction* (196).

> . . . what should we do with this play in which a father tries to murder the son . . .?
> —Pietro Pucci, *Oedipus and the Fabrication of the Father* (3).

INFANTICIDE, INFANTICIDISM, AND THE THEBAN RELIGIOUS CRISIS

*O*EDIPUS THE KING RECORDS A CULTURE IN CRISIS: THEBES IS BESET by a plague that is destroying the productive and reproductive basis of its economy. Oedipus' people want to interpret the disaster as divine punishment for an evil they might yet be able to purge from their kingdom. They do not treat the plague as a natural disaster but allegorize it as a warning from the gods that they must purify their world by rooting out a violent, contaminating presence among them. First supplicating and then identifying with the gods, they regard themselves as the agents of divine violence, which they then redirect at what they think is the profane cause of their suffering.

Oedipus would seem to reaffirm this cultural identification when he promises to track down the former king's killer, the presumptive cause of the plague. Oedipus will "fight" for the former king "as if for my own father," and to that end calls upon the retributive "justice" of the gods to destroy anyone who stands in his way. He prays, "against all those who disobey" him, that "the gods send out no harvest from their soil, nor children from their wives. Oh, let them die victims of this plague, or of something worse. Yet for the rest of us, people of Cadmus, we the obedient, may Justice, our ally, and all the gods, be always on our side!"[1] In the standard, ironic readings of these lines, Oedipus unwittingly condemns himself, for he does not know the truth of his parentage—indeed, he does not know that he does not know—and therefore does not know that he himself is the source of the contagion that is killing the city.[2] Nor does anyone else grasp the dramatic irony that escapes the king—except for the Theban seer Teiresias.[3] In the words of Charles Segal: "True vision belongs to the blind man"—the foremost guardian of Thebes' religious commitments—not Oedipus:

> The scene between Oedipus and Teiresias puts on the stage the paradoxical contrast between the king's eyes that do not see and the blind prophet's that do. But the paradoxes of blind vision are doubled by paradoxes of deaf hearing. Oedipus cannot "understand" the truth spoken in Teiresias' unambiguous words. . . . Oedipus's insistent anger even pushes Teiresias to abandon his enigmatic language of revelation (350–353) for the most open, flagrant accusation possible: "I declare you to be the killer of that man whose murderer you are seeking" (362).[4]

Accordingly, when Oedipus mutilates his eyes after he discovers his guilt, he would be acknowledging that his kingdom's central religious figure, Teiresias, has all along possessed the most secure form of knowledge—on the one hand, the self-reflexive, second-order, ironic knowledge that he does not merely think he knows the truth but that he really does know and that he knows that he knows; and on the other hand, the equally reflexive knowledge that he knows Oedipus is in the grip of a false belief, a hubristic false confidence about his knowledge, such that he does not know that he does not know (and so on) what he thinks he does.[5]

This ironic reading of Teiresias' epistemological superiority, however, is problematic. Why did Teiresias not warn the Thebans years ago against making Oedipus their king? Why has Teiresias not explained the source of the plague at its outbreak? Why does he wait until the king provokes him to speak out, and why does he respond to Oedipus with an anger that raises doubts about his motivation? Why does the figure who supposedly knows the truth disappear less than a third of the way through the drama? After Oedipus destroys his eyes, he is as blind as the seer he has traduced. Why, then, when their king faces his people, stumbling and groping in agony before them for the final 200–plus lines (14 percent of the play), does the Chorus not once invoke Teiresias' prescience or remark the terrible irony of Oedipus' self-punishment? Their king defiled beyond calculation, why would the Chorus—indeed, why would Oedipus himself—not turn to the seer? If Oedipus is, as Charles Segal affirms, "a figure whose force of personality and integrity set him . . . apart for a special destiny and enable him to confront that destiny with clarity and courage after a painfully won struggle for self-knowledge,"[6] why would he not publicly acknowledge the seer's earlier revelation? Finally, why does Oedipus not kill himself? What can he want his people to see in their king's self-mutilation that they do not already know by virtue of their seer's previous, and presumably god-inspired, indictment of him?

This chapter argues that Oedipus knows what Teiresias and the rest of Thebes do not—that their religious beliefs derive from their fear of acknowledging that the sacred cannot protect them from the costliness of existence, of which the plague is a devastating instance. Oedipus knows that this costliness—this manifestation of the world's infanticidism—is non-transcendable. He also knows that his people deny this fact and view the cause of their collective suffering not as a chance event (not, for example, as a disease that exceeds their medical expertise) but as a metaphysical disaster, a divine punishment from gods who might yet be propitiated. He knows that they are tempted to identify with the gods and to envision themselves as the agents rather than victims of divine wrath, an identification that requires them to redirect the violence of the gods against someone other than themselves, as if the death of this person would remove the cause of the plague that has left so many corpses in its wake. In this regard Oedipus knows that the metaphysical or allegorical interpretation of the plague is a means by which his people have sacralized so as to conceal the infanticidal implications of the economization that is both the catastrophe and possibility of human existence.

Oedipus wants to demystify Thebes' self-sacralization—that is, to bring his people face-to-face with the sacrificial implications of their economization in particular and the world's infanticidity in general, neither of which they have been able to think through. To this end Oedipus seeks to show that his people have projected onto the plague their deepest anxieties about the pitilessness of the economizing necessity within which human existence is inscribed, a pitilessness to which they have yielded in their religious beliefs and practices, a pitilessness which they have equated with the will of the gods and internalized. Oedipus knows that in the description they give of the plague his people are haunted by an image of themselves as pitiless, an image they do not recognize, an image of the infanticidal deadliness of their own economizations.

Oedipus understands the enormity of his task. On the one hand, he must convince his people to acknowledge their collective violence—specifically, their own infanticidal pitilessness —behind their allegorizing interpretation of the plague. On the other hand, he must convince them both to give up their desire to step beyond the economizing horizon of their existence and to abandon their practice of purifying themselves through the sacrifice of scapegoat victims. In both cases Oedipus must resist the allegorizing impulse of his people by which they are tempted to believe that the plague is the result of the unavenged murder of the former king. At the same time he must elucidate how his people's allegorizing impulse leads them, in the name of their gods, to engage in more and more virulent and explicitly infanticidal forms of violence, violence that reproduces the very destructiveness they wish to expel from their world.

At stake for Oedipus, then, is whether or not he can articulate the paradox that, in denying the infanticidism of the world—and thus in denying their participation in the necessity of an economization that can never become purely sacred, purely a force of life, purely generative—his people will engage in forms of sacrificial violence that will hasten and intensify the deadliness that "plagues" mortal beings. At stake, in other words, is whether or not Oedipus can get his culture to feel, if not understand, that in allegorizing the plague they have reproduced it in more virulent form and that they must give up their allegory.

The danger for Oedipus, however, is great. Attempting to initiate a cultural critique by articulating both the infanticidal meaning the Thebans have unwittingly projected onto the plague and the infanticidity of the gods that this projection defends against, Oedipus risks becoming the target of his people's rage at him for his message. To minimize the danger of persecution, Oedipus adopts a strategy of speaking "between the lines" and miming the ignorance of which the seer accuses him.[7] In the discursive space opened by this self-protective simulation, Oedipus gains time as he covertly tries to mirror the plague's repressed infanticidal meaning in an act that would reveal to his kingdom what its religious beliefs prevent the Thebans from grasping—namely, that there is no escaping the world's infanticidism.[8]

SPEAKING BETWEEN THE LINES

Whenever he seems to fall victim to the play's dramatic ironies (and to trip over his own angry tongue, as it were), Oedipus in fact hints at his discursive strategy of deliberately speaking by hints.[9] Consider, for example, his peculiar account to Jocasta of his sudden anxiety about his past after Teiresias and Creon have publicly fingered him as the murderer of the former king, and after he learns, supposedly for the first time, that the former king had been killed at a crossroads. When Jocasta asks what "troubles" him (Gould, line 770), he tells her that he will tell her "everything," for "who has a right greater than yours" to know, he asks rhetorically (Gould, lines 772–73). And yet for the duration of their marriage (they have been together long enough to have begotten four presumably adolescent children) he has evidently refused her this "right," since he has never before explained the circumstances under which he left Corinth and came to kill an old man and his retinue at "the exact location where, *as you tell of it*," he says to Jocasta, "the king was killed" (Gould, lines 798–99). Why does Oedipus suddenly reveal a secret he has evidently kept from his wife for so many years?

What he next says to Jocasta reinforces the strangeness—in fact, the contradictoriness—of his sudden self-disclosure about why he feels so alarmed. He recalls how, raised as the son of Polybus and Merope in Corinth, "I was first citizen, until [a] chance attacked me," he says, referring to an encounter with a drunkard who publicly accuses him of being a bastard. Although he says the accusation was "striking enough, to be sure, *but not worth all the gravity I gave it*" (Gould, lines 776–79),[10] he does not in fact dismiss the drunkard's story. Why not? Why does he introduce his back-story with an account of an event he now claims is trivial and therefore of no interest to his present listeners?

Part of the answer comes from the fate of the drunkard. When Oedipus questions his parents about the drunkard's accusation, "they made the man who let slip the word pay dearly for the insult."[11] In other words, Oedipus frames his autobiography with the account of someone who is punished for telling the truth. Here, Oedipus is redirecting the audience's gaze at themselves. He is rehearsing the scapegoating punishment that not only the Thebans but the literary tradition will soon dish out to him for attempting to reveal a truth they do not want to hear about their tendency to scapegoat.

When he continues with his story, is Oedipus taking the drunkard seriously or not? He says on the one hand that, at the time, he was "comforted" by the pitiless reaction of his parents but on the other hand that he "continued" to feel "vex[ed]" (Lloyd-Jones, 405, lines 785–86) since the drunkard's "words kept coming back" (Gould, line 786). As Gould comments, the Greek phrase "coming back" can mean either "the gossip crept abroad" or "the memory kept haunting me" (99n786). Clearly, they cannot haunt Oedipus unless he gives them credence. And why would a person crippled from birth not wonder about his origin, especially in a culture that accepted the discarding of defective newborns? Oedipus next says that Polybus and Merope denounced the accuser but does not say that they denied this man's statement. Why not? And why does he say he was "comforted" or "pleased"[12] by their response when, to the contrary, he was so riled about the rumor that he went to the oracle at Pytho "without the knowledge of my mother and my father" (Lloyd-Jones, 405, line 787)?

Oedipus introduces additional peculiarities to his back-story when he claims that Apollo sent him away "dishonoring my demand" (Gould, lines 788–89), presumably the demand to know who conceived him. However, when he then explains that Apollo had forecast his patricidal and incestuous future, Oedipus merely implies, he does not say directly, that he had posed the question of his parentage and that the god had "dishonored" him by not answering it. At this point he says that Apollo had prophesied "*other* wretched horrors," a turn of phrase implying that his conception and birth were one instance of the disastrousness he now seemingly fears is about to overtake him. Oedipus' indirection about what he did or did not ask the oracle, in other words, raises the possibility that Apollo had confirmed and so "dishonored" Oedipus' question, repeating the "dishonoring" news first brought by the drunkard, and then had "come out with other"—that is, additional—"things terrible and sad for my unhappy self" (Lloyd-Jones, 407, lines 799–800).

Most commentaries do not entertain this possibility. They take Oedipus at his (seemingly self-incriminating) word that he left Corinth "and went where I could never see accomplished the shameful predictions of my cruel oracles" (Lloyd-Jones, 407, lines 796–97). This action "might have made sense," Philip Vellacott notes, "if he had believed that Polybus and Merope were his parents; but in fact he had come to Delphi because he had strong reason to doubt if they were."[13] Following the prophecy, he had strong reasons not to kill another man, let alone someone older. And if he had, as he claims, he would have had compelling reasons to reflect on the irony of his attempts to escape his supposed fate and to be all the more cautious about marrying at all, let alone an older woman, and about admitting to his action, let alone under the present circumstances. And yet, as Oedipus now recalls aloud the fatal skirmish at the crossroads, he neglects to mention either what emotional response he had to his action or to his frame of mind when offered the opportunity to marry. To the contrary, he now fears, as if he were realizing for the first time, the meaning of his past behavior: "if this foreigner," the man he says he killed, "had any tie with Laius, who now could be more miserable, and who more hateful to the gods, than I . . .?" (Lloyd-Jones, 407, lines 814–17).[14]

The interpretive issue is not merely the problematic nature of Oedipus' past behavior, which scholars typically explain in terms that substitute the reader's mastery of Oedipus for Oedipus' loss of self-mastery,[15] but of his present narrative accounting of that behavior. Is it certain that Oedipus is reporting rather than inventing the past? Is it certain that this acknowledged master of riddling words does not have an ulterior motive for the seeming lacunae, non sequiturs, unverifiability, and other oddities of his discourse? Since the entire plot depends on Theban faith in the oracle, why does Oedipus provide an explanation of his anxieties that, in his back-story, profanes the oracle by linking the drunkard's taunt and the pythia's pronouncement at Delphi? Perhaps he perceives the institution of oracular revelation, upheld as sacred by his kingdom, to be a (subornable) system of (intoxicating) rumor.[16] If he did, how could he present his insight without arousing the furious resistance of those, like Teiresias, who identify with this system and who are dependent on the political economy this system sacralizes? If Oedipus were endeavoring to lift his culture's repression of the infanticidism through which the gods mark out the possibilities of human destiny, if he were thereby attempting to redefine his culture's understanding of the gods, would he not have had to adopt a strategic discourse in order to minimize the threat his cultural critique would pose? A first question, then is this: Does Oedipus speak from a position of dramatically ironic ignorance or from a meta-level position of discursive sophistication? This question foregrounds the economization that underwrites the traditional conception of Sophoclean irony—the reader's sense of intellectual mastery at the expense of Oedipus. It also underscores the problem of economization within Oedipus' own self-presentation: how can he use his authority to change his people's ideological investment in a belief system he knows to be inadequate in accounting for why his people are suffering?

A second question also turns on this problem of economization in Oedipus' self-interpretation as well as the reader's interpretation of Oedipus' self-interpretation. This question points toward Oedipus' discursive strategy of trying to communicate a meaning different from what he actually says: Why does Oedipus drop his defense against the charge of regicide, perhaps the most notorious interpretive crux of the play?[17] When Teiresias denounces Oedipus as the cause of the plague, Oedipus offers an explanation: he acted alone whereas the self-proclaimed eyewitness to the king's murder had reported that Laius had been killed by a band of thieves. Oedipus calls for this survivor to testify once again: "if he still gives the same number, I was not the killer, for one is not the same as many" (Lloyd-Jones, 411, lines 843–45).[18] The entire plot of the drama— the play's inexorable movement toward Oedipus' self-recognition and reversal of fortunes—hinges on the eyewitness, and yet when this man finally arrives, Oedipus does not ask him the question he has announced is the very reason for ordering him to testify. Why not? Why does he abandon the empiricism upon which he has put forward his defense? What can he possibly gain by not asking his question? What can he possibly lose by asking it?

Traditional responses ignore the second question and finesse the first by arguing that Oedipus is convinced of his guilt from irrefutable facts that need no further investigation. As Frederick Ahl points out, however, such an answer reproduces the very way the personages in the drama neglect to scrutinize the unverifiable, hearsay, fabricated nature of the evidence against Oedipus. Ahl grounds his book-length argument in a view of the massively narcissistic economization that he believes motivates Oedipus to convict himself of a crime and to accept a guilt for which there is insufficient empirical evidence. What is his payoff? The answer Ahl offers is that Oedipus harbors a (bipolar) hope of a mythic identity as his people's savior. On the one hand, "Oedipus comes to see himself as singled out to be a kind of scapegoat, a *pharmakos*, to Apollo," someone "chosen" to be a means of "atonement" for "the ills of the community" even if he is not "the real cause of the community's sufferings or guilt." Although he fears this fate, nevertheless he comes to embrace it, for, on the other hand, his "sense of personal guilt allows him to take on the responsibility for the guilt of the community as a whole." In Ahl's reading, Oedipus resolves this motivational dilemma by developing a mythomaniac "self-conviction" of his paradoxical power to save a community by acknowledging the devastating power of his violence and consequent guilt. The result is that Oedipus acts out a grandiose "self-deception" that elevates him to the status of a mythic, in fact "Christlike," redeemer.[19] If this were the case, then Oedipus would be accepting his kingdom's allegorization of the plague as caused by an individual guilty of the most extreme, the most violent impiety.

Other aspects of Sophocles' tragedy, however, suggest that Oedipus is not a victim of an impious, mythologizing impulse, one that preserves his culture's faith in their gods, but is its greatest critic. The most important of these elements is the overtly infanticidal nature of the plague, which emphasizes in yet another way the sacrificial economization Thebes represses and Oedipus wishes to expose. Thus, the third question opened by considering the strategic purposes behind Oedipus' discourse is this: Why are the infanticidal features of the plague so difficult to detect, let alone theorize, and what might be their link to the terms of Oedipus' defense?

The question of the Theban plague repeats the terms of Oedipus' defense: why should the consequences of the alleged wrongdoing of one person take the form of the suffering of many? Why would the gods make an entire city, including its children, pay such a terrible price? And why should the payment take the form of a plague?

A multiple disaster, the plague afflicts Thebes in three catastrophic ways. "A blight is on the buds that enclose the fruit, a blight is on the flocks of grazing cattle and on the women giving birth, killing their offspring; the fire-bearing god, hateful Pestilence, has swooped upon the city and harries it, emptying the house of Cadmus, and Black Hades is a plutocrat in groans and weeping" (Lloyd-Jones, 329, lines 25–30). According to Vernant, "Thebes suffers from a *loimos* that manifests itself in the traditional way, by the failure of all sources of fertility: Earth, flocks, and women are no longer productive while at the same time plague decimates the living. Sterility, disease, and death are all felt to be the power of the same defilement, a *miasma* that has disrupted the whole of life's normal course."[20] On the one hand the plague destroys the seed and thus kills off the future; on the other hand it destroys the living and kills off the present. Thebes thus finds itself imperiled in its ability to transmit itself into the next generation. The city is dying.

As the play opens the Chorus bemoans the "countless" numbers of recently dead Thebans: "Countless are [the] deaths, and the city is perishing." (Lloyd-Jones, 343, line 180). The Chorus cannot begin to calculate the destructiveness of the plague. They are brought up short by a limitless limit to their ability to imagine their loss, to conceive the total failure of conception. Because the disaster is without numerical measure, no relation of one and many, no ratio, will be able to delimit it. This strange, terrible, numberless, arrhythmic catastrophe marks the onslaught of a reproductive crisis the fatality of which has spread everywhere, reaching to the very horizon of the Theban economy.[21]

How is this reproductive crisis to be understood? What is its relation to its apparent (symbolic, not literal) cause—the "bloodshed" in the killing of Laius, "that has brought the storm upon the city" (Lloyd-Jones, 335, line 101)? Bernard Knox summarizes the traditional assessment of the plague: the "sympathetic relationship between the fruits of the soil and the fruit of the womb is reflected in the transference of agricultural terms to the involved pollution of the marriage of Oedipus and Jocasta, and what the reflection suggests is the responsibility of that unholy marriage for the stunted crops" and presumably the blight on the cattle as well.[22] Pietro Pucci echoes this view: "the plague attacks the production of children, livestock, and crops (the trinity of civilized generational continuity), as if it were intended to symbolize Oedipus's crime, the son who has defiled production by generating children with his mother."[23] According to Seth Benardete, "Thebes has been struck by a plague that exactly fits Oedipus's crimes, for defective offspring is supposed to be the consequence of incest."[24]

Perhaps, but defective offspring throughout the Theban kingdom cannot literally, but only symbolically, be the consequence of Oedipus' incest, since he is not their progenitor. What is more, the children of Thebes are never said to be defective. They are said to be dying or dead. More ominously still, their corpses are said to be unaccountably left to rot rather than to be properly attended to: "unpitied [Thebes'] children lie on the ground, carried off by death, with none to lament" (Lloyd-Jones, 343, lines 181–82).[25] Why unpitied? What does the absence of pity signify about the meaning of a plague that is "grown ingrained" or "nurtured"?[26]

The self-declared witness to Laius' murder provides the answer. Called to testify about the murder of the king, he instead bears witness to the infanticidal violence directed against Laius' (ostensible) son. Under questioning, this servant indicates that Jocasta had given him an infant "said to be [Laius'] child" (Lloyd-Jones, 449, line 1171) in order to "kill the boy" (Gould, line 1174). He confesses, however, to have given the child over to the care of a shepherd.[27] Why did he not carry out the command to leave the deliberately crippled—and therefore anathematized—child to die of exposure? The risks from disobeying would have been enormous. Why did he take them? Because, "O master, I *pitied* it, and thought that I could send it off to another country" (Gould, lines 1178–79). The servant's compassion saves the child from a cruel death by starvation, dehydration, exposure, or the attack of animals. Pity, then, is an affective force strong enough to lead a servant to overcome his fear of and disobey an infanticidal decree from the kingdom's ruler.[28] No other emotional experience in the tragedy has such power, a power that is able to call the very authority of the *tyrannos* into question. No wonder Aristotle locates pity at the emotional heart of tragedy.[29]

Once Oedipus has elicited the servant's kindness toward an infant, he abandons his defense without ever asking the question—did or did not the servant say that a band of thieves, not a lone robber, killed Laius?— which is the sole reason for summoning him. Why does he not ask this question? Because he has now gotten a member of his kingdom to confess to the infanticidal violence of the former king. Oedipus is thus on the verge of revealing how the pitiless violence of the one, of the royal family against its child (left to die of exposure on the pathless hillside of Mount Cithaeron), is now the pitilessness of the many, of numerous Theban households toward their unburied dead children (exposed on the streets of the city itself).

What is to be recognized, then, at the climax of the play's recognition scene is that Oedipus abandons his defense precisely at the juncture in the drama when he has elicited from the slave a counter-conceptive solution to the riddle of the plague, the riddle of the multiple deaths of children in relation to the single death intended by Laius and Jocasta. If the plague can be said to fit anyone's crime, it must fit the crime of Laius and Jocasta, for dead—unburied, unmourned—offspring would have been the more or less direct, immediate, and literal, not symbolic, consequence of their violence but for the fortuitous compassion of the slave. If the reproductive context of Oedipus and Jocasta's marriage can be interpreted as (metaphorically) responsible for the plague, then all the more so the reproductive context of a marriage in which the parents, plotting pitilessly against their child, attempt to undo their procreation. If the crime of the one can (symbolically) overtake the many, then all the more so the crime of the many can overtake the one. If a seeming stranger, Oedipus, is revealed to be a Theban after all, then his reappearance is, perforce, the haunting return of the unwanted child, the child intended for death, hence the return of the kingdom's infanticide-victim. In short, the plague reproduces within the city-state at large the crisis of infanticide within the house of Laius. In suffering the mutilating, murderous aggression of his parents, Oedipus survives a version of the pitilessness that now besets all of Thebes.[30]

Oedipus is a scapegoat, then, who intervenes in the sacrificiality of his kingdom to reveal the possibility of another order of economy, one investing in an affective reorientation in response to a new conception of the gods. This emotional realignment entails a paradoxical answerability: the capacity to respond with pity (like the shepherd) to the other in the other's helplessness, but also the courage to acknowledge in oneself the murderousness of a Laius against the helpless other. It involves the ability to care for and thereby invest in the other, and to do so without any guarantee of a future return; but it also entails being susceptible to a hate that can lead one to (want to) destroy the other, to (want to) protect oneself from the potentially life-threatening costs to oneself of such investment. Finally, it requires an acceptance that certain calamities are not metaphysical messages from the gods but unavoidable consequences of the fact that existence costs.

The paradoxical answerability to which Oedipus is attuned is a consequence of the infanticidism inherent to life in a Darwinian universe, where the other is always able to represent a potential menace. Because the other can be a threat, Judith Butler explains, "the desire to kill" may be "primary to human beings."[31] Even an infant can stimulate this impulse. The very extremity of the infant's precarious life can elicit not only a (loving) identification but a (furious) dis-identification. The sight or sound of the infant might evoke a fear of hurting this person—indeed, might awaken a fear of bringing harm to others more generally. However, the utter dependency of the newborn might also trigger a sense of one's own vulnerabilities and therefore of wanting to destroy this source, this unwanted reminder, of a primal anxiety.[32] As Butler notes, the "Other" calls to us in a "vocalization of agony that is not yet language or no longer language" and thereby "waken[s]" us "to the precariousness of the Other's

life, the one that rouses at once the temptation to murder *and* the interdiction against it."[33] The precariousness of which Butler writes is the
ordinary story of human existence: "One insight that injury affords is
that there are others out there on whom my life depends, people I do not
know and may never know." Having survived his victimization as an
infant, so detested as to be the target of mutilation and then a slow death,
Oedipus understands that, in Butler's words, "no security measure" can
"foreclose" this "fundamental dependency on anonymous others."[34]

In his genius — misrecognized as his (ironic, hubristic, tragic) susceptibility to a fate that overtakes him in the very act of trying to escape
it, as the susceptibility of the one rather than of the many to harm in
general — Oedipus understands that the category of "others" must be expanded to include the otherness of the sacred itself. He thus apprehends
that the gods cannot protect humans from their universal helplessness
because the sacred coincides with this very vulnerability. In consequence, Oedipus knows that the sacred cannot be approached except
in its paradoxicality — as the demand for a compassion without reserve,
for a sacrifice of self for other; but therefore as a demand that threatens
one's most basic drive to survive, one's most automatic impulses toward
self-protection.

Others, Butler notes, "make moral claims upon us, address moral demands to us, ones that we do not ask for, ones that we are not free to
refuse." To respond to these claims "means to be awake to what is precarious in another life," to "the precariousness of life itself."[35] Oedipus
offers his people the chance to rethink this precariousness in terms of its
infanticidal implications. To this end he stages his recognition in terms
of the difference between infanticide (as empirical phenomenon) and
infanticidism (as the underlying "logic" of the empirical phenomenon, a
logic that is operative even in the absence of infanticide). On the one
hand, Oedipus understands infanticide as a figure either of any strategy
for destroying the other under the illusion that one can thereby protect
oneself from the violence of the sacred (as when Laius and Jocasta try
to dispose of him, their son, through whom Apollo has cursed them), or
of the vulnerability to the other that threatens an entire people's collective survival into the future (the plague). On the other hand, he intuits
the infanticidism that his culture fears, refuses to acknowledge, and cannot name. This infanticidity encompasses the injurability and deathliness,
the non-calculable costliness of futures lost, from which not even the
gods themselves can exempt humans, no matter how intense, how sacrificially scrupulous, how devout the supplication, and how sincere the
effort at atonement might be. He knows, in sum, that the sacred calls to
humans in a double "voice" that must be recognized to be infanticidal on
the one hand (the voice of Laius and Jocasta) and life-sparing on the

other (the servant, the Corinthian shepherd to whom the servant gives the infant Oedipus, the king and queen to whom the shepherd in turn passes on the child).

In other words, Oedipus abandons his defense in order to raise into view two possible scenes. The first is the scene of a sacrificial abandonment of a child who is without defense against either the lethal action directed against his person or the desire that motivates that action. The second is a scene of the infant's rescue, thereafter repeated every day of this person's life following his adoption into Polybus and Merope's household as their son. At the climax of the drama's recognition scene, then, Oedipus succeeds in exposing the concealed exposure of the child and then the child's rescue — the temptation and the temptation overcome to destroy in the child the reproductive embodiment of an unwanted future.

Oedipus' aim, however, is not merely to identify a particular act of violence but the felt meaning of the logical form of its underlying structure. No child can ever know, in the form of first-person experience, the conditions under which it is hailed into being nor ever recall its initial vulnerability to this address from others on which the very formation of its subjectivity and future self-consciousness depends. Oedipus' cultural task, then, is to transform his kingdom's understanding of their collective vulnerability to the other — to one another, to the gods, and finally to the anonymous generality of the world's infanticidism — in order to avoid the temptation of seeing in the sacred a solution to the general problem of a pitiableness for which no human distribution of resources will ever suffice. A fourth question, then, is, How does Oedipus' act of self-blinding contribute to his infanticidal cultural critique?[36]

Oedipus specifies the infanticidal meaning of his self-blinding when, having discovered that Jocasta has hanged herself, having taken down her body, and having removed the "pins" from her robe, he "raised" the broaches and "struck into the ball-joints of his eyes" (Gould, lines 1269–70).[37] Oedipus does not destroy his *ophthalmoi* (eyes) or *kykloi* (literally circles or disks and metaphorically eyeballs) but his *arthra* (joints), "an unparalleled use of this word," Gould explains, "and very odd indeed, if we had not been prepared for it by 718 and 1032," where the word denotes ankles (145n12700). At line 718 Jocasta recalls how Laius had "fastened" (Lloyd-Jones) or "yoked the ball-joints [*arthra*] of his son's feet" (Gould). At line 1032, the Corinthian messenger indicates how "the ball-joints [*arthra*]" of Oedipus' feet "might testify" to the fate from which he was saved: "Your feet were pierced and I am your rescuer" (Gould, lines 1032 and 1034). As Gould all but acknowledges, when Oedipus blinds himself he does to his arthra-eyes what Laius had done to his arthra-ankles. Gould says that "the piercing of the eyes continues . . . the piercing of the ankles."[38] Gould points out the similarity between the two acts of violence but misses Oedipus' intention: Oedipus wants his audience to see his father's violence, and that is why he redirects it against his eyes. In other words, Oedipus repeats the infanticidal aggression—the infanticidal paternal "hailing"—that is inscribed in his ankles and swollen feet. By displacing the aggression from feet to eyes, however, he attempts to raise the father's violence into view where it can be publicly named, acknowledged, and analyzed.

Whatever Oedipus reveals about the nature of his motivation, he acts out the motivation of his parents, which the Theban kingdom has repressed. In blinding himself he provides his people with a perspicuous image of their collective blindness to their violence.[39] Pitilessly mutilating his *arthra*, Oedipus emerges from the palace "a vision even one who hates must pity," the palace messenger concedes in horror (Gould, line 1296). Although the members of the chorus acquiesce in this characterization, they cannot face the sight of the abomination before them: "Indeed I pity you, but I cannot look at you, though there's much I want to ask and much to learn and much to see. I shudder at the sight of you" (Grene, lines 1303–7).

At this moment the Chorus enact the play's catastrophe: they turn away from the terrifying sight of Oedipus. In doing so they not only refuse to acknowledge the infanticidal meaning of his act but unwittingly—ironically—act out the moral blindness of the sighted who refuse to see. Anticipating this response, Oedipus blinds himself in private—in a space unavailable to the public eye—in order to foreground the collective self-blinding that results from his culture's tragic inability to pity. Thus, just when they would turn toward Oedipus to address him, to ask for him to explain, to hear from him, to see what there is to be seen, the chorus cannot muster the requisite pity and so turn away.

Their blindness is emphatic: at the very moment they say they want to "learn" the meaning of his "miserable fate" (Lloyd-Jones, lines 1305 and 1302), they avert their eyes and try to cover their ears. In response Oedipus cries out: "Ah! Ah! I am a man of misery. Where am I carried? Pity me! Where is my voice scattered abroad on wings? Divinity, where has your lunge transported me?" To which the Chorus respond: "To something horrible, not to be heard or seen" (Gould, lines 1308–12). Oedipus here brings forth the affective meaning of the plague not as a god-sent punishment but as a crisis of compassion. The Chorus shut themselves off from the pity they claim they feel for their king, and they do so just after Oedipus has, in blinding himself, traced in reverse the actions by which his parents had sought to remove him from everyone's sight, and just after he has stumbled through the gates of the palace to expose himself to public view. For the next 230 lines of the play's extended denouement, he forces his people to behold in his *arthra* a traumatizing horror, a "suffering [that] sends terror through men's eyes, terrible beyond any suffering my eyes have touched" (Gould, line 1297–99).

The infanticidal meaning of that suffering, however, has been before the people of Thebes from the outset of Oedipus' arrival: it has been visible in his step and audible in his name. Why, then, have the Thebans not recognized this implication of "Oedipus"? "Oedipus" (from *oidein*, to swell, and *pous*, foot) means "Swellfoot."[40] This name identifies the consequences of the actions—the yoking, perhaps the piercing, of his ankles—by which his parents intended that he die. Like his feet, Oedipus' name announces that he is the child of infanticidal parents but that he has somehow survived the death sentence to which they tried to condemn him. Both his name and feet, then, record the identity-destroying condition from which he takes his identity. Both translate the interpellative riddle of his survival: How could I have lived if my ankles were hobbled and I was left to die? This riddle can be generalized: How does any child survive its defenselessness?

Since Oedipus is astute enough to solve the riddle of the Sphinx, is it believable that he has not solved the riddle of his naming? Is it believable that he does not know what his name means or how he might have received it? Since he is an immigrant, is it not possible that he has deliberately chosen this name? Bernard Knox notes that Oedipus' name "emphasizes the physical blemish which scars the body of the splendid *tyrannos*, a defect he would like to forget but which reminds us of the cast-out child he once was and foreshadows the outcast man he is soon to be."[41] Is it certain, however, that he wants to forget this defect? Is it not possible that he would want never to forget it, and that, if he could overcome the desire to make someone pay for this ontological assault, he could discover in it a destiny-defining gift by which he himself might "remind us of the cast-out child he once was"? Is his drive to solve the riddle of the plague not a concern to "save" his people—whom he repeatedly addresses as his "children"[42]—from a children-destroying attitude that leads a people to respond to what might be a natural disaster (the plague) with infanticidal actions that intensify this disaster's deadliness?

Over and over Oedipus attempts to name what his kingdom does not want to see or hear concerning the infanticidism of the sacred and the infanticide-violence that erupts when a people deny the infanticidism of the sacred. Precisely because his kingdom resists his message, precisely because he risks not merely his empirical life and limb but his name and what it will come to signify, he must adopt an elliptical communicative strategy in an effort to overcome his kingdom's resistance. One example will illustrate what is at stake in Oedipus' indirection.

When Oedipus questions the Corinthian messenger about being a foundling, he explicitly refers to his feet as sites of *kakon* (Gould, line

1033), which can mean "trouble" "pain," or "scars,"[43] and then as "tokens" (Gould, line 1035):

Messenger. I was your savior, son.
Oedipus. From what? What was my trouble when you took me?
Messenger. The ball-joints of your feet might testify.
Oedipus. What's that? What makes you name that ancient trouble [*kakon*]?
Messenger. Your feet were pierced and I am your rescuer.
(Gould, lines 1030–34)

Employing the passive voice — "Your feet were pierced" — the Messenger avoids identifying the aggressors. He withholds the name of the parents in reconstructing the origin of the name of the child. Oedipus responds by disclosing the cover-up: "A fearful rebuke those tokens [spargana] left for me!" (Gould, line 1035). Since "the word *spargana* . . . is used in tragedy and comedy to refer to tokens (usually hung around the neck) by which the parents (or others) can later identify an exposed child," the line can be rendered: "My swaddling clothes [*spargana*] brought me a rare disgrace" (Gould, 124n1035). Rather than hiding his wound, Oedipus' wrappings uncover the parental source of his crippling injury. That is why, when the messenger suggests that Oedipus is called his "present name" (1036) from the "chance" of the assault on his body, the king can finally broach the question of his parents' responsibility:

Messenger. That was the chance [*tyche*] that names you who you are.
Oedipus. By the gods, did my mother or my father do this?

According to Jeffrey Rusten, Oedipus' question is ambiguous, since it can mean either "Did I get my name from my parents?" or "Did my parents actually maim me?" (52n1037). In fact, however, the question's ambiguity is doubly self-clarifying, for he receives his name from the *kakon* bequeathed to him at birth. The "chance" that names him is the troubling mischance of having been born to infanticidal parents, who inscribe his bad luck on his body when they mutilate him. Having survived the assault, Oedipus acquires the (infanticidal) tokens (his lame feet) by which he provides a visible trace of his parents' infanticidal violence with every hobbled footstep he takes.[44]

When he asks his question about who has maimed him, Oedipus introduces a telling ambiguity through the phrase, "by the gods," to oppose one understanding of the sacred against another: he asks in the name of the gods whether or not his parents had mutilated him in the name of the gods. That is, he invokes the gods to legitimize the questioning by which he seeks to reveal the suppressed or repressed infanticidal violence of the parents, who for their part invoke the gods in pursuing their (infanticidal) self-interest. Emphasizing the annihilating intention of his parents, Oedipus rewrites the sacred not as a divine will that directs the world but as the universal vulnerability of the child the survival of which depends on "chance"—specifically, the interpellative luck of being hailed by a pitying rather than a destroying other.

Shortly thereafter Oedipus again contests his culture's conception of the sacred when he asserts himself to be "the child of Chance, the giver of good. . . . She is my mother" (Gould, lines 1080–82). When he personifies chance, Oedipus tacitly counts as mother all who have saved him from, and thus acted as surrogates for, the parents who condemned him, parents to whom he was born by chance. As an infant, Oedipus lives or dies by virtue of the care he does or does not receive from others, and the force of his insight is to equate that care with an existential principle that takes into account the infanticidism of the sacred—the chance of fatal neglect or abuse, the chance of being pitied. The equation is momentous, for by it Oedipus recognizes the infanticidism of being—here, the vulnerability to infanticide—as the condition of the possibility of compassion. When he then says that "I shall not prove untrue to such a [chance-determined] nature by giving up the search for my own birth" (Gould, lines 1084–85), he has already found what he says he is looking for—a way to articulate the parental assault on his joints, an assault that constitutes the secret that Thebes refuses to see.[45]

Renaming himself the child of chance, and thus foregrounding the status of "Oedipus" as a self-nomination, the king challenges his people to see what he already sees: "Break out what will! I at least shall be willing to see my ancestry" (Grene, 58, lines 1076–77). According to Hogan, "*Break out* occurs both of storms and of festering wounds,"[46] hence of the plague which, assailing Thebes, has left it "reeling like a wreck," scarcely able to "lift its prow out of the depths, out of the bloody surf" (Grene, 11, lines 22–24). To see Oedipus (the name and person) is to see his ancestry because his very name captures the violence that was done to him as a child by his parents. To see Oedipus is to see his parents and what they did to him. It is to see that they were infanticidal. What is more, it is to see in Thebes' own history what years later has "broken out" again, this time to plague not only Oedipus but all the "children" of Thebes whose suffering, Oedipus declares, "rouses my pity" (Gould, line 13).

The Sphinx has presaged this infanticidal "breakout." The question is, How, and why has Oedipus alone been able to solve her riddle? The Sphinx poses a thought problem: "There exists on land a thing with two feet and four feet, with a single voice, that has three feet as well. It changes shape, alone among the things that move on land or in the air or down through the sea. Yet during the periods when it walks supported by the largest number of feet, then is the speed in its limbs the feeblest of all" (Gould, 19n36). The answer, of course, is Man, who "crawls on all fours as an infant, stands firmly on his two feet in his youth, and leans upon a staff in his old age."[47] Why should Oedipus be the one of many able to solve this riddle?

According to Benardete, as the play opens "the crippled Oedipus, we must imagine, appears before the Thebans leaning on a staff." As "a support for his infirmity," the staff points to the physical weakness that "no doubt enabled him to solve the riddle of the Sphinx: a man in the prime of life but maimed since childhood and hence 'three-footed' before his time saw in himself the riddle's answer."[48] To the contrary, Oedipus' name and feet exclude him from the developmental sequence encrypted in the riddle: What is the presumptively normal course of human development?[49] Debarred from that trajectory by virtue of his parents' murderousness, Oedipus has suffered a violent developmental history; in person and in name he bears the knowledge of a maturation compromised from the first days of his precarious life. Far from seeing himself as the paradigmatic instance of the riddle's solution, he knows that, standing on claudicant legs when he answers the Sphinx, he is the riddle's paradigmatic exception. His exceptionalism enables him to understand that the violence of the Sphinx mirrors the violence of his own father.

Having had his feet bound together, Oedipus has already encountered the "binding" power of the Sphinx, whose name, from *sphingein*, to bind fast,[50] reflects the action Laius and Jocasta took against his infant body. They themselves engage in a form of the Sphinx's violence. It is the riddle of their violence, refracted in the murderous aggression of the monster who bedevils Thebes, that no one but Oedipus can solve because no one but Oedipus can recognize in the riddle the problem of disrupted childhood development. The Sphinx herself incarnates this disruption. In one legend, the Sphinx is the hybrid offspring of other hybrid monsters.[51] In other legends she is "the bastard daughter of Laios."[52] Either way this heteromorphic creature represents an abominable misconception, a reproductive catastrophe. She embodies in both her form and lineage the wrong answer to her own question. With the head of a woman and a winged lion's body, the Sphinx's hybrid or "plural" form contrasts with the "single voiced" being — *anthropos*, Man — whose name solves her riddle.[53]

Oedipus himself is sphinxed when his father "fastened [his infant] ankles and had him cast out by the hands of others upon the trackless hillside" in order to avoid an oracle. In fact, he is sphinxed even earlier since, according to Jocasta, his very begetting was cursed: "An oracle once came to Laius," Jocasta tells Oedipus, "I will not say from Phoebus himself, but from his servants, saying that it would be his fate to die at the hands of the son who should be the child of him and me" (Lloyd-Jones, 399, lines 718–19 and 711–14). When Laius and Jocasta try to avoid their prophesied fate by maiming and then ordering their child to be left to die outside the city, they themselves become a form of the monster that later afflicts Thebes with her uncanny presence. When Oedipus confronts the Sphinx at the gates of Thebes, he meets up with an allegorical figure of Laius and Jocasta, a figure through whom Oedipus symbolically overcomes the violence of his parents.

The mythic account of Laius suggests how the Sphinx is a fantastic projection of his infanticidal impulses, which she embodies in symbolic guise. As a young man, Laius violated the guest-host relationship, foundational to Greek culture,[54] when, having sought sanctuary in Pelops' kingdom, he repays his host by abducting his son, Chrysippus. Pelops prays for revenge to Apollo, who condemns Laius' son. Since Laius not only kidnaps but sodomizes Chrysippus, he is in effect a sphincter king (*sphincter* derives from the same word that is the source of *Sphinx*). When he pierces his own son's ankles, he symbolically repeats the assault on Pelops' boy, bringing this earlier nonreproductive penetration to a conclusion he intends to be infanticidal. Not surprisingly, it is a sphincter goddess who blocks the passageway, the gates, to Thebes during the reign of Laius.

It is overdetermined, then, that Oedipus, himself a *spingeined* victim of his father, not only recognizes himself in the aberrant form of the riddling monster but also apprehends the return of the father's violence in the terror the Sphinx visits on Thebes. When Oedipus defeats the Sphinx, he symbolically frees Thebes from the former king's sodomistic and infanticidal—his anti-reproductive—violence.[55] He also tries to free Thebes from the infanticidal influence of its former king in the way he designates himself "Oedipus." In person and in name, the lame-legged Oedipus poses the Sphinx's question in reverse: What creature, normally walking on four legs, two legs, and eventually three, is forced—by whom and why—to walk on three from the outset? The answer is the abused infant who grows up with a constant reminder of the signifying wound from which he has received his identity: Oedipus' Greek name, "Oidipous," the first syllable of which is less a word than an exclamation of pain, can mean "Oh, [the pain of my] two feet."[56]

Insofar as they are doubles, the Sphinx and Oedipus embody the solution, represented in the image of feet, to a cultural crisis the nature of which the people of Thebes suspect but do not want to own up to. Early on, Creon all but admits Thebes' symptomatic resistance to knowing this truth. Asked by Oedipus why Thebes failed to pursue the matter of Laius' murder, Creon alludes to the city's helplessness in the midst of "our troubles" (*kakois*), the plural form of the same word that Oedipus has, in the singular, on the tip of his tongue: "it was your very kingship that was killed! What kind of trouble (*kakon*) blocked you from a search?"

To which Creon replies: "The riddling Sphinx induced us to neglect mysterious *crimes* and rather seek solution of *troubles* at our feet" (Grene, line 130–31). These "troubles" are *to pros posi:* metaphorically, they are "right in front of us"; literally, they are "at our feet," and it is this literal meaning that the Sphinx and Oedipus both apprehend. Both know what Oedipus' name reveals—that the "evils" that bedevil Thebes are (pedagogically) encrypted in the broken body of an unwanted infant, an anonymous "Swellfoot," someone who was to have been left to die on a "pathless hillside," a place of no footprints.[57]

UNMASKING THE ALLEGORY OF THE PLAGUE

From the outset Oedipus has attempted to raise into view the "tokens" of the infanticidal "troubles" to which he was subjected as a newborn and to reinterpret not the plague itself but his kingdom's interpretation of the plague—to reinterpret this interpretation as itself a form of the same "betokening trouble" that has afflicted him from birth. That is, he has wanted to teach his people how to live with a knowledge they have been unprepared to accept—the knowledge that life is inherently infanticidal and that their belief that the gods can protect them from this existential horizon has in fact led them to engage in actions that are as deadly as, perhaps even more deadly than, the plague they are seeking to overcome.

As has been indicated, Oedipus knows that human existence is precarious, even excruciatingly so, and that no appeal to the gods can reduce one's existential dependencies, which are the cost of being alive. He understands the temptation of interpreting disasters as under the control of a divine force that might be appeased. In particular, he understands how his people fear that the gods have deliberately visited a deadly scourge on the Theban kingdom through the (alleged) impiety and violence of someone in their midst. Oedipus further understands how, in consequence, his people are drawn to supplicate the gods, to publicly identify with them, to view themselves as the instruments of divine will and the destruction this will has unleashed, and to atone for someone among them by redirecting a similar destruction against this person, whose impiety, they believe, has aroused the wrath of the gods against everyone. Oedipus knows, in other words, that his people have responded, and at the outset of the drama are continuing to respond, to what initially might have been a natural disaster with an allegorical interpretation that suggests they unconsciously regard themselves as the cause of the crisis at hand—that they are projecting onto the disaster the infanticidal pitilessness that had overtaken the previous king and that they now fear has spread throughout the kingdom.

Oedipus hears this fear in the symptomatic language of the two accounts of the plague's deadliness that are offered to him (by a priest and by the chorus) as well as in Creon's report, supposedly from the oracle, of the plague's supposed cause (the killing of the former king) and solution (sacrificing the killer for the sake of the entire kingdom). In their unselfconscious references to the plague's infanticidal character, the priest, the chorus, and Creon tacitly confess to the infanticidal violence in their midst all the while hiding the nature of this violence in the theological terms by which they explain the plague as a divine punishment brought on by one person's falling away from the gods. Oedipus is trying to show that the plague as the Thebans interpret it mirrors their pitilessness. When they describe and respond to the plague as if it were an infanticidal punishment sent by the gods, they betray their worst dread—that they are collectively without pity and that, like the infanticidal Laius, they have turned their pitilessness against themselves and have thereby exacerbated the suffering and deadliness that the plague has caused. Oedipus organizes his entire discourse, including his seemingly unknowing self-incriminations, around the aim of disclosing the mistaken—the infanticidal—theological allegorizing that keeps the people of Thebes from examining their fear. In pursuing this cultural demystification, Oedipus links the Theban investment in their allegorization of the plague to their false conception of the symbolic order, a conception that hides the infanticidism of the world and the gods.

INTERPELLATION, INFANTICIDITY, AND THE SYMBOLIC ORDER DE-TRANSCENDENTALIZED

As was discussed in chapter 6, to be interpellated is to be inscribed in the symbolic order as a subject but not necessarily as a living being. One can be hailed not only into but also out of existence. What is more, one can even be hailed out of the possibility of existing. Interpellation, then, is as much a counter-conceptive as a conceptive structure and event.

The names of both "Oedipus" and "Laius" illustrate this doubleness. As indicated above, "Oedipus" names the father's refusal to name his son. Indeed, "Oedipus" is a strange species of unnaming name that points to the father's intention that the child not survive. Whereas most "proper" names cover up the traces of the infanticidal structure of life and affirm the living presence of the persons named, the "improper" name of "Oedipus" announces those effaced traces. Insofar as "Oedipus" identifies the bearer of this name as the victim of murderous parents, it brings into the light of day the non-visibility of the infanticidism that inheres in the structure and event of interpellation. That is, in exposing

Laius' infanticidal aims, "Oedipus" reveals the other side of interpellation — the way the "expectation" of new life can just as easily be a profound aversion to it.

In this regard "Oedipus" names the father as much as it does the son. That is, it identifies the namer (as curse-giver) at the same time that it identifies the son the father names (as cursed). "Oedipus" means that "Laius" means that the father is afraid of his son and hates what his son's life signifies for him — vulnerability to a threat that is implicit in his reproductive generativity, the threat of being genealogically displaced. The name "Oedipus" thus doubles back on the father, who is not a pure source of life. In this way the name of the father, the name "Laius," refers not only to a specific person, who wants his son dead, but to the counter-conceptive force within all conception, to the life-negating potentiality within any interpellation. In other words "Laius" names an individual (Laius) but also a symbolic function (interpellation), one that announces the loss, the death, the disappearance, the otherwise untraceable elimination of life in the moment of any life's appearance.[58]

When Apollo prophesies the fate of Laius and Jocasta as well as of the child they have yet to conceive,[59] he announces the interpellative violence of the symbolic order in terms of the deathliness inhering in all genealogy, all lineage, all ancestry. Apollo hails Laius and Jocasta with the news that they will destroy themselves through their conception and birthing of a son who shall destroy himself in turn when he tries to escape his destiny (that is, his oracular interpellation by Apollo), itself a cause and consequence of his parents' attempt to escape their destiny (that is, their oracular interpellation by the same god). In other words, Apollo sets in motion an interpellative transfer of his aggression to the parents and of the parents' aggression to the child. In this way "Apollo" becomes the name of the infanticidism to which both humans and the gods are bound.

This interpellative inscription of humans and gods alike reproduces life as economization — that is, life as bearing the traces of the deathliness that is its cost, its condition of possibility — the meta-destiny that all humans share and that is the subject of Sophocles' tragedy. The name of Apollo's sanctuary suggests as much, for "Delphi" comes from the common noun *delphus*, the Greek word for *womb*.[60] It is at the crossroads of their respective journeys to and from the sacred womb-site that Laius and Oedipus seal their fates. It is back to Apollo — the phallic archer god who has taken over the temple, the matrix of conception, birth, and knowledge of the future that is metonymically associated with the newborn — that Oedipus sends Creon to discover the solution to the plague. It is to this god — whose infanticidal curses and infanticide-removing blessings define the possibility of any life's advent — that Oedipus raises his hands before striking his eyes. Damning Laius and Jocasta by means of the son, and therefore the son by means of the parents, the god identifies a structural violence within any reproductive event. He names an accursedness attaching to all human reproductivity. Connecting the destinies of both Oedipus and his parents to Apollo's difficult hailing, Sophocles' drama begins to delimit the infanticidality of the interpellation within which life is "fated" to have what "chance" it has. The source of every oracular disclosure, beneficent and destructive alike, Apollo subjects every person in advance of his or her conception and birth to a general address. Within that interpellative structure each person may or may not be welcomed into life.

The first syllable of "Oidipous" echoes this irreducible ambiguity. Joined to the semantic possibilities of the name in which it is here embedded, "oi" is evocative of the child's first signaling of the world from out of its helplessness—its automatic, inarticulate reflex of crying. Having had the good fortune of being adopted into a family under the supervision of a wife, Merope, whose name means "articulate human,"[61] Oedipus later calls himself, in a (mother-supported) articulation that announces the contingent nature of the infant's biological advent, the "child of Chance." He does so not primarily to repudiate the parents who did not want him to live but to acknowledge the way their designs against him were susceptible to unforeseeable interference, to the wayward events that "give" him his subsequent survival. The event in question is the unpredictable intervention by the herdsman who disobeys Laius' command and instead saves the infant by passing him to another herdsman, who in turn forwards this "gift" (Gould, line 1022) to the childless Corinthian leader. The Greek word for gift—∂oron—signifies not only a present but "a votive offering to the gods."[62] The ironies here rebound against Theban religious orthodoxy, for Polybus is no god, and the offering buys not a divine but a human protection. The sacrilegious acts by which Laius and Jocasta would give up their son to death become the fortuitous means by which others can give him his life. Rejected and then saved from the fatal consequences of this rejection, rescued by the kindness of strangers who might just as easily have left him to die, Oedipus is a child of the fortune or chance within which all destiny is inscribed. He is a child of an interpellative force that is greater than Apollo, or that is the new, counter-conceptive meaning Oedipus is attributing to this god.

Calling himself the child of chance, Oedipus in effect contraceives his advent. That is, he knows how easily his origin could have annihilated him. Attuned by his crippling to his vulnerability from birth, Oedipus might be understood as angry—murderously so. But he might also be understood as recognizing that the physical and psychological sufferings to which he was subjected are, in fact, the conditions of the possibility of his subsequent survival, that they are the gift of an injury without which he would not be who he is. If so, they are the gift of an injurability that precedes the specific injury that comes to designate his identity.

Oedipus lives both in spite of his parents' attempt to maim and kill him and also because of those efforts. Accordingly, he bears a name that joins his conception, the prospect of its contraceptive undoing, and his rescue, such that he is an "Oedipus," one who survives by chance the interpellative expectation that he not survive. Does Oedipus understand the contingent nature not only of his survival but of any infant's survival? Does he understand that it is not having been conceived that confers identity but having been sufficiently cared for, and that such care may or may not come from one's supposed progenitors? Does he understand that if life proceeds from out of a fortuitous hailing, it is always possible for life to have been snuffed out from an unfortuitous hailing? Does he grasp that all human reproduction occurs within a logically prior context of interpellations, of announcements that cannot be known in advance will trumpet the arrival of a new life rather than presage a deathly plague?

In the canonical readings the answer is no.[63] In the first reading to introduce Althusser's notion of interpellation into a consideration of Oedipus' identity the answer is also no. Thus, Kirk Ormand asserts that Oedipus accepts the category of "biological identity" as a natural, not a socially constructed and regulated concept; that he does not grasp how identity "becomes 'natural' through a socially accepted process of recollection and subsequent suppression of other, competing possibilities, and through masking the instability inherent in this process."[64] Ormand concludes that Oedipus unwittingly falls victim to this ideological self-mystification when he abandons his defense and "actively allows" himself to be convinced that he really is the son of Laius and Jocasta: "He never once asks the herdsman if one or more than one person killed Laius. He apparently accepts the answer to the question 'Who am I?' as sufficient answer to the question that has consumed him, 'Who killed Laius?' He actively allows his biological identity to displace the question of what he has done. Like the answer to a riddle, the discovery of Oedipus's identity changes the categories that the original question suggested."[65]

To the contrary, it is not Oedipus who accepts his supposed "biological identity," it is the long tradition of ironic commentary that takes Laius' paternity for granted. In fact, Oedipus specifically indicates his recognition that paternity is always embedded in narrative, is always dependent upon attestation, hence is never entirely empirical, hence too is always able to be contested by a counter-narrative. He does so in one of the most notorious of his supposedly ironic speech-acts when he calls forth the names of the entire line of Theban kings. Protecting the dynastic genealogy, he prays to Apollo to punish the former king's murderer: "And this curse . . . against the one who did it, whether alone in secrecy, or with others: may he wear out his life unblest and evil!" (Gould, lines 246–249). In condemning the murderer, Oedipus hails him to destruction. He does so, however, not in his own name but in the name of the "power" (Gould, 237) he has as the "holder of the office" (Grene, 21, line 259) that once belonged to Laius, and before Laius to Laius' father Labdacus, to this man's father Polydorus, and to his in turn, Cadmus, the founder of Thebes, and to his father Agenor as well (cf. Gould, lines 267–69). As the present king, Oedipus occupies the same place in the line of kings that each of his predecessors does, for the lineage in question is only incidentally a line of biological descent. After all, blood lines are established as such not by some irrefutable empirical procedure but rather by public avowal and its retransmission—that is, by speech acts that achieve their authority through various protocols of institutional legitimation. These speech acts are not necessarily true. Indeed, their constative truth is largely irrelevant to their performative felicity. Before being a genealogy of kin, any line of kings is a narratively asserted tradition of the kings' respective claims to consanguinity. These claims constitute rituals of self-authorization; they do not depend on empirical factuality. When Oedipus finds himself the king, he inserts himself into the seemingly self-begetting chain of paternal leaders as an alien ruler whose authority does not depend upon the fiction of consanguineous descent. By declaring his biological difference from this line, he highlights the self-mystifying process by which his city-state mythifies its origin and its future destiny.

By confessing responsibility for the merely alleged, never proven, crimes, Oedipus reinserts himself back into the hereditary succession of Theban kings, and when he does so it is not merely his personal authority and power that have been evacuated but that of the "office" of king itself. Insofar as it is the successor king who always supplants—kills off—the former king, all governmental transfer of power, even the most peaceable, harbors an irreducible structural violence. It is the symbolic order itself—it is the entire heritage of "fathers" going back to the very gods—that Oedipus would implicate as the cause of Thebes' plague, for when he takes responsibility for the plague, Oedipus does so not as the unique and singular individual and not as the ironically unknowing biological heir of the kingly lineage but as its metonymical representative, as one of many. Here, the tradition of Sophoclean criticism misses the point of Oedipus' identification: he risks being perceived as the biological son of Laius in his efforts to expose both the empirical infanticide-violence of a particular biological father and the structural violence, the infanticidity, that belongs to the very concept of the father. All ironic readings of the play fall victim to the empirical temptation—the desire to reduce arche-violence to empirical violence, infanticidality to infanticide, injurability (which precedes any possible injury or escape from injury) to an empirical assault.

Oedipus finally submits to his "destiny" not because he realizes that he is guilty but because he accepts this fate as the cost of trying to specify the contraceptive limit this side of which all exercise of power, all choice, all hailing, all acts of conception take place. When those who occupy privileged positions in the symbolic order take on the name of a series of fathers supposedly related by blood, they typically do so in order to establish their generative purity, the supposed purity of the symbolic order itself. When each ruler in a succession identifies himself as the legitimate patrilineal heir of the father-king he has supplanted, however, he winds up colluding in a cross-generational cultural effort to erase the cost of whatever generativity each can claim for himself, a cost that finally opens on the prospect of an infanticidality without limit, an infanticidism that extends to the gods. The effort to transcend the structural infanticidity of the world invariably implicates the father-kings in actions that are empirically infanticidal for the reasons that have been developed at length in chapter 6. Here, suffice it to recall that to be the source, the father has to be able to be the unsource; he has to have the power to destroy his creation, otherwise what he creates will come to replace, do without, or otherwise evacuate his generativity and thereby his identity as the world's paternal telos. And yet if he has such uncreative power, the father will have been constituted by precisely what removes his paternity.[66]

This structural contamination is necessary to the very conception of the father's conceptivity. It cannot be eliminated either by being reduced to an empirical violence or by being attributed to the son. For this double reason the god that uses the son to take revenge against the parents cannot be rehabilitated according to any interpretive program that seeks to understand life as a conceptive movement. Presupposing Oedipus' self-ignorance and guilt, such programs hail an Oedipus whose counter-hailing they cannot read.

At the moment when he might have been expected to question the herdsman about the number of robbers who killed Laius, Oedipus abandons his defense, cries out at the supposed revelation of his guilt, and apostrophizes himself as a child of woe: "Oh, oh!," he says, the Greek expression of his agony, "iou, iou," inverting the sound of anguish "oi," that begins his name: "O light, may I now look on you for the last time, I who am revealed as cursed in my birth" (Lloyd-Jones, 453, lines 1182–84). Before he is "cursed in my marriage, cursed in my killing" (Lloyd-Jones, 454, lines 1184–85), he is "cursed in my birth," "bred of a match accursed" (Grene), "shown monstrous in my birth" (Gould). With his parturition-miming wail, Oedipus halts all further inquiry into the causes of Thebes' plague. Having elicited the herdsman's story of his pity for the foot-crippled child, Oedipus shouts out his most pitiful of cries. When he does, he intensifies the pedagogical hailing of his community in an inter-pellative sequence that he brings to a halt when he blinds himself, thereby forcing his people to look him in his bleeding eyes. At that moment he calls out to arrest his kingdom's collective gaze. Having failed to bring his people to the necessary insights concerning the infanticide-crisis that results when one refuses the infanticidism of the sacred, he assails his own *arthra* in a last attempt to get them to see what he sees that they have not.

Oedipus fails. He fails for reasons that do not become evident until Jesus radicalizes the kind of self-sacrifice that Oedipus makes, the sub-ject of the next chapter. In the New Testament Jesus brings the infanti-cidity of life not to the eyes but to the lips and tongue under the com-mand to eat and drink his body and blood. In this commandment and the ritual he inaugurates, Jesus enables his followers to internalize his self-sacrifice in a way that Oedipus does not. When Oedipus blinds himself, he attempts to bring the infanticidity of the world before the eyes of his onlookers. However, he limits the demand he makes of his people to the visual act of beholding him—in pity, to be sure, but nevertheless at a vi-sual distance. He wants his world to open their hearts to him; and yet at the same time he presents himself as a horrifying visual spectacle, a mu-tilated figure whose violence repels his onlookers. He intends, of course, to play pity against fright and revulsion in the hope of overcoming the terror of the other; however, he winds up arousing this very terror and overwhelming his people's sense of pity. In the resulting movement of approach and avoidance on the part of those Oedipus wants to reach lies his tragedy.

Oedipus yields to the tragedy when he personalizes his self-sacrifice. On the one hand, having perceived the (infanticidal) pitilessness of his people, he clings to the possibility that he can save his "children" by evok-ing their pity for him in the knowledge that he was an unpitied infant; that he can found a new political economy by arousing his people's com-passion for him; that he can provide them the affective means of living with a difficult knowledge—the knowledge that their religious beliefs cannot protect them from, and inevitably worsen the problem of, the economizing necessity that makes life infanticidal—by eliciting their identification with him. For this very reason, on the other hand, he has too little to offer them—no teachings, no explicit principles or tenets, no faith, no binding ritual, almost nothing beyond himself—by means of which they can commemorate the gift of his self-sacrifice and them-selves attempt to give it in turn.

In the gift of his blindness, Oedipus' people can see that he gives up his sight but not necessarily that he does so in the name of revealing the cost of every waking moment. They can see that someone stands before them, someone other. They do not understand, however, that he wants them to see not himself but themselves. Indeed, the nature of the experience of sight reinforces the phenomenological difference between self and other that Oedipus is trying to remove. Oedipus wants his people to see in his bleeding eyes a sign of the economization that sustains their own existence, that informs every second of their awareness, that inheres in every act of seeing the other. What he wants, however, requires a deeply difficult and problematic act of abstraction.

In the Eucharist Jesus overcomes much of this difficulty when he commands his communicants to ingest his body. He expands one of the most basic predications humans make about themselves—we eat, therefore we live—into one of the most provocative ontological declarations: in the Eucharist, we eat the person of Jesus—we eat what is sacred, we destroy what has absolute and infinite value—therefore we live. Inserting himself as the divine essence of everything we ingest, Jesus makes explicit that in eating to live we economize by shunting the cost of our existence elsewhere (onto other people, other living things, the environment, even God). In the Eucharist, then, Jesus achieves a condensation of meaning as well as a vehicle for ritually commemorating and internalizing this meaning that are beyond Oedipus. In consequence, he brings the cost of life not before the eyes but into the mouth and then the most interior part of the body. Furthermore, he does so in the name of an affective investment far more powerful and moving, but also infinitely more problematic, than the pity that Oedipus dreams of.

9
The Infanticidity of Flesh and Word:
The Eucharistic Revision of Greek Sacrifice

From whom do kings of the earth take toll or tribute? From their children or from others?
>   —Matthew 17:26

The blind and the lame came to him in the temple, and he cured them. But when the chief priests and the scribes saw the amazing things that he did, and heard the children crying out in the temple, "Hosanna to the Son of David," they became angry and said to him, "Do you hear what these are saying?" Jesus said to them, "Yes; have you never read,
'Out of the mouths of infants and nursing babies you have prepared praise for yourself'?"
>   —Matthew 21:14–16

Go and learn what this means, "I desire mercy, not sacrifice."
>   —Matthew 9:13.

BEYOND TRANSCENDENCE: ABRAHAM, OEDIPUS, JESUS

EVOLUTIONARY THEORY FOREGROUNDS THE ECONOMIC PROBLEM of life: there can be no distribution of resources that is not differential, that does not discriminate, that does not result in a system of relative advantages and disadvantages, and therefore that does not entail costs which are ultimately sacrificial of and deadly to other life. All living things must economize in order to out-survive and out-reproduce their competitors. Survival, however, is always only temporary, and reproductive success is always only relative: neither is governed by any teleology that would guarantee the indefinite life of a group or species nor the life of life. In a dynamic biosphere, living forms eventually encounter environmental changes for which they are unsuited, and then they die out. No living form, and thus not life itself, can evolve strategies of economization that will suit it to all possible futures. Evolutionary economization is

231

another name for the death of individual living things, the extinction of groups of living things, and the eventual disappearance of life.

This side of that disappearance, life competes against life with such relentless implacability that living things drive other living things and even themselves into extinction. An insignificant fraction of the total number of forms of life remain. These forms of life and those yet to evolve have or will have their purchase on being at the cost of a deathliness—not only the loss of what has existed but the loss of possible genetic futures—that is impossible to measure mathematically or empirically. Therefore, even if the specific forms of life that exist at present and that may yet arrive were to suddenly become immortal, they would not embody any putative immortality of life itself, for even under this circumstance life itself would be marked as structurally dependent on the death that has been the economic condition of its possibility. Life is not simply life; in its origin from out of the nonliving and in its structural dependence on the death it requires, life is not a purely living force. Because life trades on death, the concept of immortal life is a contradiction in terms. Once again, then, even if it were to become immortal, which is not a possibility in a thermodynamic universe, life itself would not be, in itself, completely alive. Within evolutionary economy, not only is the life of living things precarious, fragile, transient, so too is the life of life.

Western culture has long resisted this conclusion, against which it has promulgated various conceptions of life as a transcendental force, as a power of generativity that, in its essence, is immune to the violence, the sacrificiality, the economization, the deathliness—in sum, the infanticidity of being—which institutes the possibility of life. At the same time, however, key Hebraic, Greek, and Jesusian texts have recognized and attempted to counter-conceive the ineluctable costs of existence. To this end they have sought to rethink the nature of the originary infanticidal violence of economization—the cost of existence that every individual and every grouping of individuals will inevitably if not deliberately visit on others—in a world that is constituted by this violence, this infanticidity.

Chapters 3, 4, and 5 have explored one of the most severe counter-conceptions put forth in Judaism—Abraham's vision of the infanticidity of the sacred as manifested in both God's call to sacrifice the son and his call to hold back from this sacrifice. These contradictory summons together bespeak a meta-level demand to recognize that the structure of sacrifice is irreducible and informs the most caring, the most loving identification of one person with another. That is what Kierkegaard implies when he endorses the *akeдah*'s teleological suspension of the ethical: ethics implicates one in, it does not free oneself from, the sacrificial-cum-infanticidal economy that is the non-transcendable limit condition of existence. Ethics cannot protect against the infanticidal. To the contrary, insofar as ethics provides the basis for a clear conscience, it becomes another instance of the self-interest that hides its (infanticidal) economizing. In proposing that the *akedah* suspends this economizing conception of ethics, Kierkegaard shows how the Abraham and Isaac narrative brings into the open the infanticidity that this conception covers up. Derrida raises the stakes of the Kierkegaardian critique of ethics to a pitch of excruciating intensity when he generalizes Kierkegaard's intellectual leap: there is no outside of the sacrifice of Isaac, which takes place every moment of every day, for life comes about only in relation to the gift of death.

Chapters 6, 7, and 8 have shown the difficulty the Greeks encountered in working out the possibilities of counter-conceiving the world in terms of the infanticidity of such a gift. Although the *Odyssey* glimpses the infanticidal consequences of sacralizing the demand for revenge, it directs almost all of its narrative energy to the end of satisfying this desire and falls short of imagining death as gift. The *Odyssey*'s apparent blessing of revenge repeats the self-authorizing move by which the Homeric world protects its constituting violence. The poem economizes on this violence by idealizing Odysseus' aggressions as indices of his resourcefulness, all in the context of his supposed fidelity to wife, son, father, household, and kingdom. Nevertheless, the poem interrupts this economization when Zeus forces Odysseus and the other Ithakans to negotiate their differences rather than to continue to slaughter one another. In his deliverance of a self-checking force, which checks the force of Odysseus and his opponents, Zeus forbids both sides from appealing to him for divine justification of the deaths each would impose on the other.

Sophocles' Oedipus recontextualizes Zeus's critique of the violence perpetrated in the name of this god. Oedipus does so to expose the infanticidal pitilessness of his culture's investment in the dream of a god-ensured collective purity. The Thebans believe they can deflect the costs of their existence by sacrificing not themselves but someone else. However, when Oedipus visits them as one of their own forgotten children, as the infanticidal target of the very king in whom Thebes has vested its authority, he threatens to expose the illusion of the transcendental self-protection from the enemy other that the Greeks sought in their sacrificial worship. Although Oedipus brings his world to the point of seeing the infanticidism of the gods themselves, he offers his vision as a gift of blindness, not of (infanticidal) death.

It remains for Jesus to accomplish what the Greek tradition fails to achieve—a way of confronting the immanence of the infanticidal in every breath one takes, every sip one swallows, every bite one eats, every act one performs, and thus a way of mourning the violence that is necessary

just to live. The rest of this chapter will show how Jesus disrupts by intensifying the sacrificial tradition of the Greeks. The consequence is that
he advances a new, a counter-, conception of the sacred, one that lays
bare the infanticidity of God himself, the infanticidity of the good news,
the infanticidity of the revealed mystery that constitutes the sacred. Jesus
thus reanimates the Abrahamic insight, the vision of the one to whom
Matthew traces back Jesus' descent. Jesus reinstitutes the insight of the
father of the Jews in a new covenant, a new rite, a new economy predicated on the Eucharistic gift of oneself for the other—the gift of one's
own death in the acknowledgment that no life occurs without sacrificing
others. In giving the gift of his death, Jesus marks the death of the sacred conceived as transcendental but resurrects the sacred as immanent
in a new way—that is, as precarious, as able to be destroyed, as no more
immortal nor invincible than humans, whom the sacred beckons to live
in accordance with the injunction to protect the life of life to come.

In giving his death rather than in demanding that his worshippers
give someone's death to him, as the Greeks thought their gods required,
Jesus intervenes in the sacrificial practices that assimilate the supposedly signal feature of specifically human life (reflexive self-consciousness)
to the economization that governs animal life. In giving the gift of his death,
Jesus does not offer the possibility of transcending this economization
but of resignifying it in the counter-economic terms of a self-sacrificing
love. Such a love "passes beyond understanding" in that it seeks (almost)
nothing in return—nothing except for a further sending forth or sending
out of this love by way of the gift of death.[1] Jesus' economic intervention, then, cannot be understood in the terms of transcendence—in terms
of a promise of a cost-free infinitude, of an immortalizing salvation in the
next world. To the contrary, in its generosity without expectation of (personal) return, this love opens up the aneconomic possibility of a mortal
infinity. This is the paradoxical infinite amplitude of every finite moment,
but only as every moment is bound to its expiration and the expiration
of every other moment.

In developing this argument I will first review the procedures of Greek
sacrifice and explain the transcendental economization that this ritual
performs. I will then show how the new form of sacrifice that Jesus in-
vents—his Eucharistic sacrifice of himself rather than of others—inverts
and displaces the conceptual oppositions that govern the sacrifice rituals
of the Greeks. It does so, however, at a cost the Platonizing tradition of
Christianity has resisted. That cost is the tradition's orthodox conception
of the sacred as transcendent.

In *Eros and Mourning*, Henry Staten contests this conception when he
argues that the Gospel of John locates the sacred not in a transcendence
of the flesh but in its non-transcendable mortality. Staten agrees that the

divinity of the Logos has always meant "that it is transcendent, eternal, and impassible; which is to say that its predicates are negations of the predicates that define the flesh. Conversely, flesh in its doctrinal sense is conceived by its contrast with Logos; it is all the things that Logos is not."[2] Against this view Staten reads the Gospel of John as redefining the sacred in terms of a "purely naturalistic meaning." Staten argues that, although Christianity "offers an antidote" to the "bleakness" of a "vision of a life that would at the limit be merely organic," an antidote in the form of "an immortal essence that triumphs over its reduction to nature in death," nevertheless Christianity has "not thought through" the "horror of natural reduction . . . as such." For this reason the Christian imagination "is driven by the loathing" of the body's destruction in death. Staten reads the Gospel of John as attempting to overcome this anxiety by laying bare "the innermost interior of the passion of mourning, palliated by no transcendence that would not itself be through and through the passion of living flesh." In this way, he concludes, John understands how Jesus "transfigure[s] mourning into love" not by transcendentalizing it but by accepting it as absolutely mortal.[3]

I want to contribute to Staten's demonstration by arguing that Jesus specifically opposes the *economy* of transcendence, which he displaces with a *counter-economy* of love. Jesus does not die as part of a bargain with God. He does not purchase humankind's salvation in an eternal hereafter. Rather, he teaches through the example of his death how to revalue the inescapable mortality of life. On the one hand, he teaches how to recognize that the drive for transcendence is just another baleful expression of (infanticidal) economization, the very economization that is a defining property of biological existence. On the other hand, he teaches how, by accepting the irreducible costliness of any individual's life, one may come to recognize the hereafter in every finite moment. These two recognitions are the heart of the gift of death that is, becomes, or will have been Jesus' gift only when it is no longer his, only when it has been received and given in turn.

TRANSCENDENTAL ECONOMIZATION AND GREEK SACRIFICE

As outlined by Walter Burkert in *Greek Religion,* Greek sacrificial practices rationalize the system of economization within which they take place. They immerse their celebrants in a performance that literally and symbolically reenacts the ongoing life of the community at the expense of the death of other life, metonymically figured in the sacrificial animal. Engaging the affective commitment of the community to itself, the rituals conclude with a meat meal that unites its celebrants in a feast by which they share in the most fundamental expression of the right to life. Greek sacrifice quite specifically contextualizes this sharing as a defense of the community against its enemies—that is, against the menacing economization on the part of the other. How so?

According to Burkert, the "function [of ritual] normally lies in group formation, the creation of solidarity, or the negotiation of understanding among members of the species,"[4] above all by sacralizing the act of eating. "The essence of the sacred act, which is hence often simply termed doing or making sacred or working sacred things, is in Greek practice a straightforward and far from miraculous process: the slaughter and consumption of a domestic animal for a god" (55). Thus, although the "ritual of animal slaughter varies in detail according to the local ancestral custom. . . , the fundamental structure is identical and clear: animal sacrifice is ritualized slaughter followed by a [consecrated] meat meal" (57).

The consecration observes a prescribed sequence in which action and utterance together enable the participants to have their feasting occur within the protection of a sacred space. To this end the participants demarcate the festivities from the profane space of everyday life by "washing, dressing in clean garments, and adornment" (56). They select an appropriate animal—the "most noble" is a bull ox (55)[5]—which is "entwined with ribbons" and, if horned, its horns gilded. In formal procession the participants—accompanied by flute players and headed by "a blameless maiden" who "carries on her head the sacrificial basket in which the knife for sacrifice lies concealed beneath grains of barely or cakes" (56)—then lead the animal to the altar. There they arrange themselves in concentric circles around the place of killing. As the "sacrificial basket and water vessel are borne around in a circle, the sacred is delimited from the profane" (56). The participants, each in turn, hold out their hands for water to be poured over them. Usually "the sacrificial animal is sprinkled with water, causing it to jerk its head, which is interpreted as the animal nodding its assent"; a bull, however, "is given water to drink," and when he lowers his head, he is said to be assenting to his imminent sacrifice as well (56). Next, each participant takes "a handful of barley groats . . . from the sacrificial basket." Falling silent, they listen while "the sacrificer recites a prayer, invocation, wish, and vow." Then, "as if in confirmation," the entire group "hurl their barely groats forward onto the altar and the sacrificial animal; in some rituals stones are thrown." At this point the sacrificer approaches the animal and "cuts some hairs from its forehead and throws them on the fire" that previously has been lit. Burkert does not indicate the content of the prayer and other priestly speech acts (56).

At the climax of the sacrifice, the sacrificer exsanguinates the animal and collects its blood, which he sprays over the top and the sides of the altar. During this ritual splattering the women begin to ululate, and the rite reaches its "emotional climax" as "life screams over death." The priests then promptly skin and butcher the animal, roast its organs on the altar fire, and taste the entrails. Thereafter the priests consecrate the inedible remains by laying them out "on the pyre . . . in just order" and burning the "symbolically reconstituted" animal (56–57). Having offered to the gods a nutritionally valueless gift, the priests roast or boil the edible portions of the slaughtered animal and give the participants an equal portion. In sum, the priests engage in two complementary significations—they sacralize the animal and then they desacralize it by killing, quartering, and consuming it.

Glossing this ritual, Burkert in effect explains how sacrifice reconciles its practitioners to the costliness of their lives—in particular, to the violence that is inextricable from the body's appetites. Burkert imagines prehistoric human cultures in which hunting must have been "the principal source of food for the family," and that for them "killing to eat was an unalterable commandment" but that "the bloody act must always have been attended with a double danger and a double fear: that the weapon might be turned against a fellow hunter, and that the death of the prey might signal an end with no future, while man must always eat and so must always hunt." In ritually celebrating the necessity of killing other living things, Greek sacrifice enables its participants to repeat the fundamental sociopolitical condition of their group—a "communally enacted aggression and shared guilt" through which they relieve the guilt and anxiety of the hunt and transform "the encounter with death . . . into life-affirming enjoyment" (58). The ritual, then, negotiates a basic existential ambivalence associated with the necessity of eating, especially when the source of food is an animal that must be destroyed. All eating requires extracting the life from living things, converting them into objects of ingestion, for the sake of one's own life. The violence of this appropriation is particularly evident in hunting; however, it is also a feature of all eating, even vegetarian.[6]

Greek sacrifice foregrounds the "irrevocable" nature of this violence: "The order of life, a social order, is constituted in the sacrifice through irrevocable acts" (59)—that is, of putting to death and then eating what has been slaughtered. When the rite prescribes "that no meat must be taken away," that "all must be consumed without remainder in the sanctuary," the feast celebrates not only the fatal aggression accompanying the appetite the meat meal satisfies but the annihilating violence of which the celebrants are warned to leave no telltale trace (57). Those traces remain, however, and nowhere more provocatively than in the way the sacrificial slaughter and meat meal is not alone the putting to death and consumption of the animal but a coded killing and incorporation of whatever beings or forces pose a threat to the sacrificing group, above all an enemy. The ancient Greek conception of prayer so attests. "The usual word for to pray, *euchesthai,* also means to boast, and in victory, to let out the cry of triumph" (73). The literal triumph is over the domesticated animal that is successfully led to its sacrificial slaughter. The symbolic triumph is over the world, over all that would incorporate the sacrificers themselves. Thus, the sacrificial prayers to the gods function as self-proclamations of present or future victory, of triumph accomplished or hoped for.[7]

The meaning of *ara,* which can signify either "prayer and vow" or "curse" (73), reinforces the economizing function of prayer as a means of protecting and adding to the life of the supplicant at the cost of subtracting from the life of the enemy. "Success and honour for one is usually inseparable from humiliation and destruction for another: the good *ara* and the evil *ara* go hand in hand." Success and honor cost, and praying is the ritual means of requesting that the gods deflect this cost onto the enemy. As Burkert remarks, "normally the Greeks had no qualms about praying for an other's destruction" (75). Praying is the verbal equivalent of the "irrevocable acts" by which life is sustained at the expense of other life. *Ara* "recalls the direct power which the word of prayer exercises as a blessing or as a curse which, once uttered, can never be retracted" (74). To pray (for oneself) is to curse (the other); it is to hope, want, intend, and seek to sacrifice the object of imprecation. Accordingly, praying and sacrificing are two modes of the same signifying actions: "*litai-thysiai,* prayers-sacrifices is an ancient and fixed conjunction" (73). To pray is to invoke the irrevocable death of the other as payment for the triumphant survival of those who enjoy the sacrifice rather than are excluded from it, of those who sacrifice rather than are sacrificed. It is, therefore, to know that one eats the life, and thus lives off the death, of the other, and thus to suspect the cannibalism that is implicit in the structure of the need for food.[8] When the Greeks prayed, they assimilated the demise of the enemy to the killing of the sacrificial animal and the sharing of the meat meal. That is, they tacitly acknowledged that the sacrificial ritual is not only carnivorous but cannibalistic in its structure.

The cannibalism is not of the self but of the other who is like the self. To eat is necessarily to eat the other, not oneself. The other is typically the animal. However, it is never simply the nonhuman other but potentially anyone—family member or friend as well as stranger or foe—with a hunger like one's own. The reason why is that every distribution of resources raises the possibility of being cheated or stolen from. The inequity at the heart of every division of resources is logically equivalent to having one's being, one's potential future, appropriated and in effect consumed or cannibalized by others. In other words, this inequity is logically equivalent to being sacrificed to the other's advantage.

Greek sacrifice permits the community to acknowledge the (cannibal) aggression necessary to sustain the life of the community while protecting the community from being the victims of that very aggression, either from among their own kind or from their enemies. Greek sacrifice offers the appearance of spiritualizing the community's hunger — not hunger as such, not the hunger of the enemy or the animal, only the hunger of the community. However, when this community curses its enemies in order to bless its own eating, it tacitly admits to feeding off of the corpse of those it has anathematized. At the very moment of sanctifying the need of its members while execrating that same need in their foes, the community is on the verge of acknowledging that it is enemy to its enemy and therefore potentially to itself as well. To the extent that one cannot eat for the other, all meals risk exposing those who feast together to be potential enemies.

In their sacrificial meals the Greeks respond to this difficulty by substituting the relation between community and gods for the relation between community and enemy and conceiving of the gods as beings who scarcely eat, above all else who do not eat meat. Like the enemy, the gods may bring the members of a community to their individual or collective deaths. Unlike the enemy, the gods do not profit from these deaths, they do not economize on them. In particular, they do not survive at the expense of the humans they kill, and they do not cannibalize those who worship them — those who kill and eat the sacrificial animal in the name of these gods. The enemy, by contrast, always economizes in ways the gods do not. The enemy kills, and if the enemy does not literally cannibalize its human prey, the enemy always does so indirectly, by degrees — by living off of the victim in one way or another. The relation to the enemy — kill or be killed — always implies eat or be eaten. Unlike the gods, humans, even those committed to the pacifism of a vegetarian diet, must live off of the death of the other. The quotidian act of eating, therefore, is a potential reminder of one's future death, one's vulnerability to being the object of the world's consumption, of being absorbed back into the earth, of being reduced to matter. To hunger is to desire, which is always to desire the death and incorporation of some other life. Even more, it is to desire the death and incorporation of the enemy. For this reason it is to be like the enemy other who also desires. Hence to know that one hungers is to know that one is hungered for, targeted by the enemy as an object of incorporation.

The Greeks withdrew their gods from this necessity by perceiving them as immortal and therefore as subsisting on substances unconnected with the economy of death—nectar and ambrosia. These two words appear to be the names of food but are in fact names of the immunity of the gods to the death-dealing appetite of all mortal creatures. *Nectar* (from *nek*, death, and *tar*, overcoming) means "overcoming death"; *ambrosia* (from *ambrotos: a*, not, and *mbrotos*, mortal), means that which is immortal.[9] The immortal gods do not kill to eat. The gods do not need to eat meat; they do not need to consume that which signifies mortal bondage to the necessity of economizing at the expense of other life. Not surprisingly, in Greek sacrifice the gods receive what is inedible —"thigh bones," deceptively "wrapped in fat and the long chine"—Aeschylus' Prometheus says in reporting on his prescription for the worship of the father-god.[10] In Hesiod's *Theogony*, Aeschylus' source, Prometheus attempts to deceive Zeus into selecting an offering of "the white bones of the ox, covered . . . with glistening fat" rather than the real meat of the sacrificed animal.[11]

The gods not only demand this deception, they sacralize it. Why? The answer is twofold. First, if the gods do not eat meat, they cannot suffer the economizing deception on the part of their human worshippers. This would mean that humans cannot threaten the sacred, which would remain uncontaminated by the economizing appetite that renders human existence so problematic for being sacrificial and ultimately infanticidal. Second, if the gods prescribe the deception necessary to completing the sacrifice, they would mitigate the emotional difficulties—manifest as ambivalence, shame, guilt, perhaps terror—for humans in being a creature that knows it must kill in order to eat, and that knows it is vulnerable to being killed and eaten in turn. In believing they had to deceive the gods by commandment of the gods, the Greeks economized on their double-bind. That is, in their ritual deception they heightened and intensified the burdensomeness of their self-awareness and then relieved it in a communal performance and feast. In this celebration they could solidify a *we* which might otherwise threaten itself from within itself—that is, from the conflicting appetites, needs, and self-interest of its subgroups and individuals.

James Davidson underscores this function of sacrifice—the conversion of deception toward the gods into a public display of fairness toward one another—in consolidating the Greek sense of community. The Greeks were obsessed with fairness, Davidson notes, and that "obsession . . . controls ancient sacrifice." Ritual sacrifice was conducted in strict accord with the idea of "isonomia" — "fair shares." The meat of the sacrificial animal had to be rendered "into equal portions" as did the wine. In fact, the Athenians had "officials called *oinoptai*, who watched to make sure each citizen got an equal portion of wine at public festivals."[12]

The isonomic principle of "fair shares" represents an incipient decoupling of economization (here the distribution of resources) from its sacralization, for the fairness of the sharing obtains only among the human participants, not between them and the gods, and only in a provisional, not absolute way. The Greeks were acutely aware that every distribution of resources is unfair, that there is no single criterion to ensure an equity, let alone an equity that would be sacred. The Greeks opted for a distribution based on "portions of more or less equal size," not of equivalent nutritional value. "In terms of quality . . . the ancient portions of meat were both uneven and unequal, some mostly fat and bone, some largely fillet and rump." The Greeks knew this was the case, for they decided who "among the sacrificing community" would receive which portion "by drawing lots to ensure everyone at least got an equal chance at a good piece."[13] The drawing of lots gives the lie to the lie—the deception aimed at the gods—that underwrites the principle of "fair shares" by which the ritual of sacrifice negotiated the problem of economization.

The act of cheating Zeus registers the unfairness of every division of resources: if the division of the sacrificial resource is itself sacrificial, then all the more so the division of those resources that have not been ritually sanctified. The interpretation of the act of division as sanctioned by Zeus himself protects the community from the difficulties that emerge when a group has no unanimously acceptable criterion for deciding who gets what portion of a limited and necessary resource. Again, the ritual rationing of meat dramatizes the sacrificiality of all allotments on the part of mortal hosts who, as mortal, are hostage to an appetite the injustice of which is not only inescapable but the very condition of existence. It is this condition the Greek gods escape insofar as they do not eat meat. Their freedom from a carnivorous appetite thus represents the fulfillment of the wish that the rite of sacrifice institutionalizes—the wish to escape being the target of the (carnivorous) economization of others. Zeus imposes the necessity of an economization—acted out in ritual sacrifice in the mandated lie or deception—that renders human existence vulnerable to the predatory (and ultimately infanticidal) interests of the enemy. Ritual sacrifice thus stages the economic problem of being an embodied being—namely, that to eat is, perforce, to be subjected to death and the prospect of being eaten in turn. It responds to this problem by projecting an image of an immortal being who seemingly wants to eat but who in reality has no alimentary need to do so. That is, it converts a deceptive and unjust offering of a worthless item—the thighbone wrapped in fat—to the god into the very principle of the community's offering of a purified image of their own economization to themselves.

It can do so only insofar as it can imagine the cycle of eating and being eaten brought to an end. That is why Zeus is denied the very feast the sacrificers will enjoy, the very meat meal they have asked him to consecrate. Zeus is made to forego the eating of meat so that he will be no

competitor to humans, unlike his worshippers who are by nature competitors with one another. Indeed, the feasting of his worshippers is difficult to differentiate from the feasting of their enemies. If the enemy is
the cannibalistic face of the sacrificers themselves, Zeus is that face idealized, spiritualized, an image in which the practitioners of sacrifice can
behold themselves as the *telos* of the cycle that otherwise would reduce
them to the vulnerable position of potential prey. The Greek institution of
sacrifice situates its practitioners as those who eat without being eaten —
for example, by the gods, who clearly have the power to treat humans
the way humans treat animals. Although their human worshippers kill in
order to eat, and although these people must die by virtue of what the
gods have decreed, these people are not eaten (by the gods) in the way
every other living creature is a potential prey at risk of being killed and
eaten. Not being eaten, however, does not provide the sacrificers a different ontological destiny from that of the animal. It merely signifies that
humans are more successful economizers.[14]

In the Greek myth of Prometheus the symbol of humankind's superior economization is fire. Greek myth associates this technology, which
enables humans to cook their meat rather than to eat it raw, with the advent of sacrifice, the religious practice that sacralizes human deception,
as well as with the origin of human consciousness. Through this linkage
the Greek myth indicates that consciousness is first and foremost an instrument of (sacrificial) economization, not of truth.

In Philip Vellacott's translation of *Prometheus Bound*, the Titan imparts
to "mindless" humankind "mind and reason,"[15] symbolized by fire, the
pantechnon, or "means of all arts."[16] Consuming what it feeds on, fire is
another name for human economization—that is, for the particular set
of capabilities by which humans have converted the world's resources
to their purposes. Thus, fire stands for self-consciousness as technology:
architecture, astronomy, number and arithmetical calculation, the pho-
netic alphabet, the domestication of animals, ship building, prophecy,
sacrifice, and metallurgy, and above all writing, "mother of many
arts,"[17] literally "the Muses' mother."[18] In fact, all the specific technologies
Prometheus bestows on humankind or enables them to invent are forms
of writing or are dependent on writing. Prophecy and sacrifice in particular are extensions of writing, as Prometheus indicates in his remarks on
interpretation: "I distinguished various modes of prophecy . . . interpreted the hidden sense / Of voices, sounds, sights met by chance upon
the road. / The various flights of crook-clawed vultures I defined / Exactly . . . how to interpret signs in sacrifice . . . And signs from flames,
obscure before, I now made plain."[19] Supporting all mental activity, fire
is an Ur-writing that takes the shape of flaming signs to signify the consciousness of economization as the destruction and consumption of life

so as to produce life. The carnivorous implication of this economization —
figured in the writing of sacrifice — is captured in the raptorial image of
"the various flights of crook-clawed vultures," which must be carefully,
even "exactly," "defined" and "interpreted." When Prometheus transfers
Zeus's fire to mortals and teaches them to cook with and sacrifice by
means of it, he enables humankind to represent and simultaneously to
cover up the origin of mind in the mortality of appetite and thus to figure in the writing of sacrifice the connections between self-consciousness,
symbolization, strategies of deception, and the sanctification of aggression against the enemy.

The writing of sacrifice brings the Greeks to the point of desymbol-
izing both the "theft" of life that constitutes the essence of the body's
hunger and the concealments by which they tried to posit the sacred as
beyond economization. A technology that can be used to signify itself, to
delimit the economization that enables it to function, the writing of sacrifice returns the participants of the ritual to a moment when appetite
achieves one of its earliest and most primitive articulations in the most
telling of symbolic cries. In that moment, the climax of the public slaughter, the Greeks shouted out the infanticidal cost of their collective existence, for just as the animal is killed, the women erupt in "a shrill cry, the
Oloyge," which is, Burkert explains, "the same cry of women [that] accompanies birth" (74). This ambiguous cry — "usually *a cry of joy;* but also
of *lamentation*"[20] — assimilates the wailing of the newborn child to the
agonizing moan of the slaughtered animal. Since the ululation is a yell of
victory over the enemy, it also encompasses as well the lamentation of the
defeated who have suffered the loss of their own kind. In superimposing
a scene of birth and a scene of carnivorous violence, the rhythm of the
oloyge gives vocal but not verbal expression to the most primal of intuitions — namely, that to be blessed by the gods, to share the meat of a collective sacrifice, to be victorious over the enemy, to exult in the birth of
a newborn, and thus to transmit one's rituals to the next generation are
all forms of the same fundamental predication, the same fundamental
activity of economization; and that, *mutatis mutandis,* to be unblessed, to
be unable to share the meat of one's sacrifices, to be defeated by the enemy, and to be unable to transmit one's rituals to the next generation
are all forms of the complementary predication of being victimized by
the economization of others. The ritual ululation, in other words, not only
performs the condition of its possibility but brings that condition to the
tip of the tongue where the collective crying out is on the verge of becoming articulate speech.

Such articulation would simultaneously require and enable a still
greater internalization of the sense of fault than Greek drama achieves
concerning the sacrificial and infanticidal violence of the economization

that underwrites human life. However, because Greek drama is a spectacle of the eye but not of the mouth, of being witness to the kill but not
participant in the feast, it limits the internalization of this knowledge,
which it keeps at a visual distance, and thus restricts its articulation.
Oedipus knows that every act of seeing the other, along with every act
of self-reflection, participates in a violent economy. More importantly, he
feels the implications of this knowledge, which he translates in the central affective term available to his culture: pity. The experience of pity,
however, is inadequate to the emotional challenge involved in taking
into oneself and taking onto oneself the responsibility for the implications of the fact that to be and to survive are to participate in the world's
infanticidity.

BEYOND GREEK SACRIFICE:
JESUS' NON-TRANSCENDENTAL VISION

Unlike an Oedipus, who raises before the eyes the infanticidal blindness
of his world, Jesus brings the infanticidity of being to the mouth, where
the cannibalism-cum-infanticidity of existence can be brought to consciousness in a previously inconceivable discourse of previously unimaginable affective power. Jesus specifies this infanticidity by his actions
in the Last Supper, which brings his radical critique, disruption, trans-
valuation, and reformation of the cultural practices that proceed from
pagan sacrifice and its violent economization to its most critical articulation. With the Eucharist providing the context for his subsequent self-
sacrifice, he completes his project of counter-conceiving the sacred—that
is, of refusing any transcendental solution to the (infanticidal) mortality
that comes to pass in the advent of every individual's life, including in the
life of the one in whom "the Word became flesh" (John 1:14). To this end
Jesus organizes the Eucharist around an extraordinary overturning of
Greek sacrificial practice.

The Eucharistic Reversal of Greek Sacrifice

Jesus launches his critique of pagan ritual by reversing the direction of
the address in Greek sacrifice, an action by which he discloses and disrupts
the economizing function of this rite. In the Greek ceremony, humans
petition the god, who hears their prayers and receives their deceptive
offerings. In spectacular contrast, in the Eucharist Jesus does the peti-
tioning when, in his declared identity as son of God, he directs his mortal followers to consume his body in the most shocking way—by an act
of cannibalism. In this scandalous demand Jesus removes the semiotic

protections by which the Greeks wrapped the economizing force of their appetite in the performative ambiguities and misdirections of their ritual. In their pagan rite, when the Greeks deny their god a real share of their meal, they act out the defensiveness by which a group protects itself from the appetite of the enemy. In contrast, in the Eucharist Jesus offers his body and blood in his identity as the greatest, most intimate friend of humankind. In consequence, he in effect translates the Greek *euchai*, or prayers for victory over the enemy, into *eucharia*,[21] an astonishing avowal of thankfulness and gratitude for the opportunity to give his life. In the Greek ceremony, the participants sprinkle the sacrificial animal with water, "causing it to jerk its head, which is interpreted as the animal nodding its assent" (Burkert, 56). In the Eucharist, Jesus removes the Greek pretense: he not only gives his life willingly, he announces the doctrine of love that enables him to do so. He thereby transforms the pagan vow — which is a curse or imprecation, a prayer for evil to befall one's enemies, and thus a verbal sacrifice of the other — into a call to love the other, including the enemy, without reserve. In other words, he reinterprets the real, the good, and the true (the meaning of *eu-*): he frees their meaning from their tie in Greek sacrifice to the lie by which the Greeks concealed the economizing that governs hostile relations with the enemy; he joins the real, the good, and the true to the absolute loss of the self-sacrificing divine friend.

In the Greek sacrifice, the gods retain a personified form but remain ontologically other by virtue of neither sharing nor being affected by (the cost of) human appetite. For this reason they are indifferent to the deception at the heart of the sacrificial offering. When they accept the valueless offering of thighbones in fat, they bless the mortal economization that motivates the false gift. In contrast, in the Christian sacrifice Jesus asserts his ontological sameness by virtue of his bodily existence, hence by virtue of sharing (the cost of) a mortal appetite. For this reason he is intent on removing the deception by which the Greeks sought to justify the sacrificial heart of their economization. In sacrificing himself, Jesus forces his followers to recognize that no conception of the sacred can relieve humankind of the cost of their existence. Rather than exempting humans from the costliness of corporeal appetite, Jesus brings them toward an awareness that the costliness is absolute — indeed, that it is infinite, nothing less than the death of the Son of God — and that there is no escape from it. It cannot be transcended. Jesus must die. He must disappear into his death.

This death is not and cannot be the purchase price of humankind's salvation in a supposedly eternal life that would follow the death of the body. If it were such a "ransom," as Mark (10:45) and the author of the first letter to Timothy (2:6) characterize it, Jesus' death would reconstitute the economization that underwrites Greek (and other pagan) sacrifice and the effort through such ritual to deflect the cost of life onto others—literally onto the animal and symbolically onto the enemy. To the contrary, when Jesus dies, his death, along with the Eucharistic ritual that announces it, introduces a new economy based on a love without reserve and without prospect of return. This love is not a contract of exchange. It does not come back, in the form of an eternal reward hereafter, to the one who dies in its name. It does not free one from one's finitude. Rather, it draws one into a complete identification with one's own mortality through an identification with the mortality of Jesus. Through this love Jesus inaugurates the paradoxical possibility of an economy without economy—a counter- or an-economy—of human relatedness.

This affective aneconomy has two overlapping determinations. First, it is rooted in an apprehension that all life costs, that the consequences are infanticidal, and that no one, including Jesus, can escape them. No one, not even Jesus, can completely economize these costs—that is, deflect them onto others such that they can be transcended. If one could, if Jesus could, then the costs, finally, would not be costs but the means to a gain without loss. The aneconomy of the spirit that Jesus announces requires that death be absolute, not a passage to an eternal life purified of the body's mortification. For this reason, second, the aneconomy of the spirit entails a counter-conceptive revaluation of traditional philosophical and theological categories—specifically, of the conceptual oppositions of life and death, sacred and profane, pure and impure, light and darkness, and above all Word and flesh. These two determinations come together in the Eucharist, the rite of self-sacrifice by which death is no longer a matter of victory or defeat but of an incalculable, measureless giving of oneself.

Jesus' Intimations of the World's Infanticidity

The motif of infanticide superintends Jesus' life from its inception. At first glance the birth of Jesus, like that of Oedipus, is a drama of infanticide escaped. The infant Jesus is targeted for death by a king who is "frightened" at the prospect of an infant prophesied to be "born king of the Jews" (Matthew 2:2–3). Feigning the desire to "go and pay . . . homage" to the newborn, Herod sends the wise men to "go and search diligently for the child; and when you have found him, bring me word" (2:8). When these magi come upon the child, however, "they were overwhelmed with joy" as they approached and "paid him homage" (2:10–11). Having emotionally and materially invested in the newborn, they heed a dream warning them "not to return" to Herod (2:12). Immediately after they leave, Joseph has a similar, though more explicit, dream in which "an angel of the Lord" warns him to "flee to Egypt . . . for Herod is about to search for the child, to destroy him" (2:13). Joseph responds as the wise men have—he leaves to protect the infant from Herod's violence.

And yet by this protective action the wise men and Joseph precipitate a generalized outbreak of the infanticidal violence they have sought to escape. Furious that his plans to kill the infant messiah have been circumvented, Herod "sent and killed all the children in and around Bethlehem who were two years old or under." He kills en masse and indiscriminately to increase the chances that the one child will not survive after all, and perhaps to punish his people for the infant's escape. In either case he unleashes a violence that leads to inconsolable grief on the part of his people: "Then was fulfilled what had been spoken through the prophet Jeremiah: 'A voice was heard in Ramah, wailing and loud lamentation, Rachel weeping for her children; she refused to be consoled, because they are no more'" (2:16–18). Although Jesus lives, his survival is the occasion for the innumerable deaths of those who die in his stead.

It is no accident, then, that Jesus frames his teachings in a discourse that suggests he is haunted by the specter of the children who "are no more" and that he propounds his message in terms that answer specifically for the infanticidal cost of his life. When, for example, Jesus embraces the salvific meaning of his condemnation to death, he does so in the name of the children who stand in for all of humankind. A living reminder of the innocent who could be said to have died for him at the beginning of his life, the vulnerable child is a figure of those for whom Jesus will now give his life. Thus, anticipating his crucifixion, at Capernaum Jesus "took a little child and put it among" his apostles and then, "taking it in his arms, he said to them, 'Whoever welcomes one such child in my name welcomes me, and whoever welcomes me welcomes not me but the one who sent me'" to die for you (Mark 9:36–37). Later he instructs his disciples to "Let the little children come to me; do not stop them; for it is to such as these that the kingdom of God belongs." He is emphatic on this point, insisting that one must "receive the kingdom of God as a little child" or "never enter it." Underscoring the urgency of his words, he reaches out to "them"—children, but also all those who would be children: "he took them up in his arms, laid his hands on them, and blessed them" (Mark 10:14–16; cf. Luke 18:15–17). He then warns his audiences what will happen "because you did not recognize the time of your visitation from God"; Jesus invokes the specter of an infanticidal war: "If you . . . had only recognized on this day the things that make for peace! But now they are hidden from your eyes. Indeed, the days will come . . . when your enemies will set up ramparts around you and surround you, and hem you in on every side. They will crush you to the ground, you and your children within you" (Luke 19:42–44). The rhetorical force of this announcement comes from the way Jesus evokes a specific fear—the fear of losing not only one's own life but the life of one's children—to reveal the condition of peace. Jesus knows that his audience know that the death of children in war is no surprise. What he knows they do not want to admit is that the cost of life is not limited to the overt sacrifice of the other but includes the invisible sacrifice of possible futures—the unborn "children within you," the children that might have come but will never arrive. As Oedipus knew, so Jesus: to fight against this knowledge is to blind oneself to "the things that make for peace." What "makes for war" is the impulse to cling to one's life, which is to say one's Darwinian self-interest at the expense of the other. What "makes for peace" is an altogether different attitude toward the necessity of economization, an attitude of acceptance that opens the possibility of self-sacrifice in the name of a boundless love for the other in spite of the economizing threat the other poses.

Over and over Jesus returns to the motif of the child's safety in order to figure his most urgent message. He tells the "scribes and Pharisees" of Jerusalem to "gather your children together as a hen gathers her brood under her wings" (Matthew 23:37). Imagining himself in a maternal role, he would protect Jerusalem's children from a "brood" of egg-threatening "vipers"—that is, from the infanticidal aggression of the world (Matthew 23:33). Sacrificing himself so that we "may become children of the light" (John 12:36), Jesus sees in the figure of the radiance-begotten child a reflection of God's world-creating command, "Let there be light" (Genesis 1:3). Behind this image is the dark night when no starlight guided any wise men to the homes of the infant sons that Herod destroyed. When Jesus speaks of the resurrection as the time of no more infant death, he brings the infanticidal consequences of his infancy into sharp relief. Those who "are worthy of a place in . . . the resurrection of the dead," he says, "cannot die anymore, because they are like angels and are children of God, being children of the resurrection" (Luke 20:35–36). In order to assure that these "children" will "not die any more," Jesus himself must die; moreover, he must die as the only begotten son of God and as the son of Man—twice over as child. When he does, he reencounters the infanticidal implications, the infanticidal cost, of his advent.

He evokes these implications yet again when in the Eucharist he identifies the wine as "my blood of the covenant, which is poured out for many for the forgiveness of sins. I tell you, I will never again drink of this fruit of the vine until that day when I drink it new with you in my Father's kingdom" (Matthew 26:28–29; see also Mark 14:24–25 and Luke 22:18). The primary meaning of the Greek word for fruit—*gĕnnēma*—is "offspring"; by analogy to reproduction, its other meaning is "produce," hence "fruit" or "generation." The noun derives from a verb *gennao*, "to procreate . . . bear, beget, be born, bring forth, conceive, be delivered of, gender, make . . ." and figuratively "to regenerate."[22] As was noted in chapter 3, the Old Testament and New Testament repeatedly invoke the expression "fruit [$p^e r\hat{\imath}y$]of the womb."[23] When God first addresses living creatures, he commands them to "be fruitful and multiply" (Genesis 1:22). He repeats the command to Adam and Eve (Genesis 1:28). Thereafter he frames his covenants in terms of the promise of reproductive "fruitfulness."

This promise is the other side of the infanticidal jeopardy that is implicit in all the references to fruit in the Bible and blatant in several. The voice of Lamentations expostulates: "Shall women eat their fruit [$p^e r\hat{\imath}y$] and children of a span long? (2:20, KJV). Hosea denounces the infanticidal godlessness of Israel with astonishing explicitness: "Ephraim is stricken, their root is dried up, they shall bear no fruit. Even though they give birth, I will kill the cherished offspring [$p^e r\hat{\imath}y$] of their womb" (9;16).[24] Micah asks: "Will the Lord be pleased with thousands of rams, with ten thousands of rivers of oil? Shall I give my firstborn for my transgression, the fruit [$p^e r\hat{\imath}y$] of my body for the sin of my world?" (6:7). When Jesus pointedly alludes to drinking the *genema* of the vine, then, he is invoking an action that has a literal meaning of infanticide. In referring to this "fruit," Jesus recalls the first sin, which he reinterprets in terms of his redemptive mission, as well as the first murder, for both events have profound infanticidal implications. By alluding to the fruitfulness of procreation, Jesus underscores the infanticidism of the original sin and its mimetic reenactment in the murder of Abel. Several times over, then, through the image of *genema* Jesus refigures the Eucharist as infanticidal: to eat the bread and to drink the wine is to consume the Son of God and man.

To do so is to satisfy one's hunger and thirst according to a sacred imperative by which one is instructed to adopt a new attitude toward the bodily necessity of consuming other life: like Jesus, we must "never again drink of this fruit of the vine" in denial of the infanticidal meaning of the body's thirst, the body's organic need. Only in this "never again" of Jesus' holy signature—as the sacrificed son, as the infanticidal offering, as the one who says "I am the true vine" (John 15:1)—will we win through to the "eternal life" of every mortal moment, a hereafter that does not (because it cannot) annul death but that is given through death. The "true vine" is the symbolic name of life-as-infanticidal. On the day that we are able to acknowledge the non-transcendental infanticidism of our being and its appetites, Jesus will drink this wine "*new* with you."

In his injunction to eat and drink his body and blood, Jesus indicates how the gift of "my Father's kingdom" is the gift of the Father's death— that is, the gift of infanticidity infinitized. In obeying Jesus' injunction to perform the ritual of the Mass in memory of him,[25] the communicant has a sign of the infanticidity of being placed on the tip of his or her tongue — that is, precisely where it has the chance of coming to be spoken, articulated, explicitly named. Through the Eucharist, then, Jesus both puts his worshippers in the position of internalizing the Word itself, the very Word that created the infanticidal horizon of being, and announces his repudiation of all cultural practices by which the infanticidal cost of existence would be avoided, denied, rationalized, or repressed.

Jesus further underscores how "eternity" is to be located this side of life's infanticidal horizon when he anticipates his crucifixion: "You know that after two days the Passover is coming, and the Son of Man will be handed over to be crucified" (Matthew 26:2). The Passover commemorates a night in Jewish history that anticipates the infanticidal jeopardy surrounding Jesus' birth—the night that God killed the firstborn in Egypt but passed over the houses of the Israelites who had "slaughtered" a lamb, eaten it, and smeared its blood "on the two doorposts and the lintel" (Exodus 12:6–8). After his death Jesus is remembered as "our paschal [Passover] lamb" (1 Corinthians 5:7). Dying under the shadow of two infanticidal slaughters, one initiated by God and one by a mere mortal, the "lamb of God" (John 1:29 and 36) identifies both with those victims whose deaths have paid for the lives of others and with those others—including himself—who have received the gift of the victims' deaths. In this double identification Jesus resignifies the sacred: he does not declare that it is a power which can overcome death but that it is an affective force which can transform one's death into the gift of new life—not a new life for oneself immortalized but another mortal life for someone else, someone else's chance to live.

That is why Jesus compares, even equates, his death to the birth of a child. "When a woman is in labor," he tells his followers, "she has pain, because her hour has come. But when her child is born, she no longer remembers the anguish because of the joy of having brought a human being into the world. So you have pain now; but I will see you again, and your hearts will rejoice, and no one can take your joy from you. On that day you will ask nothing of me" (John 16:21–23). One might interpret this allusion to the mother's painful parturition allegorically, as Jesus' promise that he will return in a spiritualized resurrection of a once mortal body. However, one might also read it literally, as Jesus' instruction to see him disappear into the newborn and thus reappear as this new being. "On that day" something extraordinary will happen: one will "ask nothing of me," as one asks nothing of the infant. To have a heart that rejoices is to open oneself to the extraordinary value of the most ordinary event—the birth of a child whose advent is an instance of the blessing that can come from being mortal and is always a reminder of one's mortality.

It is to give oneself for the life of the other as if the other were a newborn — that is, as if the other's economization were not a threat but a signal, like the infant's helpless cry, that were able to elicit an attitude of caring without any thought of a future reciprocation.

To have a heart that rejoices, then, is to recognize the infinite value of the most ordinary finite moment. This moment is utterly transient. It fades, passes into and perhaps out of memory, and is often lost beyond any possible retrieval. Even if it remains in memory, it must nevertheless yield to the economizing demands of existence that must be attended to — eating, sleeping, working, dividing one's attention, parceling one's energy, and so on. For the duration of an instant, however, one is released into an aneconomic infinitude of joy, a non-economizable beatitude, "which no one can take from you" but also which one cannot trade, exchange, count on, use, or otherwise convert into an instrumental gain. In this sense the infinitude of a finite moment is transcendent without being transcendental. Precisely because the joy of this moment is transient, it enables the individual to transcend the desire for transcendence. Through the Eucharist Jesus redefines the desire for transcendence as pagan and the joy that comes from giving up this desire as Christological.

This joy, Jesus says, can arise only if one asks nothing of him, most especially not an escape from death — either one's own or his. This joy depends on accepting his death — that is, loving his death and loving in the name of it — not as the promise of an "eternal life" after one dies but as the gift of a lifetime that beckons one to give this impossible gift of death in turn.

A Love that Does Not Cling to Life

Such an acceptance requires, for at least two reasons, a love that does not try to do what the tradition of Platonizing Christianity has attempted in its conceptions of Jesus — namely, to immortalize its object. The first is that immortalization as traditionally conceived is never complete. It is always partial. It always depends on a mortal remainder that cannot be made immortal and so upsets the difference between (perishable) flesh and (imperishable) spirit. How so?

As Staten explains, when Paul imagines the resurrection of the body, he posits two forms of the flesh: "Not all flesh is alike," Paul asserts. In Staten's translation, "All *sarx* is not the same *sarx*" (1 Corinthians 15:39), and only one of the two kinds of flesh is resurrected — that flesh which is spiritually transformed. Without this transfiguration by spirit (*pneuma*), "flesh and blood cannot inherit the kingdom of God, nor does the perishable inherit the imperishable" (1 Corinthians 15:50). Once transformed, however, the flesh is no longer flesh and the resurrection no longer that of the mortal body. In other words, the resurrection of the spiritualized flesh leaves behind an unspiritualized remainder in the form of the second kind of flesh that is doomed to self-obliteration.[26]

Paul cannot distinguish between two kinds of flesh without undermining his transcendental view of spirit, since in order to be transcendent, spirit must be able to transform what is not transcendent and do so without remainder. However, two problems immediately arise. On the one hand, a remainderless transformation would eliminate the difference between the transcendent and the non-transcendent that gives spirit its essential identity. Some mortal flesh must remain. On the other hand, a mortal remainder reveals an incompleteness in the reach of the spirit. This remainder must disappear into its mortality but not by virtue of its mortality, for such self-annihilation would imply a force or movement beyond the reach of spirit.

If the Logos is transcendent, it must be able to descend into the flesh and die but also survive this death. It must subject itself to a destruction that it itself initiates while rebegetting itself from out of this very death. It must be able to be both incarnate and independent of its incarnation. It must be able to live and die and live again but differently, immortally; alternatively, it must be able to live and die on one ontological plane all the while living differently, by virtue of its immortality, on a second ontological plane. The two planes must retain their differences while entering into the very communication that undermines these differences.

The result is a conceptual conundrum evident in the representational abyss that arises when the "eternal life" of the spirit is posited as the reality that transcends the finite life of corporeal being. On the one hand, the concept of eternal life—life without death—is based on an analogy with mortal life: eternal life is not life without death but *as if* life without death. The transcendentalizing interpretive move is to literalize this metaphor and posit it as the creative, generative—in a word, conceptive—ground of being. The result is that organic life becomes a shadow of eternal life. On the other hand, however, the transcendentalizing hermeneutic presupposes precisely the finitude it would negate. Because physical life is mortal, eternal life could not be life but would have to be something else. For this reason "eternal life" cannot be affirmatively represented as such, for it is nameable only by analogy to what it is not (the very analogy it denies by reversing). This means, however, that eternity cannot be conceived as a life beyond life, as a life that suspends death. To the contrary, eternal life must be counter-conceived as a possibility inseparable from the finiteness of being.[27] If eternal life happens, it does so not in a time beyond death but this side of death—that is, in the finite transience of any moment. If it happens, it is because it does not simply arrive; it does not simply come. Rather, it comes to pass: it will have come and passed away. Indeed, it will have come only insofar as it is recognized as having come to pass.

John indicates this counter-conceptive horizon to Jesus' teaching when at the beginning of his gospel he employs a verb, *gínomai*, with an ambiguous temporal meaning to characterize the descent of the Logos: "In the beginning was the Word . . . and the word became flesh" or "was made flesh" (1:14). On the one hand *gínomai* can signify a process of becoming, in which case the Logos was originally something other than the flesh it subsequently becomes. On the other hand *gínomai* can mean being made as or coming into being as, in which case the Logos does not "become" flesh but "is made as" flesh from its self-beginning. In this case the Logos is a figure of the death-bound embodiment that inscribes all existence, and even the source of that existence, within a structure of mortality borne by the Logos. If the Word occurs, if it *is*, only in its finitizing incarnation in the world it creates, then its bestowal of being "in the beginning" would be inseparable from its bestowal of the death of being. Conversely, insofar as death always overtakes the possibilities of life, possibilities that are necessarily withdrawn in the advent of whatever lives in fact, then there can be neither beginning nor "eternal life" outside of death.

The second reason why the joy Jesus proclaims requires an acceptance of the finality of organic death is that "eternal life" would be a form of the economization that characterizes organic life in general and human existence in particular. As noted above, it would be a form of the very self-interest that motivates pagan Greek sacrifice and that Jesus demystifies. On the one hand, the prospect of a future immortal life, of a presumably imperishable consciousness relieved of its incarnation in a mortal body, promises an attachment to self and others that can never be lost and so would transport one beyond all grief. On the other hand, it promises an absolute release from any and all cost of this new life. This release infinitizes the defining feature of what economization pretends to offer—a life without mortgage, a life without debt or death, hence a life without responsibility for the invisible, nonempirical, infinite loss that underwrites all mortal existence. Twice over, then, "eternal life" represents the fulfillment of the dream of a transcendental economization.

And yet, as has been demonstrated, if an immortal existence were possible, it would nevertheless retain the traces of all the untraceable potentialities for life that are foregone in the lives that come to pass. That is, it would be joined to a deathliness that would be infinitely greater than, and thus infinitely nullifying of, the infinitude of eternal life.[28] Moreover, it would threaten to precipitate the individual into a condition of perpetual mourning for which no expression of grief, not even an infinite grieving, would be adequate to the structure of loss that necessarily attaches to eternal being.

As Staten has elucidated throughout his study of *Eros in Mourning*, if one loves because of the promise of "eternal life," one loves contingently, narcissistically. Jesus is emphatic that one must love unconditionally: "As the Father has loved me, so I have loved you; abide in my love. . . . This is my commandment, that you love one another as I have loved you. No one has greater love than this, to lay down one's life for one's friends" (John 15:9 and 12–13). If Jesus gave his life but lived forever, he would give nothing of himself. The divine son would be giving up merely the appearance of his life in a mimetic inversion and repetition of the way the Greeks offered the gods merely the appearance of a valuable sacrificial gift. To the contrary, Jesus gives everything of himself, and he does so in order that those who would follow him can free themselves from the (Darwinian) temptation of sacrificing the other to their self-interest. Jesus gives his life in order that those who survive him will revalue their conception of self-interest. He sacrifices himself in order to teach that one must neither cling to one's own existence nor idealize his life, both of which must be "given up" for the other. To "abide" in Jesus' love is to retransmit it by loving the other to the point of being able to relinquish one's life for them. This greatest of all possible love requires the sacrificial death of self. Why? Because in that moment the giver's love cannot be reciprocated and therefore is able to be given and received with the least expectation or hope of return. As has been indicated in the discussion of Abraham, to the extent that the gift of death arouses the recipient's gratitude, this person has only one recourse—to rebequeath in turn but without return. By this act he does not give a particular gift but gives giving. In the asymmetry of such giving, the gift of death is the gift not of life but of the giving which makes life possible within the context of its mortal circumscription. In other words, Jesus' commandment to give oneself without the possibility of reciprocation opens the possibility of an aneconomic "payment forward," the possibility of a relation to the mortal other that might enable this person to enter into a similar affective revaluation of loss and death.

In mobilizing the community to affirm their affective investments in their own lives at the expense of the lives of others, the sacrificial economy of the Greeks forms a massive cultural barrier against just this revaluation. In contrast, Jesus mobilizes his followers to affirm not his own life but his affirmation of the lives of others. As Staten explains, in eliciting an absolute identification on the part of his disciples, in offering "an unreserved pouring-out of his substance toward them or on their behalf," Jesus "open[s] the fountains of love in their own breasts."[29] He can do so because they believe their teacher is divine, "an embodied being who can be loved as no ordinary mortal being can." They "do not know that he will die, and soon," for otherwise they would be tempted to hold back emotionally on their commitment to him, to protect themselves from the loss that his announcement at the Last Supper, followed by the crucifixion, unleashes.[30]

The loss in question is not only the loss of Jesus, the one they love, but the loss of a part of themselves. Indeed, some form of self-loss always occurs whenever one loses the object in which one has invested his or her life, his or her present and future being.[31] According to Staten, Jesus exacerbates this threat when he puts his followers in the position of suffering as they have not suffered before in order to recognize in their grief at his humiliation and death—injustice itself—the extent to which they grieve narcissistically for themselves and their future demise, the extent to which they remain caught up in the "limitless pathos" of their own "self-clinging,"[32] the extent to which they are still economizing, the extent to which they are still trading on the preciousness of their own existence.

For the apostles, as for anyone, Staten explains, the "unbearable sharpness of the pain of separation from the most loved and most loving being" might threaten to turn them against the world by arousing "the anger and resentment of aggrieved automourning, the type of self-mourning that is still in rebellion against self-loss—that still reserves itself against the absolute expenditure it has begun to taste."[33] This expenditure without reserve—the ability to turn toward others, knowing that one will both lose the world and be lost to it, infinitely so in either case, even at the very moment of one's greatest and most abiding love, hence at the moment most worthy of being remembered forever—is, Staten proposes, what the Gospel of John intuits is the meaning of "eternal life."

According to Staten, the dominant tradition of Christian thought finds it "unthinkable . . . to pour out all one's being toward merely mortal objects precisely as mortal, with no thought of any transcendence of any sort beyond that which is mortal love itself, of love for what is mortal precisely as mortal and because it is mortal."[34] And yet, Staten argues, Jesus aims precisely at persuading his believers to give themselves over to this very (unthinkable) possibility—to relinquish all their defenses against the threat of the loss of the beloved as well as of the self-loss that comes from loving another who must die and leave one bereft. If one beholds the sacred in the other whom one loves but must lose, then the death of this other would feel like the loss of the sacred itself. It is this possibility that Jesus arouses in order to push his followers not to follow him but to follow his example, not to identify with him but with his identification with the totality of humankind.

In this second-order identification, Jesus dies all over again with the advent of each new life. Once again, he thereby becomes the figure of the structural costliness of existence as such, a costliness which is equivalent to the entirety of the sacred—that is, to all life that comes into being or

that is sacrificed before it can come into being. He thereby becomes a figure not only of one who suffers unjustly at the economizing hands of
others,[35] but of one who, like everyone else, is himself an instance of the
injustice that constitutes anyone's empirical life, anyone's coming into existence, whether or not their births set off the slaughter of others already
born. In being the victim of injustice who recognizes the structural injustice of any human life—indeed, of life at its most sacred—Jesus extends his revaluation of the conceptual oppositions that the tradition of
Platonizing Christianity endeavors to keep in place. This tradition hier-
archizes each opposition and then in each case idealizes one of the terms
over the other in a conceptive vision of spirit as pure and limitless source
of eternal being. Against this interpretive strategy Jesus revalues the
terms of the oppositions and thus disrupts the system of their hierar-
chization. When he does, he reveals how, within the horizon of the economization that is not transcendable, the ransom of which Mark and others
speak can become gift—the gift of death.

Such a ransoming gift must awaken the deepest gratitude and the
greatest sense of obligation but at the risk of thereby abolishing the gift
in the desire to reciprocate, a reaction that reinscribes the gift in an economy of exchange. And yet this risk is the greatest of opportunities insofar as it arouses a desire to reciprocate but blocks all avenues for doing
so, all avenues but one. This avenue is the possibility of giving the gift
in turn and therefore without return. In this giving of giving, the ransoming gift enables one to economize without economizing on the risk by
virtue of being the gift of death that cannot be reciprocated though it can
be repeated. Indeed, in this giving of giving, the ransoming gift will not
have become the gift of death unless and until it has been repeated. The
gift of death thus comes from the futurity—not an empirical future but
an indeterminate futurity—that the gift will for its part have made possible. In this sense the gift of death would always be (yet) to come and
would thereby announce an eternity that is immanent to, not transcendent over, the finite terms of the life of the individual, the life of the group,
the life of humankind as a species, and, indeed, the life of life.[36]

To "have life in [Jesus'] name" (John 20:31) would not be to antici-
pate more life, and above all not an immortal life hereafter, for oneself. It
would be, rather, to disappear, following Jesus' example, into the promise of life for the other through the gift of death. The giving of this gift
can displace the old ways of economizing, of sacrificing, of subjecting the
world to yet more infanticide violence, however, only on the condition
that it be given unconditionally. According to Derrida, such giving must
therefore accept the risk of opening itself to the monstrous. "All experience open to the future is prepared or prepares to welcome the monstrous *arrivant*, to welcome it, that is, to accord hospitality to that which

is absolutely foreign or strange, but also . . . to try to domesticate it. . . . This is the movement of culture. . . . All of history has shown that each time an *event* has been produced . . . it took the form of the unacceptable, or even the intolerable, of the incomprehensible, that is, of a certain monstrosity."[37] It is this monstrosity that the Western cultural imagination has tried to master by conceiving of the future in the same transcendentalizing terms that it has conceived of life. The concluding chapter to this study asks how it might be possible to counter-conceive the time to come.

IV
The Inconceivable Future

10

Conceptions and Contraceptions of the Future:
Star Trek, Terminator 2, The Matrix,
and *Alien Resurrection*

The future can only be anticipated in the form of an absolute danger.
It is that which breaks absolutely with constituted normality and can
only be proclaimed, *presented*, as a sort of monstrosity.
— Jacques Derrida, *Of Grammatology* (5)

Here there is a sort of question, call it historical, of which we are only
glimpsing today the *conception*, the *formation*, the *gestation*, the *labor*. I
employ these words, I admit, with a glance toward the business of
childbearing — but also with a glance toward those who, in a company
from which I do not exclude myself, turn their eyes away in the face
of the as yet unnameable which is proclaiming itself and which can
do so, as is necessary whenever a birth is in the offing, only under the
species of the non-species, in the formless, mute, infant, and terrifying form of monstrosity.
— Jacques Derrida, "Structure, Sign, and Play in the Discourse of
the Human Sciences" (265)

. . . the future is necessarily monstrous: the figure of the future, that
is, that which can only be surprising, that for which we are not prepared . . . is heralded by species of monsters. A future that would not
be monstrous would not be a future; it would already be a predictable, calculable, and programmable tomorrow. All experience
open to the future is prepared or prepares itself to welcome the monstrous *arrivant*.
— Jacques Derrida, "Passages — from Traumatism to Promise,"
Points (386–87)

CONCEIVING AND COUNTER-CONCEIVING THE FUTURE

THE CONCEPT OF FUTURITY SHARES WITH ALL OTHER CONCEPTS
the signal connotation of the literalized metaphor that governs the concept of conceptuality itself — namely, that thought is like reproduction
in producing new life, more life, hence the future. Conceptuality itself

implies a living future, and the concept of futurity makes explicit that whatever future there is will be a scene of life producing life.

The etymology of *future* reinforces this metaphysical conception of time as a form of life. The Latin *futurus* descends from the Indo-European *bheue,* "to be, exist, grow." This stem is the source of a Germanic root meaning "to be," from which eventually arose the modern English word *be;* it is also the stem of the Latin *fieri,* "to become." The Indo-European root has led by way of German to an Old Norse term meaning "to live" and a Middle Dutch term meaning "to cultivate." It has given rise to the Greek *phuein,* "to bring forth, make grow," the nominal form of which, *phusis,* "growth, nature," is the origin of the English *physics;* to the Greek *phulon,* "tribe, class, race"; and finally to an Old English word for dwelling or house, the modern English verb *build,* and a Middle Dutch term designating riches and property.[1] The word *future* thus participates in an etymological development that affirms thinking as ontologically originary — conceptive. It inscribes within its root meaning a predicate movement by which *what will be* — the future — is conceived as being self-engendering, hence self-perpetuating.

As was argued in chapters 1 and 2, however, if the evolutionary future is inexorably extinctive (not only for the human species but for all biological life), and if to think is to conceive or self-conceive, then the evolutionary time to come cannot be thought — that is, conceived. The evolutionary future is not that which will simply "be" but also and simultaneously that which will destroy the species that posits evolution, above all the evolution of self-consciousness, as conceptive.

Because evolution entails that existence costs, no conception of the world can enable the future to be a time when life's sacrificial horizon is overcome. The very basis of evolutionary change — mutability at the level of the gene, the logical equivalence of reproductive success and reproductive failure at the level of the individual, vulnerability to extinction at the level of the species — means that evolution is not reducible to a history of life or to the future of life. Evolution is only incidentally, contingently, a matter of the living. The biblical Flood illustrates this evolutionary implication: those who survive inherit the earth not only in the present but in the future through their descendants, and those who succumb continue to die by losing not only their lives but the possible lives of the descendants they might have had.

Conceived as that which will be, the future hides the infinitely greater loss of that which will never be. The deceit within all biological or mental conceptions of the future is explicit when the death of the other is figured as a finite loss offset by a potentially infinite and thereby sacred gain in life to the surviving victors. To so conceive of the future requires covering up the (infanticidal) costliness of all life, and that cover-up condemns conception—biological or mental—to the very uncreation to which this trope would seem to be opposed. Every conception of the future implies an abortion or contraception of other possible futures.

It is difficult to think without conceiving—that is, without relying on the very conceptuality that posits thinking as conception. If it were possible to think without conceiving, the result would be, from the point of view of thought as conception, nothing less than an apocalyptic and infanticidal loss of the conceivable future—indeed, of that which can be conceived at all. The conjunction of apocalypse and infanticide thus indicates the difficult advent (not birth) of a non-conceptive thought as that thought bumps up against the traditional conceptualizations that block its articulation. *Star Trek: The Motion Picture*, *Terminator 2*, and *The Matrix* act out this problem and attempt to solve it in a conceptive manner that covers up the very problem in question.

THE FUTURE OF CONSCIOUSNESS AS AN EVOLUTIONARY BIRTHING: *STAR TREK*

Star Trek: The Motion Picture[2] begins with a threatening, nonverbal hail from a massive interstellar "energy cloud," its origin unknown, heading directly toward earth, obliterating all galactic objects in its path. Eventually Federation Admiral Kirk (William Shatner) and his crew discover at the center of the cloud humankind's long lost technological offspring, the *Voyager* satellite. Unbeknown to earth, in the several hundred years after its launch *Voyager* has evolved into "a life form of its own, a conscious, living entity," Spock (Leonard Nimoy) says, and for that reason it is initially unrecognizable when it returns to the solar system "looking for its creator." Having been rebuilt and sent "on its journey back" home by "a machine planet" it has encountered, it calls itself "VGER," its abbreviated name marking its lost memory of those who constructed it. Although it has acquired a new identity, it retains its original programming—to "collect all data possible" and to "transmit its information" to its maker, which it mistakenly "believes . . . is a machine." Once Kirk convinces VGER otherwise—that "we [humans] are the creator"—it insists that "the creator must join with VGER." So intones Ilia (Persis Khambatta), the *Enterprise* officer VGER has reduced to a data structure and then reconstituted to serve as its interface with the "carbon based units" it has not known are "true life forms." *Star Trek* ends when Kirk's First Officer and Captain, Will Dekker (Stephen Collins), and Ilia, respectively the metonymical figures of humankind and the alien consciousness, "join" in a PG-rated act of symbolic intercourse. As they stand face-to-face, Dekker and Ilia become sparkling particles of swirling light that stream outward in a scintillating explosion and diffusion. The scene condenses into a brilliant moment a cosmic conception and parturition. "Spock, did we just see the beginning of a new life form?" Kirk asks. "Yes, Captain. We witnessed a birth—possibly the next step in our evolution." To which the good doctor (DeForest Kelley) remarks, "well, it's been a long time since I've delivered a baby."

The ending of *Star Trek* depicts the fulfillment of a wish—that the future will be something like the begotten offspring of the present, and that it is "conceivable" as an extension of heterosexual generativity. That wish, however, betrays the anxiety that motivates it—the dread of a human-ending inhuman future. *Star Trek* evokes this fear, at first imagining the future as the time of a nonhuman consciousness unable to hear humankind's welcome and therefore about to obliterate the earth. *Star Trek* then converts this fear into exultant joy by revealing that the alien consciousness is seeking a human consciousness of its own in the form of the "simple feeling" that would give it the "meaning" and "hope" that it presently lacks. VGER, Spock says after melding with it, is "asking questions. . . . Is this all that I am? Is there nothing more?" The film answers with its symbolic primal scene of conceptive intercourse and the expectation of a birth to come, a birth that will perpetuate human consciousness into the distant future.

In making this primal scene, the Federation admiral and officers must first save VGER from its parricidal violence against its creators. They can do so because they recognize it as their prodigal technological child coming home at last and then teach it to recognize human consciousness as its progenitive source. In this way *Star Trek* turns the arrival of the alien into a drama of mutual recognition by which the cosmos is rebegotten. In other words, through its imagery of metaphorical copulation and its vocabulary of birth, the film conceives the future as the outcome of an evolutionary process—one modeled on the generativity of biological and mental conceptivity—that is on the verge of extinguishing humankind but that finally preserves humans from an apocalyptic demise.

The result is that the film reenacts the ideological process, described by Althusser, that makes interpellation appear to be, finally, a life-affirming expression of human subjectivity rather than the (infanticidal-cum-extinctive) condition of the human subject's possibility.

ALIEN INTERPELLATION

As was discussed in chapter 6, before there is a subject, there is subjectivation. This *subjection to* otherness can be reproductive, in which case the *subjected to* is interpellated into life and becomes a person. *Subjection to* can also be contraceptive, in which case the *subjected to* is hailed into nonexistence and does not become a person. In either case, interpellative subjectivation is the condition of the possibility of a subject's being or its nonbeing.[3]

The Western cultural tradition, however, has conceptualized and paternalized interpellation in particular and the symbolic order in general as fundamentally life-begetting. It has attempted to purify the symbolic order of the general infanticidism by which interpellation in the form of reproduction is an evolutionary force of death as much as it is an evolutionary force of life. Even if it were able to succeed in this impossible task, the tradition would "be" what it conceives itself as being (life begetting life) only in relation to what this tradition does not want to "be" (life begetting but simultaneously destroying and obstructing the production of life). Since life can be "conceived" only in relation to death, the very concept of life includes what the concept seems to exclude—its other. As Judith Butler explains about subject-formation in general: "the subject is constituted through the force of exclusion and abjection, one which produces a constitutive outside to the subject, an abjected outside, which is, after all, 'inside' the subject as its own founding repudiation."[4]

Such "exinclusion" splits the subject; it forces the subject to be what it is not. According to Lacan, this splitting constitutes the subject in the so-called mirror stage, when the young, physically uncoordinated child either encounters—jubilantly or anxiously—its own specular image or recognizes itself in the objectifying gaze of the other.[5]

Star Trek dramatizes the jubilant possibilities of this encounter insofar as it affirms humankind's conceptual mastery of VGER's (infanticide-avoidant) desire to reconnect with the maker that hailed it into existence. Miming YHWH, Kirk at the interpellative climax of the film claims for himself, as spokesperson for all of humanity, an absolute power to name humans as the creator and thus as the source of VGER's being. According to Althusser, when YHWH says "I am that I am," he "defines himself as the Subject *par excellence,* he who is through himself and for himself . . . and he who interpellates his subject, the individual[s] subjected to him by his very interpellation" ("Ideology and Ideological State Apparatuses," 179). Kirk repeats God's self-nomination, thereby turning human subjectivity into a mirror in which VGER can recognize its subjection to and origination in the seemingly divine (human) Subject. At the same time, Kirk turns VGER's subjectivity into a mirror in which humans can recognize the technological offspring they have forgotten. Such a double mirroring might have led Kirk, Spock, and McCoy to acknowledge that, despite the mimetic trick of calling themselves VGER's creator, humans are as subject to interpellative subjection as is VGER, that this shared dependency always occurs in the context of a possible hailing into death, and that this power to subject the other into nonexistence defines the most divine Subject—God—who always (and only) speaks from out of his potentially world-destroying self-sufficiency. But *Star Trek*'s mirroring scene does not lead to this counter-conceptive insight. Instead, it leads Kirk, Spock, and McCoy to celebrate humankind's seeming self-delivery into a conceptive future.

A CONTEST OF FUTURES: *TERMINATOR 2*

Staging the future as an infanticidal call from a machine world that can come into being only on the condition of humankind's present destruction, *Terminator 2* is on the verge of apprehending what *Star Trek* in its jubilation at surviving and domesticating its seeming nemesis does not about the extinctive horizon of life.

In James Cameron's film,[6] an early model of the Terminator (Arnold Schwarzenegger) has been sent back from the future to protect a teenager, John Connor (Edward Furlong), from a more advanced model of Terminator—the T-1000 (Robert Patrick)—also from the future. The mission of the protean T-1000—a metallic liquid, it has the shape-shifting ability to assume the form of the humans with which it has come into contact—is to eradicate the boy (whose initials, JC, allude to Jesus Christ) whose destiny is to lead a resistance against the sentient machines that humans will soon create. As in all science fiction films that involve time travel, the interpenetration of temporal phases in *Terminator 2* makes explicit the potentially apocalyptic and infanticidal implications of actions that would alter the world's future history, hence its past. For this reason *Terminator 2* relativizes and divides every temporal moment. Thus, for those who travel back in time, the "present" to which they return is their past. In relation to this "past," however, the time-traveler's present is the future. Time travel, in short, folds all temporal moments into one another; that is, it enables science fiction films to presence the past, the present, and the future simultaneously.

Terminator 2 equivocates in its characterization of the actions that will prevent one (machinic) future from supplanting another (fully human) future. On the one hand, it makes explicit the infanticidal mission of the T-1000—the assassination of a teenage boy. On the other hand, it covers up the infanticidal implications of the human victim who, if he survives, will bring about the demise of humankind's technological offspring. Thus, the film demonizes the T-1000, whose actions represent a robotic future world's efforts to defend itself against extinction. Thus, too, does the film sacralize the boy's life, along with the lives of his mother and the

Terminator who is assigned to protect him, even though John Connor will wage what, from the perspective of those he would defeat, is an infanticidal apocalypse—that is, death at the hands of the parental generation that has created them.

Not surprisingly, within its first minute the film depicts an infanticide holocaust. The film opens with an ominous, reverberating bass chord, repeated in two or three different keys, as the camera first shows an aerial view of a crowded freeway, automotive arterial lifeline of metropolitan civilization, and then cuts to a street-level view. The camera next cuts to a grassy playground, Edenic trees in the distance. The idyllic scene is suffused with light, the sun shining gloriously. In the foreground is a teeter-totter and behind it is a swing on which a young girl and boy facing in opposite directions are arcing up into the air. Embodying in their undeveloped sexual difference the potential for humankind's reproductive future, the children are laughing, the sound of their unselfconscious happiness, the only sound in the scene, muffled. Immersed in the thrill of swinging against the pull of gravity, they are oblivious to what a parent or other adult might experience as the preciousness, even precariousness, of their play. The physical movement of the children and their gaiety emphasize their aliveness; and yet the absence of sound casts an auditory pall over the scene.

The camera follows one child rising into the air and then the other, the first child now off screen. As the second child swings upward, the screen gradually whitens until, at the apex of her arc, she disappears without a sound into the intensifying light of a nuclear explosion and its holocaustal fire. Her dematerialization inverts the association of light and life, one of the most abiding of anthropological motifs. In the *Poetics*, Aristotle defines metaphor by analogy to the way the sun is said to "inseminate" the world by "sowing [its] god-created fire" analogously to the way a farmer "scatters" his "seed (*sperma*)."[7] Turning the screen into a kind of blank page, the sun in *Terminator 2* inscribes itself upon the earth as a writing not of life but of infanticidal death. In representing the playground as a place of almost complete silence, the camera anticipates the blotting out of the child that immediately follows. Here withdrawing the children's voices in a scene anticipating the future termination of humans, the movie shortly thereafter introduces the quest of its heroes to save those voices from this eventuality. The next scene emphasizes but then turns away from the infanticidal nature of the child's destruction and the film's vision of the Terminator future. Following the child's disappearance, the camera cuts to the unburied remains of countless humans as an inhuman foot pulverizes one skull and then as an army of machine troops crush acres and acres of skeletons. A metonymy of the collective destruction that has overtaken her world, the innocent child's pitiless death has become both generalized and lost in the indiscriminate slaughter of countless human lives.[8]

Seventy minutes later, the film completes its opening (infanticidal) sequence when Sarah Connor (Linda Hamilton) returns to the playground, this time full of children, in a dream. Having escaped from a mental hospital, she has been reunited with her son and his Terminator protector. Taking refuge in the desert, Sarah falls asleep. In her dream she stands at a chain link fence and sees a little girl on a merry-go-round. She yells out a frantic "no," the sound of which is deleted from the film track. No one in the playground hears her; like the people in her waking life, no one in her dream can imagine the cyborg future that is about to overtake humankind. No one can conceive of an apocalyptic hailing that would bring a nonhuman future into being at the cost of the human future the film's protagonists struggle to insure.

The camera does not record the vocalizations of the children at play; in relation to the Terminator future, the children are already dead. Thus, the scene unfolds in dreadful silence. Sarah looks at a young boy on a teeter-totter, then at another child, the same young girl who disappears at the beginning of the film, swinging into the air. Distraught at what is about to happen, Sarah shakes the fence, but no one sees her: she is as invisible as they will be nonexistent following the nuclear blast that will obliterate them. She next sees her infant son and then herself as a young mother. Her earlier self puts her son on one of the playground spring-horses and then, as if sensing the presence of her future self, looks in the direction of the fence but does not see the older (dreaming) person she becomes looking at her.

At that moment there is a blinding flash of light. A child falls, letting out a short scream. Other children and their mothers fall, screaming, then turning to stone from a nuclear blast in the background. Puffs of white smoke rise from where some of the kids and mothers have been vaporized. Then Sarah, screaming as she witnesses the holocaust face-on, bursts into flame. Her earlier self and her child also burst into flame. The camera then cuts to a thermal wave sweeping through the city, exploding building after building. When it reaches the park, the petrified children and mothers, including Sarah and her child, and then the dreamer herself explode. Still standing at the fence, Sarah is reduced to a skeleton as her flesh is blasted off of her body. The appalling sequence, which lasts an excruciating one hundred seconds, transforms the death of the single child in the opening scene into the death of many children. The infanticide imagery of the earlier scene is here compounded when the children — including Sarah Connor's own infant, her younger dream self, and the other mothers, all of whom are helpless to protect their kids—are shown instantly disintegrating in the aftershock of the bomb's blast.

Together, the two scenes bring the infanticidal implications of the war between humans and machines into the open. For most of its Freudian storyline, however, *Terminator 2* hides these implications in a retelling of the familiar oedipal narrative. Capitulating to the traditional misreading of Oedipus, according to which the child is the origin of the violence the parents must counter, the movie transfers the aggression of the son onto humankind's technological offspring. Thus, the film represents humankind's resistance against the Terminators as a defense of civilization— specifically, of the family values embodied in Sarah Connor's protection of her son—and its reproductive context. The movie, in other words, "conceives" of the human future in terms of safeguarding human conception from an infanticidal holocaust. The film's holocaust scenes are symptomatic expressions of this very conception—of the conceptuality within which the figure of the alien threatens to destroy the human. The film offers a counter-scene, however, in which the camera is on the verge of disclosing a "counter-conceptive" apprehension. The scene occurs at the movie's climax, when for thirty agonizing seconds the T-1000 dies. The storyline wants the death of the T-1000 to be the destruction of the nonhuman, the inhuman. In fact, however, the film comes perilously close to representing his death throes as utterly human.

At the end of the film, the T-1000 takes on the form and voice of Sarah, calling out to John in a tone that duplicates her fight-to-the-death desire to protect her son. Engaging in his deceitful mimesis, the Terminator acts out the violence implicit in all hailing, all interpellation. As the Terminator calls out to John, the boy follows the voice and is about to rush forward into the arms of his disguised enemy when a second Sarah appears behind the first. This Sarah tells her son to get down: she has a gun and needs a clear line of fire in order to shoot the false Sarah. When her gunshots fail to stop the T-1000, all appears to be lost until the dismembered Schwarzenegger Terminator, having inched his way onto a conveyor belt that has propelled him forward, comes upon his nemesis, whom he is finally able to destroy. Aiming one last time, he fires at the T-1000, splitting the head and torso of his enemy to the waist. Rocked backward, the T-1000 falls into a vat of sun-bright molten metal. In his— its—death-throes, the T-1000 takes on various human shapes, evidently those of its victims. Nearing its end, it assumes the lurid form of a Munch-like face, screaming in agony. Finally it becomes a mouth that cannot speak its termination except as an inarticulate screeching. A metonymical figure of the infant, this alien mouth vanishes when it swallows itself, leaving no interpellative trace of its existence. There is not even an echo of its death wail, only the brilliance of the liquid fire, medium of the sacrificial death that makes the human future possible.[9]

Although *Terminator 2* represents the T-1000 as nonhuman and his disappearance as the end of the nonhuman threat to the human, in fact the film renders him all too human when it depicts his agony. As he dies, the film not only identifies him with all those human victims whose identities he has destroyed and then mimetically appropriated, it identifies with him. The camera does not just show the T-1000 melting away. It pointedly depicts the T-1000 as if it were human. Here, in its most provocative, albeit unguarded, identification with the human enemy, the film thereby places the T-1000 in the position of the victim that it has placed humans. What is more, at the same time the film places itself and its viewer in the position of the Terminator. The result is that the movie twice over closes the distance between the nonhuman and human. In doing so *Terminator 2* specifies the infanticidal implications of human survival against the products of their own imagination.

Reduced to a speechless mouth, the T-1000 can only scream and then disappear into itself for another reason: it comes from a future that is in contraceptive relation to this world. The threat posed by the T-1000 is precisely the meaning of John Connor's survival, for the human son's life means the death of an alternative future, a death represented in the T-1000's agony as the silencing of another kind of being in the world. In *Terminator 2*, the future the T-1000 inhabits is literally inconceivable. It is unable to be conceived in the conceptuality that governs the past to which it has been sent except as an infanticidal threat to the order for which this conceptuality provides the philosophical foundation. Killing off one of humankind's machinic heirs, *Terminator 2* ends by militantly affirming the power of humans to survive into the future against the products of their own invention. Marking the heroic self-sacrifice of the Schwarzenegger Terminator, the film rationalizes the destruction of the T-1000—the infanticidal meaning of which it does not recognize—in the name of rescuing the human child. In the person of this child, the future has a human face, the face of a John Connor, rather than the visage of a Terminator, a cyborg that has no face of its own.

Insofar as John Connor is a Jesus Christ figure, however, the film retreats from acknowledging what the New Testament makes explicit—namely, that Christ's advent triggers Herod's massive slaughter of the innocents and that his crucifixion as the Son of God redeems humanity at the cost of another slaughter, this time of the absolutely innocent. Offering a future perfected, Jesus dies a symbolic infanticide, the condition of the possibility in Christian thought of what is and of what will be. Alluding to the Christian salvation, the film has its JC figure sacrifice the other rather than himself. The film thus backs away from the insight that it is on the verge of comprehending and that Jesus embodies—namely, that the time to come always bears an infanticidal, counter-conceptive meaning.

THE MACHINIC THREAT TO THE REPRODUCTIVE FUTURE: *THE MATRIX*

Like *Terminator 2, The Matrix*[10] is caught between conceiving and counter-conceiving the future. The storyline of *The Matrix* is well known. An ordinary computer programmer by day, Thomas Anderson, but the outlaw hacker by night, Neo (Keanu Reeves) receives a "wake up" call from a revolutionary group led by Morpheus (Laurence Fishburne). Morpheus believes the anagrammatically named Neo is "the One"—the individual destined to release humans from their imprisonment within the Matrix. The Matrix for its part is a vast artificial intelligence network that "grows" humans in placental cocoons and harvests the electrical energy that their brains produce. Unaware that they are little more than brains in a vat, humans live in a "computer-generated dreamworld" that they experience as real by virtue of direct stimulation of the brain. Morpheus wants to remove Neo from this environment, free his mind from the Matrix's years of programming, train him to combat the Matrix, and then support him in the battle to come, which takes place within the virtual terrain of the Matrix's programs.

From the outset, *The Matrix* is replete with imagery of conception and birthing. The scenes of Neo's bugging and then debugging illustrate the significance of this imagery for the film's "conception" of Neo's destiny. The scenes begin when, after the Matrix's cybermorphic constructs— the Sentinels—take Neo into custody, Agent Smith questions his captive, asking him to reveal his contacts with Morpheus. Neo refuses and gives Agent Smith the finger. He says, in effect, "fuck you," using the discourse of conception to stipulate a victory over the enemy other, a victory that would block its earth-colonizing, mechanical self-propagation. Neo's gesture encapsulates the sacrificial economy that governs reproduction since, as has been noted, any conception blocks the conceptions that might otherwise have occurred. *The Matrix* refuses to acknowledge this contamination of the conceptive by the contraceptive, instead splitting the two and attributing the contraceptive to humankind's technological enemy and reserving the conceptive for its heroic human warriors.

Disappointed in Neo's juvenile nonverbal response, Agent Smith causes Neo's mouth to seal and disappear. The suffocating scene underscores the film's subtext—the impossibility of speaking outside a signifying system conceived as conceptive. Not surprisingly, after Neo loses his mouth and hence his ability to articulate his resistance, he is physically over-powered and violated. It is as if he is raped and impregnated with a bio-mechanical bug. Agent Smith places a tracer over Neo's belly; once it is activated, it then enters him through his navel, site of each person's at-tachment to the maternal body and thus a sign of each person's concep-tive origin. In reconnecting Neo to the Matrix—the artificial *mater,* the false mother[11]—Agent Smith and his cohorts in effect return him to a technological womb which the rest of the film figures as the place of a feticidal harvest.

The debugging that follows the assault on Neo dramatizes the male hysteria that suffuses the film and specifically the resistance movement led by Morpheus. Picked up by Trinity (Carrie-Anne Moss), the central female member of Morpheus' resistance cadre, and her cohorts, Neo finally consents to having the tap removed. The resulting operation re-quires him to expose his belly and once again to be penetrated, this time by an extraction device. The procedure, replete with the sound of the quasi-living mechanism being vacuumed out of Neo's abdomen, is a kind of male abortion with the bloody bug figured as a species of artificial fetus.

The debugging anticipates the film's conflicted imagery surrounding Neo's metaphorical birthing into what Morpheus insists is "the real world." Neo's symbolic parturition begins with a mirror or identity scene during which Neo comes face-to-face with the extraordinary illusion in which he has been immersed since birth, at least according to Morpheus. As Neo touches the broken mirror into which he is gazing, it adheres to his finger.[12] Liquifying, it travels up his arm, rapidly merging with and be-coming the very substance of his entire body. As his heart is about to fib-rillate, one of Morpheus's crew "gets a lock" on Neo's place in the "fetus fields" of the Matrix. The camera cuts to those fields, where one of the Matrix's machines unhooks Neo from the artificial womb in which he has been encased in a uterine fluid. Unsnapping a series of mechanical um-bilici, the Matrix then flushes Neo from itself. From the point of view of the Matrix, Neo's release is like a miscarriage or abortion.

From the point of view of Morpheus, however, Neo's release is a birthing: "his head goes under the water three times" in accordance with the baptismal requirement that "the head . . . be cleansed three times for the father, the son, and the holy spirit."[13] Floundering in the sewer water, Neo is saved from drowning when the forceps-like claws of a crane close around him and take him upward out of the hellish dark belly of the Matrix and into the generative white light of Morpheus's scout ship. Neo's extraction from the Matrix completes the earlier extraction of the Matrix-tap from Neo.

After a period of rehabilitation, Neo is ready to train under the tutelage of Morpheus, who later in the film is revered as a "father." As Morpheus is dying from the torture of the Sentinels, his comrade-in-arms, Tank (Marcus Chong), prays: "you were more than our leader. You were . . . a father." Although no male sires any child in this film, the promise of paternal generativity underwrites the war against the inhuman, infanticidal mother-Matrix, which bypasses the conceptive role of the father to propagate its human slaves by clonal manipulation. No wonder, then, that the revolutionary father-figure, Morpheus, wages war against the Matrix from within its metropolitan simulacrum,[14] for in this virtual cityscape human consciousness believes it is in one world but is in another. It is, therefore, in exile from itself without knowing it. In placing his faith in Neo, Morpheus adopts him as his son, believing that this person will be able to save Zion from the apocalyptic threat of the Matrix and its counter-conceptive metropolis. Zion, the last redoubt against the colonizing expansionism of the Matrix, is a human space, the Matrix purified, turned conceptive. From the point of view of Morpheus and the other inhabitants of Zion, the Matrix is infanticidal and must be destroyed.

The necessity of that destruction signals the male hysteria of Morpheus and his world when confronted with a future that threatens to be inconceivable. Neo's response to this threat is to impregnate the Matrix. He does so near the end of the film by turning himself into a flash of light and then entering Agent Smith through the midriff. In this action, Neo absorbs Agent Smith's being somewhat in the way that the mirror had earlier absorbed him. The conceptive power of Neo's penetration and appropriation is signaled when Agent Smith's head explodes as Neo gets his (ejaculatory) revenge for having been earlier penetrated. (*The Matrix* here makes explicit the counter-conceptive implications of what *Star Trek* domesticates in its consummatory climax.) An extension of the anti-maternal Matrix, Agent Smith cannot withstand the paternally guided force of the son's penetration and the conceptual mastery of the Matrix which this penetration symbolizes.

That mastery comes from the father by way of what the film represents at the level of its emplotment and dialogue as the woman's heterosexual desire. On the one hand, Trinity's position in the masculine trinity to which her name alludes, along with her androgynized appearance, "especially paired with the somewhat gender and sexually ambiguous Keanu Reeves,"[15] might be read as resisting the film's heterosexual conceptual investments. And yet, by presenting its homoerotic overtones within its allusion to the trinitarian unity of Father, Son, and Holy Ghost, the film sublates gender and sexuality into the most traditional conceptual schemas—that of thought's generativity—much as Plato subordinated sexuality, homosexual or otherwise, to the idealization of mental intercourse.

On the other hand, the film emphatically endorses Trinity's hetero-sexual love for Neo, a love she believes the Oracle has sanctified. When Agent Smith kills Neo, Trinity raises him from the dead with her Oracle-inspired declaration of love and then her kiss. "Neo, I'm not afraid any-more. The Oracle told me that I would fall in love and that that man, the man that I love, would be the one. So you see, you can't be dead. You can't be, because I love you. You hear me?! I love you." A kind of Klein-ian "good mother," the Oracle provides not only physical but spiritual nourishment to those who believe in her. Thus, just as she confirms Morpheus's faith in "the One," so too does she affirm Trinity's dream of a (heterosexual) love that is so powerful it can resurrect the dead. Through the influence of the Oracle, the two faiths become "one" when, troping against the tale of Sleeping Beauty, Trinity kisses Neo. Trinity thereby transfers to or awakens in him the inseminating generativity of the Mor-pheus father-figure, whose world-saving commitment has received the divine imprimatur of the maternal, perhaps grandmotherly, seer.

In the fairy tale circumstances of Neo's rebirth, the film heterosexualizes its narrative climax. That is, it displaces the possibility of other sexual unions—signified by its diffuse intimations of homosexual inclinations, its more pointed evasion of contact between its two black figures, the paternal Morpheus and the black, maternal Oracle, and its refusal to ex-plore the currents of desire between Morpheus and any of his follow-ers—onto the white characters, Neo and Trinity. The film thus incorpo-rates the overt heterosexuality of these two figures, as well as any covert homosexuality they might embody, within the ethnocentric and phallic conceptivity that has dominated Western thought and imagination.

Not surprisingly, when Neo revives from Trinity's eroticized hailing, he transforms himself into the aforementioned phallic blaze of light and, penetrating Agent Smith, begets himself upon the Matrix. The resulting destruction of the Matrix—the technological offspring of human inven-tion, a bad seed maternalized as a Kleinian "bad mother"—acts out the infanticide-violence that propels the paternal figure whenever his con-ceptive power is at stake. His mouth now unsealed, Neo is soon shown speaking into a phone, calling humankind fully into being, the Matrix out of being. At the end, Neo cannot take an action that is absolutely con-ceptive, only relatively so. He can release humans from their imprison-ment within the "fetus fields" of the Matrix to be symbolically reborn only by killing off the AI.

What complicates Neo's victory is that the Matrix, like the Terminator technology of the earlier movie, initially is the product of human engi-neering. In consequence, the war against the Matrix is a war between a parent human generation and its cyber-offspring. Morpheus's status as father indicates the paternal aggression that the film tries to figure as salvific—conceptive. That effort bespeaks the film's difficulty in imagining the time to come except in terms of imperiled conception; it registers the film's dread at the prospect of a contraceptive rather than a conceptive future. Neo's victory thus enacts the film's "conception" of the future as a defense against a "contraceptive" possibility.[16]

ABORTING THE FUTURE: *ALIEN RESURRECTION*

The fourth *Alien* film, *Alien Resurrection*,[17] recognizes this other possibility in the repeated way that it delineates the contraceptive nature of all conception. It does so by "resurrecting" the character of Ripley (Sigourney Weaver), whose self-sacrifice in *Alien 3* saves humankind from a future in which *homo sapiens* will disappear either because humans are destroyed or because they are crossbred with aliens to form a radically hybrid species whose characteristics are unpredictable, perhaps unspeakable. To forestall either eventuality, at the end of the third *Alien* film Ripley dives backward into an inferno, similar to the one into which the T-1000 falls. Her arms extended, Christlike, she kills herself in order to destroy the alien fetus that has been implanted in her. *Alien 3* sanctifies the –cidal (suicidal, matricidal, feticidal) violence of Ripley's death.[18] Thus, in *Alien 3* Ripley kills herself in order to redeem the earth from the Frankensteinian-cum-satanic arrogance of the Terran Growth Conglomerate (TGC) scientists who play God by engineering new life forms. Moreover, she does so in the name of humanity's future reproductive purity.

By opposing the survival of the human species to the survival of a competing alien species or the advent of a new species no longer entirely human, *Alien 3* explicitly remarks the sacrificial economy of natural selection. That is why it conceives of human survival in conceptive terms. In this regard, Ripley's self-immolation is a thoroughly conservative action intended to safeguard the integrity of the human from its genetic contamination. In other words, she commits feticide under the aegis of a conceptive ideology that represents its "conceptual" articulations as a force of pure life.

The achievement of *Alien Resurrection* is its return to the scene of sacrifice and its refiguration of it, however partially and ambivalently, in terms of a "counter-conceptuality." To this end, the film raises Ripley from the dead no longer as a Christ figure but as a dark version of the Virgin Mary. Unlike her biblical precursor, bearer of the most sanctified newborn, Ripley is a surrogate mother who will be called upon to destroy her child's child. And yet Ripley is very much like the Virgin Mary insofar as the pregnancies of both figures are embedded in a contraceptive context. Immaculately conceived, the New Testament Mary sires one of the most alien conceptions imaginable. What is more, in relation to the maculate nature of all other human begettings, Mary's conception might be considered to be ironically contraceptive in its very purity, since its unblemished nature is in antithesis to—it is contra—the defilement that attaches to all other sexually conceived human pregnancies. In addition, Mary's conception is contraceptive in that her pregnancy, accomplished through the alien agency of the Holy Ghost, eventuates in the birth of a son who survives a slaughter of the innocents as an infant only to die as a symbolic infant at the direction of his Father God.

Evoking this contraceptive and infanticidal context of Mary's conception, pregnancy, and birthing, *Alien Resurrection* begins with Ripley genetically reconstructed from DNA in blood samples taken and frozen before she killed herself. Brought back to life by scientists working for United Systems Military (USM) aboard the research spacecraft *USS Auriga*, Ripley is somehow still pregnant, the research object of the scientists who are pursuing the "applications" that will follow from their program of cross-breeding humans and aliens. "The benefits," one of them exults as he spears a shrimp from Ripley's plate and then sucks it down as he talks, "go way beyond urban pacification" to include the creation of "new alloys and vaccines . . . there's nothing like this in any world we've seen." This triumphant, self-congratulatory self-absorption — embodied in the technocrat's appetite—will soon give way to the predatory screeches of the alien to which Ripley is about to give birth.

This birth takes place as a C-section. Lying on an operating table, Ripley is cut (or ripped) open in an action which inscribes her name upon her body. A captive of TGC and USM, Ripley is subject to the interpellative medical procedures that are the condition of the possibility not only of her reanimation but of her reproductivity. What Ripley — along with the film's other human simulacrum, the cyborg Call (Winona Ryder)—will soon realize is that this interpellation has "inconceivable," and therefore unspeakable, implications. This unspeakability is symbolically encoded in the physiology of Ripley's newborn "daughter." The neonatal alien is almost all mandible and maxilla. Its head, disproportionate to the rest of its prehistoric body, is taken up almost entirely by its jaws. With its first squealing cry, it opens its mouth to disclose its saliva-dripping teeth, also the initial focus of the film's second shot of the alien whose hideous double mouth is its most distinctive feature.

The alien's mouth and jaws, along with its razor-edged teeth, do not constitute primarily an organ of communication but rather of destruction. Although the alien communicates with others of its kind, making use of high-pitched signals, it does not employ its mouth to speak, let alone to articulate complex symbolic representations of the world. In fact, the alien's mouth is devoid of almost any expressivity other than indications of its murderous appetite. Whatever organs support the alien's communicative signaling, they are not buccal. The result is that the alien's voracious mouth is almost exclusively oriented to performing the most primitive of Darwininian functions—killing and eating. The alien's jaws, teeth, and mouth thus represent the other side of interpellation, the contraceptive "greeting" implicit in the most conceptive hailing. What is more, they represent the interpellative infanticidism within the encounter not only between the sentient alien and human, but between human and human since, as was explained at the outset of chapter 6, every "conceptive" interpellation is simultaneously contraceptive. The alien's face, devoid of flesh, exposes its articulated anatomical structure, and that articulation of its deadly mandibles personifies what is inarticulate and inarticulable in conceptuality—namely, the evolutionary cost of human reproductive success and the world transforming, culture imposing force of consciousness that such success has supported.

Terminator 2 and *The Matrix* also personify this reproductive costliness by embodying it in a specific, material, quasi-human form—ruthless Terminator machines and self-propagating "agents," respectively. Through such personifications the films give a simulated human face, the face of an enemy bent on defeating humans, to the infanticidal economization that makes human life possible. The personification of the alien is here an allegory of the difficulty in counter-conceiving the future. In the first place, personification forces the characters in the films to "face" the terror not only of their individual deaths but of human extinction. However, the death and extinction that comes from the alien mirrors the deathliness—all the conceptions foregone, all the futures lost—implicit in anyone's survival. In the second place, then, the personified alien would be the reflection of what no one can literally see when beholding his or her own image—the "faces," the faceless faces, of the others who have been interpellated out of existence (and therefore will never have had a face) when this person has been interpellated into existence. Again, the personified alien would be the face of a future without me. A form of mimetic figuration, personification enables the films to begin to represent the contraceptive force within human reproductivity but then to protect themselves from this representation by converting it into an enemy other, whose violence legitimizes humankind's self-protective counter-violence. The success of this defensive representational operation secures the future as conceivable even when it is threatened by the seemingly nonhuman other.

In other words, within a conceptively dominated system of thought and representation, the loathsome, imperiling, monstrous alien incarnates the very threat that is internal to this system but that the system tries to exclude from its self-representations. Such a system can register

the infanticidity of being, if at all, only as an alienness that its conceptuality excludes from itself. It can "conceive" of this (infanticidal) alienness
only as what is external to it, not as an expression of the infanticidism
that is constitutive of the system's very conceptivity. Personification here
functions as a representational means of reducing the infanticidal (the
infanticidism that is within all life and that necessarily escapes human
control) to infanticide (a potentially controllable empirical violence, here
located in the reproductive threat of the alien). In this way the personification of the alien approximates an encounter with the destructiveness
that makes of human reproductivity a force not of life but of life and
death, of lifedeath, of that for which there is no "concept."

In the cloned and genetically enhanced Ripley and the manufactured
cyborg Call, *Alien Resurrection* takes back what it has projected onto the
alien. Utterly human in appearance, Ripley and Call experience themselves to be ontologically isolated from the humans they simulate. In the
difference between their appearance and their sense of being constructed
as instruments in the service of a technocratic function that has gone
awry, they give the lie to the conceptual oppositions within which the film
represents the alien as incarnating a reproductivity which imperils the
survival of the human species. In their seemingly recognizable humanity,
they are ironic reminders that the film can deploy its strategies of resistance only from within the very conceptuality it is attempting to displace.
Although in their human appearance Ripley and Call stand as conceptively represented figures of the future as human, in their advent as manufactured beings they stand as counter-conceptive figures of a future that
is literally inconceivable.

The sequence in the space station's cloning laboratory illustrates the
film's incipient contraceptive apprehension of this future. Midway through
the film Ripley discovers her genetically engineered ancestry when she
comes upon seven generations of hideously deformed mutants, partially
human and partially alien hybrids, behind the locked doors of a laboratory. Six are dead, floating in large transparent containers filled with a
liquid preservative. The seventh, with a face recognizable as Ripley's, is
strapped to a gurney and hooked to an artificial life-support system. Her
grotesque body appears to have erupted; its torso has been stitched together with the crudest possible technique to prevent it from disintegrating. An incoherent assemblage of parts that are not viable on their
own, this corporeal frame nevertheless houses, imprisons rather, a self-
reflexive consciousness. That consciousness, located in this creature's
eyes and the gaze she directs toward Ripley, is endowed with language.
It is, however, on the verge of being strangled by the very material body
that encases it.

As Ripley slowly walks through the room, grimly moving from one abortive version of herself to another, she is stunned, appalled, and dismayed. The sequence, which lasts approximately four and a half minutes, is unrelenting in disclosing the infanticidal implications of the technology that has produced Ripley. The sequence ends when Ripley heeds the barely audible plea of the half-dead creature, whose mouth is so misshapen she can scarcely speak: "Kill me. Kill me." Approaching the suffering creature without a word, Ripley fights back tears as she touches the sheet that partially covers her clonal precursor (perhaps her "mother," perhaps her "sister"). Still without a word, Ripley slowly backs away and, when Call hands her a gun, proceeds to destroy the room, firing jets of flame everywhere. As the camera records the lurid destruction, each of the containers explodes in holocaustal fire.

What does the sequence signify? It might be Ripley's attempt to erase all trace of the violence that made her existence possible. It might be her effort to acknowledge that violence. Her existence has cost, and in the laboratory she comes face-to-face with the infanticidal consequences of that fact. When she destroys the remains of the six dead mutants and puts the living one to death, she engages in an action that completes the contraceptions she has beheld. In doing so, she discovers a counter-conceptive rather than conceptive source of mercy. Such mercy cannot occur in the name of life conceived as transcendent of death but only in the name of a life contaminated by the contraceptive deathliness that all life necessarily entails. Thus, Ripley does not just mercifully put to death a suffering being but destroys someone who is her genetic double. Recognizing herself in this person, Ripley apprehends, and provides for the film's viewers a representation of, the suicidal meaning of the destruction she is about to unleash. In obliterating the remains of the seven generations of creatures, whose cloning is perhaps equivalent to having been torn from the womb, Ripley mourns for them and for herself: their aborted lives have made her life possible.

The subsequent semiotic coding of the film's events underscores the movie's attempts to contraceive of the future. Alluding to Ripley's nature as a clone (as well as to Call's identity as a cyborg), *Alien Resurrection* looks ahead to a technological alternative to sexual reproduction—a technology of replication rather than of conceptive reproduction—as the means by which new human life is achieved. In doing so, the film marks as defunct or irrelevant the conceptual schemata by which the Western world has represented not only the onset of the individual human's life but the character of conceptuality itself. The film again displaces the conceptual framework within which life is figured as quintessentially conceptive when it evokes the death of the ship's computer system. In the previous *Alien* films, the spaceship's computer is called Mother, and it fails. In *Alien Resurrection*, the computer, "the voice of the ship" according to the script, is called Father, and it dies. "Father is dead, asshole," Call announces at one point. As technological parental imagoes, the two computers embody a conceptive ideology. According to that ideology, especially in its oedipal configurations, the deaths of the parents threaten the future; their demise betokens the loss of the gendered sexuality and conceptive biological context that have been necessary, until recently, for the production of new humans. Thus, from the point of view of the conceptuality that the film is contesting, the deaths of Mother and Father signal the death of the child that is to be, for a world that conceives of the future is a world that can greet the possibility of radical change only as a hysterical dread of wholesale infanticidal slaughter.

It is just this infanticidal prospect that the movie tries to negotiate in its astonishing climax with the harrowing death of Ripley's grandchild. In that scene, which is staged as an enactment of a partial birth abortion, the film apprehends the contraceptive violence, the contraceptive interpellation, that underwrites any and all possible futures.

Ripley's female child is a queen mother who possesses both alien and human reproductive systems. Maturing quickly, this oviparous monster lays an astonishing quantity of eggs. When they begin to hatch, the renegade space cowboys, who have made a "delivery" of frozen human bodies to the space station (the aliens will beget themselves upon these hosts), must wage an infanticidal war. Much of the film is given over to the nightmarish special effects used to dramatize the violent consequences. The violence becomes almost dumbfounding shortly after the alien mother, undergoing a human labor, gives birth to a quasi-human hybrid whom Ripley must destroy. This creature, Ripley's second-generation descendant, has an ashen-colored reptilian body but a human-like face. Indeed, it has a human infant's oversized eyes set deeply into a face that looks frighteningly skeletal. Its eyes are simultaneously terribly sad and enraged, terrified and terrifying. The result is to impart a haunting, spectral, cadaverous aspect to the creature, who is born with a seemingly boundless ferocity. It immediately directs its murderous energy against its mother, whom it savagely decapitates. Such violence, by which this creature would inaugurate a future that must not come to pass, sums up the film's worst conceptive fears.

Ripley must destroy it in what is a sacrifice, indeed a crucifixion. As Ripley distracts the monster from trying to crush Call, she approaches the newborn, mouth closed, and nuzzles it, in the process quieting the alien's rage. At one point Ripley passes her hand over the alien's saurian face, slicing her palm. She then flings the blood that oozes from her stigmata-like wound against the window of the space freighter, the *Betty*. Ripley's blood has the same corrosive biochemical characteristics as the blood of the aliens, and it begins to eat away the window. Instantly the galactic vacuum outside the spaceship pulls on the body of the alien and eventually sucks it out. The process takes several minutes: the alien's body is slowly, agonizingly eviscerated, exploding into bits as it passes through the portal. All the while, the alien is roaring, shrieking, screaming, its wailing on the verge of resolving into speech, into a verbal utterance that would give voice to what the dying sunken eyes appear to understand about its demise. What do those eyes express? A primal rage and struggle for life but also an agony of recognition that it is being deliberately killed by one whom it loves from out of its infant helplessness.

The alien's prolonged, high-pitched, neonatal screams, its preverbal horror as it is being obliterated, bespeak what the movie itself wants but hesitates to articulate in the form of discursive speech—namely, that the violence that is about to save both the human species from supercession by aliens and the earth itself from annihilation is utterly infanticidal. The scream of the alien, Ripley's quasi-human grandchild, like the scream of the T-1000 in *Terminator 2*, marks the death of the literalized metaphor of conception as a basis for representing the future. Conversely, it is to mark the sound, otherwise unvoiced, of that subjectivity that never comes into being whenever a specific subject does manage to get conceived and born and cared for.

The ending of *Alien Resurrection* develops the implications of its contra-conceptive vision of the future. In particular, it qualifies its representation of humankind's survival by linking it to the actions of two artificial female constructs—Ripley, a clone, and Call, a "synthetic," a "droid," an "auton," that is, a "robot designed by robots." First, under the gentle but firm direction of Ripley, Call accesses the ship's central computing network through a panel hidden inside a hollowed-out Bible. When she discovers that the supply ship is about to be hijacked, leaving them stranded aboard the alien-infested vessel, Call overrides the *USS Auriga's* main computer. She kills it—hence "Father is dead"—reprograms its navigational system, and sets the spaceship on a collision course with (mother) earth. Call accedes to Ripley's encouragement to "blow the ship" and destroy the entire breed of aliens who are threatening to infect the planet—to "kill them all"—now that she has killed her own descendant.

Herself programmed to protect humankind from the dangers posed by alien life forms, Call embodies the conceptive view of the future but grafted onto a cyborg frame. A hybrid being designed to protect humans from becoming hybridized, she represents Western culture's wish fulfillment translated into Darwinian terms—namely, that otherness exists to affirm human consciousness as the telos of evolution. Call is thus not a subject in her own right. Not only does she not have a fully human subjectivity, her own ontologically problematic existence pointedly "calls" such subjectivity itself into question. Here, in relation to her programming—another form of interpellation—she is an abject.

In the brief exchange that follows Ripley's command to destroy all the aliens, Call struggles to understand the abjection of her difference from the human. "How can you stand being what you are?" Call asks Ripley. In an early script she asks: "Why do you go on living? How can you stand it? How can you stand . . . yourself?" When Ripley answers "Not much choice," Call responds in dismay: "At least there's part of you that's human. I'm just . . . [fuck, she adds in the script]. Look at me, I'm disgusting." Shortly before, she has explained her revulsion at patching into "Father": "It's like . . . your insides are liquid. It's not real." In one version of the script, Ripley then asks Call if she dreams. When Call says "yes," Ripley says that she also dreams but is no longer afraid of the alien visitations that beset her sleep: "no matter how bad the dreams get . . . when I wake up it's always worse."[19]

Call despairs because she is not human and, she implies, not real. In asking Ripley to justify her existence, but doing so by means of an accusatory and dismissal tone, Call indicates the intensity of her self-loathing and the existential dread beneath it. In contrast to Call, Ripley appears to have accommodated herself to the knowledge that she was "grown," not sexually begotten and procreated, and that she is "a thing, a construct," not a person. In consequence, her gaze at the end becomes an evocative reflection of the film's attempt to contraceive of the future. With Call at her side, she watches from a window in the *Betty* as the paternal space station, a kind of machinic spermatozoa, hurtles through the terran atmosphere and then explodes on impact with mother earth. Terrestrial life has been saved through an action the final representation of which symbolically enacts a sexual union. It is not the glorious conjunction of Dekker and VGER, as in *Star Trek*, nor is it the triumphant penetration of Agent Smith by Neo in *The Matrix*. It is neither humankind's "next evolutionary step" nor its achievement of a transformed consciousness by which it regains mastery over the technological future. To the contrary, it is a cataclysmic, life-destroying disunion. In the unrepresented aftermath of the irradiating detonation that kills off the remaining aliens, countless humans and their children, and thus the futures these children would have produced, will disappear. Only Ripley and Call survive as witnesses to the nuclear explosion that protects the earth from the extraterrestrial aliens but at a cost the film does not venture to measure.

The irony of the film's ending, however, is still more forbidding. Because Ripley and Call are constructed beings, they are the otherness that has already overtaken humankind, the death of the predatory aliens notwithstanding. Paradoxically embodying a human-programmed nonhuman otherness, they turn their heads in unison and gaze out at the nuclear blast following the space station's destruction. In this moment the film explicitly figures Ripley and Call as mimetic doubles whose human appearance belies their contra-conceptive origins. Standing in for the humankind whose futurity they have assured, Ripley and Call simultaneously stand in for the alien species they have destroyed. Between them there will be no heterosexual reproductive coupling. What they signify, therefore, is an order of human-like existence — a future — no longer conceivable in conceptive terms. They bear in their respective persons the infanticidal-cum-extinctive meaning of their survival, a survival that spells the end of the human, the death of the aliens not withstanding.[20]

THE INCONCEIVABLE

Agent Smith of *The Matrix* puts this contra-conceptual recognition in the starkest terms. "Evolution, Morpheus. Evolution. Like the dinosaur. Look out that window. You had your time. The future is our world, Morpheus. The future is our time." In its narrative trajectory, *The Matrix* repudiates the agent's insight concerning the contraceptive course of evolution. It thus retreats into a chiliastic mania for the father's supremacy. In this regard *The Matrix* is a regressive cultural dream, an expression of a collective fantasy of a society hysterically protecting itself from what the end of the millennium might beget. In depicting Neo as entering Smith's belly head first, the film symbolically encodes his subsequent inseminating triumph over the Matrix in the terms of the paternalized conceptual will to power that has organized Western thought. Invented, fabricated rather than conceived, Ripley and Call, like Agent Smith, know better. Not only is it that "Father is dead," as Call declares, but that the future, which the figure of the father has been conceptualized as guaranteeing, is in principle over as well, no matter how drawn out in fact this ending will be. The future as human, the future as narratable in terms of conception, the future as conceivable, is not the future of futurity — as Ripley, Call, and Agent Smith understand. They hail from a different — inconceivable — future, the echoing cry of which can perhaps be heard if one is willing to listen to what the Western world has refused to say about the infanticidal horizon of being.

Notes

PREFACE

1. David Bakan, *Disease, Pain, and Sacrifice: Toward a Psychology of Suffering* (Boston: Beacon Press, 1971), 104.

2. David Bakan, *The Duality of Human Existence: Isolation and Communion in Western Man* (Boston: Beacon Press, 1966), 205.

3. Ibid., 223.

4. Ibid., 229.

5. Cited in David Bakan, *Slaughter of the Innocents: A Study of the Battered Child Phenomenon* (Boston: Beacon Press, 1972), 80.

6. Ibid., 20.

7. Ibid., 55.

8. Ibid., 20.

9. Ibid., 232.

10. Leo Strauss, *Persecution and the Art of Writing,* (Chicago: University of Chicago Press, 1988), 34.

INTRODUCTION

1. Matthew 2:16, *The New Oxford Annotated Bible,* New Revised Standard Version, ed. Bruce M. Metzger and Roland E. Murphy (New York: Oxford University Press, 1994). Unless otherwise specified, all citations from the Bible will be to this edition.

2. David Lee Miller, *Dreams of the Burning Child: Sacrificial Sons and the Father's Witness* (Ithaca: Cornell University Press, 2003), 1.

3. Homer, *The Odyssey,* trans. Robert Fitzgerald (New York: Vintage Classics/Random House, 1990), book 24.459.

4. Ibid., 2.2.

5. Ibid., 24.462.

6. Miller, *Dreams of the Burning Child,* 7.

7. Henry Staten, *Eros in Mourning: Homer to Lacan* (Baltimore: Johns Hopkins University Press, 1995), xii.

8. J. P. "Genesis," in Robert Alter and Frank Kermode, eds., *The Literary Guide to the Bible* (Cambridge: Belknap Press/Harvard University Press, 1987), 41.

9. Jacques Derrida, *Of Grammatology,* corrected ed., trans. Gayatri Chakravorty Spivak (Baltimore: Johns Hopkins University Press, 1997), 5.

10. Thomas Keenan, *Fables of Responsibility: Aberrations and Predicaments in Ethics and Politics* (Stanford: Stanford University Press, 1997), 4.

11. Hent de Vries and Samuel Weber, eds., *Violence, Identity, and Self-Determination* (Stanford: Stanford University Press, 1997), 2.

12. Dominick LaCapra, *Representing the Holocaust: History, Theory, Trauma* (Ithaca: Cornell University Press, 1994), 11.

13. Keenan, *Fables of Responsibility*, 3.

CHAPTER 1
EXISTENCE COSTS

1. E. O. Wilson, "Foreword," Gary Larson, *There's a Hair in My Dirt: A Worm's Story* (HarperCollins, 1998), n.p.

2. Ibid., n.p.

3. Charles Darwin, *"The Origin of Species by Means of Natural Selection or the Preservation of Favored Races in the Struggle for Life" and "The Descent of Man and Selection in Relation to Sex"* (New York: Random House/Modern Library, n.d.), 62 and 52; my emphasis.

4. Ibid., 52.

5. Ibid., 51 and 56.

6. Will and Ariel Durant, *The Lessons of History* (New York: Simon and Schuster, 1968), 18. "History is a fragment of biology," and "the laws of biology are the fundamental lessons of history," the Durants write. "We are subject to the processes and trials of evolution, to the struggle for existence and the survival of the fittest to survive. . . . So the first biological lesson of history is that life is competition. Competition is not only the life of trade, it is the trade of life" (18–19).

7. William H. McNeil, *Plagues and People* (Garden City: Anchor Press/Doubleday, 1976), 5.

8. Ibid., 12.

9. Ibid., *The Human Condition: An Ecological and Historical View* (Princeton: Princeton University Press, 1979), 74.

10. Ibid., 74.

11. Mark Nathan Cohen, *Health and the Rise of Civilization* (New Haven: Yale University Press, 1989), 53–54.

12. Darwin, *The Origin of Species*, 52.

13. Ibid., 53.

14. Bertrand Russell, *Religion and Science* (Home Universal Library, 1935; London and New York: Oxford University Press, 1961), 73.

15. Darwin, *The Origin of Species*, 90.

16. Alfred W. Crosby, *Germs, Seeds, and Animals* (Armonk: M. E. Sharpe, 1994), 192.

17. Ibid., 191.

18. *The Extant Writings of Epicurus*, trans. C. Bailey, in Whitney J. Oates, ed., *The Stoic and Epicurean Philosophers: The Complete Extant Writings of Epicurus, Epictetus, Lucretius, Marcus Aurelius* (New York: Modern Library, 1940), 4.

19. Lucretius, *On the Nature of Things — De Rerum Natura*, trans. H. A. J. Munro, in Whitney J. Oates, ed., *The Stoic and Epicurean Philosophers: The Complete Extant Writings of Epicurus, Epictetus, Lucretius, Marcus Aurelius* (New York: Modern Library, 1940), 72. For Lucretius, the very orderliness of nature depends on the "seed" of "begetting bodies": "If things came from nothing, any kind might be born of any thing, nothing would require seed." The result would be a monstrous violation of the nature of things: "Men for instance might rise out of the sea, the scaly race out of the earth, and birds might burst out of the sky; horned and other herds, every kind of wild beasts would haunt with changing brood tilth and wilderness alike. Nor would the same fruits keep constant to trees, but would change; any tree might bear any fruit. For if there were not begetting bodies for each, how could

things have a fixed unvarying mother? But in fact because things are all produced from fixed seeds, each thing is born and goes forth into the borders of light out of that in which resides its matter and first bodies. . . . We must admit therefore that nothing can come from nothing, since things require seed before they can severally be born" (72–73).

20. David J. Depew and Bruce H. Weber, *Darwinism Evolving: Systems Dynamics and the Genealogy of Natural Selection* (Cambridge: MIT Press/Bradford Book, 1995), 466.

21. Ibid., 464; my emphasis.

22. Ibid., 464.

23. Ibid., 466.

24. Ibid., 474. According to Depew and Weber, an ecosystem's degree of "ascendency" is its "total energy transfer" in relation to "the level of interconnectiveness among [its] components . . . over time." The more "ascendant" an ecosystem, the more it is able to "increase the total energy flow through the system. The effect is to increase the dissipation of energy as entropy production to the surroundings."

25. Garrett Hardin, *Living within Limits: Ecology, Economics, and Population Taboos,* (New York: Oxford University Press, 1993), 183.

26. Ibid., *The Ostrich Factor: Our Population Myopia,* (New York: Oxford University Press, 1999), 9.

27. Ibid., *Living within Limits,* 189.

28. Daniel A. Underwood and Paul G. King, "On the Ideological Foundations of Environmental Policy," *Ecological Economics* 1 (1989): 322.

29. Ibid., 323n10.

30. Ibid., 322.

31. Ibid., 331.

32. Ibid., 329.

33. Darwin, *The Origin of Species,* 374.

34. John Maynard Smith and Eors Szathmary, *The Major Transitions in Evolution* (Oxford and New York: W. H. Freeman/Spektrum, 1995), 20; see also 20–58 and 67–72 passim. Maynard Smith and Szathmary's assertion that "luck was needed" applies to the "self-regulating" operations of the Oklo atomic reaction; the fact of such operations is one of the "two general conclusions" from which they draw several "parallels with the origin of life," including, by implication, that life's onset was fortuitous (20).

35. Darwin, *The Origin of Species,*100.

36. George C. Williams, *Adaptation and Natural Selection: A Critique of Some Current Evolutionary Thought* (Princeton: Princeton University Press, 1966), xiii.

37. Richard Leakey and Roger Lewin, *The Sixth Extinction: Patterns of Life and the Future of Humankind* (New York: Doubleday, 1995), 18.

38. Ibid., 67 and 86.

39. Niles Eldredge, *The Miner's Canary: Unraveling the Mysteries of Extinction* (New York: Prentice Hall, 1991), 134.

40. Williams, *Adaptation and Natural Selection,* 121.

41. Eldredge, *The Miner's Canary,* 58.

42. William K. Purves, Gordon H. Orians, H. Craig Heller, and David Sadava, *Life: The Science of Biology,* 5th ed. (Sunderland: Sinauer Associates, Inc., 1998), 449.

43. David M. Raup, *Extinction: Bad Genes or Bad Luck?* (New York: Norton, 1991), 3 and 11.

44. Purves et al, *Life,* 433. The calculations involved in determining the parameters of extinction depend on arguable assumptions. Thus, Raup has arrived at a lower kill percentage—on average, 65 percent of all species for the five mass extinctions (*Extinction,* 85).

William Glen reports that at the time of the K/T extinction—a "Great Kill" associated with the transition between the Cretaceous and the Tertiary Periods, when the dinosaurs disappeared—"75 percent of all animal species in the seas and almost all the land animals that weighed more than 50 pounds" were destroyed ("What the Impact/Volcanism/Mass-Extinction Debates Are About," *The Mass-Extinction Debates: How Science Works in a Crisis* [Stanford: Stanford University Press, 1994], 8). Nevertheless, "The K/T mass extinction was not the only one in Earth's history, nor even the worst. That distinction goes either to the event that marked the transition from the Permian Period to the Triassic, some 250 million years ago, when as many as 96 percent of all species in the ocean vanished, or perhaps . . . to the extinction in the early Cambrian Period (end of the Botomian Stage, about 525 million years ago) that killed off 80 percent of the genera. There is evidence in the fossil record for at least nine other mass extinctions. One of the most interesting hypotheses to spring from the impact debates is the idea that these mass dyings have recurred with a regular period of 26 million years" (25).

45. Raup, *Extinction*, 85.

46. Williams, *Adaptation and Natural Selection*, 121.

47. Eldredge, *The Miner's Canary*, 125.

48. Williams, *Adaptation and Natural Selection*, 120; my emphases. In switching to the present indicative Williams not only points back toward what might have been but implicitly toward what, when sufficient time has passed, ineluctably will come to pass. If from the vantage of natural history there would have been nothing exceptional about the disappearance of homo sapiens, then there assuredly will be nothing uncommon about our future extinction: not only was it but it still is and always will remain "the statistically most likely development." Even this amendment to Williams, however, does not sufficiently identify the absolute finitude of the human species. For the language of probability in Williams' statement applies only to the timing of the extinction fate, not to the fate itself. Williams misses the structural necessity that governs the empirical certitude of extinction: that an extinctive fate will overtake humankind is not a matter of chance but of a necessity that, as the next chapter will explain, inheres in the very structure of evolutionary change.

49. Leakey and Lewin, *The Sixth Extinction*, 228 and 221.

50. Stephen Jay Gould, *Full House: The Spread of Excellence from Plato to Darwin* (New York: Harmony Books, 1996), 18; my emphasis.

51. Leakey and Lewin, *The Sixth Extinction*, 228.

52. Gould, *Full House*, 20.

53. Eldredge, *The Miner's Canary*, 172.

54. Williams, *Adaptation and Natural Selection*, 120.

55. Leakey and Lewin, *The Sixth Extinction*, 173 and 194.

56. See Peter Ward's discussion in *The End of Evolution: On Mass Extinctions and the Preservation of Biodiversity* (New York: Bantam, 1994) of Paul S. Martin's "Overkill Hypothesis" (196–203).

57. A. Hallam and P. B. Wignall, *Mass Extinctions and Their Aftermath* (Oxford: Oxford University Press, 1997), 241.

58. David Steadman, cited in "Humans Make Extinction Happen 100 Times Faster," *University of Florida News* (March 6, 1997). According to Ricklefs, the average rate of "background extinction" is on the order of one species per year: "The life spans of species in the fossil record vary according to taxon, but they generally fall within the range of 1 to 10 million years. Thus, on average, the probability that a particular species will go extinct in a single year is in the range of 1 in a million to 1 in 10 million. If, as conservative estimates have it, on the order of 1 to 10 million species inhabit the earth, this would

amount to a background extinction rate of about one species extinction per year" (*The Economy of Nature: A Textbook in Basic Ecology*, 5th ed. [New York: W. H. Freeman and Company, 2001], 487).

59. Leakey and Lewin *The Sixth Extinction*, 205.

60. Ricklefs, *The Economy of Nature*, 492.

61. Leakey and Lewin, *The Sixth Extinction*, 234.

62. Sheldon Watts, *Epidemics and History: Disease, Power and Imperialism* (New Haven: Yale University Press, 1997).

63. Leakey and Lewin, *The Sixth Extinction*, 235.

64. Purves, et al., *Life*, 1224.

65. Dawn Stover, "The Final Frontier," *Popular Science*, July 1997, 59. According to Stover, the United States alone "has lost 94 percent of its original frontier forest, and 85 percent of the remainder is threatened. . . . The forests that once covered most of Europe are nearly all gone. Except for the Congo Basin, Africa's frontier forests have all but vanished. No intact forest is left on the island of Madagascar. . . . Very little frontier forest remains in Asia. India and China have only 20 percent of their original forest cover, and almost none of it is frontier forest. The Amazon Basin is the largest intact tropical forest remaining. But Brazil alone lost more than 140,000 square miles of forest between 1980 and 1990." Only in Russia, Canada, and Alaska are there large expanses of frontier boreal forests remaining (58–59).

66. Ibid., 59.

67. Purves et al., *Life*, 1234–35 and 1226.

68. Leakey and Lewin, *The Sixth Extinction*, 245.

69. Purves, et al., *Life*, 1224.

70. Eldredge, *The Miner's Canary*, 207.

71. Ibid., 207.

72. Hallam and Wignall, *Mass Extinctions and Their Aftermath*, 241.

73. John C. Briggs, "Mass Extinctions: Fact or Fallacy?" in William Glen, ed., *The Mass-Extinction Debates*, 236.

74. Amy Coen, cited in the *Florida Times Union*, July 18, 1999, 1.13.b. At the end of *The Economy of Nature*, Ricklefs treats his title concept, which is not named in the book's index, as a subset of the "natural ecology" of nature conceived as if it were a unitary being endowed with an incipient moral sensibility: "To what degree are human values compatible with natural values?" Ricklefs asks. "Can managed ecosystems serve some of the same functions as natural ecosystems, or will nature preserves stand in stark contrast to completely altered environments dominated by humans and their domesticated species?" (500). Since "a sustainable biosphere is unlikely as long as the human population continues to grow," and since "further population increase will lead to further crowding, tearing not only the fabric of human society but also of the life-supporting systems of the environment" (500), humans are the species whose evolutionary advent now threatens the biosphere itself, the very context of evolutionary process. However, Ricklefs cannot conceive of the danger posed by humans to be a specific instance of the danger immanent to evolutionary economy in general. Thus, he concludes by invoking the "economy of nature" as the moral key to human survival. Warning of the end of the human, Ricklefs writes: "We have succeeded famously in becoming the technological species. Our survival now depends on our becoming the ecological species and taking our *proper place* in the economy of nature" (514). At this point "economy" is no longer a descriptive category, which would refer to the study of the world's (thermodynamically constrained) "primary production" (128ff), but an axiological and teleological category, which would define the "place" of humankind in terms of a teleological property of nature itself.

75. Cohen, *Health and the Rise of Civilization,* 14; my emphases.

76. Italian historian Piero Camporesi has sought to recover a sense of that suffering on the part of the masses of poor throughout early modern Europe. In *Bread of Dreams: Food and Fantasy in Early Modern Europe* (trans. David Gentilcore [Chicago: University of Chicago Press, 1989]), he suggests that, in an era "when peasants made up the over-whelming majority of [Europe's] population," the extremity of their hunger, in conjunc-tion with the toxicity of various additives to the often mouldy, verminous bread they scrabbled for, produced a stupefied mental state among the very poor (33. See also 120–30).

77. Cohen, *Health and the Rise of Civilization,* 54.

78. Ibid., 14.

79. Cited in Stover, "Endangered Speech," 34.

80. David Crystal, *Language Death* (Cambridge: Cambridge University Press, 2000), 14–15.

81. Andrew Dalby, *Language in Danger: The Loss of Linguistic Diversity and the Threat to Our Future* (New York: Columbia University Press), ix.

82. Cited in Stover, "Endangered Speech," 34.

83. Dalby, *Language in Danger,* 148.

84. Daniel Nettle and Suzanne Romaine, *Vanishing Voices: The Extinction of the World's Languages* (New York: Oxford University Press, 2000), 116.

85. Cited in Stover, "Endangered Speech," 34.

86. David E. Stannard, *American Holocaust: Columbus and the Conquest of the New World* (New York: Oxford University Press, 1992), x.

87. Ibid., xii.

88. Ibid., x.

89. Ibid., x.

90. Ibid., 95. Limiting himself to a discussion of "The Indian Population of North America in 1492" (*William and Mary Quarterly* 49.2, 3rd ser. [April 1992]: 298–320), John D. Daniels provides a comprehensive survey of the methodological issues involved in estimating pre-Columbian native populations and reviews the divergent population fig-ures various demographical historians, anthropologists, and others have offered.

91. Crosby, *Germs, Seeds, and Animals,* 25.

92. Charles Darwin, *The Voyage of the Beagle* (London: Dent/Everyman's Library, 1906, 1959), 418–19.

93. In the continuation of this passage Lyell accepts the extinctive violence within the "dissemination" that characterizes the life history of any and all species: "That minute parasitic plant, called 'the rust' in wheat, has, like the Hessian fly, the locust, and the aphis, caused famines ere now amongst the 'lords of the creation.' The most insignificant and diminutive species, whether in the animal or vegetable kingdom, have each slaugh-tered their thousands, as they disseminated themselves over the globe" (Sir Charles Lyell. *Principles of Geology: Being an Attempt to Explain the Former Changes of the Earth's Surface by Reference to Causes Now in Operation,* 3 vols., 1830–1833 [New York and London: Johnson Reprint Corporation/The Sources of Science, no. 84, 1969], 2:156).

94. Jacques Derrida, *Specters of Marx: The State of the Debt, the Work of Mourning, and the New International,* trans. Peggy Kamuf (New York: Routledge, 1994), 85.

95. Ibid., 81.

96. Ibid., 82.

97. Watt, *Epidemics and History,* 279.

98. Derrida, *Specters of Marx,* 83.

99. Ibid.

100. Ibid., 85.

101. Georges Bataille, *The Accursed Share: An Essay on General Economy,* vol. I, *Consumption,* trans. Robert Hurley (New York: Urzone, Inc., 1988/Zone Books, 1991), 23.

CHAPTER 2
THE INFANTICIDAL HORIZON OF BIOLOGICAL EXISTENCE

1. Darwin, *Descent of Man,* in *"The Origin of Species" and "The Descent of Man"* (New York: Random House/Modern Library, n.d.), 487. Darwin writes that of all the "checks" to population discussed by Malthus, infanticide "is probably *the most important of all*" (429; my emphasis). Nevertheless, whenever he broaches the subject of human infanticide, Darwin is shocked: "Infanticide was formerly practised . . . to a frightful extent" in the Sandwich, now Hawaiian, Islands, he remarks. Among West Coast Africans it was a "fearfully common practice." In South America, he reports, "some tribes . . . formerly destroyed so many infants of both sexes that they were on the point of extinction," and he adds that "in the Polynesian Islands women have been known to kill from four or five, to even ten of their children; and Ellis could not find a single woman who had not killed at least one. In a village on the eastern frontier of India Colonel MacCulloch found not a single female child" (609, 884, 897).

2. In *Slaughter of the Innocents: A Study of the Battered Child Phenomenon* (Boston: Beacon Press, 1972), David Bakan struggles with just this evolutionary conundrum: "If the person who has been abused in childhood becomes the parent of a child, the likelihood of a repetition of abusive practice is great. Here we have a relentless mechanism which continues until the aim of population reduction is achieved, until the line of child abusers is wiped out. One of the greatest ironies of evolution is that insofar as the trait with which we are concerned is natural and genetically carried, it must be carried precisely by those in whom it manifests itself least, that is, by those who reproduce effectively and who rear children effectively. The lines of child abusers must have been repeatedly wiped out in the long history of evolution, yet the trait has evidently been positively selected" (114).

3. J. T. Fraser, *Of Time, Passion, and Knowledge: Reflections on the Strategy of Existence* (New York: George Braziller, 1975), 361 and 362.

4. Ibid., 362.

5. *Aporia* is from the Greek *a-,* not, + *poros,* a stem that can signify a means of passing a river, the paths of the sea, a way through or over, a means of achieving, and a contrivance or resource (cf. Liddell and Scott, *Greek English Lexicon,* 579). An aporia, then, is a kind of no-exit, a double bind, an inescapable contradiction. Godel's famous proof that the axioms of any complex mathematical system cannot be both consistent and complete renders number theory aporetic.

6. Mark Ridley, *Evolution* (Boston: Blackwell Scientific Publications, 1993), 20.

7. Fraser, *Of Time, Passion, and Knowledge,* 222.

8. Ridley, *Evolution,* 20.

9. Ibid., 308.

10. Richard Dawkins, *The Selfish Gene,* new ed. (Oxford: Oxford University Press, 1989), 7.

11. V. C. Wynne-Edwards, *Animal Dispersion in Relation to Social Behaviour* (Edinburgh: Oliver and Boyd, 1962), 492.

12. Marvin Harris, *Culture, People, Nature: An Introduction to General Anthropology,* 6th ed. (New York: HarperCollins, 1989), 20.

13. Ibid., *Cannibals and Kings: The Origins of Cultures* (New York: Vintage/Random House, 1977), 6.

14. Ibid., *Our Kind: Who We Are, Where We Come From, Where We Are Going* (New York: Harper Perennial/Harper and Row, 1989), 211. How widespread is human infanticide? In their 1976 review of a sample of 112 "preindustrial" cultures (dispersed across 561 population groups) listed in the Human Relations Area Files (HRAF), William Divale and Marvin Harris report that forty of the sixty-six cultures for which there is information concerning the occurrence or nonoccurrence of infanticide "commonly" practice overt forms of infant killing and another fourteen "occasionally" do; in two cultures infanticide is "not common." In only ten of the cultures was overt infanticide said to be "not practiced." In forty-six of the cultures there was "no information" concerning the presence or absence of the practice of infanticide and the frequency of this practice. In other words overt infanticide —which does not include covert, passive, or deferred forms of infant killing—is reported in 81.8 percent of the sixty-six cultures for which information is available. Because much of the literature on the cultures in the HRAF was written before the "recent awakening" to the role of infanticide in population control, field observation studies no doubt under report the incidence of overt forms of infant killing, to say nothing of covert forms ("Population, Warfare, and the Male Supremacist Complex," *American Anthropologist* 78.3 [September 1976]: 521–38).

Both infanticide and abortion probably occur in all cultures. "In a study of 350 preindustrial societies, George Devereux found that direct abortion was 'an absolutely universal phenomenon'" (*Culture, People, Nature,* 222; Harris cites from "A Typological Study of Abortion in 350 Primitive, Ancient, and Pre-Industrial Societies," in H. Rosen, ed., *Abortion in America* [Boston: Beacon Press, 1967], 98). Moreover, "Some forms of infanticide are as widely practiced as abortion," and for the same reasons of economy: "the decision to make the social effort necessary to give birth to and rear children is heavily influenced by the balance of costs and benefits confronting prospective parents. We can be confident that when the balance is adverse, some form of birth or death control will be activated at some point in the reproductive process . . . . To a degree that is shocking to modern sensibilities, preindustrial and underdeveloped societies employ reproduction-regulating measures that achieve their effect *after* the birth of a child . . . . Much evidence exists that if reproduction is not limited *before* or during pregnancy, then it will be limited *after* pregnancy by direct or indirect infanticide or pedicide (the killing of young children)" (*Culture, People, Nature,* 229).

15. Suzanne Ripley, "Infanticide in Langurs and Man," in N. M. Cohen, R. S. Malpass, and H. G. Klein, eds., *Biosocial Mechanisms of Population Regulation* (New Haven: Yale University Press, 1980), 349, 350, and 383; my emphases. What makes infanticide adaptive for humans, Ripley suggests, is the double binding effect of an evolutionary history that has conferred upon this long-lived, imitative, generalist species of frugivores-omnivores "a high intrinsic reproductive rate" coupled with a "low supportive ability" ("Infanticide in Langurs and Man," 380). Because "generalist species can exploit habitats susceptible of turbulence and resource fluctuation," and because "mortality in such places is likely to be high," therefore "a compensatorily high reproductive capacity is adaptive . . . in order to recover as rapidly as possible from local population losses" (359). For most of prehistory humankind's "high maximum potential reproductive rate" (359) has far exceeded the capacity of human groups—from families to larger arrangements of allied individuals—for supporting high numbers of offspring. Because humans can produce many more children than they can adequately rear, both individually and collectively, they have needed to find ways of limiting their numbers—for example, by dispersal or migration or adoption out as well as by infanticide. "Whenever . . . infant mortality did not hold population levels sufficiently well below the low carrying capacity, local densities could be regulated through the process of pairs of spouses 'selfishly' correcting reproductive errors after the fact, as needed individually, by behavioral

means, of which the most flexible and biologically multivalued are *post*natal ones: adoption and infanticide" (380–81). If individual reproductive strategy represents the proximate cause of infanticide, its "ultimate biological value lies in retaining polymorphism of genotypes for populations of an ecological generalist reproducing within a type of social structure that otherwise rapidly leads to inbreeding." This "biological multivalue" represents another level of infanticidal causation, namely a "species-level efficient cause" (363). In controlling "excess breeding success of a high-*r* generalist faced with a low feasible overall density as a secondary consumer," infanticide in combination with deterrents to inbreeding would have fostered "genetic variability" among foraging humans who lived in "comparably small (20–60 individuals)" bands (380). Infanticide, in other words, represents a calculated response on the part of individuals to diminished availability of resources for the feeding and care of offspring; at the same time decisions to commit infanticide interact with the avoidance of incest to promote a group-level outcome in the form of increased genotypic variability for the population.

16. According to Ridley "it is now more usual (though by no means universal) for biologists to believe that group selection is a weak and unimportant process" and that it is "rarely likely," if at all, "to over-ride individual selection" (*Evolution*, 312 and 313).

17. Dawkins, *The Selfish Gene*, 7–8. John Maynard Smith has elaborated the general form of the model for this second argument ("Group Selection," *Quarterly Review of Biology* 51 [1976]: 277–83); cf. Ridley, *Evolution*, 312.

18. Ibid., 5.

19. From this point of view there is no "group as a whole" trying to maximize the overall average reproductivity of its aggregate membership. There are, rather, more or less closely related individuals — descent lines or genetic lineages — in reproductive competition with one another. It is possible that their competition will lead to one or more evolutionarily stable reproductive strategies; as will become clear in subsequent discussions, however, it is also possible that their competition will not, and even that their competition might lead to the extinction not only of one or more but of all the lineages, in other words to the extinction of "the group as a whole."

20. Dawkins, *The Selfish Gene*, 147 .

21. Ibid., *The Extended Phenotype: The Long Reach of the Gene* (Oxford: Oxford University Press, 1982), 55.

22. Glen Hausfater and Sarah Blaffer Hrdy, "Preface," in Glenn Hausfater and Sarah Blaffer Hrdy, eds., *Infanticide: Comparative and Evolutionary Perspectives* (New York: Aldine, 1984), xi.

23. Ibid., "Comparative and Evolutionary Perspectives on Infanticide: Introduction and Overview," *Infanticide*, xiii.

24. Ibid., xiv.

25. Ibid., xiii.

26. Ibid., xiv. According to Hrdy and Hausfater, the "shift in thinking about infanticide can be traced in large part to Williams' influential critique of current evolutionary thinking (1966) and to seminal writings on kin selection and sexual selection by Hamilton (1964) and Trivers (1972)" (xv). Whereas Williams refuted the principle of group selection in *Adaptation and Natural Selection* (1966), two years earlier Hamilton had published two papers on "The Genetical Evolution of Social Behaviour (I and II)" (*Journal of Theoretical Biology 7* [1964]: 1–16 and 17–52) that broadened the notion of reproductive fitness. If classical fitness refers to the individual organism's reproductive success, "inclusive fitness" takes into account the individual's degree of genetic relatedness to its kin and represents reproductive success not in terms of personal offspring but in terms of genotypes. Dawkins explains: "The organisms we see around us are descended from ancestors, and they have inherited some of the attributes that made those individuals

ancestors as opposed to non-ancestors. If an organism exists it contains the genes of a long line of successful ancestors. The [classical] fitness of an organism is its success as an ancestor. . . . But Hamilton grasped the central point . . . that natural selection will favour organs and behaviour that cause the individual's genes to be passed on, whether or not the individual is, himself, an ancestor. An individual that assists his brother to be an ancestor may thereby ensure the survival in the gene-pool of the genes 'for' brotherly assistance. Hamilton saw that parental care is really only a special case of caring for close relatives with a high probability of containing the genes for caring." In other words "the inclusive fitness of an organism is not a property of himself, but a property of his actions or effects. Inclusive fitness is calculated from an individual's own reproductive success plus his *effects* on the reproductive success of his relatives, each one weighed by the appropriate coefficient of relatedness" (*The Extended Phenotype*, 185–86).

In "Parental Investment and Sexual Selection" (in B. Campbell, ed., *Sexual Selection and the Descent of Man* [Chicago: Aldine, 1972], 136–79), Robert L. Trivers gave the concept of parental investment (P.I.) in offspring a rigorous economic definition that enabled him to specify the reproductive costs of any reproductive gain that parental investment brings.

27. See Hausfater and Hrdy, "Comparative and Evolutionary Perspectives on Infanticide," *Infanticide*, xiv.

28. Ibid., xi; my emphasis.

29. Sarah Blaffer Hrdy, *The Woman That Never Evolved*, (Cambridge: Harvard University Press, 1981), 91.

30. Ibid., 69.

31. Ibid., 80.

32. Ibid., 70.

33. Ibid., 81. As Hausfater has explained of langurs, the example being generalizable to other primates, the "suckling primate infant produces in its mother a prolonged period of lactational amenorrhea," which spontaneously ends when the infant is weaned or dies before weaning. The result is that the female "rapidly returns to breeding condition"— in the case of the infant's death, usually within a month. Thus, when an adult male kills an infant that is both unweaned and unrelated to himself, he effectively speeds the mother's return to estrus and does so at little cost to himself" ("Infanticide in Langurs," *Infanticide*, 257–58).

34. Glenn Hausfater, "Infanticide in Langurs: Strategies, Counterstrategies, and Parameter Value," in Hausfater and Hrdy, *Infanticide*, 257. For a contrary view see Barbara Burke, "Infanticide: Why Does It Happen in Monkeys, Mice, and Men?" *Science* 5.4 (1984): 26–31. See also Jane Boggess, "Infant Killing and Male Reproductive Strategies in Langurs (*Presbytis entellus*)," in Hausfater and Hrdy, *Infanticide* (283–310), which also includes responses by Yukimaru Sugiyma, "Proximate Factors of Infanticide Among Langurs at Dharwar: A Reply to Boggess" (311–14), and by Sarah Blaffer Hrdy, "Assumptions and Evidence Regarding the Sexual Selection Hypothesis: A Reply to Boggess" (315–19).

35. Hrdy, *The Woman That Never Evolved*, 85.

36. Ibid., 94.

37. "This form of selection," Darwin writes, "depends, not on a struggle for existence in relation to other organic beings or to external conditions, but on a struggle between the individuals of one sex, generally the males, for the possession of the other sex. The result is not death to the unsuccessful competitor, but few or no offspring. Sexual selection is, therefore, less rigorous than natural selection" (*The Origin of Species*, 69).

38. Carolyn M. Crockett and Ranka Sekulic, "Infanticide in Red Howler Monkeys (*Alouatta Seniculus*)," in Hausfater and Hrdy, *Infanticide*, 186.

39. Lysa Leland, Thomas T. Struhsaker, and Thomas M. Butynski, "Infanticide by Adult Males in Three Primate Species of the Kibale Forest, Uganda," in Hausfater and Hrdy, *Infanticide*, 171. Leland, Struhsaker, and Butynski also argue that "the sexual selection hypothesis encompasses most, if not all other, hypotheses as secondary effects of reproductive competition. For example, after committing infanticide, a male gains in fitness if he cannibalizes his victim. Infanticide and aggression . . . may also integrate the male socially and sexually more quickly into the group, resulting in greater reproductive success even with females who might not have had infants. At the same time, by killing infants sired by other males, an infanticidal male reduces the reproductive success of his competitors and may also increase his own fitness and that of his offspring by reducing competition for resources. While infanticide always reduces population density to some extent, this again would be a secondary effect that may further enhance survival of the infanticidal male's offspring" (164).

40. Anthony D. Collins, Curt D. and Jane Goodall "Infanticide in Two Populations of Savanna Baboons," in Hausfater and Hrdy, *Infanticide*, 215.

41. Christian Vogel and Hartmut Loch, "Reproductive Parameters, Adult-Male Replacements, and Infanticide among Free-Ranging Langurs (*Presbytis Entellus*) at Jodhpur (Rajasthan), India," in Hausfater and Hrdy, *Infanticide*, 248.

42. Dian Fossey, "Infanticide in Mountain Gorillas (*Gorilla Gorilla Beringei*) with Comparative Notes on Chimpanzees," in Hausfater and Hrdy, *Infanticide*, 222.

43. Hrdy, *The Woman That Never Evolved*, 94–95.

44. Ibid., 92.

45. Ibid., 92–93.

46. Ibid., 93.

47. Ibid.

48. Ibid.

49. Ibid., 94.

50. Hausfater, "Infanticide in Langurs," in Hausfater and Hrdy, *Infanticide*, 281.

51. Garrett Hardin, "The Tragedy of the Commons," *Science* 162 (1968): 1243.

52. Adam Smith, *An Inquiry into the Nature and Causes of the Wealth of Nations*, ed. Edwin Cannin (New York: Modern Library, 1937, 1965), 423.

53. Hausfater, "Infanticide in Langurs," in Hausfater and Hrdy, *Infanticide*, 281.

54. Hrdy, *The Woman That Never Evolved*, 94.

55. Dawkins, *The Selfish Gene*, 184–85; my emphases.

56. Ibid., 69.

57. Ibid., 186.

58. Mildred Dickemann, "Concepts and Classification in the Study of Human Infanticide: Sectional Introduction and Some Cautionary Notes," in Hausfater and Hrdy, *Infanticide*, 428.

59. William L. Langer, "Infanticide: A Historical Survey," *History of Childhood Quarterly* 1.3 (Winter 1974): 353; my emphasis.

60. Sarah Blaffer Hrdy, "Fitness Tradeoffs in the History and Evolution of Delegated Mothering with Special Reference to Wet-Nursing, Abandonment, and Infanticide," *Ethology and Sociobiology* 13 (1992): 412.

61. Dickemann, "Concepts and Classification in the Study of Human Infanticide," in Hausfater and Hrdy, *Infanticide*, 428.

62. Virginia D. Hayssen, "Mammalian Reproduction: Constraints on the Evolution of Infanticide," in Hausfater and Hrdy, *Infanticide*, 110.

63. Dickemann, "Concepts and Classification in the Study of Human Infanticide," in Hausfater and Hrdy, *Infanticide*, 428.

64. Hrdy and Hausfater, "Comparative and Evolutionary Perspectives on Infanticide," in Hausfater and Hrdy, *Infanticide*, xv). Apparently not uncommon among birds is siblicide, "a phenomenon that parents themselves facilitate by laying eggs at intervals so that the first-hatched chick is typically larger and stronger than the second. Furthermore, the parents generally do not intervene when the older chick attacks the younger." More surprising, perhaps, is siblicide among sand sharks, also known as sand tigers. Sibling sand sharks "begin to devour one another while still squirming inside the mother's oviduct, a hitherto undreamed of hazard of viviparity" (xvi).

65. Ibid., xv.

66. See Susan C. M. Scrimshaw, "Infanticide in Human Populations: Societal and Individual Concerns," in Hausfater and Hrdy, *Infanticide*, 441 and 450.

67. Harris, *Our Kind*, 211.

68. Ibid., 223. Anthropologists distinguish between emics and etics — between the perspectives of those who belong to the culture under discussion and the explanatory categories employed by outside observers of the culture.

69. Hrdy and Hausfater, "Comparative and Evolutionary Perspectives on Infanticide," in Hausfater and Hrdy, *Infanticide*, xv.

70. Trivers, "Parental Investment and Sexual Selection," in Campbell, ed., *Sexual Selection*, 139.

71. Dawkins, *The Selfish Gene*, 124.

72. Hrdy, *The Woman That Never Evolved*, 94.

73. It might be objected that extinction is not a unitary phenomenon, that the disappearance of a species might be due not to its diminished reproductivity but to the successive selection of its individual variants, such that over time the species changes and even becomes a taxonomically or cladistically new species, its earlier forms having given way to significantly different later forms. This objection, however, confirms the fact that the essence of natural selection is not in its preservation of genetic lineages but in its differential selection of some gene-lines over others. If the line of descent is thought to describe a line of life, it must also be understood to describe a line of extinction.

74. This is the case whether extinction is due to biological or physical causes. Extinction from biological causes takes place by "competitive coevolution . . . as can happen, for example, when predators, or parasites, drive their prey (or hosts) extinct, when superior competitors eliminate inferior competitors, or when a species' food supply disappears" (Ridley, *Evolution*, 592; cf. 593–601). Extinction from physical causes takes place by virtue of widespread environmental changes that destroy huge numbers of species (592 and 601–15). Subject to extinction pressures that most likely vary over the eons, species apparently "do not grow better, or worse, at avoiding extinction as they persist in time; old species have the same chance of extinction as young ones" (601). If biological extinction represents an outcome internal to the selection that governs "competitive coevolution," extinction from physical perturbations of the biosphere represents an outcome external to the processes of natural selection. Since natural selection cannot ensure a species against the indefinite and unforeseeable future possibility of the physical cataclysms associated with mass extinctions, *selection for* remains a trap for otherwise successful species that are overtaken by sudden dramatic transformations of the environment.

75. The image of evolution as an intricately branching tree of life defends against this apprehension. Not surprisingly, when Darwin has recourse to this ancient trope, he does so ambivalently. "I believe this simile largely speaks the truth," he says, even as he immediately turns from this flower of speech to the murderousness of the life this image represents: "The green and budding twigs may represent existing species; and those produced during former years may represent the long succession of extinct species. At each

period of growth all the growing twigs have tried to branch out on all sides, and to over-top and kill the surrounding twigs and branches, in the same manner as species and groups of species have at all times overmastered other species in the great battle for life" (*The Origin of Species*, 99). As Darwin expands on his simile, the specter of extinction con-tinues to supervene but always as a kind of temporary interlude between moments of life: "From the first growth of the tree, many a limb and branch has decayed and dropped off; and these fallen branches of various sizes may represent those whole orders, families, and genera which have no living representatives," (100). Even as his language reverberates with images of death and extinction, Darwin endeavors to subordinate the reality they designate to a superordinate reality of "generation," determining the former as an effect of the latter. "As buds give rise by growth to fresh buds, and these, if vigorous, branch out and overtop on all sides many a feebler branch, so by generation I believe it has been with the great Tree of Life, which fills with its dead and broken branches the crust of the earth, and covers the surface with its everbranching and beautiful ramifications" (101). Whereas God blocks Adam and Eve from access to the Tree of Life, not so Darwin, who locates this "everbranching" source of life across the entire "surface" of the earth. Unlike in Genesis, Darwin's Tree of Life rises out of the death-filled crust such that the biblical dust and ashes have become nature's fertile seed bed.

Many have repeated Darwin's image to represent life as emerging from out of itself in a process of ceaseless self-generation and self-continuity made manifest by "the total fan-out of [life's] offspring" (Daniel C. Dennett, *Darwin's Dangerous Idea: Evolution and the Meanings of Life* [New York: Simon and Schuster, 1995], 85). And yet as Dennett un-derscores, "*most* of those offspring's trajectories terminate without mating, or at least without offspring of their own. This is the Malthusian crunch. Everywhere we look, the branches and twigs are covered with the short, terminal fuzz of birth-death without fur-ther issue" (91). The evidence of death and extinction is ubiquitous, for the prolific "fan-ning out" of life's offspring "everywhere" leads to prolicide, to the massive "birth-death" of offspring "without further issue." And yet "the graph that plots the time-line trajectories of all the things that have ever lived on this planet" (85) is never saluted as the great tree of death and extinction.

76. Dawkins, *The Extended Phenotype*, 4 and 5.

77. Ibid., 5; my emphasis.

78. Ibid., 4.

79. Ibid., 292.

80. Ibid., 4. The two perspectives—that of the selfish organism and that of the selfish gene—are not necessarily at odds, since the concept of differential reproductive fitness can and has been defined "in such a way as to tend to make 'the individual maximizes its inclusive fitness' equivalent to 'the genetic replicators maximize their survival'" (7).

81. Ibid., 114.

82. Dawkins, *The Selfish Gene*, 23.

83. Dawkins, *The Extended Phenotype*, 98.

84. Ibid., 117.

85. Ibid., 134.

86. Donna J. Haraway, "Biopolitics of Postmodern Bodies: Constitutions of Self in Immune System Discourse," in *Simians, Cyborgs, and Women: The Reinvention of Nature* (New York: Routledge, 1991), 219.

87. Dawkins, *The Extended Phenotype*, 5. For a recent exposition of the extent to which the body is constituted as a site of genetic conflict, see also Austin Burt and Robert Trivers, *Genes in Conflict: the Biology of Selfish Genetic Elements* (Cambridge: Belknap Press/Harvard University Press, 2006).

88. Haraway, a hominid biologist and historian of science, reports on the work of Leo Buss, who views immune system interactions in metazoan organisms in terms of "at least two units of selection, cellular and individual," which do not necessarily "harmonize" to form an intermeshed whole but, rather, may be in conflict. "The parts are not *for* the whole." Indeed, "there is no part/whole relation at all" because there is no overarching singularity or identity (no whole) in relation to which the organism's components could be identified as such (as parts). There is, rather, an "irreducible vulnerability, multiplicity, and contingency of every construct of individuality." The disparate "units of selection" can and may "harmonize," but such harmony is not necessary; rather, such harmony is contingent and does not presuppose a prior unity. "Pathology," therefore, does not result from a breakdown of organismic integrity but rather from one or another unresolved "conflict of interests between the cellular and organismic units of selection" ("Biopolitics of Postmodern Bodies," 220).

89. Dawkins, *The Extended Phenotype*, 133 and 138.

90. Ibid., 139. In addition to having been demonstrated by computer generation, this effect has also been experimentally produced and has practical applications to pest control (139).

91. Ibid., 143.

92. Ibid., 18.

93. Ibid., 248–49; my emphases. See Burt and Trivers, *Genes in Conflict*.

94. Ibid., 230.

95. Ibid., 249.

96. Ibid., 57.

97. Ibid., 56.

98. Dawkins, *The Selfish Gene*, 25; my emphasis.

99. Ibid., 35. To persist eternally, a replicator would have to be able to duplicate itself under all future conditions. A replicator would have to be able to survive the adventitiousness introduced into any future by matter's subatomic "uncertainty." That uncertainty imposes a theoretical limit to any macroatomic replicative program.

100. Dawkins, *The Selfish Gene*, 16; my emphases.

101. Ibid., 16–17; my emphases.

102. Ibid., 322.

103. Although genes "can self-copy for ten million generations and *scarcely degrade at all*," Darwinian evolution "works only because—apart from discrete mutations, which natural selection either weeds out or preserves—the copying process is not perfect" (Richard Dawkins, *River Out of Eden: A Darwinian View of Life* [New York: Basic Books/ HarperCollins, 1995], 19).

104. A "length of DNA that codes for a polypeptide," that is, a chain of amino acids (Ridley, *Evolution*, 25).

105. Dawkins, *The Selfish Gene*, 33–34.

106. Jacques Derrida, *Speech and Phenomena and Other Essays on Husserl's Theory of Signs*, trans. David B. Allison (Evanston: Northwestern University Press, 1973), 50.

107. Ibid. "Signature, Event, Context," in *Margins of Philosophy*, trans. Alan Bass (Chicago: University of Chicago Press, 1982), 317.

108. Ibid.

109. Ibid., "Le facteur de la verité," in *The Post Card: From Socrates to Freud and Beyond*, trans. Alan Bass (Chicago: University of Chicago Press, 1987), 489.

110. Dawkins, *The Selfish Gene*, 191.

111. Ibid., 193–94.

112. Ibid., 191.

113. Ibid., 192.

114. Richard Dawkins, "The Evolution of Evolvability," in Christopher G. Langton, ed., *Artificial Life* (Redwood City: Addison-Wesley, 1988), 217.

115. Ibid.

116. Ibid. Segmentation, Dawkins notes, "may have occurred only twice in history, once in the lineage leading to annelids and arthropods and once in the lineage leading to vertebrates" (217).

117. Ibid., 218.

118. Ibid.

119. Ibid.

120. According to A. G. Cairns-Smith, the first replicators may not have been organic molecules but inorganic crystals (*Seven Clues to the Origin of Life: A Scientific Detective Story* (Cambridge: Cambridge University Press, 1985), 74–79.

121. Dawkins, *The Selfish Gene*, 193.

122. At the end of his chapter on "Memes: The New Replicators" in *The Selfish Gene*, Dawkins hints at the death-stakes involved in the competition between genetic and memic replication. Having noted that "individual man is fundamentally selfish" and that this selfishness is differentially fatal, Dawkins goes on to say, nevertheless, that we can "discuss ways of deliberately cultivating and nurturing pure, disinterested altruism — something that has no place in nature, something that has never existed before in the whole history of the world. We are built as gene machines and cultured as meme machines, but we have the power to turn against our creators. We, alone on earth, can rebel against the tyranny of the selfish replicators" (200–201). Such memic rebellion would be the attempt to transcend — to put out of play, to overcome, to destroy — the genes for genetic selfishness, which is to say genes, period. If human cognition has arisen evolutionarily, however, then to find a place for that which has "no place in nature" humans would have to displace their thinking — precisely the deconstructive project.

123. The future of such "life" — that is, of such death-life or life-death — is monstrous, a barely conceivable possibility, as the citation from Derrida at the end of the previous chapter has indicated.

On this and other counts, recent critiques of deconstruction from ardent empiricists misconstrue both Derrida's intent and the force of his demonstrations concerning not the fictionality of the empirical but its textual inscription. In *Evolution and Literary Theory* (Columbia: University of Missouri Press, 1995), for example, Joseph Carroll insists on kicking the proverbial Johnsonian stone to refute what he thinks is the patent absurdity of poststructuralism's alleged anti-scientificity. Thus, Carroll is anxious to declare how, following hard won explanatory advances in the sciences, especially in evolutionary biology, he is able to ground his interdisciplinary efforts in "Darwinian naturalism," to derive his claims to knowledge from "empirical research" on "an actual world," to "once again take the 'subject' — the living, individual, human personality — as a primary point of reference," and to this end to read texts "as the intentional productions of living, individual human beings." Thus, too, is he anxious but nevertheless determined to represent "poststructuralism" as a kind of monolithic protocol — "an alternative, competing paradigm" that "operates on principles that are radically incompatible with those of evolutionary theory" (Carroll, 94–95 and 468). As Carroll's ideological commitment to a certain positivisitic conception of the real suggests, his conclusion fails to take into account how the sensible is such only in relation to that from which it is differentiated, namely the intelligible. The reality of the "actual world," as well as of any other "primary point of reference," is not independent of such difference but constituted as an effect of it.

In *Mimesis and the Human Animal: On the Biogenetic Foundations of Literary Representation* (Evanston: Northwestern University Press, 1996), Robert Storey endorses both the substance and the rhetorical form of Carroll's consignment of poststructuralism to future oblivion, since, like Carroll, he believes that the humanities have failed to appreciate Darwin and for that reason are "paddl[ing] about in intellectual sandboxes" (207). In their contempt for poststructuralism, Storey and Carroll identify themselves with a future in which they will out-live those whose postmodern discipline is "not merely obsolete but essentially void . . . essentially a wrong turn, a dead end, a misconceived enterprise"— that is to say, an abomination or even an abortion, and in any case "a repository of delusions and wasted efforts" (Carroll, 468). Such a denunciation, of course, is not a constative but a performative utterance, not a fact but a prediction. The irony that attends this statement of revilement turns on the way the imputation substitutes claim for demonstration, aversion for understanding, attack for truth, apocalyptic tone for objectivity, and does so according to a practice that is sacrificial. A close inspection of Carroll and Storey's vocabulary would reveal the latent infanticidism of that practice.

124. Dennett, *Darwin's Dangerous Idea*, passim.

125. Steven Rose, *Lifelines: Biology beyond Determinism* (Oxford: Oxford University Press, 1998), 18.

CHAPTER 3
INFANTICIDE AND REPRODUCTION IN GENESIS

1. Unless they are referenced otherwise, citations are to *The New Oxford Annotated Bible*, The New Revised Standard Version, ed. Bruce M. Metzger and Roland E. Murphy (New York: Oxford University Press, 1991, 1994).

2. "Lexical Aids to the Old Testament," *Hebrew-Greek Key Word Study Bible*, King James Version, rev. ed. (Chattanooga: AMG International, Inc., 1991), 1607 and 1618. Subsequent references to this work will be abbreviated *HGSB*, followed by page number. Where references are to the "Hebrew and Chaldee dictionary and "Greek Dictionary of the New Testament" sections at the end of the *HGSB*, the notes will so indicate.

3. "The Hebrew word *yâda'* . . . indicates the most intimate relationship between a man and a woman, the sexual bond" (*HGSB*, 8).

4. The Hebrew word for fruit, *p^erîy*, derives from a verb, *pârâh*, to bear fruit, literally or figuratively ("Hebrew and Chaldee Dictionary," *HGSG*, 96). God's first commandment uses fruitfulness as a metaphor of reproductive success: "'Be fruitful and multiply and fill the waters in the seas, and let birds multiply on the earth'" (Genesis 1:22). God repeats the commandment to humans (Genesis 1:28). Reproductive fruitfulness continues the act of creation; it is the rhythm of the division (between male and female, a metonymy of all the divisions that emerge with the creation), which is overcome in the fruitfulness of sexual union. Thus the expression "fruit of the womb," which recurs in Genesis (30:1–2), Deuteronomy (7:12–14, 28:4, 28:11, 28:18, 30:9), Psalms (127:3, 132:11), Isaiah (13:18), and Hosea (9:16). The Greek word for fruit, *karpós*, "fruit (of his loins) fruit as plucked" ("Greek Dictionary of the New Testament," *HGSG*, 39) occurs in the phrase "fruit of your womb" (Luke 1:41–42) and in the phrase "descendants [*karpós*] on his throne" (Acts 2:30). The multiple references to fruitfulness enforce its double meaning as productivity and reproductivity. Three times God commands Noah to "be fruitful and multiply." The first time he directs Noah to "'Bring out with you every living thing that is with you of all flesh—birds and animals and every creeping thing that creeps on the earth—so that they may abound on the earth, and be fruitful and multiply on the earth" (Genesis 8:17–18). Here, the bringing out or forth is like a magnificent parturition, the ark being a kind of wondrous prosthetic womb. Later, God promises

Abraham progenerative fruitfulness as a covenantal sign: "I will make you exceedingly fruitful [*pârâh*]; and I will make nations of you, and kings shall come from you. I will establish my covenant between me and you, and your offspring after you throughout their generations, for an everlasting covenant, to be God to you and to your offspring" (Genesis 17:6–7). Leviticus repeats this covenantal promise of reproductive fruitfulness (26:9). Numerous other references define fruitfulness [*pârâh*] as or link it to fertility (cf. Genesis 26:22, 28:3, 35:11, 41:45, 48:4, 49:22; Exodus 1:7; Jeremiah 23:3; Ezekiel 19:10; Psalm 107:35–38, 128; Hosea 10:1). These references provide the reproductive backdrop for the dozens of references to fruit and fruitfulness in the Gospels.

5. David Bakan, *Slaughter of the Innocents: A Study of the Battered Child Phenomenon* (Boston: Beacon Press, 1972), ix.

6. Ibid., *And They Took Themselves Wives: The Emergence of patriarchy in Western Civilization* (San Francisco: Harper and Row, 1979), 16. The meaning of the Greek *karpos*, "fruit as plucked*," reinforces the infanticidal meaning of the first sin — plucking and eating the fruit from the Tree of Knowledge.

7. Having destroyed his potential rivals, the sons of other families in his kingdom, and having murdered several of his own sons for conspiring against him, Herod repeats his infanticidal tactics when he learns that a child of Davidic genealogy would come to rule the Jews (*The Westminster Dictionary of the Bible*, ed. John D. Davis, rev. and rewritten by Henry Snyder Gehman [Philadelphia: Westminster Press, 1944], 238–39). To forestall this eventuality, he orders his infamous slaughter of the innocents, recorded in Matthew 2:16.

8. This interpretation contests the position that religion mystifies the nature of reality. In "Genesis as Myth," Edmund Leach characterizes biblical narrative as non-rational myth: "The non-rationality of myth" is the "very essence" of religion, "for religion requires a demonstration of faith by the suspension of critical doubt" (*Genesis as Myth and Other Essays* [London: Jonathan Cape, 1969], 7). The "essence" of religion's mythological consciousness is evident in its approach to "the antinomy of life and death," one of the abiding preoccupations of "religion everywhere," Leach notes. "Religion *seeks to deny* the binary link between the two words; it does this by creating the mystical idea of another world, a land of the dead where life is perpetual" and by introducing numerous mediating categories that seem to establish that "death is *not* the necessary consequence of life" (10 and 12; first emphasis mine). This and the next two chapters, however, argue that the Bible does not deny but affirms the "binary link" between life and death — indeed, that the Bible shows this link to be infanticidal, and that it recognizes the (infanticidal) deathliness within the divine creator himself. Chapter 8 shows how Jesus attributes this very (infanticidal) deathliness to the Word, which he incarnates in his person.

9. Walter Benjamin is on the track of the infanticidal meaning of the fall when he infers that the prohibited knowing Adam and Eve gain amounts to "the *uncreative* imitation of [God's] creative verb." If the uncreating Fall is "the moment of *birth* of man's language," as Benjamin declares (my emphases), then language is stillborn, bearing but unable to name the infanticidality of which it is an expression. Thus does Benjamin's birth metaphor exemplify the very way that the prelapsarian name "steps away from itself," forced to "communicate *something* now, outside itself" (*Schriften*, 2:464–65; cited by Said, *Beginnings: Intention and Method* [Baltimore: Johns Hopkins University Press, 1975], 231). And yet it can do so only by virtue of the infanticidality within itself — that is, only by being the uncreating medium of human consciousness. Although Benjamin locates the moment of (infanticidal) uncreation in the Fall into language, I believe that Genesis situates it within the divine predication itself, and that the Bible should be read for its attempts, in fear and trembling, to understand how to live with this knowledge.

10. J. P. Fokkelman, "Genesis," in Robert Alter and Frank Kermode, eds., *The Literary Guide to the Bible* (Belknap Press/Harvard University Press, 1987), 41.

11. The priestly author of Genesis, Howard Eilberg-Schwartz writes, is preoccupied both with "the problem of tracing lines of descent" and with reproductive fertility. The Israelite priests "were urgently concerned about human sexuality and reproduction, matters that are intimately related to the problem of developing and perpetuating a lineage. Thus one of the priestly writer's favorite themes is human fertility (Gen. 1:22; 9:1, 7; 17:2, 3, 10; 28:3–4; 35:11–12; 48:4; Exod. 1:7). The priests were concerned further with possible contamination of lines of descent by incest or marrying foreign women. These concerns constantly work their way into the priestly narration of human and Israelite history and underlie many of the laws in the priestly code" (*The Savage in Judaism: An Anthropology of Israelite Religion and Ancient Judaism* [Bloomington: Indiana University Press, 1990], 166–67). They also underlie what Eilberg-Schwartz calls the Torah's "genealogy of knowledge" (see in particular ch. 9, "Creation, Classification, and the Genealogy of Knowledge," 217–34).

12. Fokkelman, "Genesis," 41.

13. Hertz notes that *bra* "is used exclusively of Divine activity. Man is spoken of as 'making' or 'forming,' but never as 'creating,' *i.e.* producing something out of nothing" (*The Pentateuch and Haftorahs,* 2n1). Paul Ricoeur underscores "that on this occasion God is not designated as father" and that the "specific verb . . . used to tell about the creative act" eliminates "any trace of begetting." Ricoeur insists that "the Creation . . . is not a piece of paternal theology" ("Fatherhood: From Phantasm to Symbol," trans. Robert Sweeney, in *The Conflict of Interpretations: Essays in Hermeneutics,* ed. Don Ihde [Evanston: Northwestern University Press, 1974], 486).

14. Fokkelman, "Genesis," 41.

15. Ibid. Eilberg-Schwartz explains why the Israelites would be hesitant to ascribe paternity to God. The Genesis account of creation "demarcate[s] and define[s]" reality. Anything that violates the classifications established in this story is treated as a flaw in creation and hence is considered abnormal and unclean. What conforms to the cherished classifications is holy" (*The Savage in Judaism,* 218). Sexuality does not so conform: "in the priestly writings, a person becomes contaminated by sexual intercourse (Lev. 15:17)." Whereas all other contaminations are involuntary, the contamination from intercourse is not: intercourse "was the one willful act that produced contamination" (204). If the origination of the world establishes the right ordering of its elements, and if the violation of categorical distinctions — between the clean and the unclean, for example — contaminates this order, then the purity of God's creative act must stand in opposition to the impurity of human procreation. Therefore, "Israelite writers were very cautious about representing God's form. Even sources that suggest that God appeared in human form hesitate to ascribe to God the necessary body parts for lower functions such as digestion, urination, defecation, and sexual intercourse. In crucial aspects of their embodiment, then, humans were not made in the image of God and human activity does not replicate divine activity. Thus while God created the world by speaking, humans procreate by joining their bodies, an act that creates contamination. Thus the divine realm served as much as an anti-image for the human realm as a mirror of it" (217).

16. John S. Kselman, "Genesis," in James L. Mays, general ed., et al., *Harper's Bible Commentary* (San Francisco: Harper and Row, 1988), 86. Writing twenty years before Fokkelman, Nahum M. Sarna denies this possibility. In polytheistic mythologies, he points out, "creation is always expressed in terms of procreation," paganism being "unable to conceive of any primal creative force other than in terms of sex. . . . The sex element existed before the cosmos came into being and all the gods were themselves creatures of sex." In contrast, "the Creator in Genesis is uniquely without any female counterpart and the very association of sex with God is utterly alien to the religion of the Bible. When, in fact, Genesis (1:27; 5:2) informs us that 'male and female He created

them,' that God Himself created sexual differentiation, it is more than likely that we are dealing with an intended protest against such pagan notions" (*Understanding Genesis* [New York: Schocken, 1966],12–13).

Why, then, does Genesis equivocate about the nature of the creation, first characterizing it as a non-sexual making but then immediately evoking the progenerativity of the heavens and the earth? Why does Genesis separate God's generativity from the reproductivity of humans but employ a word, *toledot*, that in every other use denotes the sexual origin of the begotten? In other words, why does the text move toward and away from the analogy of divine creativity to human procreativity? Accepting the "documentary hypothesis" (which asserts that the Bible was put together from documents separated in time by hundreds of years and in outlook by authors of widely divergent sensibilities), Bakan explains that "the later patrilineally, patriarchically oriented authors of the Bible found the idea of God as a sexual being intolerable, and they sought to change it. Yet their modifications were not so complete as to remove all traces of earlier meanings" (*And They Took Themselves Wives*, 103). In attempting to recover such hints, Bakan identifies numerous veiled or bowdlerized allusions to the idea of the impregnating power of divine visitations. "There are," he surmises, "two major reasons for the incomplete censorship of divine impregnation. The first is that the great respect for the text inhibited too relentless a modification. The second is that a fundamental rationale for the idea of election by God meant descent from God, and that notion needed to be retained in some form" (103). For a more recent study of the tensions in Judaism resulting from its conflicted acceptances and denials of God's sexuality, see Eilberg-Schwartz's *God's Phallus and Other Problems for Men and Monotheism* (Boston: Beacon Press, 1994).

Whether or not Genesis retains in the first appearance of *toledot* a trace of God as a sexual being, the book in fact underscores the linkage between God's creation and human procreation by representing God as father, in truth as the first and absolute father, the father of the world, a fact that David Bakan suggests ought not to be taken for granted: "So preoccupied were the authors of the Bible with fatherhood," he writes, "that even God is conceived of as father" (*And They Took Themselves Wives*, 12). Bakan finds this conception at the very center of Judaism and Christianity: "the basic theme, and seeming preoccupation, of the Bible as a whole, is paternity . . . paternity is the phenomenon around which the basic elements of biblical theology and social, political, and economic relationships are structured" (12).

In contrast to Bakan, Ricoeur observes that "in the Old Testament . . . the designation of God as father is quantitatively insignificant. Specialists in Old and New Testament scholarship are in agreement in emphasizing—and at first being surprised at—this great reserve limiting the use of the epithet 'father' in the writings of the Old Testament. Marchel [*Dieu-Père dans le Nouveau Testament*] and Jeremias [*Abba*] count less than twenty instances in the Old Testament" ("Fatherhood: From Phantasm to Symbol," *The Conflict of Interpretations*, 482–83).

For a recent review of the scholarship on the theme of God as father, see Mary Rose D'Angelo, "*Abba* and 'Father': Imperial Theology and the Jesus Traditions," *Journal of Biblical Literature* 111.4 (1992): 611–30. D'Angelo includes a discussion of "'Father' as an Address to God in Ancient Judaism and Earliest Christianity" (617–22). See also Peter Widdicombe, *The Fatherhood of God from Origen to Athanasius* (Oxford: Clarendon Press, 1994).

17. According to Bakan, the Bible is so concerned with working out the ramifications of the male's role in conception that it "may be interpreted as a document representing the crisis of paternalization," which turns on "all the changes involved in the male's assumption of the various obligations of fatherhood" (*And They Took Themselves Wives*, 13). To this end the Bible, Bakan argues, records the transition from a "matrocentric" to a

"patrocentric" form of cultural organization. "Unquestionably, the general impact of the text is to promote patrocentrism, and the associated patrilineality and patriarchy. . . . However, there are strong traces of a prior matrocentrism, with matrilineality and perhaps even matriarchy, in the text" (66). The overcoming of these matrocentric, matrilineal, and matriarchal traditions "made possible the unification of a state beyond the limits set by the matrilineal descent" (172). Bakan finds in such unification the signs of a psychological development he associates with the recognition of "the abiding contingency of the welfare of the total society on the quality of individual human beings, and the contingency of the quality of human beings on appropriate care, especially in childhood" (175). Thus, according to Bakan, the movement toward patrilineal social patterns was "in the direction of bringing about a condition of greater care for children" (175). Because the difficulties that arose from the assumption of responsibility by males for their biological offspring "also gave rise to a temptation to kill their children," Bakan asserts that "a large part of the Bible's moral burden is to prevent infanticide from actually taking place" (15).

For other discussions of descent in Judaism see, for example, Shaye J. D. Cohen, "The Origins of the Matrilineal Principle in Jewish Law," *AJS Review* 10.1 (1985): 19–54; Lawrence A. Hoffman, *Covenant of Blood: Circumcision and Gender in Rabbinic Judaism* (Chicago: University of Chicago Press, 1966), esp. 42–48; Nancy Jay, "Sacrifice, Descent, and the Patriarchs," *Vetus Testamentum* 38.1 (1988): 52–70, and *Throughout Your Generations Forever: Sacrifice, Religion, and Paternity* (Chicago: University of Chicago Press, 1992); and Savina J. Teubel, *Sarah the Priestess: The First Matriarch of Genesis* (Athens: Swallow Press, 1984).

18. Genesis 2:7 emphasizes Adam's relation to the earth when it says that God "formed man [*adam*, human being, is akin to *adam*, red or ruddy] of dust from the ground ['*adāmāh*, soil, specifically red earth]" (*HGSB*, 1595 and 1646–47). The verb *vayyitzer* ("formed") reinforces this relation, since it derives "from the same root, *yatzar,* as is used of the potter moulding clay into a vessel" (Hertz, *The Pentateuch and Haftorahs*, 7n7). The verse also hints ever so elliptically that Adam (perhaps from the Akkadian *adāmu*, "make, produce," and akin to *admu*, "child") is formed in the way children are (see *The Westminster Dictionary of the Bible*, 10).

19. "Hebrew and Chaldee Dictionary," *HGSG*, 37.

20. Hertz, *The Pentateuch and Haftorahs*, 14n10.

21. Cited by Hertz, *The Pentateuch and Haftorahs*, 14n10.

22. The narrative highlights the relation of knowing and lying when Adam and Eve withhold the fact of their disobedience from God. At that instant they achieve a second-order or reflexive knowledge: they know something about the nature of knowing—about the way knowledge can be simulated or feigned, for example, or the way it requires signs in order to be signified, hence the way it can be symbolically encoded. They themselves institute such a mode of signification when, their eyes "opened," they then cover themselves with "loincloths" (3:7); they close off from physical sight the nakedness that their clothing thereafter represents and symbolically repeat their act of avoiding God's sight. When God asks, "Where are you?" his question enforces the connection between reflexivity, signification, and the non-presentative implications (lying, hiding, indirection, withholding, shame, self-protectiveness, and so on) of representation. To this end the "where" is literal and metaphorical: Adam and Eve have hidden themselves someplace, somewhere, and they have thereby resituated themselves morally. God underscores this consequence of their concealment when he exiles them, their removal from Eden a physical enactment of the way their knowledge has already moved them out of their previous relation to the garden. Adam recognizes the existential import of this change of relation when he confesses his newly discovered trepidation of his creator: "I heard the sound of you in the garden, and I was afraid, because I was naked; and I hid myself."

At this point the narrative has begun to merge its first two predications (to know and to lie) with its third (to conceive) by awakening Adam and Eve's self-consciousness about their sexuality. The narrative intensifies the association when it cites God's response to Adam's admission of fear: "Who told you that you were naked?" God demands. The narrative does yet again when it represents Adam and Eve's conception as an act of metaphorical knowing: "Now the man knew [*yâda'*] his wife Eve and she conceived [*hârâh;* "Hebrew and Chaldee Dictionary," *HGSB*, 33] and bore Cain" (4:1).

The narrative immediately amalgamates its third predication with its fourth when, playing on the sound of Cain's name, *Qayin,* Eve says, "'I have produced [*qânâh,* homophonically echoing *Qayin*] a man with the help of the Lord.' Next she bore his brother Abel" (4:1; "Hebrew and Chaldee Dictionary," *HGSB,* 103 and 104). The begetting of Cain, however, is the bringing into the world of a killer. Following the murder of Abel, God asks Cain a version of the double question he has earlier asked Adam and Eve: "Where is your brother Abel?" Cain's duplicitous answer, "'I do not *know* [*yâda'*]'" (4:9; my emphasis), seals the transposition of the three predications. Within that seal is inscribed the infanticidality of genesis, as the details of Cain's murder suggest.

23. Concerning the "sevenfold" nature of the vengeance of which the mark of Cain forewarns, Hertz notes that "The number 'seven' is occasionally used in the Bible to express an indefinite large number; cf. Lev. xxvi,27; Prov. xxiv,16. Cain's murderer shall be visited with a punishment far greater than that exacted of Abel's, as God had now made manifest His abhorrence of bloodshed to all" (*The Pentateuch and Haftorahs,* 15n15).

24. René Girard has made two somewhat contradictory but nevertheless provocative suggestions concerning Cain's murderousness. The first is that Cain's aggression is a symptomatic expression of a "mimetic crisis" of escalating retributive or "reciprocal violence," which the institution of sacrifice, here represented by Abel's burnt offering, deflects. "One of the brothers kills the other, and the murderer is the one who does not have the violence-outlet of animal sacrifice at his disposal. This difference between sacrificial and nonsacrificial cults determines, in effect, God's judgement in favor of Abel. To say that God accedes to Abel's sacrificial offerings but rejects the offerings of Cain is simply another way of saying—from the viewpoint of the divinity—that Cain is a murderer, whereas his brother is not" (*Violence and the Sacred,* trans. Patrick Gregory [Baltimore: Johns Hopkins University Press, 1977]), 4; cf. Girard's characterization in *The Scapegoat* (trans. Yvonne Freccero [Baltimore: Johns Hopkins University Press, 1986]) of Abel as one of the numerous persecuted victims to whom Christ likens himself and is likened by others (117).

If all religious practices aim, as Girard insists, at converting violence against others of one's kind into collective celebrations of the community's harmony with itself, those practices revolve around the power of sacrificial rites to unite a people in an act of unanimous, and thereby culturally productive or generative, violence against a scapegoat victim. On the one hand Girard believes that Cain represents a people who have not discovered the efficacy of sacrifice; on the other Girard also asserts that the story of his murderousness repeats the violent persecution that is the bedrock of this mechanism of social cohesion. In this case the story of Cain in fact describes precisely the discovery of the efficacy of sacrificial victimage. Here Girard's suggestion seems to be that Cain's violence inaugurates the sacrificial means by which the Canaanite heritage is able to found and institute itself (cf. Girard's *Things Hidden Since the Foundation of the World,* trans. Stephen Bann and Michael Metteer [Stanford: Stanford University Press, 1987], 144–46).

25. God marks [*vayasem'ôth,* sets a sign on, from *sûm,* sets, and *'ôth,* a sign, token, symbol, warning] Cain (4:15; "Hebrew and Chaldee Dictionary," *HGSB,* 113 and 10).

26. The next verses continue to interweave the prospects of generational survival and reproductive ruination the one within the other. On the one hand, Genesis emphasizes

Cain's reproductive success when it lists his descendants through the sixth generation (4:17–22). On the other hand, Genesis conspicuously avoids using the term *toledot* to describe Cain's offspring. Plaut suggests that the omission of the word *toledot* may have functioned to isolate Cain genealogically. The similarity between the names of Cain's descendants and Seth's (cf. 4:17–22 and 5:1–31) suggests that the variations on the first listing introduced by the second were "probably due to the understandable disinclination to have all men appear to be descended from a murderer. It may also be that for this reason the term . . . (*toledot*) is denied the Cain line" (*The Torah: A Modern Commentary* [New York: Union of American Jewish Congregations, 1981], 54n1). In deviating from its typical employment of the word at the beginning of genealogical listings, the narrative marks the memory of Cain with its version of the textual mark God has put on him.

Genesis links reproductivity to reproductivity threatened when, five generations into Cain's lineage, Lamach tropes against God's earlier mathematical admonition against those who would take revenge against Cain. Reminding his wives of his quickness to anger, Lamech declares: "I have slain a man for wounding me, a young man for striking me. If Cain is avenged sevenfold, truly Lamech seventy-seven fold" (4:23–24).

In several commentaries on the story of Lamech (in the apocryphal I Enoch, the Genesis Apocryphon, the Targum Pseudo-Jonathan, Pseudo-Philo, and the Book of Jasher), Bakan finds evidence that "what has been included in the [biblical] text may perhaps be a threat song by a male addressed to the female, a threat to kill the child which might be the product of an unfaithful union, a threat almost carried out by Abraham against Isaac" (*And They Took Themselves Wives*, 160–61).

27. The continuation of the verse says that these early humans "were of old ['*ôlām*, "most distant times"], men of renown." The Hebrew '*ôlām* means "hidden, concealed (i.e. to the vanishing point); time immemorial, time past, antiquity. . . . The KJV translates the word as 'beginning of the world'" (*HGSB*, 1643). Deriving from '*âlam*, "to veil from sight, i.e. conceal" ("Hebrew and Chaldee Dictionary," *HGSB*, 89), '*ôlām* here points to the veiled nature of the wickedness, which for its part echoes a time immemorial when Adam and Eve attempt to hide their initial sin from God.

28. Plaut, *The Torah*, 61 and 61n2.

29. Not etymologically related, *∂hor* and *toledot* are conceptually akin, since *∂hor* signifies one link in the chain of *toledot*.

30. The Hebrew word for descendants derives from *zera'*, seed, semen (*HGSB*, 1610).

31. In "Finders Keepers: Preservation and the Biblical Foundling" (*Mosaic* 11.1 [Fall 1977]), Barbara L. Estrin explains how a loss in the past overtakes the future in what might be called an infanticidal-cum-chrono-cidal pattern of obliteration. She takes as her example Moses' address to the tribe of Korah, in which he threatens that they "shall die a death *not* like the 'common death of all men'" but rather "shall disappear en mass from the earth," their past as well as their future erased (63). Moses warns the tribe: "if the Lord creates something new, and the ground opens its mouth, and swallows them up, with all that belongs to them, and they go down alive into Sheol, then you shall know that these men have despised the Lord" (Numbers 16:30). In the next two verses the threat is carried out. Estrin comments: "As punishment for their transgression, Korah and his men are so totally absorbed that *no trace* of them is left. Like Enoch, who 'was not; for God took him' (Genesis 5:24), *the tribe's past is retroactively annihilated and its future projectively thereby destroyed;* nothing remains to verify an entire communal life" (63–64). Since Korah is introduced as son — "the son of Izhar, son of Kohath, son of Levi" (Numbers 16:1) going back three generations — the "swallowing up" of him and all the households of his tribe represents an infanticidal extinction of both past and future. The image of the "ground opening its mouth" here anticipates the figure of the Dragon in Revelation, through whom the Bible reveals the entire sweep of its concern with the infanticidal.

32. Plaut, *The Torah*, 70.

33. The Talmud, Plaut notes, records an argument concerning whether Noah had been castrated or sexually abused by Ham. The narrative traces back to a Canaanite myth and a Hurrian legend, in each of which a son castrates his father (*The Torah*, 70 n 2).

34. Commenting on the curse against Canaan, Hertz says: "It was firmly held in ancient times . . . that the blessing or curse which a father pronounced upon a child affected the latter's descendants. We, therefore, have here in effect a forecast of the future, that the Canaanites would be a servile and degraded race" (*The Pentateuch and Haftorahs*, 34 n 25). In asking why Noah should curse not his son but his grandson, and Canaan in particular, Bakan recalls the "rabbinical explanation," which is that "the castrated Noah, deprived of his capacity to have a fourth son, puts a curse on Ham's fourth son (BT, Nezikin: Sanhedrin 70a)" (*And They Took Themselves Wives*, 79).

35. *The New Oxford Annotated Bible*, 14, nll.1–9.

36. "Numerous interpreters have noted that in the ancient Near East cutting an animal in half was the act by which a covenant or treaty was ratified" (Eilberg-Schwartz, *The Savage in Judaism*, 168). In the case at hand Eilberg-Schwartz believes that the cutting served to identify Abraham as the founder of a new lineage, to distinguish him "from all humans who had come before" (167). To that end "the division of the animals alludes directly to the substance of the divine promise. God promises that Abraham, not his father, brothers, or their descendants, would inherit the land. Cutting the animal in two (presumably longitudinally through the genitals) symbolizes the split that initiated this genealogical division" between Abraham and Lot. "Significantly, in the Jahwist narrative, this symbolic act follows directly upon the dispute over land between the herdsmen of Abraham and Lot, Abraham's patrilineal cousin. The quarrel ends with Abraham and Lot agreeing to live in different parts of the land. But the quarrel is symptomatic of the potential for Lot and his descendants to lay claim to Abraham's inheritance. Immediately after this incident, the Jahwist inserts the covenant between Abraham and God and the act of cutting the animals in half" (168).

If the ritual bisection of animals enacts the covenantal promise of a separate descent, if it communicates as well the entire set of values associated with fertility, inheritance, genealogical identity, community, and homeland, then its counterpart would be the test of Solomon's judgment (1 Kings 16–28), in which the king of wisdom resolves to cut in two a child each of "two harlots" claims as her own. Each woman has recently given birth, but one of the infants has unaccountably "died in the night." In the morning the women dispute possession of the still living child, each claiming it for herself. Solomon settles the matter when he asks for a sword and issues his notorious order: "Divide the living child in two, and give half to the one, and half to the other." The narrating voice says that "the woman whose son was alive said to the king, because her heart yearned for her son, 'Oh my lord, give her the living child, and by no means slay it.' But the other said, 'It shall be neither mine nor yours; divide it.'" Thereupon Solomon declares the first woman to be the child's mother and gives it over to her care. Marc Shell cautions that "the sword-wielding Solomon does not figure out which of the two claimants is the literal mother, only which wants the child to live" (*Children of the Earth: Literature, Politics, and Nationhood* [New York: Oxford University Press, 1993], 5). Such a determination is crucial if children are to serve as the covenantal blessing, for their deaths would signify, indeed would be, the loss of the covenant. In affirming the child's claim to life and someone's care against the sacrificial counterclaim, Solomon exercises a "wisdom" and "justice" that draws out the infanticidal implications of the rite of animal sacrifice by which Abraham seals the covenant cut by God.

37. The Hebrew word translated as *made* is *kârath*, "to cut (e.g., a covenant), cut out; to cut off a part of the body (e.g. head, hand, foreskin); maim, castrate; to cut down trees,

cut down idols; to root out; to eliminate, kill, destroy; to be consumed; to be exiled, to be destroyed; to withdraw, be withdrawn" Sometimes *kârath* "has metaphorical meanings of elimination or removal." At other times the cut is literal. "'Cutting a covenant' was literal, because animals had to be slaughtered in order to ratify the agreement" (*HGSB*, 1624). Abram completes the ritual slaughtering when he passes a "flaming torch" between the two cut pieces of the animals (Genesis 15:17).

The covenantal language of cutting is akin to the "dream-work's singular tendency to disregard negation and to employ the same means of representation for expressing contraries." In this regard "the behaviour of the dream-work . . . is identical with a peculiarity in the oldest languages known to us" (Sigmund Freud, "The Antithetic Sense of Primal Words," *Standard Edition of the Complete Psychological Works of Sigmund Freud*, vol. 10, trans. James Strachey [London: Hogarth Press and the Institute of Psycho-Analysis, 1966], 156). From a psychoanalytic view it is, therefore, overdetermined that Abram should receive the covenant only after he falls asleep—that is, in a dream—and that God's words should announce both freedom and slavery, the promised land and exile.

38. The antithetical power of the covenant here turns in upon itself: because the covenant opens a way, through the detour of exile, from God to God, it is a cut that heals by means of the wound it inflicts. In other words the cut simultaneously cuts off its power of cutting. This cut cuts itself; such a cut is, perforce, a cut without cut. The covenant thus preserves in a single textual stroke both its power to open and its power to cut out or cut off from.

In a hermeneutic gesture that has enormous political implications, biblical exegesis has located the meaning of covenantal wounding in the meaning of covenantal healing. As the rest of this chapter and the next will argue, however, the "cut of the covenant" should be interpreted in the way it reverses and displaces this hierarchical valuation.

39. Baskin alludes to the attitude of *b. Pesah.* (113b). *Menuddeh* is the passive form of *niddah*, to distance, push away, excommunicate, remove someone from the community. It is used of menstruation as well as incest—in either case with failed or contaminated reproduction. Etymologically unrelated but conceptually akin to Hebrew words for cutting off, *niddah* designates an action that is an instance of a larger category of separations or severings and their reproductive consequences. See Judith R. Baskin, "Rabbinic Reflections on the Barren Wife," *Harvard Theological Review* 82.1 (1989): 101–14.

40. Baskin, "Rabbinic Reflections on the Barren Wife," 108.

41. Fokkelman, "Genesis," 43.

42. Estrin, "Finders Keepers," 71.

43. According to Mara E. Donaldson, "two unacceptable forms of marriage" threaten the genealogical dream—"those which are incestuous (too closely related) and those which are exogamous (not related at all)" ("Kinship Theory in the Patriarchal Narratives: The Case of the Barren Wife," *Journal of the American Academy of Religion* 49.1 [1980]: 79). In order to mitigate this threat, the Genesis narratives prescribe the correct form of marriage—unions between cross-cousins, with matrilateral cross-cousin marriage (between a son and his mother's brother's daughter) appearing "to be the best arrangement in a patrilineal society for establishing a complex cycle of alliances" (82).

Drawing on Lévi-Strauss's argument in *The Elementary Structures of Kinship* "that *exchange* and *alliance* are the keys to understanding kinship," Donaldson reads barrenness "as the key indicator of an 'incorrect' relationship" (79 and 83). Although God intervenes to make each of the barren matriarchs (Sarah, Rebekah, and finally Rachel) fertile, the subtext of the narrative sequence points to the increasing "correctness" of the marriages. In other words the narrative handling of barrenness in the context of alliance-formation represents the consolidation of the patriarchal prerogative of men to "define and exchange women" (85).

44. Howard Eilberg-Schwartz, *God's Phallus and Other Problems for Men and Monotheism*
(Boston: Beacon Press, 1990), 140–41.
45. Ibid., 140.
46. Ibid., 141.
47. "Lexical Aids to the Old Testament," *HGSB*, 1626.
48. Much scholarship has been devoted to the meaning of circumcision in Judaism,
which is to occur on the eighth day of the newborn's life (Genesis 17:12), in contrast
to its role in pagan cultures, which carry out the surgery when the boy becomes a man.
Eilberg-Schwartz disputes the contention that "this rite served as a purely arbitrary sign
of God's covenant with Abraham" (146). In addition to its spiritualized significance as
an act that initiates the male child into the covenant, Israelite circumcision draws on its
reproductive meaning in other cultures: "for the priestly community the practice of circumcision, despite its role in symbolizing the covenant and despite its performance just
after birth, nonetheless symbolized the fertility of the initiate as well as his entrance into
and ability to perpetuate a lineage of male descendants" ("The Fruitful Cut," *The Savage
in Judaism*, 143).
    In Hebrew, the word for *commemorate* retains precisely this reproductive signification.
The "stem for 'commemorate' or 'remember' (*zkr*)," Eilberg-Schwartz points out, "is
etymologically related to the word for male (*zkr*). Both derive from the same Semitic root.
. . . In Arabic, one of Hebrew's cognate languages, the word for male also means "male
organ" and "call upon in worship." The priestly symbol of the covenant [circumcision]
ties together these themes, for only a male's body can bear the symbol of the covenant.
To put it another way, in the priestly community, remembering the covenant requires
having the appropriate member ("The Fruitful Cut," 172).
    Troubled by the gendered nature of the covenant, Hoffman echoes the insight that
inspires Eilberg-Schwartz's pun: inextricable from the covenantal relation to God, circumcision carves into the body of the male the "extreme sexist symbolism" of its vision.
For historically circumcision is the ritual surety "that has initiated a male lifeline, that
once called on boys entering puberty to wash their hands in a mixture of circumcision
blood and water, that contrasted male blood that saves with female blood that pollutes,
and that became the dominant male ritual from which women were eventually forcefully
excluded, even though the infants they nursed were required to undergo it" (*Covenant of
Blood*, 210–11).
    49. Hoffman, *Covenant of Blood*, 11.
    50. So designated in the "documentary hypothesis" concerning the Bible's multiple
authorship. According to the classic formulation of this hypothesis, the Pentateuch was
composed by a number of hands over a span of some six hundred years. The last of the
authorial voices, P, identifies with the theocratic authorities following the Babylonian
exile. There is "an earlier corpus normally called D, generally held to reflect pre-exilic
monarchical interests as well as the prophets who opposed that very monarchy," although
the D (Deuteronomy) document may have been assembled not before but during the
time of exile. "Classical theory supposes also a J and an E narrative, these being the two
most ancient and independent documents ultimately subsumed under D. The status of
these two strands is most in question. They may or may not have existed independently
before D. Either way, however, we have a sharp break between D (and including J and
E, if they existed independently) and P" (Hoffman, *Covenant of Blood*, 28–29).
    Hoffman highlights the differences between the J and P visions of the covenant: "Hav-
ing no notion that the covenant has something to do with circumcision . . . J marks it by
an elaborate animal sacrifice. By contrast, for P, circumcision is the very essence of the
covenant. Whereas for J the sacrificial ritual is merely a secondary event made to serve
the primary concern of covenant, P's rival chapter 17 almost makes the covenant second-

ary to the ritualistic concern for circumcision" (34). Why? Because, Hoffman suggests, each version responds to a different sociopolitical need. "J's version . . . quickly departs from its original problem, Abraham's desire for children, and introduces an allied interest, the justification of Israel's political independence, an issue that faced the Davidic-Solomonic monarchy when J wrote his account. Thus J concludes, 'To your offspring I will give this land, from the river of Egypt to the river Euphrates' (Gen. 15:18–21). But not so P, for whom monarchic interests are absent. In P's day there was no empire save the Persian, to which the newly constituted Judean state (and P) owed fealty. And the monarchy, once represented alongside the priesthood by the joint rulership of Joshua and Zerubbabel, is exactly what P and one hundred years of priestly ancestry have managed to replace with a thoroughgoing theocracy." Whereas J presents the covenantal sacrifice as "the means to fulfill the promise of Israelite hegemony in Canaan," P "has no need to establish an ideological basis for that hegemony." In consequence "the covenantal act that matters is not Abraham's sacrifice but his circumcision, which is never severed from the story's original problematic: his childlessness, which requires for its solution that he complete his own body by paring away his foreskin and then appearing before God *tamim,* 'whole'" (*Covenant of Blood,* 35–36).

51. Ultimately the P narrative will assimilate the two forms of separation; it will do so by extending the language of circumcision to the horticultural working of the land, so that, for example, the pruning of trees will be understood as a form of circumcision (see Eilberg-Schwartz's discussion of "Uncircumcised Fruit Trees" in his chapter "The Fruitful Cut" in *The Savage in Judaism,* 149–54).

52. Daniel Boyarin, "'This We Know to Be the Carnal Israel': Circumcision and the Erotic Life of God and Israel," *Critical Inquiry* 18 (Spring 1992): 492. In order to be able as an adult voluntarily to open himself to God, the male child was first involuntarily opened and feminized, Boyarin says, through the ritual cutting of circumcision: "at a traditional circumcision ceremony the newly circumcised boy is addressed: 'And I say to you [feminine pronoun!]: In your [feminine] blood, you [feminine] shall live'" (496; his interpolations). Circumcision here brings the newborn infant into an initial, involuntary communion with God by "rendering the male somewhat feminine" (496); it provides an initial model for the adult male's voluntary communion.

Elliot Wolfson explains that the Rabbinical tradition emphasized "the nexus between circumcision and the appearance of God" ("Circumcision, Vision of God, and Textual Interpretation: From Midrashic Trope to Mystical Symbol," in *Circle in the Square: Studies in the Use of Gender in Kabbalistic Symbolism* [Albany: State University of New York Press, 1995], 31). Following Wolfson, Boyarin interprets circumcision as providing Abraham with just this (feminized) ability to see God. To this end Boyarin cites from *Genesis Rabbah:* "It is written, 'This, after my skin will have been peeled off, but from my flesh, I will see God?' (Job 19:26). Abraham said, after I circumcised myself many converts came to cleave to this sign. 'But from my flesh, I will see God,' for had I not done this [circumcised myself], on what account would the Holy Blessed One, have appeared to me? 'And the Lord appeared to him'" (*Midrash Bereshit Rabbah,* 479/48:1 and 485/48:9; cited in "'This We Know to Be the Carnal Israel,'" 492). When such a mystical vision "is interpreted as a penetration by the divine word or spirit into the body and soul of the adept," the result is "an image of sexuality in which the mystic is figured as the female partner." For this reason, Boyarin writes, "circumcision is understood by the midrash as feminizing the male, thus making him open to receive the divine speech and vision of God." For the male to be divinely penetrated, is, in the words of another midrashic text cited by Boyarin, for him to become one of "the Daughters of Zion" ("'This We Know to Be the Carnal Israel,'" 494–95).

53. That the infant God rescues is female reinforces the rite's feminizing motifs. It also brings into the open what Nancy Jay has called the "final patrilineal triumph" of

the Torah's P redactor ("Sacrifice, Descent, and the Patriarchs," 70; cited in Hoffman, *Covenant of Blood*, 44), a view Hoffman endorses: "my whole point is that the Rabbis made Judaism inseparable from the male lifeline. Like it or not, they had no idea of a female lifeline. They identify Jewish culture in its fullness only with men's concerns, men's growth, men's maturity; women exist officially only insofar as they enter the orbit of men" (*Covenant of Blood*, 25). The circumcision ceremony, itself an identity rite, repeats this expropriating identification when it inserts verse 16:6 from the longer Ezekiel narrative. That is, the ritual citation of a single verse cuts off that part of the narrative which foregrounds the female lifeline.

54. Such recognition is part of a complex semiotic system that links covenant, circumcision, cutting off, exile and exile overcome, different actions of opening or being opened, different actions of closing or sealing, signs, revelatory vision, the mouth, the gift, receptivity, paternal transfer, and so on. Several linkages in this system are evident when Ezekiel opens himself to God. "In the thirtieth year, in the fourth month, on the fifth day of the month . . . the heavens were opened [*pâathach*], and I saw visions of God," he declares (1:1). God directs him to "Open [*patsah*] your mouth, and eat what I give you," and thereupon stretches out a hand with a written scroll (2:8–9). "So I opened my mouth, and he gave me the scroll to eat" (3:2). Having eaten, Ezekiel here accepts and countersigns the divine gift by committing himself to a life of retransmitting the divine words, giving them to be eaten in turn, in a process of witnessing that opens the eyes of others to the possibility of being opened to "visions of God."

Wolfson underscore the visionary power of circumcision, which "is the vestibule or portal through which one must pass if one is to have a visionary experience of God. The *opening* of circumcision results in an *opening up* to God, a receptivity, that enables one to stand in God's presence and to behold the glory." By this reasoning, "in a fundamentally ontological sense, only one who is circumcised has an eye that is *open*." Again, circumcision "is an *opening*, a removal of closure, which corresponds objectively to a disclosure of God" ("Circumcision" in *Circle in the Square*, 34–35; my emphases).

According to Wolfson, circumcision "opens" the male to "the visualization of God" in multiple ways. Deontologically, circumcision reminds the male that "through the doing of good deeds, that is, through fulfilling God's commandments, one is rewarded" with an "epiphany of God." Ontologically, circumcision signifies "that only one whose sexual organ is circumcised can stand in the presence of God's glory." Hermeneutically, circumcision involves "the movement from closure to openness," of which the study of the Torah is "a structural re-enactment" ("Circumcision," in *Circle in the Square*, 47).

It also participates in the establishment of "male descent lines" and "is of a piece with P's lengthy male-only genealogies." Again, "a covenant made with Abraham, but not with Sarah, is sealed with a sign that is itself an iconic reminder that being male, not female, is what matters." Over time the rabbis "elaborate the covenantal sign of circumcision into a lengthy ritual from which women as mothers will eventually be eliminated altogether" (Hoffman, *Covenant of Blood*, 44, 42, and 47–48).

Although circumcision may be understood as "a male erasure of the female role in procreation" ("'This We Know to Be the Carnal Israel,'" 496n64), Boyarin is inclined to interpret the ritual surgery "not as exclusion of the female so much as inclusion of the male in filiation" (497)—that is, as the inclusion of the male in the reproductive enterprise of assuring a genealogical future.

55. Bakan, *And They Took Themselves Wives*, 141–42.

56. Bakan, *The Duality of Human Existence: Isolation and Communion in Western Man* (Boston: Beacon Press, 1966), 217.

57. Freud, *Introductory Lectures on Psychoanalysis, Standard Edition*, vol. 15, 165.

58. Bakan, *The Duality of Human Existence*, 216.

59. Eilberg-Schwartz, *God's Phallus*, 141.

60. Karen Ericksen Paige and Jeffery M. Paige, *The Politics of Reproductive Ritual* (Berkeley: University of California Press, 1981), 128.

61. Ibid., 149 and 156–57.

62. Ibid., 147. The Paiges oppose their "kin-group loyalty hypothesis" to the psychoanalytic explanation. Because the prospect of lineage fission involves issues of "kin-based power," the conflicts associated with it pertain to "adults, not children, and rational questions of power and success, not children's dreams of omnipotence and revenge. The dilemma of fission, then, unlike the dilemma of Oedipus, is a problem for adults and is rooted in the social structure of adult society. If the dilemma of fission is the source of circumcision or any other ritual practice, it will not require a theoretical detour through infant personality, Oedipal rebellions against the primal father, or neurotic primitives" (125).

63. Ibid., *The Politics of Reproductive Ritual*, 147.

64. "The absence of castration in strong fraternal interest group societies actually indicates the political weakness of these systems. Patriarchs must extend the right to ultimate power to their descendants and collaterals in order to win their loyalty even though this means sharing power and, if a lineage fission occurs, losing some" (Paige and Paige, *The Politics of Reproductive Ritual*, 144).

65. *Midrash Bereshit Rabbah*, 480 (48:5); cited in Wolfson, "Circumcision," 32–33. See also Bakan, who notes that "commentary has often identified the circumcision ceremony with the almost-sacrifice of Isaac on Mt. Moriah" (Bakan, *And They Took Themselves Wives*, 142).

66. Wolfson, "Circumcision," 144 n 26.

67. Cited in *And They Took Themselves Wives*, 142. More recently Hoffman traces the development by which the Rabbis came to symbolize the blood of the paschal lamb by the blood of the circumcision, and then to symbolize this blood by wine, in the process "replac[ing] the fertility symbolism of the Bible with blood as a symbol of salvation. In this blood symbolism, they merged the two biblical concepts of covenant—sacrifice (from Genesis 15) and circumcision (from Genesis 17). Blood now became the dominant symbol of covenant, both sacrificially (as the lamb) and through circumcision." What is more, if "one form of blood recalls the other," if "the blood of the paschal lamb and the blood of circumcision become merged because both are items given by God specifically to effect salvation," both are "recollected" in each rite's respective use of wine (*Covenant of Blood*, 109).

68. Commenting on Exodus 13:13, Hertz claims that the law of redemption "is in direct opposition to the practice of the heathen Semitic peoples of sacrificing their firstborn" (*Pentateuch and Haftorahs*, 262 n 13). Birnbaum explains that the law in question requires an investment: "Originally, the first-born sons belonged to the service of God. Later, instead of the first-born of all the tribes, the Levites were chosen for service in connection with the sanctuary. In return for this, every first-born Israelite was to be redeemed by paying five shekels to a *kohen* [priest], descendant of Levi" (*Daily Prayer Book/Ha-siddur Ha-shalem*, trans. Philip Birnbaum [New York: Hebrew Publishing Company, 1949], 749–50n). If an economic obligation here replaces the practice of infanticide sacrifice, such payment nevertheless reveals the infanticidism of the law.

69. Eilberg-Schwartz, "The Fruitful Cut," *The Savage in Judaism*, 146.

70. Ibid., 146–47.

71. In his commentary on God's covenant with Abraham, Hertz provides another example of the deep association between circumcision and infanticide, this time with circumcision serving as the stimulus for the infanticidal persecution of the Jew. Listing the atrocities that Jews have suffered for defending the fundamental rite of Judaism, Hertz

includes not only their own deaths but the deaths of their infants: "Jewish men and women have in all ages been ready to lay down their lives in its defence. The Maccabean martyrs died for it. The officers of King Antiochus put to death the mothers who initiated their children into the Covenant—'and they hanged their babes about their necks' (I Maccabees I,16)" (*The Pentateuch and Haftorahs*, 58n10). Whether it is too much to suggest that the fatal ligature marks around the infant's neck left by the noose bespeak the killer's rage at the sight of the circumcised body of the Jew, the involuntary martyrdom of these child victims testifies to the infanticidal violence that circumcision and the faith it symbolizes here have not been able to avert. Indeed, in Hertz's remarks the image of the hanging child stands for the entire spectrum of persecutions, for persecution itself, turning the attribution of child murder back on the European tradition that so accused the Jew. On this matter, see, for example, R. Po-chia Hsia, *The Myth of Ritual Murder: Jews and Magic in Reformation Germany* (New Haven: Yale University Press), 1988.

72. Leo Strauss, "The Beginning of the Bible and Its Greek Counterparts," in Harold Bloom, ed., *Genesis*, (New York: Chelsea House, 1986), 37.

73. The word for overthrowing, *haphak*, signifies a turning about or over and can mean "opposite" ("Hebrew and Chaldee Dictionary," *HGSB*, 33). God opposes and overturns the cities by means of a holocaustal action, the "rain of fire," that is itself oppositional in its imagery. As will become evident in the next chapter, this oxymoron unites what is kept separate in the stories of Ishmael and Isaac—the water (below ground) Ishmael and Hagar discover when they chance upon a well and the ritual conflagration Abraham is to set atop Mount Moriah.

74. The Hebrew for *grew* derives from *tsamach*, to sprout ("Hebrew and Chaldee Dictionary," *HGSB*, 100).

75. Eilberg-Schwartz, "Creation, Classification, and the Genealogy of Knowledge," *The Savage in Judaism*, 218–21.

76. Bakan, *The Duality of Human Existence*, 216.

77. Perhaps in deference to the covenant given to her and Abram, Sarai holds back from seeking the boy's destruction.

78. Kselman, "Genesis," 100.

79. Although Abraham gives some bread and water to Hagar when he sends her away, his provisioning is insufficient to insure her survival or that of her son (21:14). The difference in timing between his gift and God's underscores the life-threatening aggression embodied in his dispatch of the mother and child.

80. Sarah is Abraham's half sister: she is, Abraham tells Abimelech, "the daughter of my father but not the daughter of my mother" (20:12).

81. Estrin, "Finders Keepers," 69.

82. Estrin believes that, "as father, [Abraham] saves the son he himself condemned" but does so "unawares." And yet she sees no irony in crediting Abraham for having *inadvertently* provided the means of saving his son from death—a death, she neglects to mention, to which he had *deliberately* given him over. "The well of water [Abraham] provides signifies at once man's creative and procreative powers. With it, Abraham ensures Ishmael's manhood; his sexual future is guaranteed by the narrator. As Ishmael's father, Abraham gives to his son his future, baptising him and restoring him to his position as seed bearer" ("Finders Keepers," 70). In eliding the mediating intervention of God in Ishmael's salvation, she transforms what would have been Abraham's fatal repudiation of his son into a transitive gift of generativity: Abraham does not condemn but rather "insures" his son's "manhood"; not God but Abraham gives Ishmael his life and future paternity. Readings like Estrin's evade the issue of the father's orphaning violence.

83. Other challenges to primogeniture—Jacob's deception in order to receive the birthright belonging to his older brother Esau (25:29–34 and 27:1–45) and Jacob's bless-

ing at the end of his life of the younger of his grandsons over the older (48:1–22) — also complicate the coming to pass of the covenantal beatitude.

84. *Abimelech* means "the father is king"; *Abraham* means "the father is high" or "exalted." Both names, then, denote precisely what is in doubt for the respective bearers of those names — paternal generativity. The doubt appears to be removed when Abimelech returns Sarah to Abraham. Thereafter Abimelech and the other members of his household bear children, and so too does Sarah. However, the bearing of children solves the problem of fertility but not of responsibility, the political question that transforms the matter of consanguinity into a matter of descent and that determines Abraham's "fatherhood." Sarah's insistence that Hagar and Ishmael be exiled so attests.

In the relation of Abraham and Abimelech, each a would-be father, control over Sarah's reproductivity is the other side of the alliance between the two men. That alliance is the textual condition of the future paternity that is inscribed in their respective names. Ishmael's survival, however, recalls the sacrificial context of the father's name and the paternity it would safeguard. What neither party to the treaty acknowledges, and what the narrative itself states only by indirection, is that kinship, alliance, and descent take place against an infanticidal backdrop. To the contrary, the narrative, and perhaps each party to the pact, intends the well and its life-giving water to serve as the symbol of the paternity-protecting alliance. And yet the site of the well is the place where the father-abandoned son and his mother would have died but for the intervention of God. The well thus functions as an architectural memorial to the reproductive politics — which is to say, the infanticidal politics — involved in the establishment of Isaac's birthright at Ishmael's expense.

85. Estrin, "Finders Keepers," 71.

86. Ibid.

87. Fokkelman, "Genesis," 42–43.

CHAPTER 4
REFUSING THE INFANTICIDAL

1. Erich Auerbach, *Mimesis: The Representation of Reality in Western Literature*, trans. Willard R. Trask (Princeton: Princeton University Press, 1953), 23. "The two styles, in their opposition, represent basic types: on the one hand fully externalized description, uniform illumination, uninterrupted connection, free expression, all events in the foreground, displaying unmistakable meanings, few elements of historical development and of psychological perspective; on the other hand, certain parts brought into high relief, others left obscure, abruptness, suggestive influence of the unexpressed, 'background' quality, multiplicity of meanings and the need for interpretation, universal-historical claims, development of the concept of the historically becoming, and preoccupation with the problematic" (23).

2. Ibid.

3. Moriah borders the valley of Hinnom, the name of which was later corrupted into "Gehenna," meaning hell. Hinnom was the place where children were made to pass through the sacrificial fire to Molech. "Ahaz and Manasseh were guilty of this abomination (II Chron. 28:3; 33:6). Jeremiah foretold that God would visit this awful wickedness with sore judgment, and would cause such a destruction of the people that the valley would become known as the valley of slaughter (Jer. 3:31–34; 19:2, 6; 32:35)" (John D. Davis, *The Westminster Dictionary of the Bible*, rev. and rewritten by Henry Snyder Gehman [Philadelphia: Westminster Press, 1944], 235).

4. The text uses *Elohim*, "the generic term for God or Gods" (W. Gunther Plaut, ed., *The Torah: A Modern Commentary* [New York: Union of American Hebrew Congregations, 1981], 149). The text also uses a verb, *nāsāh*, sometimes translated as "tempted" in the sense of putting Abraham to the test (see *HGSB*, 1637, and J. H. Hertz, ed., *The Soncino Edition of the Pentateuch and Haftorahs*, 2nd ed [London: Soncino Press, 1971], 74n1.

5. J. P. Fokkelman, "Genesis," in Robert Alter and Frank Kermode, eds., *The Literary Guide to the Bible* [Belknap Press/Harvard University Press, 1987], 39.

6. Ibid., 50.

7. Barbara L. Estrin, "Finders Keepers: Preservation and the Biblical Foundling," *Mosaic* 11.1 (Fall 1977): 70.

8. Fokkelman, "Genesis," 50.

9. Louis Jacobs, "The Problem of the *Akedah* in Jewish Thought," in Robert L. Perkins, ed., *Kierkegaard's "Fear and Trembling": Critical Appraisals* (University: University of Alabama Press, 1981), 1. Jacobs identifies sixteen passages in which the Bible condemns child sacrifice: Leviticus 18:21 and 20:1–8, Deuteronomy 12:31 and 18:10, 2 Kings 3:27, 16:3, 17:17, 17:31, 21:6, and 23:10, 2 Chronicles 28:3 and 33:6, Jeremiah 7:31 and 19:5, Ezekiel 20:31, and Micah 6:7. Bakan, who infers from the repeated injunctions against infanticide that the image of the holocaustal sacrifice of the child represented "not only a psychological tendency, but one which was at least sometimes 'acted out,'" lists several additional passages: Judges 11:3–40, 1 Kings 11:7, Psalms 106:37–38, Isaiah 57:5, and Jeremiah 32:35 (*Duality of Human Existence*, 205 and 205n4). In *Slaughter of the Innocents* Bakan recalls that the origin of the New Testament word for hell, *Gehenna*, derives from *Ge-Hinnom*, with *Hinnom* being the name of "a valley near Jerusalem which the prophets railed against as the place where the children were destroyed" (28–29).

10. Jacobs, "The Problem of the *Akedah* in Jewish Thought," 1.

11. In the future, Job will be rewarded for having "spoken of me *what is right*" in contrast to his interlocutors who, because they have not so spoken, are condemned to "offer up for yourselves a burnt offering" (Job 42:7–8; my emphasis). In other words, God demands sacrifice not from Job—whose "righteousness" leads to the blessing of living long enough that he "saw his children, and his children's children, four generations" (42:16)— but from those whom he declares have spoken amiss. The implication is that generativity comes to those who can see their way beyond sacrifice, unlike Job's interlocutors, who remain trapped in a sacrificial ideology. If it is not right to sacrifice, what does Abraham's willingness to obey an infanticidal order indicate vis-à-vis Job's exemplarity?

For the infanticidal implications of sacrifice in the book of Job, see David Bakan, *Disease, Pain, and Sacrifice: Toward a Psychology of Suffering* (Boston: Beacon Press, 1971), 93–128.

12. Søren Kierkegaard, *"Fear and Trembling" and "The Sickness Unto Death"*, trans. Walter Lowrie (Garden City: Doubleday/Anchor Books, 1954), 67.

13. Kierkegaard, *Fear and Trembling*, 41. Kierkegaard adds that this is the case insofar as the ethical "reposes immanently in itself" and "has nothing without itself which is *telos*, but is itself *telos* for everything outside it" (41).

14. In the "Prelude" to *Fear and Trembling* Kierkegaard imagines how Abraham might seek to protect his son from losing faith in a God who turned out to be murderous—that is, by pretending that the call to sacrifice is his own desire, not God's. "Then for an instant [Abraham] turned away from [Isaac], and when Isaac again saw Abraham's face it was changed, his glance was wild, his form was horror. He seized Isaac by the throat, threw him to the ground, and said, 'Stupid boy, dost thou then suppose that I am thy father? I am an idolater. Does thou suppose that this is God's bidding? No, it is my desire.' Then Isaac trembled and cried out in terror, 'O God in heaven, have compassion upon me. . . . If I have no father upon earth, be Thou my father!' But Abraham in a low voice

said to himself, 'O Lord in heaven, I thank Thee. After all it is better for him to believe that I am a monster, rather than that he should lose faith in Thee'" (27). In this fictional exegesis, Kierkegaard's Abraham renounces his own fatherhood and assumes the mask of a monstrous idolater in order to motivate his son to seek in God the paternal "compassion" that the terrified boy thinks is his last hope.

15. Jacobs, "The Problem of the *Akedah*," 1. But see Plaut, who writes that because "the practice of human sacrifice . . . was well-known to the ancients and central to the cults of Israel's neighbors," Abraham might very well "have considered the command to sacrifice his son entirely legitimate," for it is a command that "other elohim could and did make" (Plaut, *The Torah*, 149). Perhaps for this reason Abraham responds immediately, apparently without question, and evidently too familiar with the ritual prescriptions surrounding holocaustal sacrifice to need briefing on the requisite protocol. "So Abraham rose early in the morning, saddled his ass, and took two of his young men with him, and his son Isaac; and he cut the wood for the burnt offering, and arose and went to the place of which God had told him" (22:3).

16. Milton Steinberg, "Kierkegaard and Judaism," in *Anatomy of Faith* (New York: Harcourt, Brace, 1960), 147.

17. Nahum M. Sarna, *Understanding Genesis* (New York: Schocken, 1966), 159.

18. Jon D. Levenson, *The Death and Resurrection of the Beloved Son: The Transformation of Child Sacrifice in Judaism and Christianity* (New Haven: Yale University Press, 1993), 113.

19. YHWH or JHWH—Yehôwâh—is the Jewish national name for God. "In the late Hellenistic period the stage is reached when the use of the name JHWH was forbidden to the people on the ground of shielding it from irreverence. The name was still pronounced in the temple by the high priest when blessing or in prayer, but in the synagogue, in prayer and in reading from the OT, it was pronounced *Adhonai* (Lord) . . . A consequence of this close association of the divine name with *Adhonai* was that, when the Massoretes (sixth to seventh centuries AD) supplied vowels to the Hebrew consonantal text, they gave JHWH the vowels of *Adhonai*," which "produced the form *Jehovah*" (Alan Richardson, ed., *A Theological Word Book of the Bible* (New York: Macmillan, 1955), 96.

20. Plaut, *The Torah*, 149. For a recent overview of the "source-critical" issues involved in the names of God in the *akedah* narrative, see James R. Davila, "The Name of God at Moriah: An Unpublished Fragment from 4QGenExoda," *Journal of Biblical Literature* 110.4 (1991): 577–82.

21. E. Wellisch, *Isaac and Oedipus: A Study in Biblical Psychology of the Sacrifice of Isaac— The Akedah* (London: Routledge and Kegan Paul, 1954), 91.

22. Ibid.

23. The concept of an "exchange" of gods is itself a rationalized form of the very sacrifice Wellisch sees this exchange as foreclosing. In replacing Elohim by the real God, God Himself, Abraham would be giving up his allegiance to a sacrificial god in order to obey a God who commands this mortal not to sacrifice. How should this relinquishment be characterized? If it is a surrender, a renunciation, or an abandonment, is it not also a sacrifice? Would not Abraham's action of giving up the inferior deity in order to give himself to the true God be tantamount to sacrificing the god of sacrifice? And would not this commitment be demanded of him in the name of the non-sacrificial God whose truth, insofar as Wellisch and others locate God's truth in the divine injunction against sacrifice, nevertheless manifested a sacrificial nature? Wellisch wants the *akedah* to be about the transcendence of sacrifice. But the means of transcendence— giving up faith in the elohim and putting faith in Yehôwâh (Adonai)—relies on the sacrificial movement, which it unselfconsciously incorporates.

24. Plaut, *The Torah*, 149. And yet, in the same breath Plaut suggests that because "the practice of human sacrifice . . . was well-known to the ancients and central to the cults

of Israel's neighbors," Abraham might very well "have considered the command to sacrifice his son entirely legitimate," for it is a command that "other elohim could and did make" (149). On the one hand, then, Plaut denies that "Abraham's religion" countenances the very command that, on the other hand, he here speculates Abraham might take for granted. Plaut's (unacknowledged) interpretive ambivalence characterizes the commentary on the *akedah* in general.

25. Hertz, *The Pentateuch and Haftorahs*, 201.

26. Sarna, *Understanding Genesis*, 161 and 162.

27. Shalom Spiegel, *The Last Trial: On the Legends and Lore of the Command to Abraham to Offer Isaac as a Sacrifice: The Akedah,* trans. Judah Goldin (Woodstock, NY: Jewish Lights, 1993), 63–64.

28. Ibid., 73.

29. Paul G. Mosca, "Child Sacrifice in Canaanite and Israelite Religion: A Study of *Mulk* and *mlk*," Ph.D. diss., Harvard University, 1975, 237; cited in Levenson, *The Death and Resurrection of the Beloved Son*, 112.

30. According to Levenson, "the major etiological function of the story of the binding of Isaac" is not to explain the advent of the taboo against child sacrifice but "to account for the establishment of a particular cult-site" (*The Death and Resurrection of the Beloved Son,* 114). To this end the story only partially repudiates the practice of child sacrifice: it responds with aversion to the prospect of the child's immolation while yet incorporating the specter of just that form of burnt offering as a divinely sanctioned responsibility.

31. Sarna, *Understanding Genesis*, 161; my emphasis.

32. When God says "Abraham," Abraham answers without the slightest hesitation and with an absolute openness to whatever order is to come: "Here I am," he says, in Hebrew "*Hinne-ni*," which means something like "behold me," Auerbach notes. In other words, Abraham is avowing his "moral position in respect to God . . . Here am I awaiting thy command" (*Mimesis*, 8). As soon as he is told what he is to do, Abraham immediately "rose early in the morning . . . and set out and went to the place in the distance that God had shown him" (22:3). According to Auerbach, "'early in the morning' is given, not as an indication of time, but for the sake of its ethical significance; it is intended to express the resolution, the promptness, the punctual obedience of the sorely tried Abraham" (*Mimesis*, 10). Hertz, too, emphasizes the promptitude of Abraham, who "lost no time in obeying the will of God" (74 n 3).

Wellisch, however, believes Abraham is deeply troubled by God's instruction. Although Abraham "set out on his journey immediately, he did not obey the command to kill Isaac simply and blindly as some commentators describe. He began his journey with an agonizing conflict. It was an inner struggle as agonizing and important as the struggle of Jesus when he set out on his way to Gethsemane" (*Isaac and Oedipus*, 82). In supplying what the narrative does not about Abraham's state of mind, Wellisch is able to read the narrative as Abraham's moral revelation, the "realization that God demanded life and not death" (89).

33. Hertz, *The Pentateuch and Haftorahs*, 74 n 1.

34. Immanuel Kant, *The Philosophy of Law: An Exposition of the Fundamental Principles of Jurisprudence as the Science of Right,* trans. W. Hastie (Edinburgh: T. & T. Clark, 1887; rpt. Clifton: Augustus M. Kelley, 1974), 115.

35. Jacobs, "The *Akedah* in Jewish Thought," 7.

36. Franz Rosenzweig, *Star of Redemption*, 2nd ed., trans. William W. Hallo (London: Routledge and Kegan Paul, 1971), 266.

37. Ibid.

38. Rosenzweig here rewrites the cognitive consequence of the fall from grace: unable to know God but able to know that they cannot know him, humans can transcend the limits to their self-consciousness by trusting a God who clothes himself in layers of de-

ception. Chapters 8 and 9 will return to the question of irony in the Greek depictions of the gods and their calls for sacrifice.

39. Emmanuel Levinas, *Noms propres* (Montpellier: Fata Morgana, 1976), 113; cited in Derrida, *The Gift of Death*, 78n6.

40. As Martin Buber has written, to Isaac, God must appear as a "sublime 'Terror.'" Why? "It is part of the basic character of this God that he claims the entirety of the one he has chosen; he takes complete possession of the one to whom he addresses himself. . . . Such taking away is part of his character in many respects. He promises Abraham a son, gives him and demands him back in order to make a gift of him afresh; and for this son he remains a sublime 'Terror'" (cited in *The Book of J,* trans. David Rosenberg, interpreted by Harold Bloom [New York: Grove Weidenfeld, 1990], 207).

41. Spiegel, *The Last Trial,* 3.

42. Ibid., *The Last Trial,* 3–4, 7, and 7.

43. Cited in Avivah Gottlieb Zornberg, *Genesis: The Beginning of Desire* (Philadelphia and Jerusalem: Jewish Publication Society, 5755, 1995), 125.

44. Ibid., 124; Zornberg's interpolation.

45. Ibid., 123.

46. In *Isaac and Oedipus,* E. Wellisch interprets the *akedah* as an allegory of psychosocial, specifically moral, development in which Abraham lets go of his infanticidal hostility toward his son: "When in the last moment God commanded him not to lay his 'hand upon the lad' he could not fully accept this immediately but wanted to shed at least a little of Isaac's blood. Abraham, in this impulse, wanted to modify the infanticidal act by at least inflicting a vicarious injury to the son. . . . But God said further: 'Neither do thou any thing unto him.' This changed Abraham's heart completely and extinguished the last trace of his Laius Complex" (76).

The ending of Leonard Cohen's song "Story of Isaac" tropes against the kind of salute Wellisch and others find in Abraham's victory over his infanticidal violence. In the fourth stanza of Cohen's lyric Abraham overcomes his ambivalence to openly avow his desire to slay his son: "When it all comes down to dust, / I will kill you if I must, / I'll help you if I can. / When it all comes down to dust, / I will help you if I must, / I'll kill you if I can" (*Stranger Music* [Leonard Cohen, Stranger Music, Inc., 1993; New York: Vintage/Random House, 1994], 140. Cohen here attests to an anxiety not included in Harold Bloom's catalogs of influence-injuries (see, for example, *The Anxiety of Influence: A Theory of Poetry,* 2nd ed. [New York: Oxford University Press, 1997] and *Poetry and Repression: Revisionism from Blake to Stevens* [New Haven: Yale University Press, 1976]). If the so-called "strong poet" must protect against the overwhelming power of the precursor, this same writer must also try to escape being supplanted by successor writers. Such efforts invariably involve symbolic forms of infanticide—that is, forms of silencing in advance the voices of writers-to-come.

Why did Freud not explore this tactic of defense? Indeed, why did he never attempt a reading of the *akedah?* Yael S. Feldman touches on the connection between the two questions: "if Freud was—consciously or unconsciously—searching for a masterplot that would represent the Romantic defiance of authority which he saw as the motive force of his life (and which he generalized for the experience of secular modernism at large), he could not have found it in a monotheistic tradition that made the *Akedah* . . . its centerpiece. Greek mythology, with its 'vertical' generational struggle, with its potential and actual infanticides and patricides, offered a better fit. Even here . . . Freud had to perform a little cosmetic surgery, ignoring Laius' initial action against his son and . . . locating his own starting point for the drama in Oedipus himself. Biblical narrative, on the other hand, particularly at the height of its stylistic austerity in the *Akedah* episode, could offer no such resource. Despite its dramatic potential (developed more fully in the various midrashic retellings of the story . . .), its textual repressions seem to be too successful to allow a full psychoanalytic interpretation, namely a meaningful analysis of unconscious fantasy and instinctual desire" ("'And Rebecca Loved Jacob,' but Freud Did Not," in Peter L. Rudnytsky and Ellen Handler Spitz, eds., *Freud and Forbidden Knowledge* [New York: New York University Press, 1994], 8–9). Behind Feldman's euphemism concerning Freud's "little [bit of] cosmetic surgery" in "ignoring Laius' initial action against his son," of course, is the (infanticidal) cutting that Laius performs or has his servants perform on his son's ankles prior to directing that the child be left to die of exposure on the barren slopes of Mount Cithaeron.

47. Spiegel, *The Last Trial*, 8.

48. See "Lexical Aids to the Old Testament," *HGSB*, 1606. *Dhāvar* "occurs more than 1400 times and is translated by no less than eighty-five different English words in the KJV! Some of the major meanings are: word, saying, speech, news, command, promise; thing, incident, occurrence, history, concern, cause, question, and lawsuit. The Ten Commandments are actually ten declarations or statements, words. . . . Sometimes *dhavar* is what is done, and sometimes it is a report of what is done. . . . The essential content of God's revelation is described by the phrase, 'the word of God came' (1 Chr. 17:3). 'The word of the Lord' was a technical expression for prophetic revelation 225 times in singular form" (*HGSB*, 1606).

49. Fokkelman, "Genesis," 50.

50. Estrin, "Finders Keepers," 70.

51. Wellisch, *Isaac and Oedipus*, 96.

52. Jacobs, "The *Akedah* in Jewish Thought," 9.

53. The infanticidal is not ontologically nihilating for the reason that it participates in what Derrida calls the quasi-transcendentalism of the *yes* that "opens the eventness of every event" without itself being an event ("A Number of Yes," trans. Brian Holmes, *Qui Parle?* 2.2 [Fall 1988]: 129).

CHAPTER 5
THE MOST COMMON EVENT IN THE WORLD

1. Rolf Rendtorff, "'Covenant' as a Structuring Concept in Genesis and Exodus," *Journal of Biblical Literature* 103.3 (1989): 387.

2. Søren Kierkegaard, *"Fear and Trembling" and "The Sickness Unto Death"*, trans. Walter Lowrie (New York: Doubleday/Anchor Books, 1954), 84, 86, and 77. Subsequent references to this work, abbreviated *FT*, will be included in the text.

3. Jacques Derrida, *The Gift of Death*, trans. David Wills (Chicago: University of Chicago Press, 1995), 67. Subsequent references to this work, abbreviated *GD*, will be included in the text.

4. Thus, the "paradoxical opposition" between the love of God and the love of Isaac is an opposition within love as such—within the love of either God or Isaac—between love and hate. That is, the purity of each relation is affected by the relation between one relation and another, such that the Kierkegaardian opposition turns in on itself, reduplicating its paradoxical effect within each of the opposing acts of love. In other words, if Abraham must love and hate, at one and the same moment, both God and Isaac, then his affective life becomes abyssal. The result is that as Abraham approaches "the great Other," in Derrida's phrase, the wholly alien nature of God forces Abraham to feel together what the ordinary meanings of love and hate hold apart.

5. Here, the *akedah* poses the problem of mimesis—Auerbach's representation of reality—with a vengeance.

6. Avivah Gottlieb Zornberg, *Genesis: The Beginning of Desire* (Philadelphia and Jerusalem: Jewish Publication Society, 5755, 1995), 121.

7. Ibid., 121.

8. Ibid.

9. Ibid.

10. Ibid., 122.

11. The death of the ram signifies the sacrificial economy of the world even when the world is conceived as consecrated by God. The death of Sarah repeats this signifying implication. In commenting on the midrashim that variously explain Sarah's death as a reaction to news of the *akedah*, Zornberg explains: "Isaac is saved, and the Shofar announces the possibility of redemption, of symbolic substitutions. But Sarah is not saved, and, in the world of her mind, Isaac is not saved, and yet the cries of her—and his— despair are retained in the liturgy and ritual, 'as an atonement' for her descendants" (*Genesis*, 124). The exegetical tradition knows what Zornberg here resists—that the sacrificiality of human sacrifice takes place in the very moment of the so-called "symbolic substitutions" by which human sacrifice is avoided. Insofar as the concept of "symbolic substitutions" conceals the cost of the life that a substitutive killing is instituted to protect, the concept partakes of the fatal literalism it would metaphorize away.

12. E. M. Cioran, *The Trouble with Being Born*, trans. Richard Howard (New York: A Richard Seaver Book/Viking, 1976), 4.

13. Derek Attridge, "On Mount Moriah—The Impossibility of Ethics," paper presented at the twenty-second annual English Department symposium, University of Alabama, Tuscaloosa, September 28–30, 1995.

14. As wholly other, God must die and nevertheless survive in every sacrifice, completed or withheld. An otherness that includes not only the living and the dead but that which can never exist, God "is" that which cannot be reduced to empirical existence, even of an infinite sort. If all that exists does so by virtue of the infinite loss that takes place through the infinite sacrifice of being, then as source of the world, God "is" its sacrificial condition of possibility. Chapter 9 will investigate how Jesus finds the greatest of good news only in an unswerving acceptance of God's infanticidity, the paradoxical source of his most radical teaching.

15. Jacques Derrida, "A Number of Yes," trans. Brian Holmes, *Qui Parle?* 2.2 (Fall 1988): 131.

16. A version of this gate reappears in the Passover celebration, which celebrates the redemption of the Israelites at the cost of their enemy's generativity, overtly figured in the infanticidal deaths of the firstborn Egyptian children.

17. The narrating voice in Graham Greene's novel *The Power and the Glory* (New York: Viking, 1968, Uniform ed.) bespeaks the anguish that comes from being unable not to sacrifice the other others: "he remembered his child . . . . He said, 'Oh God, help her . . . let her live forever.' This was the love he should have felt for every soul in the world. . . . This is what I should feel all the time for everyone, and he tried to turn his brain away towards . . . a long succession of faces . . . for those were all in danger too. He prayed, 'God help them,' but in his moment of prayer he switched back to his child beside the rubbish-dump, and he knew it was for her only that he prayed. Another failure" (249–50). The sum of all souls for which love "should be felt all the time" is unreachable except by an act of (sacrificial) abstraction. Such an act asks the impossible. It requires one to apprehend the singularity of each individual's suffering; and yet it denies "everyone" his or her singular suffering precisely to the extent that it acknowledges the collective "all" rather than each one individually.

Suffering is cognate with *fertile*. Both ultimately derive from an Indo-European root meaning "to carry; also to bear children" (*The American Heritage Dictionary of Indo-European*

Roots, rev. and ed. Calvert Watkins [Boston: Houghton Mifflin Company], 7]. As its etymology indicates, *suffering* always remains linked to the evocation of the individual's reproductive advent and thus to the specter of infanticide. That is why Greene's narrator "switched back" from the "long succession of faces" to the person of the one child, "his" child, the "child beside the rubbish-dump," the incarnation of Job but in the figure of a young girl, who will not be rewarded as her biblical counterpart was after his afflictions. In memory it will be this impoverished child who will stand in for the impossible remembrance of everyone else; and it will be a place of waste that substitutes for all the other places of suffering. To be called to take account of the unknowable number of these sites in human history and prehistory is to confront the frightful prospect, in George Bataille's words, that "the ground we live on is little other than a field of multiple destructions" (*The Accursed Share: An Essay on General Economy*, vol. I, *Consumption*, trans. Robert Hurley [New York: Zone Books, 1991], 23). As the protagonist of *The Power and the Glory* apprehends, this field is infanticidal.

18. "We know that justice—justice to the absolute singularity of the other, the person, the case, the text—is impossible, and that it happens. Abraham does justice to the absolute singularity of Jehovah, of the command, the call. We can't say how he does it, he can't say how he does it, but he does it, and without hesitation. But he also decides, and it is the same decision to do the worst possible *injustice* to his son. And if the act of doing justice is always also the act of doing an injustice, ethical acts—acts which involve no injustice—cannot happen" (Attridge, "On Mount Moriah").

19. The association of fatherhood and ascension is thematic as well as etymological. According to J. H. Hertz the second half of Abram's new name, *raham*, "is an Arabic word for 'multitude.' The change of name emphasizes the mission of Abraham, which is 'To bring all the peoples under the wings of the Shechinah'" (*The Pentateuch and Haftorahs*, 2nd ed [London: Soncino Press, 1971], 58 n 5). The Shechinah, the (high, soaring, or exalted) emanation of God's spirit, seeks the father who is able to transcend the differences that would otherwise divide his people, the father who is able metaphorically to rise above these differences on "the wings of the Shechinah."

20. Zornberg, *Genesis*, 21.

21. I have been told there is a midrashic commentary which affirms this connection.

22. Preparatory to Hagar's expulsion (21:14) "Abraham places (Heb. *sam*) bread and water on Hagar's back"; in preparation for the burnt offering of his second son (22:6), "Abraham places (Heb. *yasem*) the wood for the holocaust upon Isaac." The parallel actions suggest that each exposure to death is equivalent to the other. "In chap. 21, Ishmael's expulsion, demanded by Sarah and approved by God, is carried out by Abraham, although it means the death of the child who was legally Sarah's. In chap. 22, Isaac, born to Sarah after long infertility, now is taken from her by Abraham's obedience to his apparent death. Both Ishmael and Isaac are exposed to death by the patriarch's obedience to God" (John S. Kselman, "Genesis," in James L. Mays, general ed., *Harper's Bible Commentary* [San Francisco: Harper and Row, 1979], 100).

Together, the two stories dramatize the general infanticidity of the world. In the story of Ishmael's expulsion, God's blessing precedes Abraham's action against his son; in the story of Isaac, God's blessing follows. The two stories justify the father's empirical violence in the name of a sacred blessing that is associated with the cause of that violence in the first narrative and its consequence in the second. The two stories thus distribute God's blessing before and after the paternal violence that would, in any naturalistic sense, ruin the very possibility of that blessing. In this way the two stories end with compensatory images of the future reproductively promised and preserved just when the human instantiation of the future is most threatened by the anti-reproductive action that God ordains. In other words the two episodes safeguard (genealogical) time itself by means of the infanticidal violence that would otherwise destroy the possibility of cross-generational transfer. Negating the paternal negations they demand, the blessings transform the threat of infanticide into the occasion and means of transgenerational survival. Israel's history thereafter proceeds from out of Abraham's violence against each of his two "only sons."

This contradiction—which permeates the organization, economy, and value of both narratives—cannot be explained away without aggressing against the two texts. The contradiction must be honored. The two narratives show how. In particular, they reprieve Abraham from the consequence of his violent intentions (exile for Ishmael, sacrifice for Isaac), in order to compel this father to imagine infanticidism without infanticide. The two episodes force the father to recognize that his hand has already been uplifted and bloody in his treatment of Ishmael, even if he has not actually held a knife to this son's throat. Since both sacrifices proceed under God's aegis, they confront the father with his guilt at the very moment of his obedience—in other words throughout the entirety of his faithfulness. The two episodes, then, call Abraham to put a face—the face of his own sons—to the infanticidism that, when it does not eventuate in a literal death, must remain faceless.

23. The movement anticipates the cutting of the newborn Solomon orders when he submits two women, each claiming motherhood of the baby, to his notorious infanticidal testing (2 Chronicles 3–8). Solomon himself "used to offer a thousand burnt offerings," and did so "at the high places" (3:3–4). This is the same Solomon who built the temple, "the house of the Lord" (3:1), in the part of Jerusalem occupying Mount Moriah, the place where God appeared to his father, David. Solomon's threat to destroy the child in order to test the two women thus echoes the terms of God's test of Abraham and relies on the same instrument for the child's deliverance.

24. B. Gittin 43a; cited by Zornberg, *Genesis*, 33; Zornberg's interpolation.

25. Zornberg, *Genesis*, 33.

26. Ibid., 35; Zornberg cites from Bereshit Rabbah 27:4.

CHAPTER 6
COUNTER-CONCEIVING THE LAW OF THE FATHER

1. Louis Althusser, "Ideology and Ideological State Apparatuses (Notes towards an Investigation)," in *Lenin and Philosophy and Other Essays*, trans. Ben Brewster (New York: Monthly Press, 1971), 176.

2. Ibid.

3. *Subjectibility* might better designate the condition of the possibility of subject-formation. Subjectivation might be an alternative for the way a subject is subject to life-determining influences before it is a consciousness, before it is a person, and even before it is a living entity.

4. It is an indeterminate mark that determines his being as the mark personified. Because it is unspecified, however, it is a mark without mark, and it traces in the empirical destruction he has caused the more general infanticidism of anyone's life, of anyone's claim to existence, of anyone's God-proclaimed right to be. Since infanticidism is not something that exists but is the condition of the possibility of existence, it cannot be represented by conventional referential marks or signs.

5. Jacques Derrida, *Archive Fever: A Freudian Impression*, trans. Eric Prenowitz (Chicago: University of Chicago Press, 1995), 4 n 1.

6. Ibid., 3.

7. George Lakoff and Mark Johnson, *Metaphors We Live By* (Chicago: University of Chicago Press, 1980), 3.

8. Ibid., 5. Lakoff and Johnson employ this same vocabulary in their more recent

work, *Philosophy in the Flesh: The Embodied Mind and Its Challenge to Western Thought* (New York: Basic Books, 1999).

9. Jacques Derrida, "White Mythology: Metaphor in the Text of Philosophy," in *Margins of Philosophy*, trans. Alan Bass (Chicago: University of Chicago Press, 1982), 224.

10. As the third epigraph indicates, through its etymology the word *metaphor* delivers a reproductive image of the linguistic generativity that metaphor is typically conceived as producing. The concept of metaphor thus reproduces the metaphor of the concept. It does so, however, by hiding (from) its own metaphoricity.

11. Page duBois, *Sowing the Body: Psychoanalysis and Ancient Representations of Women* (Chicago: University of Chicago Press, 1988), 169–83.

12. Plato, *Phaedrus and Letters VII and VIII*, trans. Walter Hamilton (Harmondsworth: Penguin, 1973), 57.

13. Ibid., 98–99.

14. Plato, *Theaetetus*, trans. F. M. Cornford, in Edith Hamilton and Huntington Cairns, eds., *The Collected Dialogues of Plato* (Princeton: Princeton University Press/Bollingen Series 71, 1961), 918–19/210b-c.

15. Ibid., 918–19/21b–c.

16. Plato, *Symposium*, 206c; cited in duBois, *Sowing the Body*, 182; her trans. DuBois' translation underscores the maternal nature of the "procreancy" Socrates is eager to hear Diotima attribute to males. The more usual translations do not recognize this possible implication. In Walter Hamilton's translation Diotima says that "All men, Socrates, have a procreative impulse, both spiritual and physical, and when they come to maturity they feel a natural desire to beget children" (Plato, *The Symposium* [Harmondsworth: Penguin, 1951], 86). In Michael Joyce's translation: "We are all of us prolific, Socrates, in body and in soul, and when we reach a certain age our nature urges us to procreation" (in Hamilton and Cairns, *The Collected Dialogues of Plato*, 558/206c).

17. Ibid., trans. Joyce, 560/208e–209a.

18. Ibid., 561/209c.

19. Plato, *Laws*, trans. A. E. Taylor, in Hamilton and Cairns, *The Collected Dialogues of Plato*, 1404/VIII.838a.

20. Ibid., 1404/VIII.839a–b.

21. Jacques Derrida, "Plato's Pharmacy," *Dissemination*, trans. Barbara Johnson, (Chicago: University of Chicago Press, 1981), 153.

22. Plato, *Theaetetus*, 149c–d; cited in Derrida, "Plato's Pharmacy," 153; his trans.

23. Robert Con Davis, *The Paternal Romance: Reading God-the-Father in Early Western Culture* (Urbana: University of Illinois Press, 1993), 6.

24. Aristotle, *Generation of Animals*, rev. ed., trans. and ed. A. L. Peck (Cambridge: Harvard University Press, 1953), 385/4.2.765.b.

25. Davis, *The Paternal Romance*, 86.

26. Aristotle, *Generation of Animals*, 385/4.1.765b.

27. Ibid., 403/4.3.767b.

28. Ibid., 390/4.1.766a (note a).

29. Ibid., 403/4.3.767b.

30. Because the woman is, Aristotle says, "the opposite of the male," she lacks the metaphysical principle of the male's form. In consequence, she produces only an impure kind of semen that she is "unable to cause . . . to take shape or to discharge" (*Generation of Animals*, 385–871/4.767b). Due to her failure to "effect concoction" of her "residual" semen, she "does not succeed in reducing the material into its own proper form." She is, then, the negative image of the male, a near-eunuch, Aristotle claims (391/4.1.766a). Once again: "the female is as it were a deformed male; and the menstrual discharge is semen, though in an impure condition; *i.e.*, it lacks one constituent, and one only, the prin-

ciple of Soul" (175/2.3.737b). This principle, the generative force within reproduction, is male.

Aristotle's argument, duBois points out, relies on the trope of metonymy in contrast to Plato's argument, which relies on the trope of metaphor. Plato's metaphors initially set forth female fertility as the basis of the philosopher's analogous conceptual power. Aristotle, however, metonymically reclassifies the difference between male and female as a relation of whole to part: "the male body is whole and complete, having come to its *telos*, having achieved perfection; the female body is a part for the whole, a thing lacking completion . . . lacking soul" (*Sowing the Body*, 184).

31. Aristotle, *The Metaphysics*, trans. John H. McMahon (Buffalo: Prometheus Books, 1991), 83/4.5.1010a.

32. Medieval scholars formalized Aristotle's logic in diagrammatic "squares of opposition."

33. Aristotle, *Generation of Animals*, 255/2.8.748a.

34. Aristotle, *Metaphysics*, 24/1.5.986b.

35. In *Speculum of the Other Woman* (trans. Gillian C. Gill [Ithaca: Cornell University Press, 1985]), Luce Irigary explains how Plato grants to the father an epistemological privilege which enables him to survey the totality of the world and to control the field of representation through operations that are principally sacrificial.

36. Davis, *The Paternal Romance*, 84.

37. Derrida, "Plato's Pharmacy," 81.

38. *The Republic of Plato*, trans. Francis MacDonald Cornford (Oxford: Oxford University Press, 1945), 217/VI.506e.

39. *Tokos* can mean "a bringing forth, birth, the time of delivery" as well as "offspring, young child, son." In its metaphorical extension to economics, it signifies "the *produce* or *usance* of money lent out" (Liddell and Scott, *Greek-English Lexicon*, abridged ed. (Oxford: Clarendon Press, 1984), 709.

40. Derrida, "Plato's Pharmacy," 82.

41. Plato, *Republic*, VI.508c; cited in Derrida, "Plato's Pharmacy," 82; his trans.

42. Derrida, "Plato's Pharmacy," 82.

43. In "Structure, Sign, and Play in the Discourse of the Human Sciences" (in Richard Macksey and Eugenio Donato, eds., *The Structuralist Controversy: The Languages of Criticism and the Sciences of Man* [Baltimore: Johns Hopkins University Press, 1970]), Derrida explains the seemingly transcendental power of the concept of the center: "it has always been thought that the center, which is by definition unique, constituted that very thing within a structure which governs the structure while escaping structurality. This is why classical thought concerning structure could say that the center is, paradoxically, *within* the structure and *outside* it." And "because it can be either inside or outside," the center "is as readily called the origin as the end, as readily *arche* as *telos*." Nothing can substitute for the center; its singularity and irreplaceability therefore entail its presentability, and for this reason the concept of center inaugurates "a history of meaning [*sen* — that is, history, period—whose origin may always be revealed or whose end may always be anticipated in the form of presence" (248). And presence has always been paternal: it is the figure of the father, already manifest or about to be, who stands at the center that forms around and emanates from his being.

44. Derrida, "Plato's Pharmacy," 146.

45. Davis, *The Paternal Romance*, 4 and ix.

46. Jacques Derrida, *Of Grammatology*, corrected ed., trans. Gayatri Chakravorti Spivak (Baltimore: Johns Hopkins University Press, 1997), 20.

47. Ibid., *Speech and Phenomena and Other Essays on Husserl's Theory of Signs*, trans. David B. Allison (Evanston: Northwestern University Press, 1973), 77.

48. Ibid., 76.

49. Ibid., 77.

50. Ibid., *Of Grammatology*, 20.

51. Ibid.

52. Louis J. Sass, "Deep Disquietudes: Reflections on Wittgenstein as Antiphilosopher," in James C. Klagge, ed., *Wittgenstein: Biography and Philosophy* (Cambridge, New York: Cambridge University Press, 2001), 103. Troping against Plato's discussion of the form of the bed, Wittgenstein repeatedly uses the metaphor of sleep to register his ambivalence about the nature of philosophical thinking. "Sometimes he describes sleep, which involves release from self consciousness and other distractions, as a desirable state: 'And being able to work is in so many ways similar to being able to fall asleep.' . . . At other times he describes it as a kind of living death: 'One could imagine a person who from birth to death is always either sleeping or lives in a kind of half-sleep or daze. This is how my life relates to one that is really alive (I am just now thinking of Kierkegaard' . . ." (cited in Sass, 142n22).

53. Hannah Arendt, *The Life of the Mind*, vol. 1, *Thinking* (New York: Harcourt Brace Jovanovich, 1971), 78 and 197. In "Thought as Conception, Thought as Counter-Conception: The Example of Freud's Wolf-Man," I analyze Freud's notion of the death instinct as a "counter-conception," by which Freud resists the "archaic" tropology of philosophical conceptuality.

54. Paul Feyerabend, *Against Method* (London: Verso, 1978), 330 (my emphasis), 30, and 114.

55. Wittgenstein, cited by Sass, "Deep Disquietudes" 110.

56. Wittgenstein, cited by S. Stephen Hilmy, *The Later Wittgenstein: The Emergence of a New Philosophical Method* (New York: Basil Blackwell, 1987), 39.

57. Plato, *Timaeus*, trans. Benjamin Jowett, in Hamilton and Cairns, *The Collected Dialogues of Plato*, 776/89a.

58. Remarking the figurative nature of "conception," it would precipitate what Derrida calls "the metaphoric catastrophe" (*The Post Card: From Socrates to Freud and Beyond*, trans. Alan Bass [Chicago: University of Chicago Press], 46), which would disclose what the trope of conception hides—namely, the (infanticidal) deathliness within thought as such.

59. Marc Shell, *The End of Kinship: "Measure for Measure," Incest, and the Ideal of Universal Siblinghood* (Stanford: Stanford University Press, 1988), 4.

60. Ibid.

61. Some anthropologists believe that the so-called atom of kinship is "not the incest taboo, not the nuclear family, and not reciprocal exchange" but "the avunculate," the relation between the mother's brother and his nephew (Fox, *Reproduction and Succession: Studies in Anthropology, Law, and Society* [New Brunswick: Transaction, 1993], 231). The positions of the nephew and uncle, however, are no less social constructs, no less inscribed within a system of differential relations, than are any other kinship positions.

62. Davis, *The Paternal Romance*, 101.

63. Ibid.

Chapter 7
Sacrifice, Revenge, and a Justice Beyond Justice

1. Economization means, therefore, that the essential characteristic of life is not that it is alive but that in producing itself it simultaneously produces death. Indeed, life pro-

duces a general deathliness on which it depends in order to be what it is—alive. The consequence of this dependence, however, is that life contaminates itself through, alternatively that life is contaminated by, a nonliving element, a general -cidism that makes life infanticidal. No living thing—not life itself—can come into being except by bearing the constitutive trace of what it is not, except by a withdrawal of (infinite possibilities of) being simultaneous with the movement by which anything comes into its being.

2. Insofar as the futures in question are unknowable, so too is the loss. In consequence, the losses in question are themselves lost. The economy of lost opportunity is abyssal in its negativity.

3. Hugh Lloyd-Jones, *The Justice of Zeus* (Berkeley: University of California Press, 1971), 29.

4. George E. Dimock, *The Unity of the Odyssey* (Amherst: University of Massachusetts Press, 1989), 4 and 26.

5. Seth L. Schein, "Introduction," *Reading the Odyssey: Selected Interpretive Essays* (Princeton: Princeton University Press, 1996), 15, 6, and 5.

6. In other words, they economize on the hero's economization.

7. Richard Seaford, *Reciprocity and Ritual: Homer and Tragedy in the Developing City-State* (Oxford: Clarendon Press, 1994), 24.

8. *The Odyssey*, trans. Robert Fitzgerald (New York: Vintage Classics/Random House, 1990), 1.61 (book 1, lines 61). Subsequent references to this translation will include book number, for the first citation in a paragraph, followed by line number.

9. Zeus intervenes in and breaks the cycle of what Girard, in *Violence and the Sacred*, calls reciprocal violence. Zeus thus exhibits the sacrificial origin and nature of the power that, in Girard's view, underwrites judicial practices, which require "an independent legal authority" that has the right and power to punish without exciting a counter-violence in turn (21).

10. Sacralizing interpretations of the death Odysseus inflicts on the Suitors have difficulty analyzing the furious grief of the surviving relatives of the Suitors. Dimock, for example, acknowledges the suffering of the kinsmen but neither their sense of being terribly wronged nor their honor-bound duty to seek revenge. "On the one hand, there is the justice of Odysseus's punishment of the suitors; on the other, the terrible pain and anger of the fathers and brothers of the dead. How can these two claims ever be reconciled? The assembly of the suitors' kinsmen itself suggests two methods, and these are ultimately one and the same: recognition of the will of the gods, and recognition that the dead deserved to die—in other words, that justice takes precedence over vengeance" (*The Unity of the Odyssey*, 331). As has been argued, however, the will of Zeus is that the bloodshed cease before it destroys the entire kingdom, not that the kinsmen adopt the perspective of the victor, for whom Dimock believes "the dead deserved to die." Because the dying seldom pass this judgment on themselves, the view that they deserve the death penalty reveals not the truth but the economizing nature of an identification with the victor —here Odysseus.

The law may permit such one-sided identification. Justice does not. What Dimock calls "justice" is not justice at all but the revenge-driven quest to impose one's will on the other, which is precisely what Zeus remarks as the injustice that must stop. Odysseus is no different from the Suitors in his desire, only in his success, and then only until the kinsmen retaliate and a force greater than either must intervene to save everyone, not just the hero, at which point Odysseus is no different from his enemies in the eyes of Zeus. The new sense of justice that Zeus introduces requires mourning the dead, even, if not especially, the enemy dead, for the reason that any coming into being is unjust in the sense of occurring within an economy of infinite loss. Because life is a consequence of the infinite structural deathliness that the living beget in every moment of surviving, because life is a gift of death, neither the chance to live nor the loss of this chance can ever be a matter of the "good conscience" that believes in deservedness. Except for its two framing moments when the poem invokes a conception of justice as revenge only to introduce Zeus's repudiation of this conception, the *Odyssey* refuses to acknowledge the incalculable cost of the hero's restoration to power, for to do so would risk introducing a potentially inconsolable identification with the dead, hence would risk recognizing that the ostensible justice associated with Odysseus' triumph—his survival, his life—is an absolute injustice.

11. Joseph Russo, Manuel Fernandez-Galiano, and Alfred Heubeck, *A Commentary on Homer's Odyssey*, vol. 3, Books XVII–XXIV (Oxford: Clarendon Press, 1992), 96. According to Norman O. Brown, Autolykos is a man given to "stealthy appropriation" of property and "stealthiness and skill at the oath" (*Hermes the Thief: The Evolution of a Myth* [New York: Vintage/Random House, 1947], 6–8 and 11).

12. Russo, Fernandez-Galiano, and Heubeck, *A Commentary on Homer's Odyssey*, vol. 3, 97. See also Ralph Hexter, *A Guide to the Odyssey: A Commentary on the English Translation of Robert Fitzgerald* (New York: Vintage/Random House, 1993), 251.

13. Dimock, *The Unity of the Odyssey*, 13). According to Russo, Fernandez-Galiano, and Heubeck, "Because all occurrences" of the verb *odussamenos* "are in the aorist or perfect tense, we can only conjecture a present *odu(s)omai,* whose meaning is 'to become angry at' or 'to take a dislike to,' with some uncertainty as to whether *anger* or *hatred* (a possible cognate with Latin *odium*) or *pain* (a possible cognate with *oduma* or *oduromai*) is the fundamental meaning of this word." These meanings make Odysseus both "The Hater" and "The Hated," hence both the source of pain and a recipient of it. "Acknowledging the simultaneous presence of an active and passive meaning in Odysseus' name allows us to see him as a distant relative of the Trickster figure of folklore and mythology, who is both deceiver and victim of deception, both the cause of pain to others and the recipient of pain" (*A Commentary on Homer's Odyssey*, vol. 3, 97).

14. Russo, Fernandez-Galiano, and Heubeck note that "the boar's lair . . . closely resembles the shelter at the end of [book] v . . . in which the exhausted Odysseus finds protection from the cold by burying himself in the leaves, like a seed of fire to be reborn the next day. . . . It is surprising that there should be an underlying connection between the lair of Odysseus and the lair of the boar that gave him his identifying wound. The poet has perhaps made an unconscious association based on the concept of birth/rebirth. Just as the 'seed of fire' ensures that a new fire will be born, so Odysseus, in his encounter with the boar, will be (re)born as the man with the scar, which becomes the sign of his identity for those closest to him" (*A Commentary on Homer's Odyssey*, vol. 3 98).

15. See Hexter, *A Guide to the Odyssey*, 251, and Russo, Fernandez-Galiano, and Heubeck, *A Commentary on Homer's Odyssey*, vol. 3, 98.

16. Hexter, *A Guide to the Odyssey*, 249. Hexter notes that the stabbing by the boar "is only the first of the grooves in a narrative with several more insets or wounds, each of which has left its scar or groove" (249). He then all but identifies the infanticidal jeopardy signified by the wounding and its relation to the name given to Odysseus "in other regions and other traditions"—the name *Oulixes*, source of the English Ulysses. Odysseus, Hexter says, "receives this name, after a fashion, when the boar gives him his 'wound' (*oule*)." In punning on the injury that nearly destroyed his life and removed his identity, *Oulixes* emphasizes the nature of the name itself as a violent cutting, a symbolic inscription literalized in the physical injury. As Hexter writes, "a hero's name is like a deep wound: [Odysseus] can no more escape the fate of his name (a victim of odium and suffering) than erase the trace left by the wound, the scar" (250). Thus, *Oulixes* embodies the paradox of all proper names, which is that in conferring identity, they simultaneously

communicate the precariousness of the person's life, especially in infancy, when the withdrawal of recognition would spell its death.

17. Homer, *The Odyssey*, 2 vols., trans. A. T. Murray, rev. George E. Dimock (Loeb Classical Library/Harvard University Press, 1990), vol. 2, 269; see Fitzgerald, 19.560–61. Subsequent references to Murray and Dimock's translation will include the name of the authors, volume, and page number. Unless otherwise noted, all emphases are mine.

18. Dimock, *The Unity of the Odyssey*, 195.

19. At the end, the *Odyssey* emphasizes the infanticidal character of vengeance when it insists on the familial positions of Odysseus (who is the "dear father" of Telemakhos and twice called the "Son of Laertes"), Telemakhos (who is twice referred to as "son," once as "grandson," and once as a member of the "house of your forefathers"), Athena (who is six times identified as Zeus's child or daughter), the Suitors (who are on at least three occasions called "sons"), and Zeus himself (who is twice identified as "Father Zeus" as well as "son of Kronos") (24.385ff). The references to familial roles underscore the cross-generational context of Odysseus' violence. They also reflect the mythic lineage of Zeus himself, who escapes his father's infanticidal aggression just as Kronos had survived a similar fate at the hands of his father, Ouranos (see Hesiod's *Theogony* in *Hesiod: "Theogony," "Works and Days," "Shield,"* trans. Apostolos N. Athanassakis [Baltimore: Johns Hopkins University Press, 1983], in particular lines 126–210, 453–506, and 615–733). Having survived his divine father's aggression, Zeus in the *Odyssey* becomes "'Father of us all'" (line 64 and 24.522), "the father of gods and men" (1.44), whose interdiction of further violence reveals the infanticidal nature of vengeance, a nature Odysseus does not want to acknowledge.

20. Karl Reinhardt, "The Adventures in the *Odyssey*," in Schein, *Reading the Odyssey*, 79 and 81. (The verses in Fitzgerald's translation are at 9.187–88. Fitzgerald translates "without justice" as "lawless.")

21. They evidently have not mastered the technology of fire, live alone, and have only a rudimentary capacity for deception in particular and symbolic representation in general. See Claude Levi-Strauss, *The Raw and the Cooked: Introduction to a Science of Mythology: 1*, trans. John and Doreen Weightman (Chicago: University of Chicago Press, 1983).

22. Other references to olive trees, especially to the one that anchors Odysseus' marriage bed (23.181–204), reinforce its phallic connotations in the Kyklops episode.

23. See Marvin Harris, *Cannibals and Kings: The Origins of Cultures* (New York: Vintage/Random House, 1977) and *Good to Eat: Riddles of Food and Culture* (New York: Simon and Schuster, 1985).

24. See Seaford, *Reciprocity and Ritual*, especially ch. 1, "Polis, Household, and Reciprocity in Homer" (1–29) and ch. 2, "Marriage, Sacrifice, and Reciprocity in Homer" (30–73).

25. The losses — of vision and of his herd, his source of meat — Odysseus forces on the Kyklops allegorize the developmental process of introjecting the world. According to Nicolas Abraham and Maria Torok: "the initial stages of introjection emerge in infancy when the mouth's emptiness is experienced alongside the mother's simultaneous presence. The emptiness is first experienced in the form of cries and sobs, delayed fullness, then as calling, ways of requesting presence, as language. Further experiences include filling the oral void by producing sound and by exploring the empty cavity with the tongue in response to sounds perceived from the outside. Finally, the early satisfactions of the mouth, as yet filled with the maternal object, are partially and gradually replaced by the novel satisfactions of a mouth now empty of that object but filled with words pertaining to the subject. The transition from a mouth filled with the breast to a mouth filled with words occurs by virtue of the intervening experiences of the empty mouth. Learning

to fill the emptiness of the mouth with words is the initial model for introjection" ("Mourn-ing *or* Melancholia: Introdjection versus Incorporation," in *The Shell and the Kernel*, vol. 1, ed. and trans. Nicholas T. Rand [Chicago: University of Chicago Press, 1994], 127–28). Once the subject converts "the absence of objects and the empty mouth . . . into words," and then these words into still other words, "the wants of the original oral vacancy are remedied by being turned into verbal relationships with the speaking community at large" (128). The result is a social economy predicated on the symbolic exchange of losses: "In-trojecting a desire, a pain, a situation means channeling them through language into a communion of empty mouths" (128). Language provides a compensatory gain in the form of the cooperation and sharing that is the basis of Homeric reciprocity and ritual.

The monster's cannibalism, however, is a reminder of the (infanticidal) costliness that can never be expunged from existence, no matter how much that cost is channeled through the forms of its symbolic deflections. The empty mouths in communion with one another form a community acting out in a symbolic register the sacrificial exchange of death for life that Odysseus witnesses in the Kyklops' cave. Mortal existence is inscribed within the symbolic order, but that order itself submits to the infanticidality that trav-erses nature and culture and disrupts the effort to establish the generative purity of the law. The law of law is the dependence of lawfulness and the justice it regulates on the general infanticidism that is its condition of possibility.

26. Dimock, *The Unity of the Odyssey*, 111.

27. To be born is to be born into language, more generally into the symbolic order, more generally still into the infanticidality that underwrites the "self's cognizance of its absence." In Polyphemos' cave, Odysseus knows that his identity is a fiction, that his name has a "life" not limited to his corporeal frame, and that this "life" is simultaneously his—infanticidal—death.

This death is the necessary condition of all signifying activity, including the symbolic reference that constitutes the possibility of self-reflective self-consciousness. As Derrida has shown, the ontological predication "I am" does not and cannot arise from out of itself—for example, from out of its immanence in or to the self-reflecting cogito; rather, it derives from the general textual necessity that "I am dead" (*Speech and Phenomena and Other Essays on Husserl's Theory of Signs*, trans. David B. Allison [Evanston: Northwestern University Press, 1973], 52–54 and 93–97)—the necessity, as Odysseus says, that "I am nobody, no man, no one." As Odysseus' proleptic self-representation indicates, "I am no-body" does not specify the empirical condition of the speaking *I*, even if it anticipates the cannibalistic demise the Kyklops has in store for Odysseus. Rather, it designates the textual inscription of this empirical condition.

The predication "I am dead" is the logical condition of the predication "I am," and this necessity announces the ontological catastrophe of the being that cannot pronounce its existence except by virtue of the death that is "structurally necessary" to any and every self-representation (Derrida, *Speech and Phenomena*, 96). The predication "I am dead" means "I am dead before I am born," "I am dead as I am born," hence "I am born dead." This "structural necessity" translates the general infanticidality of being and its representation.

28. Walter Burkert, *Structure and History in Greek Mythology and Ritual* (Berkeley: Uni-versity of California Press, 1979), 55. Burkert notes that the practice of "collecting the bones, especially the thighbones, of the victim and depositing them in some holy place, and setting the skull of the animal on a tree or on a pole . . . is attested since the Pale-olithic period" (55).

29. The narrative never refers to Odysseus' thigh as such but rather to his wound "above the knee," where the boar "with his tusk tore a long gash in the flesh, but did not reach the bone of the man" (Murray and Dimock, 267). That the narrative mentions the

uninjured bone reinforces the meaning of Odysseus' injury as the mark not merely of the sacrificial but, once again, infanticidal burnt offering he avoided becoming.

CHAPTER 8
THE WOUNDED INFANT AND THE INFANTICIDISM
OF THE GODS

1. Thomas Gould, trans., *Oedipus the King by Sophocles: A Translation with Commentary* (Englewood Cliffs: Prentice Hall, 1970), lines 264–75. Subsequent references to Gould's translation will be included in the text. So too will subsequent references to his commentary (page number followed by the line number in the play to which Gould adds his note).

2. As Paul Ricoeur notes, "At the beginning of the play Oedipus calls down curses upon the unknown person responsible for the plague, but he excludes the possibility that that person might in fact be himself. The entire drama consists in the resistance and ultimate collapse of this presumption. Oedipus must be broken in his pride through suffering" (*Freud and Philosophy: An Essay on Interpretation,* trans. Denis Sav⸱re [New Haven: Yale University Press, 1970], 516).

3. According to Jean-Pierre Vernant, "Oedipus himself does not understand the secret speech that, without his realizing, lurks at the heart of what he says. And except for Tiresias, no witness to the drama on stage is capable of perceiving it either" ("Ambiguity and Reversal: On the Enigmatic Structure of Oedipus Rex," in Jean-Pierre Vernant and Pierre Vidal-Naquet, *Myth and Tragedy in Ancient Greece,* trans. Janet Lloyd [New York: Zone Books, 1990], 116). Charles Segal develops this insight: "The famous 'tragic ironies' of the play are so powerful," he writes, "because they are doubled by the theatrical situation" such that "what is in plain sight of the audience is hidden from the participants" ("Freud, Language, and the Unconscious," *Sophocles' Tragic World: Divinity, Nature, Society* [Cambridge: Harvard University Press, 1995], 162).

4. Segal, "Freud, Language, and the Unconscious," *Sophocles' Tragic World,* 163.

5. For Ricoeur, Oedipus eventually sees that he has not seen the truth of his desire as it is figured in the fatal blows he delivers at the crossroads (to the man he had not recognized was his father), in his marriage (to the woman he has never recognized is his mother), and in his misplaced confidence that because he has rescued the city once before (from the Sphinx) he can do so again. Three times blinded by patricidal rage, incestuous longing, and hubristic self-assertion, Oedipus finally apprehends what he has not wanted to see, and when he does, he suddenly sees with Teiresian eyes: "The underlying link between the anger of Oedipus and the power of truth . . . is the core of the veritable tragedy. This core is not the problem of sex, but the problem of light. The seer is blind with respect to the eyes of the body, but he sees the truth in the light of the mind. That is why Oedipus, who sees the light of day but is blind with regard to himself, will achieve self-consciousness only by becoming the blind seer." Thus does Oedipus darken his sight to mark his inner transfiguration. At the moment of greatest suffering, greatest darkness, there is greatest illumination: "What is punishment in the tragedy of sex is the dark night of the senses in the final tragedy of truth" (*Freud and Philosophy,* 517).

Most readings of the play advance some version of this insight. Richard S. Caldwell, for example, explains that "On the thematic and dramatic level, the self-blinding appears as a metaphorical representation of the acquisition by Oedipus of internal knowledge. A central theme of the play, the source of Oedipus' greatness and his downfall, is his power of intellect, his relentless search for the knowledge which will save his city and reveal his identity" ("The Blindness of Oedipus," *International Review of Psycho-Analysis* 1 [1974]: 208). Such statements typify the modern commentary on Oedipus.

6. Charles Segal, *Oedipus Tyrannus: Tragic Heroism and the Limits of Knowledge*, 2nd ed. (New York: Oxford University Press, 2001), 120.

7. "Persecution," Leo Strauss argues, "gives rise to a peculiar technique of writing, and therewith to a peculiar type of literature, in which the truth about all crucial things is presented exclusively between the lines" (*Persecution and the Art of Writing* [Chicago: University of Chicago Press, 1988], 25).

8. Sandor Goodheart ("Ληστας' Εφασχε: Oedipus and Laius' Many Murderers," *Diacritics* 8.1 [Spring 1978]: 55–71) and Frederick Ahl (*Sophocles' Oedipus: Evidence and Self-Conviction* (Ithaca: Cornell University Press, 1991) argue that there is no credible empirical evidence in the play to convict Oedipus of Laius' murder and that Oedipus either accepts or convinces himself of his guilt in order to achieve a mythic identity. In fact, there is no evidence, only his self-incriminating assertion, that Oedipus has killed anyone. If the meaning of the drama depends on understanding Oedipus' psychology, and if that psychology disposes Oedipus to the (perhaps hubristic) aim of becoming a cultural leader, it is possible that he might be willing to risk defeat in order to actualize a potentially transformative cultural vision. History, after all, is filled with examples of religious martyrs, military leaders, emperors, and others, even scholars, who have entertained such ambitions.

9. In *Sophocles and Oedipus: A Study of "Oedipus Tyrannus" with a New Translation* (Ann Arbor: University of Michigan Press, 1971), Philip Vellacott examines six sets of questions in arguing that Oedipus has known from the time of his marriage the truth about his identity, and thus about his real relation to Jocasta and Laius, but that he has "built up for himself" a "sort of defence-system," a cover story "which made plausible sense, and which he trained himself and others to accept" (119). Against this interpretation, I am arguing that Oedipus is attempting to lead his people to see through not his but their collective "defense-system," and that he can do so only indirectly. Although I disagree with Vellacott's construal of Oedipus' motivation, Vellacott's questions are an early stimulus for the present study.

10. Oedipus here describes the (supposedly trivial) "chance" event in the same language of aggression that he soon uses to speak of the (ultimately destiny-shaping) attack at the crossroads, when an old man in a carriage "tried violently to force me off the road" and then "lunged down with twin prongs at the middle of my head" after he, Oedipus, had "struck" the old man's driver "in anger" (Gould, lines 805–9). The similarity of vocabulary and its tenor turns the two events into versions of the same experiential assault. Why does Oedipus link the two events linguistically but differentiate their value?

11. Hugh Lloyd-Jones, ed. and trans., *Sophocles: Ajax, Electra, Oedipus Tyrannus*, vol. 1 (Cambridge: Harvard University Press/Loeb Classical Library, 20, 1994), 405, lines 783–84. Subsequent references to this translation (including page number followed by line numbers) will be included in the text.

12. Jeffrey Rusten translates the Greek to read: "'I was pleased by them,' i.e. satisfied with their response" (*Sophocles: Oidipous Tyrannos: Commentary* [Bryn Mawr: Bryn Mawr Greek Commentaries, 1990], 40). Subsequent references to Rusten's translation (including page number followed by line numbers) will also be included in the text.

13. Vellacott, *Sophocles and Oedipus*, 115.

14. For Vellacott, Oedipus' suspicions concerning his parents are not sufficient to overcome his rage and ambition. Driven by these two motives, he kills a man and then marries after having received a warning about killing and marrying (*Sophocles and Oedipus*, 118). Although Vellacott disputes the presumption that Oedipus unwittingly enacts

his fate in resisting it, he assents to the view that the king's tragic shortcomings impel him toward "risks it was criminal to take" (119). According to Vellacott, Oedipus has hidden his past behind a false autobiography, to which others have acceded, and lived a lie. When the plague descends, Oedipus realizes "[t]here was only one way to save Thebes" —namely, to have the truth brought out" and himself, "the polluted man," brought to account and "banished, if not killed" (120).

15. The irony would be compounded if Oedipus were losing control of his present narration at the very moment he details how he may have lost control over his life. Such irony presupposes that readers have access to the protagonist's psychology—to the tragic shortcomings of his character, to his unconscious motivation—which he himself does not. Thus, one might suppose that Oedipus is ensnared in his hubristic quickness to take offense and to react with misplaced anger: "King Oedipus can be rash and destructive when opposed," writes Mark Ringer, who perceives Oedipus to have a "stubborn determination" by which he "forces the action of the play to its horrible conclusion" (*Electra and the Empty Urn: Metatheater and Role Playing in Sophocles* [Chapel Hill: University of North Carolina Press, 1998], 79). One might then interpret this motivation psychodynamically: "Sophocles does not tell us what Oedipus's conscious motives may be," Segal writes, "but, thanks to the very abruptness and illogicality of the oracular response, the scene does follow the Freudian model of the unconscious, and specifically in the area of the oedipus complex, that is, concern with desire for the mother and hostility to the father. The man who asks about his hidden origins receives from a mysterious divine voice the reply that he is doomed to have union with his mother and kill his father. . . . He at once denies that knowledge by headlong flight from it, only to fulfill it without consciously knowing that he is doing so" ("Freud, Language, and the Unconscious," *Sophocles' Tragic World*, 173). Such explanations are circular: Oedipus cannot recognize the illogicality of the oracle because he cannot recognize his unconscious desire; readers can know that Oedipus does not recognize his desire because he does not see through the illogicality of the oracle.

Circular or not, ironic readings presume that Oedipus must be accountable to gods in whom the western world no longer believes. If Oedipus himself does not believe in the Theban conception of the sacred, the ironic readings of his guilt would block access to the king's cultural critique.

16. As Walter Burkert has explained, at Pytho, the Delphian sanctuary, the Pythia received the divine logos while entranced. She then communicated her "utterances" to her priestly handlers, who in their turn "fixed" them "in the normal Greek literary form, the Homeric hexameter" (*Greek Religion*, trans. John Raffa [Cambridge: Harvard University Press, 1985], 115–16). This versification thus culminated the communicative relay by which a supplicant such as Oedipus would have been delivered to a manifestly edited statement concerning his fate. Is it not possible that Oedipus is deliberately embedding his report, many times removed from the Pythia's own mouth, in an unreliable narrative in order to highlight the dubiousness, not to mention the subornability, of the oracle? "Admittedly it was also regarded as possible to bribe the Pythia," Burkert notes (116).

17. See, for example, Harshbarger, "Who Killed Laius?" *Tulane Drama Review* 9.4 (Summer 1965): 120–31; Girard, "Oedipus and the Surrogate Victim," *Violence and the Sacred*, trans. Patrick Gregory (Baltimore: Johns Hopkins University Press, 1977), 68–88 and *Oedipus Unbound: Selected Writings on Rivalry and Desire*, ed. Mark R. Anspach (Stanford: Stanford University Press, 2004); and Goodhart, "Ληστας' Εφασχε: Oedipus and Laius' Many Murderers," *Diacritics* 8.1 (Spring 1978): 55–71.

18. Oedipus continues: "But if he speaks unmistakably of one solitary man, then at once the balance tilts towards me." Jocasta immediately objects: "Well, know that that is how the word was made known, and he cannot take back that word, for the whole city

heard it, and not I alone" (Lloyd-Jones, 411, lines 846–50). He cannot recant without impeaching his credibility and motivations. Were he now to accuse Oedipus of being the lone murderer, Oedipus would have additional evidence of the very conspiracy he earlier accused Creon and Teiresias of fomenting.

19. Ahl, *Sophocles' Oedipus*, 262 and 263. "When someone chooses a painful and apparently humiliating path despite numerous opportunities to escape it," as Ahl spends his book demonstrating is the case with Oedipus, "people strongly incline to accept that he must be either what he proclaims himself to be, as Sophocles' readers generally believe, or a madman, as Creon suggests to the chorus. And this is where there is a curiously Christlike element in the Oedipus myth. Crucial to Christ's claim to be the Messiah . . . is his willingness to accept public humiliation and execution, to become a scapegoat and be a ritual offering for the community's sins. To be god, he must also be the lamb of god and fulfill even the most terrifying prophecies in conformity with messianic expectations. He must, then, make himself the slave of 'the word,' of destiny. That . . . is his 'heroic' choice of achieving divinity through suffering" (263).

Ahl's interpretation follows in the steps of Girard (*Violence and the Sacred, Oedipus Unbound*), who has propounded the thesis, elaborated by Goodhart and anticipated by Francis Fergusson (*The Idea of a Theater: The Art of Drama in Changing Perspective* [Garden City: Doubleday Anchor, n.d.]) among others, that Oedipus is a scapegoat for the plague and that he colludes in the process by which Thebes selects him as their sacrificial victim for the guilt of those who persecute him. Participating in "the universal matrix of scapegoat politics," Oedipus "discovers he is guilty of parricide and incest . . . less by uncovering certain hitherto obscure empirical facts than by voluntarily appropriating an oracular logic which assumes he has always already been guilty." In other words, "Oedipus becomes 'Oedipus'" not by divine ordinance but by accepting a mythic role: he is "guilty" not of patricide and incest as such but of these two crimes insofar as they stand for a people's own violence against themselves, for it is not Oedipus alone but all of Thebes who "are identically 'murderers of Laius'" (Goodhart, "Ληστας' Εφασχε: Oedipus and Laius' Many Murderers," 67). In this reading, Oedipus is the one who stands for the many, his defense functioning as a symptomatic expression of what is under collective repression.

20. Vernant, "Ambiguity and Reversal," 128.

21. As Bernard Knox puts the matter, for Thebes "the normal cycle of ploughing, sowing, and increase has broken down—'the fruit of our famous land does not increase' (171–2)—and this is accompanied by an interruption of the cycle of human procreation and birth—'the land is dying . . . in the birthless labor pangs of the women' (25–7)" (*Oedipus at Thebes: Sophocles' Tragic Hero and His Time* [New York: Norton, 1971], 114).

22. Knox, *Oedipus at Thebes*, 114.

23. Pietro Pucci, *Oedipus and the Fabrication of the Father: "Oedipus Tyrannus" in Modern Criticism and Philosophy* (Baltimore: Johns Hopkins University Press, 1992), 91.

24. Seth Benardete, "Sophocles' *Oedipus Tyrannus*," in Thomas Woodard, ed., *Sophocles: A Collection of Critical Essays* (Englewood Cliffs, NJ: Prentice Hall, 1966), 107. Pucci believes that Sophocles' "audience knows" that incest is "the epitome of moral pestilence" (113). Along with patricide, incest is "the most violent inversion of all relationships, the epitome of lawlessness" (138). Again, "incest was an even worse transgression" than patricide: "in the absence of a generic name for incest in the fifth century, Oedipus produces a compound word to describe the act. But the messenger cannot repeat the word. This notion is unfathomable; it is impiety itself (*anosia*, 1289)" (143).

25. In the *Antigone*, Oedipus' daughter resists to the end of her life the authority of Creon, who decrees Antigone's brother anathema and "proclaim[s] to the city that this man shall no one honor with a grave and none shall mourn. You shall leave him without

burial; you shall watch him chewed up by birds and dogs and violated" (*Antigone*, trans. David Grene, in *The Complete Greek Tragedies: Sophocles I*, 2nd ed., ed. David Grene and Richmond Lattimore (Chicago: University of Chicago Press, 1991), 168).

26. The first phrase is Grene's translation of line 97 (*Oedipus the King*, in *Sophocles I*, 58); the second is Pucci's (*Oedipus and the Fabrication of the Father*, 6). Subsequent references to Grene's translation will be included in the text.

27. The Corinthian messenger, who brings news of King Polydorus' death, claims to be the shepherd who received the foot-pierced infant.

28. The scene of compassion introduces the possibility of a sociality—an ethical tie or bonding—that would be beyond Theban law, for as the servant, bound by law to his (infanticidal) master, loosens the cords that bind the infant's ankles, he becomes bound by compassion to the child.

29. In the *Poetics*, Aristotle argues that the central force of tragedy is its power of catharsis, its capacity for "effecting through pity and fear the purification of such emotions" (*Aristotle: Poetics*, trans. Malcolm Heath [New York: Penguin, 1996], 10/1449b). As Martha Nussbaum explains, "Aristotle shows . . . that the ethically controversial material of pity and fear is not a kernel of content inside the tragic form; it forms the [very] form" of tragedy. "It informs the choice of the hero, the type of story chosen, and the causal structure linking its events." Moreover, "it also shapes two further features of tragic plot . . . reversal (*peripetia*) and recognition (*anagnorisis*)" ("Tragedy and Self-sufficiency," in Amélie Oksenberg Rorty, ed., *Essays on Aristotle's Poetics* [Princeton: Princeton University Press, 1992], 279). Because pity is at the very heart of tragedy, it is crucial to know what evokes this emotion. "What we pity," Aristotle says in his *Rhetoric*, "is stated clearly in the definition. All unpleasant and painful things excite pity if they tend to destroy and annihilate . . . including mutilation" (114, 1386a)—that is, precisely the injuriousness that Oedipus educes from the servant.

30. According to Knox, in "the standard version of the story, the version used by Aeschylus," Oedipus "is paying for the sins of his father." Knox summarizes the interpretive position of most modern readings of the play when he asserts that in *Oedipus the King* Sophocles "resolutely ignores this traditional burden of the myth . . . . At point after point Sophocles remains silent on the question of Laius' responsibility, a silence all the more noticeable and emphatic because he was addressing an audience familiar with the Aeschylean handling of the material" (*Oedipus at Thebes*, 101).

31. Judith Butler, *Precarious Life: The Powers of Mourning and Violence* (New York: Verso, 2004), 137.

32. At the end of Updike's *Rabbit is Rich* (New York: Ballantine/Fawcett Crest, 1981) the narrating voice alludes to an unstated complex of emotions in the response of Rabbit to what his newborn granddaughter signifies for him: "Fortune's hostage, heart's desire, a granddaughter. His. Another nail in his coffin. His" (437).

33. Butler, *Precarious Life*, 139.

34. Ibid., xii.

35. Ibid., 131 and 134.

36. Oedipus's recognition leads to "*the* act of the play," Alister Cameron writes (*The Identity of Oedipus the King: Five Essays on the Oedipus Tyrannus* [New York: New York University Press, 1968], 99), which is also "one of the most familiar and most 'overinterpreted' symbolic acts in literature"—his self-mutilation (Richard Caldwell, "The Blindness of Oedipus," 207). Caldwell reviews the psychoanalytic elaborations of Freud's interpretation. According to Freud, "the blinding in the legend of Oedipus, as well as elsewhere, stands for castration" (*Interpretation of Dreams* [1900], *Standard Edition*, vol. 5 [1900], 398 n 1). Such self-aggression is "the appropriate punishment for incest," Caldwell explains, since "it is through the eyes that the child's sexual curiosity and incestuous wishes

are first expressed; thus the punishment which necessarily follows upon the achievement of these desires is inflicted upon the eyes as both sexual organs themselves and as symbolizing the genitals." In other words, the displacement from genitals to eyes obeys the principle that "similarity of punishment indicates similarity of transgression." In the example Caldwell examines, the future seer Teiresias loses his sight after an act of "illicit looking" the object of which in the various legends is either the mother's naked body or the genitalia of a maternal substitute ("The Blindness of Oedipus," 207, 212, and 209).

George Devereux demonstrates that the psychoanalytic interpretations "could have been advanced also on purely philological grounds," for blinding in the ancient world "was deemed to be so appropriate a penalty for sexual trespass as to be quite frequently inflicted, even by legal process" ("The Self-Blinding of Oidipous in Sophokles: *Oidipous Tyrannos*," *Journal of Hellenic Studies* 93 [1973]: 26–27 and 42). Devereux goes on to suggest how the act of self-blinding could serve as the appropriate punishment for the crime of patricide as well as of incest, especially if the slaying is understood to have been part of a "patrilineal succession, temporarily disguised as one of matrilineal succession" (47).

37. Segal emphasizes the common language of phallic penetration ("bursting," "striking," "lunging") in Oedipus' description of the fatal confrontation at the crossroads and in the Corinthian messenger's report on Jocasta's suicide, Oedipus' discovery of her body, and Oedipus' self-violence. Segal interprets this language as one of the meta-dramatic means by which Sophocles links Oedipus' self-punishment and his patricide and thereby "calls attention to the representational power of drama, through which a single action unfolding onstage can contain, symbolically, the meaning of an entire lifetime" (*Oedipus Tyrannus*, 129). I agree, except that I believe this meaning must be reexamined in terms not just of the son's violence but the father's.

Gould notes the recurrence of a "group of words meaning to "leap," "lunge," "thrust," "swoop," and "hit," are repeated in such a way as to equate all the various "chances"— the patricide, the incest, the plague, etc., even the malicious taunt by the drunken man" (102 n 807). Gould might have extended his "etcetera" to include Laius's aggression against his son's ankles.

38. James C. Hogan historicizes the aggression against Oedipus. Citing from W. K. Lacey's, *The Family in Classical Greece,* Hogan says that "'There can be little doubt that the exposure of surplus children was practiced throughout antiquity' . . . and just as little doubt that no family, much less a royal one, would expose its first and only male heir unless extraordinary circumstances compelled it." He then accepts that Oedipus' ankles were "pierced and tied together to lessen still further the chances of survival. . . . This vile work was entrusted to the hands of others to avoid the guilt of killing one's own kin and, no doubt, from more personal scruples" (*A Commentary on the Plays of Sophocles* [Carbondale and Edwardsville: Southern Illinois University Press, 1991], 49–50).

P. G. Maxwell-Stuart denies that Oedipus' ankles were pierced. They were "yoked" by constricting cords that caused his joints to swell: "Oedipus has his feet tied together and that is that" ("Interpretations of the Name Oedipus," *Maia* 27 [1975]: 39 and 39n14). Not recognizing the infanticidal context of Oedipus' birth, Maxwell-Stuart asserts that "whatever tokens Oedipus needs to discover the truth about himself they are not at the end of his legs" (39).

39. This image is a screen memory with a vengeance. According to J. Laplanche and J.-B. Pontalis, a screen memory is "a childhood memory characterised both by its unusual sharpness and by the apparent insignificance of its content. The analysis of such memories leads back to indelible childhood experiences and to unconscious phantasies. Like the symptom, the screen memory is a formation produced by a compromise between repressed elements and defence" (*The Language of Psychoanalysis*, trans. Donald Nicholson-Smith [New York: Norton, 1973], 410–11).

40. According to Pucci, "everyone [in the Theban audience] knows—as Aristophanes also testifies—that his name comes from his swollen feet" ("The Tragic *Pharmakos* of the *Oedipus Rex*," *Helios* 17.1 [1990]: 44; Pucci's reference is to *Frogs*, lines 1182ff.). Leonard Shengold has pointed out that Laius, who taught Chrysippus the art of charioteering, "promoted locomotion in his catamite" but "inhibited it in his son, Oedipus, whom he crippled" ("Oedipus and Locomotion," *Psychoanalytic Quarterly* 63 [1994]: 24 n 1).

41. Knox, *Oedipus at Thebes*, 182.

42. Oedipus' first words—"*o tékna*," "my children"—are the first words of the play.

43. According to Gould, "it is impossible to tell from this word whether Sophocles meant us to think of a painful or even crippling infirmity or merely disfiguring marks (perhaps even very slight ones) of which Oedipus was ashamed . . . . Indeed, this line just might mean 'What is this ancient trouble you speak of?'" (123 n 1033).

44. In the *Rhetoric*, Aristotle explains that the best speakers are "especially successful in exciting pity," for they "put the disasters before our eyes, and make them seem close to us, just coming or just past." They do so by presenting "the *tokens* and the actions of sufferers—the garments and the like of those who have already suffered; the words and the like of those actually suffering" (*Rhetoric and Poetics*, trans. W. Rhys Roberts and Ingram Bywater [New York: Modern Library, 1954], 1386b). The key "tokens" in *Oedipus the King* are not those that recall the death of Laius but the infanticidal aggression he directs against his newborn son's body.

45. Knox argues that Oedipus' deification of Chance is an index of how this agency became transformed in the fifth century from an "instrument of divine purpose, 'daughter of Foreknowledge,'" into "an autonomous goddess who personifies the absence of causal order in the universe." If "the very existence of this new goddess Chance makes the existence of the old gods meaningless," then Oedipus' identification with her signals his atheism (*Oedipus at Thebes* 166).

To the contrary, Oedipus restores to Chance one of "her" previously essential functions—safeguarding the child and its future. This function is at the heart of the attitude Knox believes Oedipus has abandoned: "in the Herodotean account of the founding of the Cypselid tyranny at Corinth, the child Cypselus, later to be *tyrannos* of Corinth, is spared by his ten appointed executioners because when the first man of the ten took hold of the child, 'by divine chance' it smiled, and the man had not the heart to kill it, nor had the others. The child 'chanced' to smile, but this was not blind chance, for if the child had been killed the oracles predicting its eventual seizure of power in Corinth could not have been fulfilled" (166). The child's smile here constitutes a sacred interpellation of the other. Oedipus, I am arguing, generalizes the sacredness of the neonatal beckoning to include its pitiable cries of helplessness as well as the pitying response of those who might hear those cries.

46. Hogan, *A Commentary on the Plays of Sophocles*, 63.

47. Robert Graves, *The Greek Myths*, vol. 2, amended 1957, rev. 1960 [New York: Penguin, 1960), 10, 105e.

48. Benardete, "Sophocles' *Oedipus Tyrannus*," 106.

49. Behind the developmental question of the Sphinx's words there is, according to Freud, "the riddle of where babies come from," a "distorted form" of "the same riddle that was propounded by the Theban Sphinx" (*Three Essays on the Theory of Sexuality, Standard Edition*, vol. 7 [1943], 92). This question about reproduction is also about what can go wrong with reproduction. Thus, embedded in "the first problem" with which the instinct for knowledge deals, the question of conception and birth, are still other questions concerning the violent possibility of something going amiss in the making of a baby. For example, Freud notes that children represent the primal scene of sexual intercourse in terms of sadistic violence. If children at an early age "witness sexual intercourse between

adults . . . they inevitably regard the sexual act as a sort of ill-treatment or act of subjugation: they view it, that is, in a sadistic sense" (94). The scene of conception is a scene of violent sexual difference—that is, a scene of castration and the horror it arouses (cf. "Some Psychical Consequences of the Anatomical Distinction Between the Sexes," *Standard Edition,* vol. 19 [1925], 252ff). Joined within a single reproductive problematic, the questions about birth and sexual difference present the child with converging scenarios of violence against his or her person. One does not have to agree with Freud's remarks on sexual difference to envision, as he does, a child wondering whether or not she or he has turned out wrong in some way, is or will be defective, even monstrous, is or is not loved and wanted.

50. *The Oxford Companion to Classical Literature,* ed. M. C. Howatson, 2nd ed. (Oxford: Oxford University Press, 1989), 537. Subsequent references to the *OCCL* will be included in the text.

51. In Hesiod's *Theogony* the Sphinx is "the child of Chimaera and Orthrus; according to others she was the child of Echidna and Typhon." The Chimaera was "a fire-breathing monster with the head of a lion, body of a she-goat, and tail of a snake." Echidna was half woman and half serpent. Typhon, or Typhoeus, had a hundred serpent heads (*OCCL,* 207, 125, 201, and 585).

52. Pausanias, *Description of Greece,* 9.26.2–3; cited in Ahl, *Sophocles' Oedipus,* 11.

53. Ahl notes that "the Sphinx is a *gynê lêistris,* 'a woman brigand'" whose identity is "strangely echoed" in the rumor that "Laios was killed by a band of *lêistai* (plunderers), as Creon points out in line 122, at the very time when the . . . Sphinx was at large" (*Sophocles' Oedipus,* 12). In other words, the relation between the Sphinx and Laius repeats the terms of the defense Oedipus drops: "one is not the same as many" (Lloyd-Jones, 411, line 845).

54. See Richard Seaford, *Reciprocity and Ritual: Homer and Tragedy in the Developing City-State* (Oxford: Clarendon Press, 1994).

55. The possibility of a "Laius Complex" has been suggested and developed by George Devereux in his 1953 article, "Why Oedipus Killed Laius: A Note on the Complementary Oedipus Complex in Greek Drama" (in George H. Pollack and John Munder Ross, eds, *The Oedipus Papers* [Madison, CT: International Universities Press/Chicago Institute for Psychoanalysis, 1988], 97–116), as well as by others, including John Munder Ross, in "Oedipus Revisited: Laius and the 'Laius Complex,'" (in Pollack and Ross, *The Oedipus Papers,* 285–316) and Jaap van Heerden, in "Suppose the Oedipus Complex were Just a Projection," *Inquiry* 21 [1979]: 461–72.

56. Cf. Liddell and Scott, *Greek-English Lexicon,* 476. Oedipus here models for his kingdom the kind of empathic—that is, pitying—perception that might bring them to recognize their interpellative violence toward Thebes' children, who "lie unpited on the ground . . . unmourned" (Gould, lines 181–182).

57. Each mention of Oedipus' name voices his personal vulnerability as a child but also the defenselessness of children in general. Every child is an "Oedipus."

58. This function overtakes a new life *in advance* of—that is, before it is born or conceived—and therefore as if *from behind* it. For Althusser, the paradigmatic example of interpellation is any act of hailing by which an individual is accosted "usually [from] behind" ("Ideology and Ideological State Apparatuses (Notes towards an Investigation)," in *Lenin and Philosophy and Other Essays,* trans. Ben Brewster [New York: Monthly Press, 1971], 174). For this reason Laius would be the exemplary interpellator, for he abducts King Pelops' son behind the king's back and then accosts the boy from behind.

59. As Derrida explains, "a letter"—including an intention, name, cry, or hailing—"does not always arrive at its destination, and from the moment that this possibility be-

longs to its structure one can say that it never truly arrives, that when it does arrive its capacity not to arrive torments it with an internal drifting" ("Le facteur de la verité," 489). Readings of *Oedipus the King* neglect the "internal drifting" or "destinerring" effect at work within a fate that only appears to be Oedipus' own but that, in fact, is part of a fortuitous concatenation of "destinies" — for example, the bad luck that overtakes Jocasta when she marries a man who has incurred the wrath of the gods. Miller, however, has underscored the way the play "is made up of more or less fortuitous and discontinuous encounters" ("Aristotle's Oedipus Complex," in *Reading Narrative* [Norman: University of Oklahoma Press, 1998], 40; cf. Ahl, *Sophocles' Oedipus*). The chance arrival of the Corinthian messenger, with the news that Polybus has died; this person's subsequent ability to recognize the shepherd from whom he had allegedly received a swollen-footed infant at least three, perhaps as many as five, decades previously; the shepherd's ability, in turn, to recognize the adult Oedipus as the same individual he had rescued as a child; all this is the context of a play in which Oedipus years earlier had left the home of his surrogate parents in order to verify a "rumor" that he was a "bastard" and then, when the oracle had not confirmed the rumor but rather announced Oedipus' destiny, had proceeded to leave the safest possible place for him to be, Corinth, in the process meeting by chance a man who apparently had goaded him into a fatal confrontation; Oedipus' subsequent victory over a Sphinx that, seemingly without cause, had beleaguered Thebes and defeated every challenger from this city-state — where in the play's ostensibly unified mimetic action is the necessity by which Oedipus' fate belongs to him? To presume that Oedipus meets *his* fate is to acquiesce in the general form of the infanticidal violence by which Laius and Jocasta would have killed their child.

60. *American Heritage Dictionary of Indo-European Roots*, 24.

61. Ahl, *Sophocles' Oedipus*, 256.

62. Liddel and Scott, *Greek-English Lexicon*, 187.

63. The name "Oedipus" includes a complex pun on two words related to the verb "to see": *oida*, "I know," and *eidos*, "knowing." When Teiresias calls Oedipus ignorant and then accuses him of being "the unholy polluter of this land," Oedipus recalls how the seer had not been able to solve the riddle of the Sphinx. The king then sarcastically refers to himself as *ho meden eidos Oidipous*, "Oedipus who knew nothing" (Lloyd-Jones, 359, line 353 and 366, line 397). For Pucci, Sophocles' text "shows a consistent irony and duplicity against Oedipus's pretensions of knowledge, for Oedipus's pun on *oida* contradicts the correct etymology of his name" ("The Tragic *Pharmakos*," 43).

64. Kirk Ormand, "Nature and Its Discontents in the *Oedipus tyrannus*," in *Exchange and the Maiden: Marriage in Sophoclean Tragedy* (Austin: University of Texas Press, 1999), 126.

65. Ibid., 128.

66. Infanticidism is here a name for what contaminates any *conception* of the father as a pure source of life. As is argued in chapter 6, the *concept* of the father requires, contradictorily, that he be able to kill his offspring as well as commit incest. In either case the father's power implicates him in a general -cidal and incestuous destructiveness that threatens to overtake the furthest reaches of the paternal order — the gods themselves. Thus, on the one hand, infanticide implies patricide, matricide, suicide, and deicide; in the logical "kinship" of these -cides, each act of erasure implies the others. So, too, on the other hand, does incest. Like Laius and Jocasta's attempted infanticide, and like Oedipus' alleged patricide, Oedipus and Jocasta's incest also functions as a doubly contradictory erasure — of the mother as mother and of the son as son, hence of the intrafamilial difference between son and mother. The structure of incest here duplicates and refracts the structure of infanticidality.

CHAPTER 9
THE INFANTICIDITY OF FLESH AND WORD

1. In his letter to the Philippians, Paul says that "the peace of God, which surpasses all understanding, will guard your hearts and your minds in Christ Jesus" (4:7). From the perspective of the self-interest posited by game theory, Jesus' gift of death would be the ultimate example of a sucker-strategy.

2. Henry Staten, *Eros in Mourning: Homer to Lacan* (Baltimore: Johns Hopkins University Press, 1995), 50. Staten cites Augustine's fear that "Even the righteous man himself will not live the life he wishes unless he reaches that state where he is wholly exempt from death, deception, and distress, and has the assurance that he will for ever be exempt. This is what our nature craves, and it will never be fully and finally happy unless it attains what it craves" (*Concerning the City of God Against the Pagans*, 14:25; cited in *Eros and Mourning*, 9). Staten cites as well Rudolf Bultmann's belief that "'existence' is 'sheerly unintelligible' if it is not enlightened by the transcendent light that 'necessarily includes freedom from death'" (Bultmann, *The Gospel of John: A Commentary*, 43; cited in *Eros and Mourning*, 48). Staten also refers to the similar attitudes of two other theological scholars: "If, as Jaroslav Pelikan says, the 'content of the salvation for which he became incarnate' is 'freedom from corruption,' then 'the Word became flesh' means that the Word traversed the *sarx*, sojourned in it, precisely in order to annul its sarctic essence. 'What Jesus lays aside,' as Edward Schillebeeckx tells us, 'is not his humanity, but the transitoriness of the *sarx*'" (Pelikan, *The Emergence of the Catholic Tradition*, 272, and Schillebeeckx, *Christ: The Experience of Jesus as Lord*, 426; cited in *Eros and Mourning*, 50).

3. Ibid., 48.

4. Walter Burkert, *Greek Religion*, trans. John Raffa (Cambridge: Harvard University Press, 1985), 54. Subsequent references will be included in the text.

5. The most common sacrificial animal, Burket notes, "is the sheep, then the goat and the pig; the cheapest is the piglet. The sacrifice of poultry is also common" (*Greek Religion*, 55).

6. Jesus underscores the aggression of even a vegetarian meal when he compares himself to the "bread of life" (John 6:35 and 48). By identifying himself as this bread — indeed, as the very grain from which it is made — Jesus locates his death in the most seemingly nonaggressive act of eating possible. Jesus thereby drives home the point that the most basic act of survival depends on the gift of death.

7. *Euchesthai* includes the meaning of making a vow: "Usually the prayer includes within it the vow — which is likewise called *euche*" (Burkert, *Greek Religion*, 73). Insofar as to pray is both to promise and to predict future triumph, it is a means of ventriloquizing the gods, another technique of rationalizing the violence of one's economizations.

8. Praying acknowledges and protects against the fact that, in Moleschott's pun, "*Der Mensch is was er isst,*" that man is what he eats. Moleschott's aphorism is a source of an eighteenth-century German work on sacrifice, Friedrich Dicke's *Über isst und ist: Ein Erklärung des Ursprungs des Opfers,* or *Concerning eats and is: An Explanation of the Origins of Sacrifice,* which is virtually the same title of Feuerbach's 1862 work *Die Geheimniss des Opfers oder der Mensch ist was er isst (The Mystery of Sacrifice or Man Is What He Eats)* (see Marx W. Wartofsky, *Feuerbach* [Cambridge: Cambridge University Press, 1977], 451 n 6).

9. *American Heritage Dictionary of Indo-European Roots,* 44 and 42.

10. *Aeschylus: "Prometheus Bound," "The Suppliants," "Seven Against Thebes," "The Persians",* trans. Philip Vallacott (New York: Penguin, 1988), 35.

11. *Hesiod: "Theogony," "Works and Days," "Shield",* trans. Apostolos N. Athanassakis (Baltimore: Johns Hopkins University Press, 1983), 26/540–41. Athanassakis wonders

at the "unfair division of portions, with the inedible parts given to the gods and the edible flesh to men," since "one gives the best to those he honors and not the worst." This "inequity was strongly felt by the Greeks," he notes, "who not infrequently considered themselves hosts of the gods at the religious feasts held in their honor"—an honor that is tantamount to dishonor. "I venture to suggest that the sense of guilt and embarrassment engendered by the unfairness of the division of the sacrificial victim may be responsible for the attribution of the unflattering prototype to Prometheus as a way of self-exoneration" (*Hesiod*, 49).

12. James Davidson, *Courtesans and Fishcakes: The Consuming Passions of Classical Athens* (New York: HarperCollins/HarperPerennial, 1999), 290–91. Davidson goes on to argue that "the true foundation of Athenian democracy" is the idea of "*isonomia*, 'fair shares,'" an older principle than "*demokratia*, 'people power,'" and one that was "directly related to *kreanomia*, the distribution of meat at sacrifice, with a punning reference" both to "*nemo* ('distribute')" and "nomos ('law')": "It is *isonomia*, not democracy, that the 'tyrant-slayers' Harmodius and Aristogiton brought to Athens when they 'ended the tyranny' at the end of the sixth century.... Cleisthenes, the democracy's founder, is in fact much better seen as a fair and equal distributor than a people's revolutionary" (291). Davidson's argument implies that democracy begins when the economic principle of "fair shares" is secularized—that is, stripped of the sacralized deception by which the Greeks previously rationalized their efforts at deflecting the costs of their group existence—and collectively internalized in a new form of political economy.

This secularization is not the loss of the sacred, however, but rather the redefinition of the sacred—specifically, the de-personification of the sacred and its transference from a relation between humans and gods to the political relation among humans. The result is that what is typically called a movement of secularization is in fact the revelation of the sacred as a spiritual power immanent in the cooperation that is potentially available when groups recognize and attempt to mitigate rather than cover up, rationalize, and pursue the sacrificial effects of their economizations.

13. Ibid., 15.

14. In Hesiod's *Theogony*, Zeus sacralizes this offering when he is supposedly duped by Prometheus into choosing the inedible portion of the slaughtered animal. But this deception is itself a cover for the deeper concealment of the economization that is before everyone's eyes, the same economization Oedipus seeks to name as infanticidal.

15. *Aeschylus: "Prometheus Bound"*, trans. Vellacott, 34.

16. John Herrington, *Aeschylus* (New Haven: Yale University Press, 1986), 159/7.

17. *Aeschylus: "Prometheus Bound"*, trans. Vellacott, 34.

18. Aeschylus, *Prometheus Bound*, trans. David Grene, in David Grene and Richmond Lattimore, eds., *The Complete Greek Tragedies: Aeschylus II* (Chicago: University of Chicago Press, 1956), 156.

19. Ibid., 35.

20. Liddell and Scott, *Greek-English Lexicon*, 484.

21. *Euchai* is the noun form of the verb *euchomai*, to pray, pay one's vows, avow, proclaim, boast, and so on. Eucharist derives from *eu*, good or well, and *kharis*, grace, favor (see Liddell and Scott, *Greek-English Lexicon*, 291 and 778).

22. *Gennao* is a variant of *genos*, which developed out of *ginomai*, "to *cause to be*," to "'*gen*'-erate," and "to *become (come into being)*." The term was "used with great latitude" to signify, literally or figuratively, the following: "arise, be assembled, be (-come, -fall, -have self), be brought (to pass), (be) come (to pass), continue, be divided, draw, be ended, fall, be finished, follow, be found, be fulfilled." In conjunction with other Greek terms it could mean "God forbid, grow, happen, have, be kept, be made, be married, be ordained to be, partake, pass, be performed, be published, require, seem, be showed." Finally, it

was employed idiomatically to signify "soon as it was, sound, be taken, be turned, use, wax, will, would, be wrought" ("New Strong's Concise Dictionary of the Words in the Greek Testament," *The New Strong's Exhaustive Concordance of the Bible,* 19).

23. See note 4 to chapter 3.

24. The preceding verses from Hosea reinforce the infanticidal context of the references to fruit: "Like grapes in the wilderness, I found Israel. Like the first fruit on the fig tree, in its first season, I saw your ancestors. But they came to Baal-poer, and consecrated themselves to a thing of shame, and became detestable like the thing they loved. Ephraim's glory shall fly away like a bird—no birth, no pregnancy, no conception! Even if they bring up children, I will bereave them until no one is left. . . . Once I saw Ephraim as a young palm planted in a lovely meadow, but now Ephraim must lead out his children for slaughter. Give them, O Lord—what will you give? Give them a miscarrying womb and dry breasts" (9:10–14).

25. The "vehicles of memory," Freud notes in *Project for a Scientific Psychology,* are "probably [the vehicles] of psychical processes in general" (*Standard Edition,* vol. 1, 300). If there is no psychic life without memory, there is no memory that does not involve a work of mourning. The etymological kinship of *memory* and *mourning* so attests, for their respective Latin and German roots derive from the same Indo-European stem, *(s)mer-,* to remember (*The American Heritage Dictionary of Indo-European Roots,* 62).

For Freud mourning is the labor through which the grieving individual economizes on an experience of losing some valued or cathected "object." Libidinally attached to or invested in an object of desire, the grieving individual must negotiate the affective consequences of being separated from it. The individual must convert the once living object into a memory of a now dead object. Memory defends against or economizes on the particular loss. Since the structural possibility of loss necessarily precedes any actual loss, it also precedes the formation of any cathexis to begin with. In this way psychic life is mortgaged from its beginning to all its future losses through which it will glimpse the shadow of its original susceptibility to loss in general.

26. See Staten, *Eros in Mourning,* 49–52 and 60–61.

27. This is why, according to Staten, "the real descent of the divine Logos into the flesh sets off a general deconstruction of all the oppositions that belong to the system of the original distinction between Logos and flesh. After it is asserted that the Logos became flesh, in the very act of assertion, neither Logos nor flesh can any longer mean what it meant before, nor can the transformation be elucidated by means of the other concepts"—such as the literal and the metaphorical—"that are themselves placed under erasure by the transformation they would be called on to explain." If "the history of Christian doctrine is the history of the containment of this general deconstruction," the gospel of John shatters this containment (*Eros in Mourning,* 49–50).

28. It would transcend transcendence, which is to say it would undo and be undone by its transcendental nature.

29. Staten, *Eros in Mourning,* 11.

30. Ibid., 10.

31. The literature on the experience of self-loss in mourning is enormous. Much of this literature responds to the psychoanalytic inquiry Freud sets forth in "Mourning and Melancholia" (*Standard Edition,* vol. 14, 281–397). See, for example, the five chapters in part 4, "New Perspectives in Metapsychology, Cryptic Mourning and Secret Love," in Nicolas Abraham and Maria Torok, *The Shell and the Kernel,* vol. 1, ed. and trans. Nicholas T. Rand (Chicago: University of Chicago Press, 1994), 99–164, and John Bowlby, *Attachment and Loss* (New York: Basic Books, 1969). Staten's work provides an especially powerful analysis of "the dialectic of mourning: the field of movement of all affective phenomena determined by the mortality of a love object" (*Eros in Mourning,* xi). Among other

works, Judith Butler's *Precarious Life: The Powers of Mourning and Violence* (London and New York: Verso, 2004), Shoshana Felman and Dori Laub's *Testimony: Crises of Witnessing in Literature, Psychoanalysis, and History* (New York: Routledge, 1992), and Juliana Schiesari's *The Gendering of Melancholia: Feminism, Psychoanalysis, and the Symbolics of Loss in Renaissance Literature* (Ithaca: Cornell University Press, 1992) provide converging deconstructive investigations of mourning.

32. Staten, *Eros in Mourning*, 10.

33. Ibid., 11.

34. Ibid., xii.

35. These include the Pharisees, for example, whose commitment to the economiza-tion Jesus repudiates is evident in their belief "that men are rewarded or punished in the future life, according as they have lived virtuously or viciously in this life" (Davis, *The Westminster Dictionary of the Bible*, 476).

36. In the imagery of nourishment, Jesus translates this ransoming gift as the Eu-charistic "bread of life," a figure of literality, Staten has shown, that relocates the sacred not in a transcendental realm beyond death but in the fatally organic nature of the mortal body.

He does so when, during his forty day fast in the wilderness, the devil tempts him to "command these stones to become loaves of bread." Jesus refuses to perform this mira-cle: "One does not live by bread alone," he answers, "but by every word that comes from the mouth of God" (Matthew 4:1–4). What are those words? In the Eucharist they take the form of the imperative to eat the "bread" that "is" the body of Jesus. In the equivalence between his body and the ordinary bread he breaks off for each of his communicants, Jesus affirms the literality of the bread and makes it function as a trope: he turns it into a figure of meat and more generally into a metonymy of the entire process by which living things, plant or animal, are killed and converted into food. Jesus' Eucharistic words — his self-translation into the edible substances of the host — clarify the literal-cum-meta-literal meaning of his earlier repudiation of the temptation to turn stone into bread: humans do not live by bread as bread alone, as if the bread were able to appear miraculously from out of the inorganic (the stones); rather, humans exist by feeding off of once-living things that have passed through the violence of human-inflicted death. Hu-mans live by eating another kind of bread, here figured in the supreme being who must nevertheless die.

The Gospel of John might appear to refute such a reading of the bread Jesus offers. "I am the living bread that came down from heaven," Jesus avows. "Whoever eats of this bread will live forever" (John 6:51). What is alive about this bread and what is meant by the "eternal life" it promises? Does "living bread" refer to a spiritual substance which is not of this world and which is to be found beyond the cycle of mortal life? Staten sug-gests otherwise by reading this bread in relation to Jesus' parable of the grain of wheat: "Very truly, I tell you, unless a grain of wheat falls into the earth and dies, it remains just a single grain; but if it dies, it bears much fruit" (John 12:24). The "fruitfulness" of the "seed" requires the (infanticidal) death of the seed. According to the orthodox theologi-cal decoding of this passage, the death in question is not really death at all but the life be-yond this life, real life, life after death — in a word, salvation — the way to which is through the life of Jesus. "The spiritual reading," Staten says, "is obvious: as applied to Jesus, death here refers to his coming martyrdom; in its application to the believer, it means dying to the world that does not know the Savior; and in both cases bringing forth fruit means doing the works of God and thus bringing others to salvation" (*Eros in Mourning*, 62).

Nevertheless, Jesus' parabolic — that is, figurative — announcement retains a "hyper-literal" signification. "Since the tenor of the metaphor bears on the death of human beings, the vehicle suggests the image, grotesque from the spiritual perspective, of an interred human body that putrefies and out of which new life springs" (Staten, *Eros in Mourning*,

62). Read hyperliterally, the spirituality of Jesus' life does not transcend the naturalism of this world but is immanent in it. According to this possibility, when Jesus says that he is the "bread of life" he is identifying the inseparability of spirit from matter, from the entire organic process by which the grain of wheat becomes the bread that sustains a human life until this life dies and returns to the earth from whence some other germ in turn sprouts and brings forth its fruit.

"Is this not what Jesus says" in the parable at hand, Staten asks? "What Christianity calls the corruption of the flesh is nothing but an effervescence of new life at a non-human level, and when the individual life ruptures it does so because organic life has passed through it as its momentary instrument on its way to new configurations" (*Eros in Mourning*, 59–60). Thus, in the same breath that Jesus announces he is the "bread of life" he also declares that this bread must be eaten and converted into the flesh of the new life that must die in its turn. Notwithstanding what one might wish to be one's immortality, the life which this bread signifies, Jesus declares, must enter into the organic round of consumption: "the bread that I will give for the life of the world is my flesh" (John 6:51). There will be an exchange that costs, and the cost will be Jesus' life.

In this reading Jesus submits to the transaction not as a way of freeing humankind from the mortality of the flesh but in order to relocate the sacred precisely in its thanatotic inescapability. Thus, Jesus' gift of "eternal life" does not refer to the destiny of a self that, in fulfillment of its narcissistic grief at the anticipation of its own demise, imagines itself being the recipient of a divine grace which would confer an otherworldly immortality following the death of the body. Rather, according to Staten, Jesus' gift refers to "this very life that we live, only under a different aspect" (*Eros in Mourning*, 63) —one informed by the gift of death.

By insisting that "my flesh is true food and my blood is true drink," on the one hand, and that "[t]he words I have spoken to you are spirit [*pneuma*] and life" (John 6:55 and 63), Jesus advances just this non-transcendence. He is "proposing a difficult new thought," Staten writes, "one that minds accustomed to the distinction between flesh and spirit cannot grasp so long as they cling to this distinction in its old form. What if it were the thought that *pneuma is* flesh and blood . . . only seen with new eyes and consecrated by the passage into death that is an act of love? Jesus' words will bear this meaning quite easily; what is difficult is the mental act that could overcome the repugnance of such a meaning and think this most intolerable thought" (*Eros in Mourning*, 65). What is intolerable is that each individual "must undergo a dissolution that is unbearable and that yet must be endured, an absolute humiliation of substance and an expenditure of self that is absolutely without return." In relation to this possibility, the Eucharist would become "the communion of universal mortality" (63) —of a universal gift of death.

37. Jacques Derrida, "Passages —from Traumatism to Promise," *Points . . . Interviews, 1974–1994*, ed. Elisabeth Weber, trans. Peggy Kamuf and Others (Stanford: Stanford University Press, 1995), 387.

CHAPTER 10
CONCEPTIONS AND CONTRACEPTIONS OF THE FUTURE

1. *American Heritage Dictionary of Indo-European Roots*, 8.

2. *Star Trek: The Motion Picture*, dir. Robert Wise (1979). Subsequent references to the screenplay, available at http://www.dailyscript.com/scripts/startrek01.html 17.234ff, will be included in the text.

3. As Derrida writes of Walter Benjamin, "[t]hat which exists . . . and that which at the same time threatens what exists . . . belong inviolably . . . to the same order." —which is to say, to the same interpellative order ("Force of Law: The Mystical Foundation of Authority," trans. Mary Quaintance, *Cardozo Law Review* 11.5–6 [July–August 1990], 275).

4. Judith Butler, *The Psychic Life of Power: Theories in Subjection* (Stanford: Stanford University Press, 1997), 3.

5. In "The Mirror Stage as Formative of the Function of the I as Revealed in Psychoanalytic Experience" (*Écrits: A Selection*, trans. Alan Sheridan [New York: Norton, 1977]), Lacan twice uses the metaphor of pregnancy to describe the "Gestalt" that signifies nothing less than the child's future: "this *Gestalt*—whose pregnancy should be regarded as bound up with the species . . . symbolizes the mental permanence of the *I*, at the same time as it prefigures its alienating destination; it is still pregnant with the correspondences that unite the *I* with the statue in which man projects himself, with the phantoms that dominate him, or with the automaton in which, in an ambiguous relation, the world of his own making tends to find completion" (2–3). Lacan's insight has wide applicability to science fiction, which dramatizes the struggle to master the "alienating destination" of the *I* by submitting it to the conceptuality the symbolic order has generated, especially as this conceptuality has been paternalized.

6. *Terminator 2: Judgment Day*, dir. James Cameron, written by James Cameron and William Wisher (Canal + Distribution, 1991). Subsequent references to the screenplay, which is available at http://screentalk.biz/moviescripts/Terminator%20II.pdf, will be included in the text.

7. Aristotle, *Poetics*, trans. Hippocrates G. Apostle, Elizabeth A. Dobbs, and Morris A. Parslow (Grinnell: Peripatetic Press, 1990), 25/57b.

8. The scene recalls the choral wailing in *Oedipus the King*, analyzed in chapter 8: "In the unnumbered deaths of its people the city dies," they say, adding that "those children that are born lie dead on the naked Earth, unpitied" (lines 178–81).

9. In an unpublished manuscript, "Undoing the Eucharist: The Abject Mouth from Jonathan Edwards to Contemporary American Science Fiction Films," I explore the anti-Eucharistic implications of the terrified mouth attempting to hail the other out of existence.

10. *The Matrix*, dir. and written by Larry Wachowski and Andy Wachowski (Warner Brothers, Inc., 1997). Subsequent references to the screenplay, slightly different versions of which are available at http://dailyscript.com/scripts/the_matrix.pdf and http://screentalk.biz/ moviescripts/The%20Matrix.pdf, will be included in the text.

11. *Matrix*, cognate with *mother, material,* and *matter,* derives from the Latin *mater,* which translates the Greek *meter,* mother (*American Heritage Dictionary of Indo-European Roots,* 39).

12. In *Terminator 2,* the quicksilver T-1000 is a mirroring machine that is able to assume the form of the person whose image it reflects. In *The Matrix,* the mirror (the filmic generation of which, I have been told, is based on an advanced form of the same special effects technology used in *Terminator 2* to produce the T-1000) merges with Neo's body without having to first kill him. The mirror enables Neo to pass not through but into the looking glass and to take on the hyper-mimeticism that characterizes the Matrix in its ability to propagate endless numbers of human simulacra, its Agents. Once again, then, a mirroring scene remarks the breakdown of the differences—between the flesh-and-blood person and the mimetic replication of an image of the human—that Morpheus wants to preserve in order to protect "the real." In other words, in both films mirroring reflects the struggle of humans to see themselves seeing, to see in their seeing the "conceptive" wish to find in their reflection an assurance that the future will be the time and place of human survival, not extinction.

13. "Trivia for *Matrix, The* (1999)." http://us.imdb.com/Trivia?0133093.

14. *Matrix* is also etymologically related to *metropolis* by way of the Greek *meter* (*American Heritage Dictionary of Indo-European Roots*, 39).

15. Lynne Joyrich, personal communication, July 15, 2001.

16. In "Sleeping with the Enemy: Fighting and Fucking in the Three *Matrix* Films" (unpublished ms.), Shep Shepard and I argue that *Matrix Revolutions* represents the invasion by the mechanized Matrix army as a spermatic invasion: "a huge drill, literally screws its way into the domed wall of Zion's ovum-shaped docking port to release swarm after ejaculatory swarm of 'squiddies.'" Their victory, we wrote, "would be the demise of the very sexual reproducibility the entire scenario associates with the Matrix's genocidal threat to humans."

In this regard, we argued, *Matrix Revolutions* "acts out the Darwinian scene of 'sperm wars,' described by Robin Baker in his book of that title (*Sperm Wars: The Science of Sex* [New York: Basic Books/HarperCollins, 1996]). There, Baker argues that 'evolutionary forces' have programmed human sexual behavior in terms of 'sperm warfare' such that 'whenever a woman's body contains sperm from two (or more) men at the same time, the sperm from those men compete for the "prize" of fertilizing her egg. The way these sperm compete is akin to warfare.' Indeed, 'very few (less than 1 percent) of the sperm in a human ejaculate are elite, fertile "egg-getters." The remainder . . . we now know to be infertile by design, "kamikaze" sperm' (xiv), either 'blockers' or 'killer sperm' the function of which is, as their names suggest, to block alien sperm from fertilizing the egg or to destroy this sperm altogether (42). In glorifying the supposedly revolutionary ethos of humans defending themselves against their technological offspring by mowing down and finally annihilating them, *Matrix Revolutions* indulges in a symbolic spermaticidal slaughter. In doing so the film denies while hysterically acting out a fear that is literally inconceivable according to the terms that have governed the history of western conceptuality." As Shepard and I underscored, "the fear in question is not a fear *of* death but an inarticulate apprehension that life itself *is* death, a possibility here represented in the spermatic lethality of the machines with which the Matrix penetrates Zion. In the threatened womb-like space of the battle scene, the film not only permits humankind to win but to do so in terms of a semiosis that retrieves the human body—and with it sexual difference and the biological reproductivity this difference supports—from the fate of being reduced to a biological anachronism in a digitized world where the logic of the future is no longer conceivable in terms of biological conception. *Matrix Revolutions* thus completes the trilogy with an ideological regression of the most archaic sort: it projects onto the human enemy that which characterizes the human itself—namely, a lethality at the heart of human conception. It is a lethality the film cannot 'conceive,' let alone articulate, except in the phantasmatic violence it attributes to that which it wants to believe is non-human."

17. *Alien Resurrection*, dir. Jean-Pierre Jeunet, written by Joss Whedon (20th-Century Fox, 1997).

18. In fact, it represents her self-sacrifice as an antitypal fulfillment of the New Testament's eschatological trajectory toward humankind's collective salvation.

19. For the version of the script in which Ripley asks if call dreams, see http://home. hawaii.rr.com/alienaffiliation/scripts/script1.html, accessed 6 March 2006; for later versions of the script, see http://www.planetavp.com/amr/scripts/alien42.txt, accessed 6 March 2006.

20. In the alternative ending of the film, Ripley and Call land on the now desolated earth to silently behold the specter of planetary lifelessness. The deletion of this ending "reproduces" the contraceptive force which this deletion apparently wants to avoid.

Bibliography

Abraham, Nicolas, and Maria Torok. "Mourning *or* Melancholia: Introjection *versus* Incorporation." *The Shell and the Kernel.* Vol. 1. Ed. and trans. Nicholas T. Rand. University of Chicago Press, 1994. 125–38.

Abraham, Nicolas, and Maria Torok. "New Perspectives in Metapsychology, Cryptic Mourning and Secret Love." Part 4 in Nicolas Abraham and Maria Torok, *The Shell and the Kernel.* Vol. 1 Ed. and trans. Nicholas T. Rand. Chicago: University of Chicago Press, 1994. 99–164.

Aeschylus. *Prometheus Bound.* In *Aeschylus: "Prometheus Bound," "The Suppliants," "Seven Against Thebes," "The Persians".* Trans. Philip Vallacott. New York: Penguin, 1988.

Ahl, Frederick. *Sophocles' "Oedipus": Evidence and Self-Conviction.* Ithaca: Cornell University Press, 1991.

Alien Resurrection. Dir. Jean-Pierre Jeunet. Written by Joss Whedon. 20th-Century Fox, 1997. Versions of the screenplay are available at http://www.geocities.com/scifiscripts/alien resurrection_early.txt and www.screentalk.org/moviescripts/Alien %20Resurrection.pdf.

Alter, Robert, and Frank Kermode, eds. *The Literary Guide to the Bible.* Cambridge: Belknap Press/ Harvard University Press, 1987.

Althusser, Louis. "Ideology and Ideological State Apparatuses (Notes towards an Investigation)." *Lenin and Philosophy and Other Essays.* Trans. Ben Brewster. New York: Monthly Press, 1971. 127–86.

The American Heritage Dictionary of Indo-European Roots. Rev. and ed. Calvert Watkins. Boston: Houghton Mifflin, 1985.

Arendt, Hannah. *The Life of the Mind.* Vol. 1, *Thinking.* New York: Harcourt Brace Jovanovich, 1971.

Aristotle. *Generation of Animals.* Rev. ed. Trans. and ed. A. L. Peck. Cambridge: Harvard University Press, 1953.

——. *The Metaphysics.* Trans. John H. McMahon. Buffalo: Prometheus Books, 1991.

——. *Poetics.* Trans. Hippocrates G. Apostle, Elizabeth A. Dobbs, and Morris A. Parslow. Grinnell: Peripatetic Press, 1990.

——. *The Poetics.* Trans. Malcolm Heath. London, New York: Penguin, 1996.

——. *Rhetoric and Poetics.* Trans. W. Rhys Roberts and Ingram Bywater. New York: Modern Library, 1954.

Attridge, Derek. "On Mount Moriah—The Impossibility of Ethics." Paper presented at the twenty-second annual English Department symposium, University of Alabama, Tuscaloosa, September 28–30, 1995.

Auerbach, Erich. "Odysseus' Scar." *Mimesis: The Representation of Reality in Western Literature.* Trans. Willard R. Trask. 1946. Princeton: Princeton University Press, 1953. 3–23.

Bakan, David. *Disease, Pain, and Sacrifice: Toward a Psychology of Suffering.* Boston: Beacon Press, 1971.

———. *The Duality of Human Existence: Isolation and Communion in Western Man*. Boston: Beacon Press, 1966.

———. *Slaughter of the Innocents: A Study of the Battered Child Phenomenon*. Boston: Beacon Press, 1972.

———. *And They Took Themselves Wives: The Emergence of Patriarchy in Western Civilization*. San Francisco: Harper and Row, 1979.

Baker, Robin. *Sperm Wars: The Science of Sex*. New York: Basic Books/HarperCollins, 1996.

Baskin, Judith R. "Rabbinic Reflections on the Barren Wife." *Harvard Theological Review* 82.1 (1989): 101–14.

Bataille, George. *The Accursed Share: An Essay on General Economy*. Vol I. *Consumption*. Trans. Robert Hurley. 1967. Urzone, Inc., 1988/Zone Books, 1991.

Benardete, Seth. "Sophocles' *Oedipus Tyrannus*." *Sophocles: A Collection of Critical Essays*. Ed. Thomas Woodard. Englewood Cliffs: Prentice Hall, 1966. 105–21.

Benjamin, Walter. *Schriften*. Ed. Theodore W. Adorno, Gretel Adorno, and Frederich Podszus. Frankfurt: Suhrkamp Verlag, 1955.

Birnbaum, Philip, trans. *Daily Prayer Book/Ha-siddur Ha-shalem*. New York: Hebrew Publishing Company, 1949.

Bloom, Harold. *The Anxiety of Influence: A Theory of Poetry*. 2nd ed. 1973. New York: Oxford University Press, 1997.

Bloom, Harold. *Poetry and Repression: Revisionism from Blake to Stevens*. New Haven: Yale University Press, 1976.

Boggess, Jane. "Infant Killing and Male Reproductive Strategies in Langurs (*Presbytis entellus*)." In Hausfater and Hrdy, eds. *Infanticide*. 283–310.

The Book of J. Trans. David Rosenberg. Interpreted by Harold Bloom. New York: Grove Weidenfeld, 1990.

Bowlby, John. *Attachment and Loss*. New York: Basic Books, 1969.

Boyarin, Daniel. "'This We Know to Be the Carnal Israel': Circumcision and the Erotic Life of God and Israel." *Critical Inquiry* 18 (Spring 1992): 474–505.

Briggs, John C. "Mass Extinctions: Fact or Fallacy?" In Glen, William, ed. *The Mass-Extinction Debates: How Science Works in a Crisis*. Stanford: Stanford University Press, 1994. 230–36.

Brown, Norman O. *Hermes the Thief: The Evolution of a Myth*. New York: Vintage/Random House, 1947, 1969.

Burke, Barbara. "Infanticide: Why Does It Happen in Monkeys, Mice, and Men?" *Science* 5.4 (1984): 26–31.

Burkert, Walter. *Greek Religion*. Trans. John Raffa. 1977. Cambridge: Harvard University Press, 1985.

———. *Structure and History in Greek Mythology and Ritual*. Berkeley and Los Angeles: University of California Press, 1979.

Burt, Austin and Robert Trivers. *Genes in Conflict: The Biology of Selfish Genetic Elements*. Cambridge: Belknap Press/Harvard University Press, 2006.

Butler, Judith. *Precarious Life: The Powers of Mourning and Violence*. London and New York: Verso, 2004.

———. *The Psychic Life of Power: Theories in Subjection*. Stanford: Stanford University Press, 1997.

Cairns-Smith, A. G. *Seven Clues to the Origin of Life: A Scientific Detective Story.* Cambridge: Cambridge University Press, 1985.

Caldwell, Richard S. "The Blindness of Oedipus." *International Review of Psycho-Analysis* 1 (1974): 207–18.

Cameron, Alister. *The Identity of Oedipus the King: Five Essays on the Oedipus Tyrannus.* New York: New York University Press, 1968.

Camporesi, Piero. *Bread of Dreams: Food and Fantasy in Early Modern Europe.* Trans. David Gentilcore. Chicago: University of Chicago Press, 1989.

Carroll, Joseph. *Evolution and Literary Theory.* Columbia: University of Missouri Press, 1995.

Cioran, E. M. *The Trouble with Being Born.* Trans. Richard Howard. New York: A Richard Seaver Book/Viking, 1976.

Coen, Amy. Cited in *Florida Times Union,* July 18, 1999. A.13b.

Cohen, Leonard. "Story of Isaac." *Stranger Music.* Leonard Cohen, Stranger Music, Inc., 1993; Vintage/Random House, 1994. 139–40.

Cohen, Mark Nathan. *Health and the Rise of Civilization.* New Haven: Yale University Press, 1989.

Cohen, Shaye J. D. "The Origins of the Matrilineal Principle in Jewish Law." *AJS Review* 10.1 (1985): 19–54.

Collins, D. Anthony, Curt D. Busse, and Jane Goodall. "Infanticide in Two Populations of Savanna Baboons." In Hausfater and Hrdy, eds. *Infanticide.* 193–215.

Crockett, Carolyn M., and Ranka Sekulic. "Infanticide in Red Howler Monkeys (*Alouatta Seniculus*)." In Hausfater and Hrdy, eds. *Infanticide.* 173–91.

Crosby, Alfred W. *Germs, Seeds, and Animals: Studies in Ecological History.* Armonk, NY: M. E. Sharpe, 1994.

Crystal, David. *Language Death.* Cambridge: Cambridge University Press, 2000.

Daily Prayer Book/Ha-siddur Ha-shalem. Trans. Philip Birnbaum. New York: Hebrew Publishing Co., 1949.

Dalby, Andrew. *Language in Danger: The Loss of Linguistic Diversity and the Threat to Our Future.* New York: Columbia University Press, 2003.

D'Angelo, Mary Rose. "*Abba* and 'Father': Imperial Theology and the Jesus Traditions." *Journal of Biblical Literature* 111.4 (1992): 611–30.

Daniels, John D. "The Indian Population of North America in 1492." *William and Mary Quarterly* 49.2, 3rd ser. (April 1992): 298–320.

Darwin, Charles. *"The Origin of Species by Means of Natural Selection or the Preservation of Favored Races in the Struggle for Life" and "The Descent of Man and Selection in Relation to Sex."* 1859 and 1871. New York: Random House/Modern Library, n.d.

———. *The Voyage of the Beagle.* London: Dent/Everyman's Library, 1906, 1959.

Davidson, James. *Courtesans and Fishcakes: The Consuming Passions of Classical Athens.* 1997. HarperCollins/HarperPerennial, 1999.

Davila, James R. "The Name of God at Moriah: An Unpublished Fragment from 4QGenExoda." *Journal of Biblical Literature* 110.4 (1991): 577–82.

Davis, John D. *The Westminster Dictionary of the Bible.* Rev. and rewritten Henry Snyder Gehman. Philadelphia: Westminster Press, 1944.

Davis, Robert Con. *The Paternal Romance: Reading God-the-Father in Early Western Culture.* Urbana: University of Illinois Press, 1993.

Dawkins, Richard. "The Evolution of Evolvability." In *Artificial Life*. Ed. Christopher G. Langton. Redwood City, CA: Addison-Wesley, 1989. 201–20.

———. *The Extended Phenotype: The Long Reach of the Gene*. Oxford: Oxford University Press, 1982.

———. *River Out of Eden: A Darwinian View of Life*. New York: Basic Books/ HarperCollins, 1995.

———. *The Selfish Gene*. New ed. 1976. Oxford: Oxford University Press, 1989.

Dennett, Daniel C. *Darwin's Dangerous Idea: Evolution and the Meanings of Life*. New York: Simon and Schuster, 1995.

Depew, David J., and Bruce H. Weber. *Darwinism Evolving: Systems Dynamics and the Genealogy of Natural Selection*. Cambridge: Massachusetts Institute of Technology Press/ Bradford Book, 1995.

Derrida, Jacques. *Archive Fever: A Freudian Impression*. Trans. Eric Prenowitz. Chicago: University of Chicago Press, 1995.

———. "Le Facteur de la Verite." In *The Post Card: From Socrates to Freud and Beyond*. Trans. Alan Bass. 1980. University of Chicago Press, 1987. 411–96.

———. "Force of Law: The 'Mystical Foundation of Authority.'" *Acts of Religion*. Ed. Gil Anidjar. Trans. Mary Quaintance. New York: Routledge, 2002. 230–98.

———. *The Gift of Death*. Trans. David Wills. 1992. Chicago: University of Chicago Press, 1995.

———. "A Number of Yes." Trans. Brian Holmes. *Que Parle?* 2.2 (Fall 1988): 120–33.

———. *Of Grammatology*. Corrected ed. Trans. Gayatri Chakravorty Spivak. 1967. Baltimore: Johns Hopkins University Press, 1997.

———. "Passages—from Traumatism to Promise." Trans. Peggy Kamuf. *Points . . . Interviews, 1974–1994*. Ed. Elisabeth Weber. Stanford: Stanford University Press, 1995. 372–95. 386–87.

———. "Plato's Pharmacy." *Dissemination*. Trans. Barbara Johnson. 1972. Chicago: University of Chicago Press, 1981.

———. *The Post Card: From Socrates to Freud and Beyond*. Trans. Alan Bass. 1980. Chicago: University of Chicago Press, 1987.

———. "Signature Event Context." *Margins of Philosophy*. 309–30.

———. *Specters of Marx: The State of the Debt, the Work of Mourning, and the New International*. Trans. Peggy Kamuf. 1993. New York: Routledge, 1994.

———. *Speech and Phenomena and Other Essays on Husserl's Theory of Signs*. Trans. David B. Allison. 1967. Evanston: Northwestern University Press, 1973.

———. "Structure, Sign, and Play in the Discourse of the Human Sciences." In Richard Macksey and Eugenio Donato, eds. *The Structuralist Controversy: The Languages of Criticism and the Sciences of Man*. Baltimore: Johns Hopkins University Press, 1970. 1972. 247–65.

———. "White Mythology: Metaphor in the Text of Philosophy." In *Margins of Philosophy*. Trans. Alan Bass. 1972. Chicago: University of Chicago Press, 1982. 207–71.

Devereux, George. "The Self-Blinding of Oidipous in Sophokles: *Oidipous Tyrannos*." *Journal of Hellenic Studies* 93 (1973): 36–49.

———. "A Typological Study of Abortion in 350 Primitive, Ancient, and Pre-Industrial Societies." In Rosen, H., ed. *Abortion in America*. Boston: Beacon Press, 1967. 95–152.

———. "Why Oedipus Killed Laius: A Note on the Complementary Oedipus Complex in Greek Drama." *The Oedipus Papers*. Ed. George H. Pollack and John Munder Ross.

Madison, CT: International Universities Press/Chicago Institute for Psychoanalysis, 1988. 97–116. Originally published in *The International Journal of Psycho-Analysis* 34 (1953): 132–41.

De Vries, Hent, and Samuel Weber, eds. *Violence, Identity, and Self-Determination.* Stanford: Stanford University Press, 1997.

Dickemann, Mildred. "Concepts and Classification in the Study of Human Infanticide: Sectional Introduction and Some Cautionary Notes." In Hausfater and Hrdy, eds. *Infanticide.* 427–37.

Dimock, George E. *The Unity of the Odyssey.* University of Massachusetts Press, 1989.

Divale, William Tulio, and Marvin Harris. "Population, Warfare, and the Male Supremacist Complex." *American Anthropologist* 78.3 (September 1976): 521–38.

Donaldson, Mara E. "Kinship Theory in the Patriarchal Narratives: The Case of the Barren Wife." *Journal of the American Academy of Religion* 49.1 (1980): 77–87.

duBois, Page. *Sowing the Body: Psychoanalysis and Ancient Representations of Women.* Chicago: University of Chicago Press, 1988.

Durant, Will and Ariel. *The Lessons of History.* New York: Simon and Schuster, 1968.

Eilberg-Schwartz, Howard. *God's Phallus and Other Problems for Men and Monotheism.* Boston: Beacon Press, 1994.

———. *The Savage in Judaism: An Anthropology of Israelite Religion and Ancient Judaism.* Bloomington: Indiana University Press, 1990.

Eldredge, Niles. *The Miner's Canary: Unraveling the Mysteries of Extinction.* New York: Prentice Hall, 1991.

Epicurus. *The Extant Writings of Epicurus.* Trans. C. Bailey. In Oates, Whitney J., ed. *The Stoic and Epicurean Philosophers: The Complete Extant Writings of Epicurus, Epictetus, Lucretius, Marcus Aurelius.* New York: Modern Library, 1940.

Estrin, Barbara L. "Finders Keepers: Preservation and the Biblical Foundling." *Mosaic* 11.1 (Fall 1977): 61–75.

Feldman, Yael S. "'And Rebecca Loved Jacob,' but Freud Did Not." In Rudnytsky, Peter L., and Ellen Handler Spitz, eds. *Freud and Forbidden Knowledge.* New York: New York University Press, 1994. 7–25.

Felman, Shoshana, and Dori Laub. *Testimony: Crises of Witnessing in Literature, Psychoanalysis, and History.* New York: Routledge, 1992.

Fergusson, Francis. *The Idea of a Theater: The Art of Drama in Changing Perspective.* Garden City, NJ: Doubleday Anchor, 1949.

Feyerabend, Paul. *Against Method.* 1975. London: Verso, 1978.

Fokkelman, J. P. "Genesis." In Alter, Robert, and Frank Kermode, eds. *The Literary Guide to the Bible.* Belknap Press/Harvard University Press, 1987. 36–55.

Fossey, Dian. "Infanticide in Mountain Gorillas (*Gorilla Gorilla Beringei*) with Comparative Notes on Chimpanzees." In Hausfater and Hrdy, eds. *Infanticide.* 217–35.

Fox, Robin. *Reproduction and Succession: Studies in Anthropology, Law, and Society.* New Brunswick: Transaction, 1993.

Fraser, J. T. *Of Time, Passion, and Knowledge: Reflections on the Strategy of Existence.* New York: George Braziller, 1975.

Freud, Sigmund. "The Antithetical Meaning of Primal Words." (1910) *SE.* Vol. 11.

———. *The Interpretation of Dreams* (1900). *SE.* Vols. 4–5.

———. *Introductory Lectures on Psychoanalysis. SE.* Vol. 15.

———. "Mourning and Melancholia" (1917). *SE.* Vol. 14.

————. *Project for a Scientific Psychology* (1895). *SE*. Vol. 1.

————. "Some Psychical Consequences of the Anatomical Distinction between the Sexes." *SE*. Vol. 19.

————. *Standard Edition of the Complete Psychological Works of Sigmund Freud*. Trans. James Strachey. London: Hogarth Press and the Institute of Psycho-Analysis, 1966.

————. *Three Essays on the Theory of Sexuality*. *SE*. Vol. 7.

Girard, René. "Oedipus and the Surrogate Victim." *Violence and the Sacred*. 68–88.

————. *Oedipus Unbound: Selected Writings on Rivalry and Desire*. Ed. Mark R. Anspach. Stanford: Stanford University Press, 2004.

————. *The Scapegoat*. Trans. Yvonne Freccero. 1982. Baltimore: Johns Hopkins University Press, 1986.

————. *Things Hidden Since the Foundation of the World*. Trans. Stephen Bann and Michael Metteer. 1978. Stanford: Stanford University Press, 1987.

————. *Violence and the Sacred*. Trans. Patrick Gregory. 1972. Baltimore: Johns Hopkins University Press, 1977.

Glen, William. "What the Impact/Volcanism/Mass-Extinction Debates Are About." *The Mass-Extinction Debates: How Science Works in a Crisis*. Stanford: Stanford University Press, 1994. 8–38.

Goodhart, Sandor. "Λήστας' Εφασχε: Oedipus and Laius' Many Murderers." *Diacritics* 8.1 (Spring 1978): 55–71.

Gould, Stephen Jay. *Full House: The Spread of Excellence from Plato to Darwin*. New York: Harmony Books, 1996.

Graves, Robert. *The Greek Myths*. Vol. 2. 1955. Amended 1957. Rev. 1960. London and New York: Penguin, 1960.

"Greek Dictionary of the New Testament." In *The Hebrew-Greek Key Word Study Bible: King James Version*.

Greene, Graham. *The Power and the Glory*. New York: Viking, 1940, 1968, Uniform edition. 1982.

Hallam, A., and P. B. Wignall. *Mass Extinctions and Their Aftermath*. Oxford: Oxford University Press, 1997.

Hamilton, Edith and Huntington Cairns, eds. *The Collected Dialogues of Plato*. Princeton: Princeton University Press/Bollingen Series 71, 1961.

Haraway, Donna J. "Biopolitics of Postmodern Bodies: Constitutions of Self in Immune System Discourse." *Simians, Cyborgs, and Women: The Reinvention of Nature*. New York: Routledge, 1991. 203–30.

Hardin, Garrett. *Living within Limits: Ecology, Economics, and Population Taboos*. New York: Oxford University Press, 1993.

————. *The Ostrich Factor: Our Population Myopia*. New York: Oxford University Press, 1999.

————. "The Tragedy of the Commons." *Science* 162 (1968): 1243–48.

Harris, Marvin. *Cannibals and Kings: The Origins of Cultures*. New York: Vintage/Random House, 1977.

————. *Culture, People, Nature: An Introduction to General Anthropology*. 6th ed. New York: HarperCollins, 1993.

————. *Good to Eat: Riddles of Food and Culture*. New York: Simon and Schuster, 1985.

———. *Our Kind: Who We Are, Where We Come From, Where We Are Going.* New York: Harper Perennial/Harper and Row, 1989.

Harshbarger, Karl. "Who Killed Laius?" *Tulane Drama Review* 9.4 (Summer 1965): 120–31.

Hausfater, Glenn. "Infanticide in Langurs: Strategies, Counterstrategies, and Parameter Value." In Hausfater and Hrdy, eds. *Infanticide.* 257–81.

Hausfater, Glenn, and Sarah Blaffer Hrdy. "Comparative and Evolutionary Perspectives on Infanticide: Introduction and Overview." In Hausfater and Hrdy, eds. *Infanticide,* xiii–xxxv.

———. "Preface." In Hausfater and Hrdy, eds., *Infanticide* xi–xii.

———. eds. *Infanticide: Comparative and Evolutionary Perspectives.* New York: Aldine, 1984.

Hayssen, Virginia D. "Mammalian Reproduction: Constraints on the Evolution of Infanticide." In Hausfater and Hrdy, eds. *Infanticide.* 105–23.

"Hebrew and Chaldee Dictionary." In *The Hebrew-Greek Key Word Study Bible: King James Version.*

The Hebrew-Greek Key Word Study Bible: King James Version. Rev. ed. Chattanooga: AMG International, Inc., 1991.

Herrington, John. *Aeschylus.* New Haven: Yale University Press, 1986.

Hertz, J. H., ed. *The Pentateuch and Haftorahs.* 2nd ed. 1936 (5696). London: Soncino Press, 1971 (5732).

Hesiod, *Theogony.* In *"Theogony," "Works and Days," "Shield".* Trans. Apostolos N. Athanassakis. Baltimore: Johns Hopkins University Press, 1983.

Hexter, Ralph. *A Guide to the Odyssey: A Commentary on the English Translation of Robert Fitzgerald.* New York: Vintage/Random House, 1993.

Hilmy, S. Stephen. *The Later Wittgenstein: The Emergence of a New Philosophical Method.* New York: Basil Blackwell, 1987.

Hoffman, Lawrence A. *Covenant of Blood: Circumcision and Gender in Rabbinic Judaism.* Chicago: University of Chicago Press, 1996.

Hogan, James C. *A Commentary on the Plays of Sophocles.* Carbondale and Edwardsville: Southern Illinois University Press, 1991.

Homer. *The Odyssey.* Trans. Robert Fitzgerald. 1961, 1963. New York: Vintage Classics/Random House, 1990.

———. *The Odyssey.* 2 vols. Trans. A. T. Murray. Rev. George E. Dimock. Cambridge: Loeb Classical Library/Harvard University Press, 1995.

Hrdy, Sarah Blaffer. "Assumptions and Evidence Regarding the Sexual Selection Hypothesis: A Reply to Boggess." In Hausfater and Hrdy, eds. *Infanticide.* 315–19.

———. "Fitness Tradeoffs in the History and Evolution of Delegated Mothering with Special Reference to Wet-Nursing, Abandonment, and Infanticide." *Ethology and Sociobiology* 13 (1992): 409–42.

———. *The Woman That Never Evolved.* Cambridge: Harvard University Press, 1981.

Hsia, R. Po-chia. *The Myth of Ritual Murder: Jews and Magic in Reformation Germany.* New Haven: Yale University Press, 1988.

Irigary, Luce. *Speculum of the Other Woman.* Trans. Gillian C. Gill. 1974. Ithaca: Cornell University Press, 1985.

Jacobs, Louis. "The Problem of the *Akedah* in Jewish Thought." In Perkins, Robert L. ed. *Kierkegaard's Fear and Trembling.* 1–9.

Jay, Nancy. "Sacrifice, Descent, and the Patriarchs." *Vetus Testamentum* 38.1 (1988): 52–70.

————. *Throughout Your Generations Forever: Sacrifice, Religion, and Paternity.* Chicago: University of Chicago Press, 1992.

Kant, Immanuel. *The Philosophy of Law: An Exposition of the Fundamental Principles of Jurisprudence as the Science of Right.* Trans. W. Hastie. Edinburgh: T. and T. Clark, 1887. Rpt. Clifton, NJ: Augustus M. Kelley, 1974.

Keenan, Thomas. *Fables of Responsibility: Aberrations and Predicaments in Ethics and Politics.* Stanford: Stanford University Press, 1997.

Kierkegaard, Soren. *"Fear and Trembling" and "The Sickness Unto Death."* Trans. Walter Lowrie. 1843. Doubleday/Anchor Books, 1954.

Kimball, A. Samuel. "Thought as Conception, Thought as Counter-Conception: The Example of Freud's Wolf-Man." Unpublished ms.

Kimball, A. Samuel. "Undoing the Eucharist: The Abject Mouth from Jonathan Edwards to Contemporary American Science Fiction Films." Unpublished ms.

Kimball, A. Samuel and Shep Shepard. "Sleeping with the Enemy: Fighting and Fucking in the Three *Matrix* Films." Unpublished ms.

Knox, Bernard. *Oedipus at Thebes: Sophocles' Tragic Hero and His Time.* New York: Norton, 1971.

Kselman, John S. "Genesis." In Mays, ed. *Harper's Bible Commentary.* 85–128.

Lacan, Jacques. "The Mirror Stage as Formative of the Function of the I." *Ecrits: A Selection.* Trans. Alan Sheridan. New York: Norton, 1977.

LaCapra, Dominick. *Representing the Holocaust: History, Theory, Trauma* (Ithaca: Cornell University Press, 1994).

Lakoff, George and Mark Johnson. *Metaphors We Live By.* Chicago: University of Chicago Press, 1980.

————. *Philosophy in the Flesh: The Embodied Mind and Its Challenge to Western Thought.* New York: Basic Books, 1999.

Langer, William L. "Infanticide: A Historical Survey." *History of Childhood Quarterly* 1.3 (Winter 1974): 353–65.

Laplanche, J. and J.-B. Pontalis. *The Language of Psycho-Analysis.* Trans. Donald Nicholson-Smith. 1967. New York: Norton, 1973.

Leach, Edmund. *Genesis as Myth and Other Essays.* London: Jonathan Cape, 1969.

Leakey, Richard, and Roger Lewin. *The Sixth Extinction: Patterns of Life and the Future of Humankind.* New York: Doubleday, 1995.

Lechte, John. *Julia Kristeva.* London and New York: Routledge, 1990.

Leland, Lysa, Thomas T. Struhsaker, and Thomas M. Butynski. "Infanticide by Adult Males in Three Primate Species of the Kibale Forest, Uganda: A Test of Hypotheses." In Hausfater and Hrdy, eds. *Infanticide.* 151–72.

Levenson, John D. *The Death and Resurrection of the Beloved Son: The Transformation of Child Sacrifice in Judaism and Christianity.* New Haven: Yale University Press, 1993.

Levi-Strauss, Claude. *The Raw and the Cooked: Introduction to a Science of Mythology: 1.* Trans. John and Doreen Weightman. Chicago: University of Chicago Press, 1983.

"Lexical Aids to the Old Testament." In *Hebrew-Greek Key Word Study Bible: King James Version.*

Lidell and Scott. *Greek-English Lexicon.* Abridged ed. Oxford: Clarendon Press, 1984.

Lloyd-Jones, Hugh. *The Justice of Zeus.* Berkeley: University of California Press, 1971.

Lucretius. *De rerum natura—De Rerum Natura*. Trans. H. A. J. Munro. In Oates, Whitney J., ed. *The Stoic and Epicurean Philosophers: The Complete Extant Writings of Epicurus, Epictetus, Lucretius, Marcus Aurelius*. New York: Modern Library, 1940.

Lyell, Sir Charles. *Principles of Geology: Being an Attempt to Explain the Former Changes of the Earth's Surface by Reference to Causes Now in Operation*. 3 vols. 1830–1833. New York and London: Johnson Reprint Corporation/The Sources of Science, no. 84, 1969.

Marks, Herbert. "Biblical Naming and Poetic Etymology." *Journal of Biblical Literature* 114.1 (1995): 21–42.

The Matrix. Written and Dir. Larry Wachowski and Andy Wachowski. Warner Bros., Inc., 1997. Versions of the screenplay are available at http://dailyscript.com/scripts/the_matrix.pdf and http://screentalk.biz/moviescripts/The%20Matrix.pdf.

Matrix Revolutions. Written and Dir. Larry Wachowski and Andy Wachowski. Warner Bros., Inc., 1997. Versions of the screenplay are available at http://www.remoteviewinglight.com/html/revolutions-transcript-1.html

Maxwell-Stuart, P. G. "Interpretations of the Name Oedipus." *Maia* 27 (1975): 37–43.

Maynard Smith, J. "Group Press Selection." *Quarterly Review of Biology* 51 (1976): 277–83.

Maynard Smith, John and Eors Szathmary. *The Major Transitions in Evolution*. Oxford and New York: W. H. Freeman/Spektrum, 1995.

Mays, James L., general ed., et al. *Harper's Bible Commentary*. San Francisco: Harper and Row, 1988.

McNeil, William H. *The Human Condition: An Ecological and Historical View*. Princeton: Princeton University Press, 1979.

———. *Plagues and People*. Garden City: Anchor Press/Doubleday, 1976.

Miller, David Lee. *Dreams of the Burning Child: Sacrificial Sons and the Father's Witness*. Ithaca: Cornell University Press, 2003.

Miller, J. Hillis. "Aristotle's Oedipus Complex." *Reading Narrative*. Norman: University of Oklahoma Press, 1998.

Mosca, Paul G. "Child Sacrifice in Canaanite and Israelite Religion: A Study of *Mulk* and *mlk*." Ph.D. diss., Cambridge: Harvard University, 1975.

Nettle, Daniel, and Suzanne Romaine. *Vanishing Voices: The Extinction of the World's Languages*. New York: Oxford University Press, 2000.

The New Oxford Annotated Bible. New Revised Standard Version. Ed. Bruce M. Metzger and Roland E. Murphy. New York: Oxford University Press, 1991, 1994.

"New Strong's Concise Dictionary of the Words in the Greek Testament." *The New Strong's Exhaustive Concordance of the Bible*. Nashville: Thomas Nelson Publishers, 1995, 1996.

Nussbaum, Martha C. "Tragedy and Self-sufficiency: Plato and Aristotle on Fear and Pity." *Essays on Aristotle's Poetics*. Ed. Amelie O. Rorty. Princeton: Princeton University Press, 1992. 261–90.

Ormand, Kirk. "Nature and its Discontents in the *Oedipus tyrannus*." *Exchange and the Maiden: Marriage in Sophoclean Tragedy*. Austin: University of Texas Press, 1999. 124–52.

The Oxford Companion to Classical Literature. Ed. M. C. Howatson. 2nd ed. Oxford: Oxford University Press, 1989.

Paige, Karen Ericksen, and Jeffery M. Paige. *The Politics of Reproductive Ritual*. Berkeley: University of California Press, 1981.

Perkins, Robert L., ed. *Kierkegaard's "Fear and Trembling": Critical Appraisals*. University: University of Alabama Press, 1981.

Plato. *Laws*. Trans. A. E. Taylor. In Hamilton and Cairns, eds. *The Collected Dialogues of Plato*.

———. *Phaedrus and Letters VII and VIII*. Trans. Walter Hamilton. Harmondsworth: Penguin, 1973.

———. *The Republic of Plato*. Trans. Francis MacDonald Cornford. Oxford: Oxford University Press, 1945.

———. *Symposium*. Trans. Michael Joyce. In Hamilton and Cairns, eds. *The Collected Dialogues of Plato*. 526–74.

———. *The Symposium*. Trans. Walter Hamilton. Harmondsworth: Penguin, 1951.

———. *Theaetetus*. Trans. F. M. Cornford. In Hamilton and Cairns, eds. *The Collected Dialogues of Plato*. 845–919.

———. *Timaeus*. Trans. Benjamin Jowett. In Hamilton and Cairns, eds. *The Collected Dialogues of Plato*. 1151–1211.

Plaut, W. Gunther, ed. *The Torah: A Modern Commentary*. New York: Union of American Hebrew Congregations, 1981.

Pucci, Pietro. *Oedipus and the Fabrication of the Father: "Oedipus Tyrannus" in Modern Criticism and Philosophy*. Baltimore and London: Johns Hopkins University Press, 1992.

———. "The Tragic *Pharmakos* of the *Oedipus Rex*." *Helios* 17.1 (1990): 41–49.

Purves, William K., Gordon H. Orians, H. Craig Heller, and David Sadava. *Life: The Science of Biology*. 5th ed. Sunderland, MA: Sinauer Associates, Inc., 1998.

Raup, David M. *Extinction: Bad Genes or Bad Luck?* New York: Norton, 1991.

Reinhardt, Karl. "The Adventures in the *Odyssey*." Schein, *Reading the Odyssey*, 63–132.

Rendtorff, Rolf. "'Covenant' as a Structuring Concept in Genesis and Exodus." *Journal of Biblical Literature* 108.3 (1989): 385–93.

Richardson, Alan, ed. *A Theological Word Book of the Bible*. New York: Macmillan, 1955.

Ricklefs, Robert E. *The Economy of Nature: A Textbook in Basic Ecology*. 5th ed. New York: W. H. Freeman and Co., 2001.

Ricoeur, Paul. "Fatherhood: From Phantasm to Symbol." Trans. Robert Sweeney. *The Conflict of Interpretations: Essays in Hermeneutics*. Ed. Don Ihde. Evanston: Northwestern University Press, 1974. 468–97.

———. *Freud and Philosophy: An Essay on Interpretation*. Trans. Denis Savage. New Haven: Yale University Press, 1970.

Ridley, Mark. *Evolution*. Boston: Blackwell Scientific Publications, 1993.

Ringer, Mark. *Electra and the Empty Urn: Metatheater and Role Playing in Sophocles*. Chapel Hill: University of North Carolina Press, 1998.

Ripley, Suzanne. "Infanticide in Langurs and Man: Adaptive Advantage or Social Pathology?" In N. M. Cohen, R. S. Malpass, and H. G. Klein, eds. *Biosocial Mechanisms of Population Regulation*. New Haven: Yale University Press, 1980. 348–90.

Rose, Steven. *Lifelines: Biology Beyond Determinism*. Oxford: Oxford University Press, 1998.

Rosenzweig, Franz. *Star of Redemption*. 2nd ed. Trans. William W. Hallo. 1930. London: Routledge and Kegan Paul, 1971.

Ross, John Munder. "Oedipus Revisited: Laius and the 'Laius Complex.'" *The Oedipus Papers*. Ed. George H. Pollack and John Munder Ross. Madison: Ct: International Universities Press/Chicago Institute for Psychoanalysis, 1988. 285–316. Originally published in *The Psychoanalytic Study of the Child*. Ed. A. Solnit, R. Eissler, A. Freud, and P. B. Neubauer. Vol. 37. New Haven: Yale University Press, 1982.

Russell, Bertrand. *Religion and Science.* Home University Library, 1935; Oxford University Press, 1961.

Russo, Joseph, Manuel Fernandez-Galiano, and Alfred Heubeck. *A Commentary on Homer's Odyssey.* Vol. 3, Books XVII–XXIV. Oxford: Clarendon Press, 1992.

Rusten, Jeffrey. *Sophocles "Oidipous Tyrannos": Commentary.* Bryn Mawr, PA: Bryn Mawr Greek Commentaries, 1990.

Said, Edward W. *Beginnings: Intention and Method.* Baltimore: Johns Hopkins University Press, 1975.

Sarna, Nahum M. *Understanding Genesis.* New York: Schocken, 1966.

Sass, Louis J. "Deep Disquietudes: Reflections on Wittgenstein as Antiphilosopher." In James C. Klagge, ed., *Wittgenstein: Biography and Philosophy.* Cambridge [England]: New York: Cambridge University Press, 2001. 98–155.

Schein, Seth L. "Introduction." Schein, *Reading the Odyssey,* 3–31.

———. ed. *Reading the Odyssey: Selected Interpretive Essays.* Princeton: Princeton University Press, 1996.

Schiesari, Juliana. *The Gendering of Melancholia: Feminism, Psychoanalysis, and the Symbolics of Loss in Renaissance Literature.* Ithaca: Cornell University Press, 1992.

Scrimshaw, Susan C. M. "Infanticide in Human Populations: Societal and Individual Concerns." In Hausfater and Hrdy, eds. *Infanticide.* 439–62.

Seaford, Richard. *Reciprocity and Ritual: Homer and Tragedy in the Developing City-State.* Oxford: Clarendon Press, 1994.

Segal, Charles. "Freud, Language, and the Unconscious." *Sophocles' Tragic World: Divinity, Nature, Society.* Cambridge: Harvard University Press, 1995. 161–79.

———. *Oedipus Tyrannus: Tragic Heroism and the Limits of Knowledge.* 2nd ed. New York: Oxford University Press, 2001.

Shell, Marc. *Children of the Earth: Literature, Politics, and Nationhood.* New York and Oxford: Oxford University Press, 1993.

———. *The End of Kinship: "Measure for Measure," Incest, and the Ideal of Universal Siblinghood.* Stanford: Stanford University Press, 1988.

Shengold, Leonard. "Oedipus and Locomotion." *Psychoanalytic Quarterly* 63 (1994): 20–28.

Smith, Adam. *An Inquiry into the Nature and Causes of the Wealth of Nations.* Ed. Edwin Cannin. New York: Modern Library, 1937, 1965.

Sophocles. *Antigone.* Trans. David Grene. In *The Complete Greek Tragedies: Sophocles I.* 2nd ed. Ed. David Grene and Richmond Lattimore. Chicago: University of Chicago Press, 1991.

———. *Oedipus the King.* Trans. David Grene. In *The Complete Greek Tragedies: Sophocles I.* 2nd ed. Ed. David Grene and Richmond Lattimore. Chicago: University of Chicago Press, 1991.

———. *Oedipus the King.* Trans. Thomas Gould. Englewood Cliffs: Prentice Hall/Greek Drama Series, 1970.

———. *Oedipus the King.* Trans Hugh Lloyd-Jones. In *Sophocles: Ajax, Electra, Oedipus Tyrannus.* Vol. 1. Ed. Hugh Lloyd-Jones. Cambridge: Harvard University Press/Loeb Classical Library, 20, 1994.

Spiegel, Shalom. *The Last Trial: On the Legends and Lore of the Command to Abraham to Offer Isaac as a Sacrifice: The Akedah.* Trans. Judah Goldin. 1950. Woodstock: Jewish Lights, 1993.

Stannard, David E. *American Holocaust: Columbus and the Conquest of the New World.* New York: Oxford University Press, 1992.

Star Trek: The Motion Picture. Dir. Robert Wise. Written by Alan Dean Foster (story), Harold Livingston (screenplay), and Gene Roddenberry (story). Paramount, 1979. The screenplay is available at http://www.dailyscript.com/scripts/startrek01.html.

Staten, Henry. *Eros in Mourning: Homer to Lacan.* Baltimore: Johns Hopkins University Press, 1995.

Steadman, David. In Adams, Scott. "Humans Make Extinction Happen 100 Times Faster." University of Florida News. March 6, 1997. http://www.napa.ufl.edu/oldnews/extinct1.htm

Steinberg, Milton. "Kierkegaard and Judaism." *Anatomy of Faith.* New York: Harcourt, Brace, 1960. 130–52.

Storey, Robert. *Mimesis and the Human Animal: On the Biogenetic Foundations of Literary Representation.* Evanston: Northwestern University Press, 1996.

Stover, Dawn. "Endangered Speech." *Popular Science* (July 1997): 34.

———. "The Final Frontier." *Popular Science* (July 1997): 58–59.

Strauss, Leo. "The Beginning of the Bible and Its Greek Counterparts." In Harold Bloom, ed. *Genesis.* New York: Chelsea House, 1986. 23–42.

———. *Persecution and the Art of Writing.* 1952. Chicago: University of Chicago Press, 1988.

Sugiyama, Yukimaru. "Proximate Factors of Infanticide Among Langurs at Dharwar: A Reply to Boggess." In Hausfater and Hrdy, eds. *Infanticide.* 311–14.

Terminator 2: Judgment Day. Dir. James Cameron. Written by James Cameron and William Wisher. Canal + Distribution, 1991. The screenplay is available at http://screentalk.biz/moviescripts/Terminator%20II.pdf.

Teube, Savina J. *Sarah the Priestess: The First Matriarch of Genesis.* Athens: Swallow Press, 1984.

Trivers, Robert L. "Parental Investment and Sexual Selection." In *Sexual Selection and the Descent of Man.* Ed. B. Campbell. Chicago: Aldine, 1972. 136–79.

"Trivia for *Matrix, The* (1999)." http://us.imdb.com/Trivia?0133093.

Underwood, Daniel A., and Paul G. King. "On the Ideological Foundations of Environmental Policy." *Ecological Economics* 1 (1989): 315–34.

Updike, John. *Rabbit Is Rich.* New York: Ballantine/Fawcett Crest, 1981.

Van Heerden, Jaap. "Suppose the Oedipus Complex were Just a Projection." *Inquiry* 21 (1979): 461–72.

Vellacott, Philip. *Sophocles and Oedipus: A Study of "Oedipus Tyrannus" with a New Translation.* Ann Arbor: University of Michigan Press, 1971.

Vernant, Jean-Pierre. "Ambiguity and Reversal: On the Enigmatic Structure of *Oedipus Rex.*" Vernant and Pierre Vidal-Naquet. *Myth and Tragedy in Ancient Greece.* Trans. Janet Lloyd. 1988. New York: Zone Books, 1990. 113–14.

Vogel, Christian, and Hartmut Loch. "Reproductive Parameters, Adult-Male Replacements, and Infanticide among Free-Ranging Langurs (*Presbytis Entellus*) at Jodhpur (Rajasthan), India." In Hausfater and Hrdy, eds. *Infanticide.* 237–55.

Ward, Peter. *The End of Evolution: On Mass Extinctions and the Preservation of Biodiversity.* New York: Bantam, 1994.

Wartofsky, Marx W. *Feuerbach.* Cambridge: Cambridge University Press, 1977.

Watts, Sheldon. *Epidemics and History: Disease, Power and Imperialism.* New Haven: Yale University Press, 1997.

Wellisch, E. *Isaac and Oedipus: A Study in Biblical Psychology of the Sacrifice of Isaac — The Akedah.* London: Routledge and Kegan Paul, 1954.

Widdicombe, Peter. *The Fatherhood of God from Origen to Athanasius.* Oxford: Clarendon Press, 1994.

Williams, George C. *Adaptation and Natural Selection: A Critique of Some Current Evolutionary Thought.* 1966. Princeton: Princeton University Press, 1992.

Wilson, E. O. "Foreword." Larson, Gary. *There's a Hair in My Dirt!: A Worm's Story.* New York: HarperCollins, 1998.

Wolfson, Elliot R. "Circumcision, Vision of God, and Textual Interpretation: From Midrashic Trope to Mystical Symbol." *Circle in the Square: Studies in the Use of Gender in Kabbalistic Symbolism.* Albany: State University of New York Press, 1995. 29–48 and 140–55. Originally published in *History of Religions* 27 (November 1987): 189–215.

Wynne-Edwards, V. C. *Animal Dispersion in Relation to Social Behaviour.* Edinburgh: Oliver and Boyd, 1962.

———. *Evolution Through Group Selection.* Oxford: Blackwell Scientific Publications, 1986.

Zornberg, Avivah Gottlieb. *Genesis: The Beginning of Desire.* Philadelphia and Jerusalem: Jewish Publication Society, 5755, 1995.

Index